WHO WROTE THE BEATLE SONGS?

A History of Lennon-McCartney

Todd M. Compton

PAHREAH PRESS
San Jose, California

Published by Pahreah Press
http://toddmcompton.com/pahreahpress.html

17 16 15 14 13 1 2 3 4 5

Publisher's Cataloging-in-Publication data
Compton, Todd M., 1952—
     Who Wrote the Beatle Songs? A History of Lennon-McCartney / Todd M. Compton
     p. cm.
     Includes bibliographical references and index
     ISBN: 978-0-9988997-0-1 (paperback)
     ISBN: 978-0-9988997-1-8 (e-book)
     ISBN: 978-0-9988997-2-5 (hardcover)

1. Beatles. 2. Rock music—1961-1970—Analysis, appreciation. 3. Rock music—Writing and publishing. 4. Lyric writing (Popular music).

ML421.B4.C66 2017
782.4/2166/0922
Library of Congress Control Number: 2017905995
Todd M. Compton, San Jose, CA

Cover photo "Press photo of The Beatles during Magical Mystery Tour"
courtesy Wikimedia Commons

Contents

Acknowledgments

My debts in this book are many. First, to my wife who has endured my Beatle files through the years, and was the book's first reader and editor. She improved it in many ways, large and small. I would also like to thank Zach and Wes for their interest and inspiration, and for requiring me to play the White Album perhaps a million times while driving in my car. Distinguished musicologist Michael Hicks, who teaches the history of rock music at Brigham Young University, was kind enough to read parts of the book and provide a generous blurb. Lisa Fahey gave valuable graphics advice on the cover. Les Gripkey, a dedicated Beatles aficionado, was an early reader who has often provided background into the Beatles and their era in our far-ranging conversations. I appreciate Tim Compton, Tamara Hauge, Terry Harward, Tina Wilmore, Sandra Zapf, Frances Salas, Ron Kapf, Frank LaPallo, Craig Miller, Max Gaertner, Greg Dalgliesh, Alisa Tangredi, Terry Szink, Sterling Augustine, Krys Corbett, Mark Davis, Karoline Hausted, Ken Arconti and Nancy Lim, friends at work and school who have provided help and encouragement. I am especially indebted to Beatles researcher Sebastian Mora, who has generously provided me with numerous corrections and improvements.

All scholarship is based on previous scholarship and I should mention those debts. Mark Lewisohn's massive, detailed books on the Beatles have been foundational reference works, often providing unique insights into the Beatles' personalities and creativity. Walter Everett's *Beatles as Musician* books have been pioneering in their scholarship and depth, and I've often worked my way back to primary sources through his exhaustive documentation. Others books that have been enormously helpful to me are Steve Turner, *A Hard Day's Write: The Stories Behind Every Beatle Song*; Doug Sulpy and Ray Schweighardt, *Get Back: The Unauthorized Chronicle of the Beatles' Let It Be Disaster*; and Richie Unterberger, *The Unreleased Beatles*. I should also thank Jan Wenner, Ray Connolly, Mike Hennessey, David Sheff, Joan Goodman, Miles, and many other journalists, who in interviews with Paul and John, asked the right questions that gave us all of the maddeningly contradictory evidence for the writing of the Beatle songs . . .

I should add that I expect readers will already know the basic story of the Beatles. If they don't, they will be well served to read some standard books on the group for more depth on biographical issues. Mark Lewisohn's *The Beatles Recording Sessions* (1988) is my favorite book on the Beatles. His three-volume biography of the group is unfortunately not yet complete, though the first volume, *The Beatles: All These Years, Volume One – Tune In* (2013), is magnificent. For a one-volume biography of the Beatles, the reader can do much worse than the second edition of Hunter Davies's *The Beatles* (1986). I've limited my focus in this book to the Beatles' songwriting, as a conscious narrowing of my narrative lens. However, I've often been painfully aware that a number of issues I mention briefly deserve extensive treatment. I could have written chapters on John's relationships with Cynthia Lennon and Yoko Ono, on Paul's relationships with Jane Asher and Linda McCartney. I could have easily written a chapter (or a book) on the Beatles breakup as background for the *Let it Be* and *Abbey Road* albums. Drugs impacted the Beatles, and the Beatles' songs, in ways that have been viewed as positive and negative; I could have written a full chapter on that story. I should say that I find each of the Beatles utterly likeable, and flawed, at the same time. However, it was never my intention to look at these issues in depth, or to write a full biography of the Beatles. Hopefully, my book will incline future Beatle biographers to make songwriting more important in their research and longer narrative canvas.

Pahreah Press has kindly allowed me to fix typos and make corrections in the text on an ongoing basis. This text has been corrected as of December 9, 2017.

1

INTRODUCTION

The Enigma of "Lennon-McCartney"

Who wrote the Beatle songs? More specifically, who wrote the Lennon-McCartney songs? And why is the question important?

Once at a party, I was telling a friend about my views of Paul and John as individual songwriters, and about how many songs attributed to "Lennon-McCartney" were actually written mainly or entirely by Paul or John, and that this analysis contradicted many of the stereotypes about the two main Beatles. My friend became increasingly annoyed. Finally, he said, "Okay, but one thing you have to admit. John wrote and sang 'Helter Skelter'" — that hard rock masterpiece from the White Album — "and Paul wrote and sang 'Good Night'" — the lushly orchestrated ballad that ends the White Album. My friend had just put his finger on the unrecognized complexity of Paul and John as songwriters: *Paul* had written and sung "Helter Skelter" while *John* had written "Good Night," and had asked George Martin to orchestrate it in "Hollywood" style. (Ringo sang it).

As this anecdote shows, if one does not understand who wrote the Beatle songs, one can misunderstand the group pretty thoroughly. In the movie *Backbeat*, the writers drew on widespread stereotypes of Paul and John, portraying Paul as an ambitious, shallow entertainer, while John was the artist who loved hard rock. In keeping with this perspective, at one point they had John perform Little Richard's rave-up "Long Tall Sally." As Paul has pointed out, he always sang this song when the Beatles performed it. That song was his specialty.[1] But this did not fit the bludgeon-like schematic stereotyping of Paul and John that the screenwriters drew on to create a plot and conflict for their movie.

---

[1] *Anthology*, 96. "I was not amused. I always sang that: me and Little Richard." See also Coleman, *Yesterday and Today*, 100.

Given the overwhelming impact the Beatles have had on popular culture in our generation, one might expect that the question, "Who wrote the Beatle songs?" would have an obvious, good, thorough answer. But surprisingly, it does not — in part because of information and misinformation provided by the Beatles themselves (aided and abetted by their inner circle), and in part because of lack of focus on what is arguably the central contribution of the Beatles — their songwriting.

Everyone but the Beatles neophyte knows that Lennon and McCartney wrote many of their songs separately. True, some songs, especially in the early Beatle period, were "full" collaborations, written in three hour sessions, "eyeball to eyeball," as Lennon put it in a 1980 interview.[2] Other songs were written separately by Paul or John, and then the other helped finish them with "supportive" collaboration. (This was the most common form of Lennon-McCartney songwriting.) At least one song, "In My Life," was written by Paul adding music to John's words (as Paul tells the story). In a few cases, Paul and John wrote entirely separate songs, or parts of songs, then stuck them together to create one finalized Beatles song (e.g., "Baby You're a Rich Man"). Sometimes Paul would add a counter-melody to one of John's songs (as in "Help"), and sometimes John would do the same thing for one of Paul's (as in "She's Leaving Home").

The necessary foundation for an understanding of the Beatles' creativity is looking at every song separately and finding out who wrote it, and who wrote what part of it, if possible. Performance of the song is an important area of study, but is secondary to the actual songwriting. Much of the Beatles' personal lives are even more secondary to the songwriting (though certainly relevant and important). The Beatles' central story is a songwriting story.

The task of discovering who wrote the Beatles songs leads the researcher into a morass of difficulties. It has been made both easier and harder by the fact that both of the two main songwriters in the group have given extensive interviews discussing the writing of the songs. We are

---

[2] Sheff, *The Playboy Interviews*, 150.

grateful for this information; we are less grateful for numerous contradictions in the principals' statements. Sometimes John or Paul contradicts the other. Often, they contradict themselves.

A few examples:

"Eleanor Rigby" started as a McCartney song, as everyone agrees, with Paul writing the music and the beginnings of the lyrics. However, Lennon, in a 1971 interview, said that he wrote "about 70 per cent" of the lyrics.[3] Not so, says John's close friend, Pete Shotton, who was present at a work session on the song: "My own recollection is that 'Eleanor Rigby' was one 'Lennon-McCartney' classic in which John's contribution was virtually nil." McCartney, in a 1981 interview, more or less agrees with Shotton. "I saw somewhere that he [John] says he helped on 'Eleanor Rigby.' Yeah. About half a line." Shotton (who one would expect to be biased toward John) and McCartney's memories coincide in a convincing way, especially given that McCartney was the main writer of the song.

But wait — in an interview in which Paul was asked to name his favorite songs *that he wrote with John*, he mentioned three: "In My Life," "Norwegian Wood," and "Eleanor Rigby." This sounds like more input than "half a line."

Or take "In My Life." In a 1980 interview, John gave this as an example of how he could write melodies, not just over the top rock 'n' roll. He often described the song as entirely his own. However, Paul has maintained in numerous interviews that John wrote all or most of the words for this song, and he, Paul, wrote all the music. His account of sitting down at the Mellotron at John's house and working out the melody for the song is quite anecdotally convincing.

And in a 1970 interview, Lennon said that Paul "helped with the middle eight" on this.

Then there is the title song of the Beatles' most critically acclaimed album, *Sgt. Pepper's Lonely Hearts Club Band*. This is a song that is generally credited to Paul, not John, and there is no dispute on that front. However,

---

[3] For the precise documentation on the quotes in this section, see the sections on the relevant songs in the following chapters.

how much of the song was written by Mal Evans, the Beatles' bear-like, bespectacled roadie? In the official biography of Paul by his close friend Miles, based on hours of interviews with Paul, Miles writes that Paul got the title while brainstorming with Mal Evans. We also have a possible diary (whose authenticity is disputed) written by Evans in which he mentions working on the song with Paul. And Ringo said, "Paul wrote a song with Mal Evans called 'Sgt Pepper.' I think Mal thought of the title. Big Mal, super roadie!" By this account, the first two words of the title song of the album did not even come from a Beatle. (However, Ringo was not a first-hand witness of the songwriting session.)

Paul disputes that Evans was the source of the name "Sgt. Pepper." Naturally, he would know better than Ringo. Or did he just forget? It doesn't help that the Ringo quote appears in one of those Beatles books without footnotes and without dates for many quotes. If Ringo's quote was quite a bit earlier than Paul's, it would have added weight.

In 1971 John put "Cry Baby Cry" on a list of songs which he said were written by himself. When asked about the song in 1980, however, Lennon said brusquely, "Not me. A piece of rubbish."

Members of the Beatles inner circle often got Lennon-McCartney song attributions wrong. For example, George Martin, who often heard the Beatles songs very soon after they were composed, or heard them being finished in the studio, simply referred to "Lucy in the Sky with Diamonds" as a Lennon song. In 1995, Paul pointed out that he had co-written the song. He said, "Now, John will have told George Martin that he had this great new song. He won't have told him: 'Hey, yesterday Paul came to my house and we wrote it together.' You don't. You just say: 'I've got this new one.' George would say: 'Super, John, it's lovely.'"

These are just a few random examples of variation in song attribution.

In fact, the Beatles and their inner circle have given countless interviews, and have produced an ever-growing number of books. Many of these sources are flatly contradictory, as Lennon and McCartney, then the other Beatles, and members of the inner circle, give widely varying testimony.

Sometimes Lennon or McCartney will speak in terms of possibility (e.g., "I may have thrown something in"), probability ("I think I threw something in") or seeming certainty. One of the two main songwriters may use all three approaches in reference to the same song.

Thus, for certain key songs, we will have, not just a conflict in opinion between Lennon and McCartney; we will have a range of contradictory opinions from either Lennon or McCartney alone. From the corpus of Lennon and McCartney interviews, we don't have simply two contrasting opinions on a song; we may have eight to ten opinions.

One obvious, important tool the historian uses when assessing contradictory data is chronology. The earlier the testimony, the sharper the witness's memory. Thus, as a general rule, the earliest evidence is the most reliable. This applies to the evidence of the Beatle songs, to a certain extent, and early data is very desirable.

However, bias and misinformation can still be present in very early evidence. A person who has been in a car accident, if questioned immediately after the accident, may tell his or her story in such a way as to cover his or her own errors, if he or she caused the accident. In the case of the Beatle songs, because of their phenomenal cultural, critical and popular impact, clearly a member of the inner circle might want to connect him or herself with them as closely as possible. In addition, the Beatles became a partisan phenomenon, as they feuded with each other after the breakup, and every element of the group came to be viewed with partisan bias. Claiming a stake in a Beatle song obviously also might even have financial repercussions.

Thus a chronological view of the Beatle song evidence is fraught with bias and complexity (and occasional misinformation) at every step of the way. We may look at Beatle song perception by stages:

Period one: the Beatles era, dominated by the standardized "Lennon-McCartney" credit itself. For most Beatle songs (putting the Harrison and Starr songs to the side for the moment), this credit was misinformation, straight out of the gate. From very early on, Brian Epstein directed Paul and John to describe all their songs as collaborations. According to

Beatles publicist Tony Barrow, "When press or others questioned John or Paul about who wrote what, each would claim the other had contributed when this was very often quite untrue. It was the easy way out and they'd been told to do it by Brian Epstein."[4] In 1964 Paul said, "Sometimes maybe he'll write a whole song himself, or I will, but we always say that we've both written it."[5] In 1966, when asked if he'd written 'Here, There and Everywhere' by himself, Paul replied, "We both work on all our songs."[6] I know my experience, growing up with the Beatles, was to think of the Lennon-McCartney songs as completely co-written. I didn't even pay much attention to who was singing lead in different songs.

As the Beatles developed, they chafed against the idea that all songs had to be considered co-written, and Paul and John began to talk about how some of their songs were not written in collaboration. They were more open about separate authorship of songs after Brian Epstein's death in August 1967, as they reached the maturity of albums such as *Revolver* and *Sgt. Pepper.* And some of the tensions of the Beatles breakup were already present toward the end of the "Beatles era" — from the *White Album* on. In addition, some insiders were apparently following the party line in stating that all Lennon-McCartney songs were co-written while other insiders weren't.

Period two: after the breakup. Fairly soon after the breakup, in 1970 and 1971, Lennon gave interviews in which he discussed the authorship of all the Lennon-McCartney songs. A decade later, he admitted that he intentionally overemphasized separate authorship of songs immediately after the breakup, because he was tired of the idea of writing with Paul:

> "I said that [that they wrote separately in early Beatle days] but I was lying. [laughs] By the time I said that, we were so sick of

---

[4] Barrow, "Why John and Paul," 21.

[5] The Beatles Ultimate Experience website. In the Beatles' first interview (October 27, 1962, for Radio Clatterbridge), Paul simply said that he and John had written most of the Beatle songs.

[6] Response to letter to the editor in *Beatles Book Monthly* 41 (Dec. 1966): 19. We should remember that sometimes material in these fan magazines was ghost-written.

this idea of writing and singing together, especially me, that I started this thing about, 'we never wrote together, we were never in the same room.' Which wasn't true. We wrote a lot of stuff together, one-on-one."[7]

During this period, John and Paul were publicly and heatedly disagreeing about many things, and attacked each other in interviews, at the same time that they were discussing authorship of songs. Naturally, bias would be present during a time of such heated emotional conflict.

So in period two, the misinformation is the mirror image of the distortions in the first period. Collaboration might be under-emphasized.

Period three: 1980s to the present. When, in 1980, John admitted overemphasizing separate authorship in period two, in theory he presented a more balanced picture. At this time, he commented on the entire Lennon-McCartney canon once again.

Paul, on the other hand, also reacted against Lennon's characterization of the authorship of many specific Beatles songs in period two. The biography of Paul by his friend Miles, *Paul McCartney: Many Years From Now* (published in 1997, but based on interviews from previous years), includes quotations from hours of interviews in which Paul commented on the writing of the Lennon-McCartney songs in detail.

Paul has said that he disagreed with Lennon on song attribution on only two songs.[8] This is a curious, even bizarre statement — Paul actually disagreed with John on dozens of songs, as we will see. (Of course, Paul disagreed with himself on numerous songs, as did John.)

Interestingly, Paul in the *Many Years From Now* interviews, has tended to emphasize collaboration in the writing of many Beatles songs, but only in selected songs. Others he fully admits were individually written.

In theory, then, by the standards of bias, period three should contain the most reliable evidence. But by the standards of chronology and memory, this period is the least reliable. (And John's tragic death in De-

[7] Sheff, *The Playboy Interviews*, 149-50.
[8] Miles, *Many Years From Now*, 278.

cember 1980 robbed us of any further comments on the Beatle songs from him.) When, in 1988, Paul was asked about "Hold Me Tight," from 1963's *With the Beatles* album, he said, "I can't remember much about that one. Certain songs were just 'work' songs, you haven't got much of a memory of them. That's one of them."[9] If Paul and John had discussed the writing of the song, in a holistic and frank way in the sixties, obviously, we would have been better off.

───────⊃◉⊂───────

Another way writers have analyzed authorship of Lennon-McCartney songs is by performance: the person who sings lead in a song. This method obviously has some validity — when Paul or John wrote songs more or less separately, they usually sang their own songs — but in some cases the lead singer was not the main writer. Only in interviews do we find this out.

For example, if a song was a collaboration with a Paul emphasis, and if Paul and John sang it together, often Paul would sing the harmony, as he enjoyed working out harmony parts, or because his voice could sing in a higher range than John's. "*Q: 'Who decides who's going to sing the lead of a particular song you may do?* **John:** It depends on a lot of things. . . . If we write 'em together, he sings higher than me so basically I normally sing lead and he sings harmony. If I can't make it he sings on-tone." (*laughter*)."[10] A simplistic analysis, then, might conclude, incorrectly, that since John is singing lead on a song, it was necessarily written primarily by John (and vice versa).

The following songs show that it is impossible to judge from lead vocals alone:

"In Spite of All the Danger" was entirely a Paul song. However, John sings the lead, Paul sings harmony.[11] Paul and John both worked on "Love Me Do," but John referred to the song as mainly Paul's ("Paul's song"). However, Lennon sang the lead on a crucial section of this until Martin switched him to harmonica.

---

[9] Lewisohn, "The Paul McCartney Interview" (1988), 10.
[10] See Beatles, Indianapolis Press Conference, September 3, 1964.
[11] Lewisohn, *Complete Beatles Chronicles*, 363.

John said, of "Every Little Thing": "His (Paul's) song; maybe I threw something in." Nevertheless, again, Lennon sings lead.

———————◖◦◗———————

Partially because of such complexities in the evidence, and partially because many writers on the Beatles have not been too interested in the Beatles' actual songwriting, when we look at work previously done on this issue, we find a long list of typical errors:

1. Authors state that Paul or John was the main writer of a song without citing any source. Whatever they may base their opinion on, conclusions without evidence are not valid. We should trust no unsupported ascription of a Beatle song.

2. Authors assume the authorship of a song based on the song's lead singer. As I've stated above, for many songs, especially in the early Beatles albums, this method can lead one astray.

3. Sometimes an author will quote useful evidence on the authorship of a song — a quote by Lennon or McCartney, say — but will not date it. A date for a quote is necessary to establish crucial chronological context.

4. Sometimes an author will quote useful evidence on the authorship of a song, but will not give a source for it (by a footnote or its equivalent). This is better than no evidence at all, but is still far from the ideal. For example, we cannot check the quote against its original source to make sure that the writer has transcribed it correctly. (And when checking quotes from Lennon and McCartney interviews, I have found many statements have been misquoted, sometimes in significant ways.) And, for a controversial quote, it is important to read it in its full context. In addition, a footnote usually gives a date for the quote.

Many Beatle books that are otherwise valuable lack footnotes. For example, Turner's *A Hard Day's Write*, an important book that focuses on the Beatles' songwriting, has no footnotes, so the researcher can't check quotes. Sometimes Turner might tell you that a quote came from an interview in a certain year. Similarly, Badman's *The Beatles: Off the Record* is a treasure chest of Beatle data, and includes quotes on specific songs for the entire Beatles canon. But the quotes are undated and unfootnoted.

A Hard Day's Write and *The Beatles: Off the Record* remain valuable, and I have been indebted to them, but the researcher can't check their quotes to make sure the writer has reproduced them accurately, the researcher can't check context, and there is no chronological placement. Why not provide a footnote? When using these books, a researcher is forced to try to find the original source through detective work.

5. Sometimes a writer, instead of providing evidence that Lennon or McCartney wrote a song, will appeal to authority. The writer may cite Ian MacDonald or Tim Riley, writers of important books on the Beatles, on who wrote a song. But then you find that neither MacDonald nor Riley has given actual primary evidence on the songwriting process. So the "appeal to authority" fallacy turns out to be a circular path to nowhere instead of a path to actual evidence.

6. Sometimes a writer will cite a valid piece of evidence for a song's authorship. He or she may even footnote it. But he or she cites only that one quote. When there are ten relevant quotes, some of them more or less contradictory, citing one quote may give a view of the topic that is holistically not correct, or possibly reflects partisan bias.

For example, if you happen to come across one of the easiest, most accessible sources for the authorship of the Beatles songs, Lennon's 1980 *Playboy* interview, and are writing on "Eleanor Rigby," you might quote Lennon's statement that "the first verse was his [Paul's] and the rest [of the verses] are basically mine." As we have seen above, McCartney, in a 1981 interview, strongly disputed that Lennon wrote more than a few words of the song. An author, when discussing "Eleanor Rigby" seriously, should reflect both points of view. And if there are six contrasting quotations, he or she should reflect the range of opinion. (Incidentally, since Lennon has given a number of easily available book-length interviews, his views on the Lennon-McCartney songs have been very influential. However, they should be tempered with McCartney's views, especially now that Miles' *Paul McCartney: Many Years From Now* has been published.)

Introduction

7. Since the breakup of the Beatles, there has been an inescapable partisan element to the Beatles phenomenon, both among rock critics, and among fans. When Lennon and McCartney had their public feud, Beatle fans often took sides, and love for the Beatles as a whole became splintered. Lennon sought to position himself with the counter-culture, and associate Paul with the commercial musical mainstream. In the same interviews in which John credited the Beatles songs to himself or Paul, he often took the opportunity to criticize Paul's songs, and portrayed many of them as trivial and shallow. (And these critiques garnered more attention that John's generous praise for some Paul songs.) Rock critics have often viewed Paul's songwriting through Lennon's eyes.

Ideally, the Beatle historian should not be swayed by pro or anti-Lennon or pro- or anti-McCartney bias. This is obviously easier said than done, for many fans of these great, but very human, songwriters.

Hopefully, we are in the third period of Beatle appreciation now, when we can enjoy and respect the songs of both Lennon and McCartney. Both men (as Beatles) had admirable traits, and both had major character flaws. Both wrote great songs and lesser songs. There is nothing wrong with a critic leaning toward the music or lyrics of one or the other; but in assessing the authorship of the Beatle songs, statements by both should be considered in an evenhanded way.

Incidentally, some have criticized McCartney for taking the opportunity to describe his contribution to the Beatle songs, in the Miles book. However, Lennon went over the Lennon-McCartney corpus *three times*, at least, once when the feud between him and Paul was at its height, and these interviews were widely published — why shouldn't McCartney go over the same territory? Any reasonable historian will gratefully welcome two sides of a story, especially such an important story.

In the interest of full disclosure, and as a case history of one Beatle fan's response to the Lennon-McCartney feud after the breakup, my experience is as follows. I was a fan of the Beatles since I saw them on the Ed Sullivan show when I was in sixth grade. I followed them as a fan through their increasingly mature albums. I didn't think deeply or critically about their songwriting during this period. They were the Beatles, with songs written by Lennon-McCartney, and Harrison.

My favorite Beatle was John, whom I perceived as being more intellectual than Paul. His offbeat verbal humor was also very appealing to me.

When the Beatles formally broke up, I shared the pain of millions of Beatle fans. However, since I've always been interested in songwriting, I waited for the early solo albums with great interest.

The first Lennon single, "Instant Karma," didn't do anything for me, musically. The lyrics were striking.

Then the *McCartney* album was released, and when I heard it, I was floored. Though in format it is often an unassuming, homemade album, the music was brilliant, melodic, deeply felt at times, playful at times, often with remarkably complex, unexpected harmonies. It was a revelation to me. (And, viewing the Paul solo albums from a musical perspective, they have continued to strike me in the same way. His main weakness as a songwriter is his lyrics, which are sometimes good and carefully wrought, but sometimes seem quickly written, an afterthought to the music.)

Lennon's first solo album, *Plastic Ono Band*, was brilliant, especially on the level of lyrics. The music was curiously non-Beatlish.

So as the Lennon-McCartney feud developed, I found myself unexpectedly on Paul's side — I believe mainly because of my interest in music. Most rock critics however, ended up on John's side, for a number of reasons — his emphasis on lyrics (which coincided with the interests of many critics), his counter-cultural, avant-garde positioning, his search for high seriousness, rather than for commercial success. And because John attacked Paul, John's adherents saw Paul and his music as the opposite of these things.

As an admirer of Paul's music, I was amazed at how his complex talent came to be viewed simplistically. He, too, had his counter-cultural, avant-garde component. He certainly was often a comic artist, but I saw him as a great comic artist in the popular, Charlie Chaplin tradition, doing light-hearted farce at times, then turning to moments of penetrating seriousness.

For example, in the schematic view of John and Paul as good and bad opposites, John wrote and performed the screaming hard rock songs (for the rock community, "good"), while Paul sang and wrote the ballads (for the rock community, "bad"). However, in reality, from the early Beatle days, Paul sang both screamers and ballads and John sang both screamers and ballads.

Though I came to object strenuously to oversimplifications and misinformation related to Paul, I probably ended up viewing John too unsympathetically, at first.

Throughout the post-Beatle period, as the Beatle albums continued to have an astounding impact, the Beatle songs became contested territory. John gave his three interviews in which he discussed song authorship. These interviews, though they overemphasized individual authorship in the Beatle songs, were an important step in understanding more fully the creativity of the Beatles.

I started to emerge from the Paul-John partisan divide when I read Paul's interviews in response to John's. He often mentioned John's positive impact on many songs that were mostly his (Paul's) own. However, he also ascribed a number of songs fully or mainly to John, and I was reminded that these were some of my favorite Beatles songs: "I'm Only Sleeping," "I'm So Tired," "Dear Prudence," along with famous songs such as "Strawberry Fields Forever" "Because," and "Across the Universe." Turning to more collaborative compositions, John was the main writer of a number of obvious great songs: "Please Please Me," "I Call Your Name," "If I Fell," "Girl," and "Norwegian Wood."

So I came to see both John and Paul as great, complex, songwriters, as well as complex human beings. Hopefully this book will help to solve the enigmas behind the personalities and songs of John and Paul; and will draw us away from the many still-prevalent oversimplifications concerning them.

8. We should be skeptical of numerical attributions for Beatle songs — for example, saying that a certain song is 70% Lennon and 30% McCartney. This is the method used by William Dowlding in his *Beatlesongs*

(a book, which, again, I am indebted to). Songwriting is not such an exact, numerical science. In addition, often simple numerical attributions do not take into consideration the relative importance of music and lyrics. For instance, if the music is written by one writer, and there is collaboration on the lyrics, shouldn't you say that the song is a 100/0 collaboration on music and a 50/50 collaboration on lyrics? If you believe that music is the most important part of popular songwriting, you might say that the song, holistically, is 80-20; but if you think that lyrics are dominant, you might say the song is 80-20 toward the other writer. Such numerical summaries do not reflect the complexity of the Beatles' songwriting.

McCartney himself used numerical attributions sometimes in *Many Years from Now*. I think he would have been well advised to avoid them, but since he used them, we can only try to interpret them as best we can.

9. One reason that the question of the Beatles as songwriters has not been treated fully is because of disinterest in songwriting, as opposed to treatments of the Beatles as people, or as performers. These latter subjects are obviously important and interesting (and can be treated responsibly or shallowly), but they are arguably not as central to the Beatles phenomenon as their music and lyrics.

Songwriter Steve Earle has written,

> In retrospect, some have attributed the boys' preeminence to a simple twist of fate, the right band coming along at the right moment in history. As a songwriter who grew up on the Beatles, I subscribe to an alternate theory. It was the songs.[12]

Clearly, many writers have been more or less uninterested in the Beatles' songwriting. Sometimes even purported serious analysis of the Beatles' music rests on oversimplifications of Paul and John as people.

Serious treatment of the Beatles, as an artistic phenomenon, should look *first* at their songwriting, their music, their lyrics. Clearly, other parts

---

[12] Earle, "The Ten Most Important Beatles Songs," 309.

of their lives are important, and related to their songwriting, but this is where the focus should be.

10. And as a subcomponent of accepting the importance of songwriting, we must go one step further, and look at music and lyrics separately. It is possible to have a song that has great music and hackneyed, run-of-the-mill lyrics. Or it is possible to have great music and lyrics that are good, not especially great. The song will still work. In fact, I am very used to pop songs with good music and bad lyrics. Bad lyrics can be part of the charm of popular music.

And it is possible to have bad music and good, striking lyrics. I draw the line there, as I find bad music actively off-putting.

Of course, the ideal is to have great music and great lyrics, a remarkable accomplishment, when actually achieved, by people such as Paul Simon, Richard Thompson, and Bruce Springsteen.

Thus, a critic or listener might be interested in music or lyrics separately. This will depend on the interests and focus of the critic. For example, if you are interested in Schubert, the lyrics of his lieder are important and contribute to the total effect of the song. However, Schubert didn't write the lyrics; if we are assessing Schubert, we will be more interested in the music. He, and other great lieder composers, often chose lyrics by mediocre poets, and made great songs with them.

In the same way, George and Ira Gershwin worked together on songs, but if you're interested in music, you will be primarily interested in George Gershwin and his gift for melodies, harmonies, rhythm, his use of the idioms of jazz and popular music. If you're interested in lyrics, you will look at Ira Gershwin and his interests, life and gifts.

If you're interested in a sociological study of the cultural content of lyrics in a certain era and place, analysis of music might be entirely secondary.

Composer Ned Rorem, in a classic 1968 article, "The Music of the Beatles," argued that the "essential quality" that set the Beatles apart from their competition was the high quality of the music they composed. "Most of the literary copy devoted to the Beatles extols the timely daring of the group's lyrics while skirting the essential quality, the music," he wrote.[13] Rorem was a classical musician, and so was naturally interested in music, though he also composed songs, so would have been attuned to the aesthetic heights that a combination of word and music can achieve.[14]

On the other hand, rock critics naturally tend to be interested in lyrics of songs, which connect the song with the artist's life and thought. Talking about a song's use of harmony can be technical and academic. For example, one critic wrote of "All My Loving," "The next cluster of chords consists of the relative Major chords — the supertonic II, the submediant VI and the mediant III."[15] This is not the kind of gripping prose that sells magazines. On the other hand it makes valid musicological points.

Critics and listeners will come to rock, folk and popular music from different backgrounds — some will focus on music, others on words. Because of this, it will be important to understand who wrote the music and who wrote the lyrics in the "Lennon-McCartney" songs, to the extent that it is possible, so we can understand the idiosyncratic achievement of each of these great songwriters.

In the following pages I will look at the corpus of Beatle and Lennon-McCartney songs. Having surveyed all the relevant valid quotes about authorship that I have been able to find, I will briefly tell the story of how the song was written (which gives evidence on who wrote the song), then summarize evidence on who wrote the song.

As I did my research, I produced a register of all quotations on a particular song, arranged chronologically. In my book, I will quote and cite liberally from these quotes, choosing the most important ones. I will give each quote in its earliest extant appearance, to the best of my ability. I will include some quotes that are unfootnoted in their source books; if they are

---

[13] Rorem, "The Music of the Beatles," 149.
[14] I also come to the Beatles from a classical music background, so I tend to listen to rock and pop music first, and lyrics second.
[15] Tillekens, "Word and Chords."

relevant quotes, I have no choice, and look forward to finding their first appearance at some future time.

If a song has a main writer, I will focus first on the statements of that writer, then the statements of the other member of the Lennon-McCartney team. Then I will include statements by the other Beatles and George Martin, ending with statements by members of the inner circle. I will try to avoid, for the most part, statements from people who were not eyewitnesses to the songwriting in some way.

I will include some quotes that indirectly indicate authorship. For instance, if Paul or John comments extensively on a song, saying what the lyrics meant, that could be evidence that they were involved in the writing of the song, even if they do not explicitly say they wrote it.

I regard important experimental sections of such Beatle songs as "Tomorrow Never Knows" and "Day in the Life" as composed, and so will try to reflect the source of experimental features in such songs.

Though my primary interest is in songs by Paul and John, I will look at all Beatle songs. This allows one to look at the Beatle albums holistically; but in addition, I also include the songs by Harrison and Starr because one finds that the songwriting of one Beatle bleeds into another. For example, Lennon stated that he helped write the words to Harrison's "Taxman." Harrison, in turn, contributed lyrics to some Lennon-McCartney songs.

I will discuss the range of possibility, probability and seeming certainty in the relevant statements on the writing the Beatle songs, and attempt a synthesis, ascribe each song to collaboration, collaboration John emphasis, collaboration Paul emphasis, Lennon-McCartney, McCartney-Lennon, Lennon, McCartney (or to Harrison or Starr, or Beatle insiders occasionally). "Collaboration" means extensive collaboration between John and Paul, usually writing 50-50 from the ground up, though the finished song might "lean" toward John or Paul in some way, so we occasionally have "collaboration, John emphasis" or "collaboration, Paul emphasis." "Lennon-McCartney" or "McCartney-Lennon" mean songs in which one writer is clearly dominant, even though the other writer also contributed to the song.

I should emphasize that *my ascription is not meant to be authoritative or certain* — when you're dealing with eight conflicting statements, certainty is impossible. Nevertheless, I will make an educated attempt at a valid ascription, based on the evidence I've been able to find.

Some readers — including some Beatle fans — will inevitably look at this project as an excessive focus on one narrow aspect of a rock group, important as that group is. But, in my view, not looking at the Beatles' songwriting, music and lyrics, is a way of not taking them seriously. Given their impact on modern popular culture, and given the continued popularity and reputation of their songs and albums, the Beatles' songwriting cries out for our painstaking attention.[16]

---

[16] For the Beatles' impact on popular culture, see McGrath, "Cutting up a glass onion." For the impact of the Beatles' music, see the prologue to the *Sgt. Peppers* album, below.

2

"The result wasn't a bit like 'Apache'"

THE EARLY BEATLES

Paul McCartney and John Lennon began writing songs when they were young teenagers, before they met each other. Soon after they met, on July 6, 1957 (John was sixteen, Paul was fifteen), they began writing together "eyeball to eyeball," creating songs from scratch, completing songs that one or the other had started, or adding minor edits to songs the other had written. Some songs that later entered the Beatles canon, such as "Love Me Do," "When I'm 64," and "One After 909," date from this era. Many other songs fell by the wayside, and have never been heard again. The Beatles would sing snippets of some of the obscure early songs in the Get Back rehearsals in 1969. They had a certain affection for them, but knew that most of them were very much apprenticeship work.

Paul and John wrote many unreleased songs during the Beatles period, both individually and together, that have been mentioned in interviews, have been played live, played in rehearsals, or recorded as demos. I am intentionally excluding such unreleased Lennon-McCartney and Harrison or Starr songs from the overview of Beatle songs that I make in this book. In theory, there was a valid winnowing process that kept these songs from being released, or that kept the Beatles from even giving them away to other groups. I believe the Beatles should be judged primarily on the songs they thought were worthy of release.

I say in theory. In reality, sometimes this process was not at all straightforward. For example, some songs from the *McCartney* album, from Lennon's *Plastic Ono Band* and *Imagine*, and from Harrison's *All Things Must Pass* (including the title cut), albums I regard very highly, were written long before the Beatles breakup, were played in Beatle rehearsals, and somehow never made it onto a Beatles record, while lesser songs did achieve release.

(For example, Harrison's "All Things Must Pass," played during the Get Back rehearsals, entirely overshadows his "For You Blue," which was released on *Let It Be*.) So I will look at songs that were released after the Beatles period if it is well documented that they were written before the breakup. I will treat them formally at the time of their release, though sometimes I will refer to early songs briefly at the time of their creation or early performance. Thus I will formally look at some of the Decca audition songs, recorded on January 1, 1962, at the time a few of them were finally released, on *Anthology 1* in 1995. However, I'll refer briefly to the Decca audition at the time it occurred.

"That'll Be the Day" / "In Spite of All the Danger" recording, 1958

On July 12, 1958, the proto-Beatles (at the time, The Quarrymen) recorded a demo single, "That'll Be the Day," a Buddy Holly cover with John singing lead, and "In Spite of All the Danger," a Paul song attributed to McCartney-Harrison, again with John singing lead. (Paul sings harmony and melodic embellishments.) These songs show up on *Anthology 1*. The Beatles era in modern recorded music begins here.

Buddy Holly was one of the Beatles' great inspirations. John once said that most of the early Beatle songs were "Buddy Holly rip-offs."[1] Paul remembered that in the early songwriting sessions he and John would listen to a Holly song over and over, then try to write something like it.[2] "That'll Be the Day" had been the first song John had learned on guitar.

---

[1] Beatles interview, Jerry G. Bishop, Aug. 13 to Sept. 1, 1965, in Winn, *Way Beyond Compare*, 359. See also Chris Roberts, "John Lennon," *Melody Maker* 39 (April 4, 1964) (Sandercombe, *The Beatles: Press Reports*, 57); Lewisohn, *Tune In*, 11. Du Noyer, *Conversations*, 33.
[2] Elson, *McCartney — Songwriter*, 24.

Home rehearsal tape, 1960.

We have a tape of a home rehearsal of the Beatles, without drummer, from spring-summer 1960. It has historical interest and little musical value. Three of these songs can be found on *Anthology 1*.

The Hamburg sessions with Tony Sheridan, June 22-23, 1961

The first professional recordings of the Beatles are the Hamburg sessions with Tony Sheridan in June 1961, during which they recorded nine songs. According to Beatles historian Mark Lewisohn, at these sessions the Beatles recorded, with Sheridan on lead vocal, "My Bonnie," "The Saints," "Why (Can't You Love Me Again)," "Nobody's Child," and "Take Out Some Insurance on Me Baby."[3] Without Sheridan, the Beatles recorded "Ain't She Sweet" and "Cry for a Shadow." All of these have been commercially released. At a later date, May 24, 1962, the Beatles and Sheridan recorded "Swanee River" and "Sweet Georgia Brown."[4]

These recordings have limited musical value, except for completists. First, the great majority of the seven songs had Sheridan singing lead, and the Beatles were merely playing backup. John correctly said: "It's just us banging about in the background as an accompaniment to Tony. I wish they'd shut up about it. It's terrible. It could be anybody and we think it's unfair on the fans to put it out as a genuine release by us."[5] Second, Pete Best, not Ringo, played drums. Third, with one exception, "Cry for a Shadow," the songs were not written by the Beatles.

Nevertheless, the "My Bonnie" single attracted the interest of Brian Epstein, an important milestone in the Beatles' career. As John said, in 1964, "We'd already made 'My Bonnie,' and all those other rubbishy records for Polydor. And kids from the Cavern, 'round about Liverpool, were

---

[3] Lewisohn, *The Complete Beatles Chronicle*, 42.
[4] Lewisohn, *Tune In*, 629. "Swanee River" has been lost.
[5] Lennon in 1963, see Shepherd and Dean, "Behind the Spotlight," *The Beatles Book Monthly* 24 (July 1965): 24. See also Paul's comments in *Anthology*, 59.

going into his record shop and saying 'Have you got 'My Bonnie' by The Beatles?' So he [Brian Epstein] got interested and he asked one of the kids who we were. He thought we were German. And he came 'round when we were playing at the Cavern."[6]

"Ain't She Sweet," with Lennon, not Sheridan, on vocals, is the earliest commercial recording of the near-standard lineup Beatles. And "Cry for a Shadow" is the first commercial recording of a song written by the Beatles, though it is rather atypical, an improvised instrumental.

―――――――〇〇―――――――

"My Bonnie (Mein Herz ist bei dir nur) / The Saints" single, Germany — Tony Sheridan, backed by the "Beat Brothers," October 23, 1961

Someone walked into Brian Epstein's record store and asked for this record on October 28, 1961. The rest is history. After this German release, the song was also released as a single in the U.K. on January 5, 1962.

○ My Bonnie (Mein Herz ist bei dir nur) (COVER) (traditional)

During this time period, British groups often played older, traditional songs in rock style. "The group also derive a great deal of pleasure from re-arranging old favourites ('Ain't She Sweet' . . .)," Paul wrote in about 1959.[7] Apparently, producer Bert Kaempfert had heard the Beatles perform this song, and thought a version with Sheridan singing lead would work well.[8] This is available on *Anthology 1*.

○ The Saints (COVER) (traditional)

Another traditional song ("When the Saints Come Marching In") in rock style.

---

[6] Beatles, Press Conference, Adelaide, Australia, June 12, 1964. See also Epstein, *A Cellarful of Noise*, 40-42; *Anthology*, 66. When "My Bonnie" was first released, the Beatles were much more enthusiastic about it, Lewisohn, *Tune In*, 493.

[7] Paul to Mr. Low, in Davies, *The Beatles*, 63.

[8] Lewisohn, *Tune In*, 447. Ray Charles and Gene Vincent had recorded it earlier.

Mister-Twist EP, including "Cry for a Shadow," released in France in January 1962[9] — When the Saints / Cry for a Shadow / My Bonnie / Why

- Cry for a Shadow — (Harrison-Lennon)

"Cry for a Shadow," originally called "Beatle Bop," an instrumental, was the first song attributed to the Beatles as songwriters that was released commercially. However, it was more an improvisation than a real act of songwriting. In fact, the song allegedly derived from a failed attempt to play someone else's song, the instrumental, "Apache," by the Shadows.[10] The Shadows, often with lead singer Cliff Richards, were probably the major British rock group in the years before the Beatles; "Apache," written by British songwriter Jerry Lordan, and released in July 1960, was the Shadows' first major hit.

"Cry" was "written" in this manner. In Hamburg, Rory Storm, the band leader of Ringo's group at the time, Rory Storm and the Hurricanes, asked the Beatles if they knew the recently released "Apache."[11] They didn't, but just "to take the mickey out of" Storm,[12] John began playing something that sounded like the song on a new guitar he'd bought, a Rickenbacker with "a funny kind of wobble bar on it," and George added the lead guitar part, making it up on the spot. "The result wasn't a bit like

---

[9] January 1962, Polydor no. 21914, according to Stormo, "Lennon's first published song." "A copy of the EP was officially given to the 'Bibliothèque nationale de France' on January 26th, 1962, and the receival date was stamped on the record's back." Some sources give April 1962 as the release date.

[10] According to Harrison in 1963, Smith, "Close-up on a Beatle: George Harrison." Pete Best, in 1985, remembered the Shadows' 1961 hit "Frightened City" as the source. *Beatle! The Pete Best Story*, 104-5. Or the Shadows tune was the November 1960 single "Man of Mystery," Lewisohn, *Tune In*, 381.

[11] George remembered "someone" asking; Pete Best said it was Storm.

[12] According to Best.

'Apache,'" George said in 1963, "but we liked it and we used it in the act for a while."[13]

The attribution "Harrison-Lennon" is thus correct. In the 1963 interview, George said, "I did actually write one number, if you could call it 'writing.'" So he definitely dominated, though Lennon was part of the original improvisation. In 1987, George told the story again, and said that the song was "really a joke."[14] Paul, in 1962, agreed the song was one that "George and John wrote themselves."[15]

After the Beatles made their first big splash, "Cry for a Shadow" was released as a single in England, in March 1964. It is now available on *Anthology 1*.

- ○ "Ain't She Sweet" (COVER) (Milton Ager, Jack Yellen) (lead vocals: John)

"Ain't She Sweet" was a pop standard, first published in 1927. Gene Vincent had recorded a fairly slow version in 1956, which John had originally followed, but the pressure for more rhythmic performances in Germany had caused the Beatles to quicken the tempo.[16]

This recording has historical importance, as the first all-Beatles recording (pre-Ringo) with vocals. And it was a staple of the early Beatles' live shows.[17] It was not released until May 29, 1964, in England. It is available on *Anthology 1*, while another version of the song, recorded in 1969 in the Get Back sessions, is on *Anthology 3*.

Other songs from the Hamburg sessions, all with Sheridan singing lead and the Beatles as backing band, were:

- ○ Take Out Some Insurance on Me Baby (aka, If You Love Me Baby) (COVER) (Charles Shingleton, Waldenese Hall), first released in 1959 by Jimmy Reed.

---

[13] Smith, "Close-up on a Beatle: George Harrison." Best remembered that George started playing and John joined in.
[14] Forte, "George Harrison," 107.
[15] Beatles, Radio Interview, October 28, 1962.
[16] According to John, as quoted in Lewisohn, *Tune In*, 449.
[17] Lewisohn, *Tune In*, 237, 440, 449.

- ○ <u>Why (Can't You Love Me Again)</u> (COVER) (Tony Sheridan, Bill Crampton)
- ○ <u>Nobody's Child</u> (COVER) (Cy Coben, Mel Foree), recorded by Hank Snow in 1949
- ○ <u>Swanee River</u> (COVER) (Stephen Foster), written in 1851. The Sheridan-Beatles recording of this has been lost.
- ○ <u>Sweet Georgia Brown</u> (COVER) (Ben Bernie, Maceo Pinkard, Kenneth Casey), written in 1925.

The Decca Audition, January 1, 1962

About half a year after the Hamburg sessions, Brian Epstein got the Beatles an audition with Decca. It was recorded, and represents another important historical record of the early Beatles. This audition included twelve covers and, most importantly, three songs written by Paul and/or John (though none of these are top-drawer Lennon-McCartney songs). The Decca audition is inferior to the recordings that the Beatles would make at EMI, but is nevertheless a fascinating recording.[18] The songs recorded were:

"<u>Like Dreamers Do</u>" (Lennon–McCartney). Paul sings lead. The song was first released by the Applejacks in 1964, see below. The Decca performance can be found on *Anthology 1*.

"<u>Money (That's What I Want)</u>" (Berry Gordy, Janie Bradford). John sings lead. See *With the Beatles*, below.

"<u>Till There Was You</u>" (Meredith Willson), from the musical, *The Music Man*. Paul sings lead. See *With the Beatles*, below.

"<u>The Sheik of Araby</u>" (Harry B. Smith, Francis Wheeler, Ted Snyder). George sings lead. The song, written in 1921 as a tribute to Rudolph Valentino, became a jazz standard. This can be found on *Anthology 1*.

---

[18] For the Decca sessions, see Unterberger, *Unreleased Beatles*, 18-25; Lewisohn, *Tune In*, 539-42.

"To Know Her Is to Love Her" (Phil Spector). John sings lead. This was released in 1958 (as "To Know Him Is to Love Him") by Phil Spector's group, the Teddy Bears. Another version of this by the Beatles is on *Live at the BBC*.

"Take Good Care of My Baby" (Gerry Goffin, Carole King). George sings lead on this song, which was a hit for Bobby Vee in 1961. No Beatle version of it has been released. John and Paul revered Goffin and King as songwriters, and John once said, "When Paul and I first got together, we wanted to be the British Goffin and King."[19]

"Memphis, Tennessee" (Chuck Berry). John sings lead. Chuck Berry was another leading inspiration of the early Beatles. John usually sang lead vocals on Berry songs, but Paul was also a committed fan.[20] Other versions of this are on the *Live at the BBC* compilations.

"Sure to Fall (In Love with You)" (Carl Perkins, Bill Cantrell, Quinton Claunch). Paul sings lead. Perkins, representing the rockabilly genre, was another major inspiration for the early Beatles. Other versions of this are on the *Live at the BBC* collections.

"Hello Little Girl" (Lennon–McCartney). John sings lead. This song was first released by the Fourmost in 1963, see below. The Decca performance can be found on *Anthology 1*.

"Three Cool Cats" (Jerry Leiber, Mike Stoller). George sings lead. The Coasters released this as the B-side of their single "Charlie Brown" in 1959. The Decca version can be found on *Anthology 1*.

"Crying, Waiting, Hoping" (Buddy Holly). George sings lead. This Buddy Holly song was released in 1959 as the B-side to "Peggy Sue Got Married." A different Beatle version is on *Live at the BBC*.

"Love of the Loved" (Lennon–McCartney). Paul sings lead. The Beatles gave this to Cilla Black, who released it in 1963, see below. The Decca audition version has never been released.

---

[19] Interview with Raoul Pantin, *Trinidad Express*, May 4, 1971, as quoted in Lewisohn, *Tune In*, extended, 2:1344. Wenner, *Lennon Remembers*, 47.

[20] For example, on January 20, 1982, on the BBC Desert Island Discs program, Paul picked Berry's "Sweet Little Sixteen" as one of his ten favorite songs. See also "I Saw Her Standing There" and "Back in the U.S.S.R.," below.

"September in the Rain" (Harry Warren, Al Dubin). Paul sings lead. This song was a standard, first published in 1937. No Beatle version of this has been released.

"Bésame Mucho" (Consuelo Velázquez). Paul sings lead. The Beatles followed the Coasters' version of the song. Other Beatle versions can be found in the *Let It Be* movie and on *Anthology 1*.

"Searchin'" (Jerry Leiber, Mike Stoller). Paul sings lead. A Coasters single, released in 1957, this was another key rock song for the Beatles.[21] The Decca version can be found on *Anthology 1*.

The Decca Audition has been released, without the three Beatle-written songs. Five of the songs performed at the audition can be found on *Anthology 1*, including two of the Beatle songs.

The contrast between this and the next major Beatle recording — the album *Please Please Me*, recorded only about a year later — is remarkable. The Lennon-McCartney originals in the later recording are mature and substantial, in contrast to the three lesser Lennon-McCartneys here. The performance of a cover song such as "Money" — later the final cut on *With the Beatles*, the Beatles' second album — is also startlingly different and more powerful in the later recording.

Some blame the selection of songs for the Decca audition's weakness. By some accounts, Brian Epstein chose the songs,[22] and he highlighted ballads and novelty songs rather than American rhythm and blues numbers more characteristic of the early Beatles. Nevertheless, there were some hard rockers included ("Money" and "Searchin'") along with Buddy Holly, Chuck Berry and Motown songs. And all of these songs were in the Beatles' live repertoire. In addition, George Harrison remembered that each Beatle chose a number he wanted to do.[23]

John Lennon, in 1972, said, "When you hear the tape, it's pretty good. It's not great, but it's good and it's certainly good for then, when you con-

---

[21] *Anthology*, 22. Another pick for Paul's Desert Island Discs.
[22] Best, *Beatle! The Pete Best Story*, 144. According to Best, "Eppy and Mike Smith chose a mixture of songs that they calculated would have the Decca bigwigs standing on their heads." The emphasis on standards was "I remember, . . . mainly at Brian's insistence."
[23] *Anthology*, 67.

sider that all that was going on was The Shadows — especially in England."[24] That's about right.

---

[24] Ibid., 68.

3

"I knew at that moment that this was going to be a good collaboration"

PLEASE PLEASE ME

With the Beatles' first single, "Love Me Do," and their first album, *Please Please Me*, the real Beatles canon begins. Remarkably, given that for many years the Beatles were a "cover" band, the early singles and albums are dominated by songs John and Paul wrote, and this creativity impressed the decisionmakers at EMI and helped the Beatles obtain their first recording contract.

As early as the first albums and singles, all the patterns of Lennon-McCartney songwriting were present. Thoroughgoing collaboration (as in the case of "I Want to Hold Your Hand" or "She Loves You") is more common now than in any other period. "Finishing" collaboration (in which one writer substantially began a song, and the other helped finish it, as in "I Saw Her Standing There") is perhaps the most common type of collaboration now, and throughout the Beatles' career. There is some collaboration with non-Beatles, also a persistent pattern, though this kind of collaboration is usually confined to outsiders filling in holes in a song's lyrics. In addition, some songs, such as "All My Loving" or "All I've Got to Do," were written entirely separately, by Paul or John alone.

"Love Me Do / P.S. I Love You" single, October 5, 1962

"Love Me Do" doesn't seem much of a song now, compared to later Beatle masterpieces, but it electrified the young Sting, who first heard it in a changing room at a swimming pool:

> We were drying ourselves off and, as was our custom, flicking towels at each other's genitals. It was at this point that we

29

heard the first bars of 'Love Me Do' from a transistor radio in the corner. The effect was immediate. There was something in the sparseness of the sound that immediately put a stop to the horseplay. John's lonely harmonica and Paul's bass played 'two to the bar,' and then the vocal harmony moved in modal fifths up to minor thirds and back again to a solo voice on the refrain. Not that I could articulate any of this at the time, but I recognized something significant, even revolutionary, in the spare economy of the sound, and the interesting thing is, so did everyone else.[1]

- **Love Me Do — (McCartney-Lennon)**
  (lead vocals: Paul and John) (recorded on September 4 and 11, 1962)

Paul wrote the main part of "Love Me Do," in 1958, when he was sixteen,[2] in the parlor of the McCartney home, 20 Forthlin Road.[3] Like many early Beatle songs, it was written in the Buddy Holly style of three or four simple chords.[4] According to Paul, "Love Me Do" "was us trying to do the blues."[5]

Paul then brought the song to John, and they worked on it extensively together, with John contributing especially to the middle part.[6] So it's an example of a common pattern in Lennon-McCartney songwriting, in fact, probably the most common pattern — collaboration, extensive or limited, after one person started a song.

---

[1] Sting, *Broken Music: A Memoir*, 80.

[2] Lennon, in Hennessey, "Who Wrote What," *Record Mirror*. Miles, *Many Years from Now*, 37. See also p. 83, for the story of how the Beatles recorded "Love Me Do" as their first single, instead of George Martin's choice, the cover "How Do You Do It."

[3] Pete Best has different memories: "The number was conceived in the course of one afternoon in our flat opposite the club." *Beatle! The Pete Best Story* (1985), 155-56.

[4] Read, "McCartney on McCartney," episode 1.

[5] "The Paul McCartney Interview," (1988), 7.

[6] Garbarani, "Paul McCartney: Lifting the Veil," (1980), p. 49: "When we started with the Beatles, John and I sat down and wrote about fifty songs, out of which I think 'Love Me Do' is the only one that got published."

As primitive as this song is, compared to later Beatle accomplishments, it marked a culmination for the early Lennon-McCartney songwriting partnership. Lennon remembered that it was the first Lennon-McCartney song they dared perform live (a new, traumatic experience).[7] Paul later called it "'our greatest philosophical song.'"[8]

Despite this song being originally written by Paul, John sang the lead for the crucial "Love me do" line until George Martin asked John to play the harmonica part, which required Paul to sing it.[9]

The evidence for the authorship of this song is somewhat contradictory. John's statements ascribe the song mostly to Paul, Paul's to collaboration. In 1971, Lennon stated that Paul wrote the "main structure," of this song when he (Paul) was sixteen, though he thought he (John) had something to do with the "middle."[10] The following year, he wrote that "Paul started [it] when he must have been about fifteen" but then they collaborated on it, and it became "one of the first ones we wrote."[11] By 1980, John ascribed the song almost completely to Paul (it was "Paul's song") and was less sure that he had contributed anything — he "might" have contributed to the middle section.[12] (Incidentally, John's use of "middle eight" did not mean a short transitional passage, eight measures, between two major sections of the song, as the name suggests, and as its synonym, "bridge," also suggests. For the Beatles, middle eight meant a middle, contrasting section, often fairly long.[13])

---

[7] *Anthology*, 68.

[8] Aldridge, "Beatles Not All That Turned On," 143.

[9] McCartney, Letter to John on John's Induction (1994). Miles, *Many Years From Now*, 91.

[10] Hennessey, "Who Wrote What," *Record Mirror*.

[11] *Anthology*, 68.

[12] Sheff, *The Playboy Interviews*, 23.

[13] For form in Beatles songs, see Everett II, 15-16; Covach, "From 'Craft' to 'Art'"; Fitzgerald, "Lennon-McCartney and the "Middle Eight." Fitzgerald emphasizes that the Beatles often used the AABA form (in which B is the "middle eight," an extended middle section) typical of many Tin Pan Alley songs, rather than "verse-chorus" songs with added "middle eight" as a short bridge (C after repetitions of AB) leading from the chorus back to the main verse melody.

In Paul's earliest comment on the song, in 1965, he reflects his own main authorship: "I wrote a couple of songs. One was 'Love Me Do.'"[14] However, after this, he generally described the song as a pure 50-50 collaboration. In 1966, also very early, he remembered collaboration: "We started off first with songs like 'Love Me Do,' with easy, stupid rhymes that didn't mean very much."[15] Paul also described collaboration in 1969: "Yeah, we used to sag off every school day, go back to my house and the two of us would write: 'Love Me Do,' 'Too Bad About Sorrows.' ['Just Fun']. . . ."[16] In 1987, he said, "I know that I sat there and we wrote 'Love Me Do'."[17] Two years later, he was asked about early collaboration with Lennon, and said, "The first thing we got, again it wasn't that good, but it was recordable, was 'Love Me Do.'"[18]

"'Love Me Do' was completely co-written," he said in 1995. "Some of them were really 50-50s, and I think that one was." He also floated the possibility that the song may have been started "without either of us having a particularly original idea."[19] However, here he admitted the possibility that the song might have been his "original idea," but only as a possibility.[20]

In 2000, Paul remembered collaboration on this, and said that "'Love Me Do' and 'I Saw Her Standing There,' . . . got the basis of a [songwriting] partnership going." However, then he added, "One of us would come up with an idea and then it would see-saw. So there was a mild competitiveness in that we were ricocheting our ideas."[21] So here, Paul emphasizes

---

[14] Wyndham, "Paul McCartney As Songwriter."

[15] Lydon, *Flashbacks: Eyewitness Accounts of the Rock Revolution*, 12.

[16] Cott and Dalton, *The Beatles Get Back*, 85. A similar statement from Paul from the same period in Aldridge, *Beatles Illustrated Lyrics*, 92.

[17] Interview, June 1987, in deCurtis, *In Other Words*, 61.

[18] Read, "McCartney on McCartney," episode 1. Cf. Garbarani, "Paul McCartney: Lifting the Veil," (1980), 49.

[19] Miles, *Many Years from Now*, 36.

[20] Ibid.

[21] *Anthology*, 23.

that, even though this was collaboration, one of the writers would have the original idea.[22]

Ironically, Paul, in 1995, claimed more of a John influence on this song than John did in 1980. John seemed certain that the main song was Paul's, while Paul emphasized collaboration.

I think the earliest interviews of John and Paul give clear evidence that this was a song Paul came up with first, then it was finished with extensive collaboration.

The Beatles performed it at the EMI audition on June 6, 1962, with Pete Best on drums; this is available on *Anthology 1*.[23] The single version was recorded on September 4 (with Ringo on drums), and can be found on *Past Masters 1*. The album version was recorded on September 11 (with session player Andy White on drums, while Ringo played tambourine).

- **P.S. I Love You — (McCartney-Lennon)**
  (lead vocal: Paul) (recorded on September 4 and 11, 1962)

According to John, Paul wrote this song in Hamburg, or on the way to Hamburg (which would be spring or summer, 1962, as they were in Hamburg April 13 to May 31).[24] Paul's girlfriend at the time, Dorothy "Dot" Rhone, later said that Paul told her that he had written the song for her.[25] It apparently was finished with some polishing from Lennon.

According to one report, Paul and John wrote this when EMI requested new material after they were offered an audition on May 9, 1962.[26] According to Miles, Paul wrote "P.S. I Love You" "not long before the recording test" on June 6.[27] They played it at the June 6 auditions, but that recording has been lost.

---

[22] One of the Beatles' friends, Bernie Boyle, remembers Paul and John working on this song together in Hamburg. Lewisohn, *Tune In*, extended, 2:1196.

[23] Pawlowski, *How They Became the Beatles*, 74. They played four songs: "Besame Mucho," "Love Me Do," "P.S. I Love You," and "Ask Me Why." Only "Besame Mucho" and "Love Me Do" survive, and both appear on *Anthology 1*.

[24] Sheff, *The Playboy Interviews*, 178.

[25] Shea and Rodriguez, *Fab Four FAQ*, 362.

[26] Lewisohn, *Tune In*, extended, 2:1192-93.

[27] Miles, *Many Years From Now*, 90.

The evidence, reflecting both Paul's writing the song and subsequent collaboration, is not too difficult. John vaguely remembered that the other Beatles contributed to it. "Paul. But I think we helped him a bit."[28] In 1980, his memories are more vague: "That's Paul's song. . . . I might have contributed something. I can't remember anything in particular. It was mainly his song."[29]

Paul claimed the song in 1995, though he left open the possibility that John made a slight contribution to it: "I don't think John had much of a hand in it."[30] While "Please Please Me" was more John, he said in 2000, "'PS I Love You' was more me."[31] That language "more me" again suggests that John might have made a contribution.

So it was substantially Paul's song, but there was probably some finishing collaboration with John.[32]

"Please Please Me / Ask Me Why" single, January 11, 1963

- **Please Please Me — (Lennon-McCartney)**
  (lead vocals: John, Paul) (recorded on November 26, 1962)

John wrote this in his bedroom at Menlove Avenue, Woolton, his Aunt Mimi's house. "I remember the day and the pink eiderdown, the bed," he said in 1980.[33] He wrote it as a slow song, consciously modeling it on Roy Orbison songs such as "Only the Lonely." The lyrics were also influenced by Bing Crosby's 1932 hit, "Please."

After John's substantial start on this song, he and Paul continued on it together. Two fifteen-year-old girls accompanied John and Paul home from a Cavern performance on June 9, 1962, and watched as the two Beat-

---

[28] Hennessey, "Who Wrote What," *Record Mirror.*
[29] Lost Lennon Tapes, Oct. 21, 1991, cf. Sheff, *The Playboy Interviews,* 178.
[30] Miles, *Many Years From Now,* 38.
[31] *Anthology,* 94.
[32] Bernie Boyle, one of their early friends, also remembered Paul and John working on this in Hamburg. Lewisohn, *Tune In,* extended, 2:1196.
[33] Lost Lennon Tapes, Oct. 21, 1991, cf. *The Playboy Interviews,* 179.

les developed "Please Please Me" on the piano. They were "mostly work-ing on the chord changes, with a lot of joking and messing about," said one girl. According to Lewisohn, the teens "dozed under the piano while Lennon-McCartney explored chords above their heads."[34] Apparently mu-sical elements of the song were not finalized when John brought it in, and they were developed in collaboration.

The Beatles played the song to George Martin, but he thought it was dragging, and was tempted to pass on it. He suggested they speed it up. The band at first resisted the idea, but eventually re-arranged it as a more uptempo song. After they finished recording it, George Martin congratu-lated them on having produced their first number one hit. He was right.[35] Paul said that this was the first time Martin "really ever showed that he could see beyond what we were offering him."[36] The Beatles were indeed very fortunate in the producer they found themselves teamed up with. A former producer of Spike Milligan / Goon Show recordings, he under-stood the Beatles' off-the-wall humor. As is shown by the *Please Please Me* album, he was able to bring the Beatles' power as a rock group to stunning life in the studio. A musician with classical musical training, he later suc-cessfully translated the Beatles' ideas into classical instrumentations. His contribution to selected Beatle songs was so substantial that it raises the question of whether he deserves co-writing credits on some songs.

The evidence for the authorship of "Please Please Me" is slightly con-tradictory, as John sometimes claimed 100% songwriting credit for the song. In John's earliest comments, in January 1963, however, he reflected both his original writing of the song, and the collaboration. "I tried to make it as simple as possible. Some of the stuff I've written has been a bit

---

[34] Lewisohn, *Tune In*, extended, 2:1235.
[35] Smith, "Beatles Almost Threw 'Please Please Me' Away." Gambaccini, "The Rolling Stone Interview" (1973); Read, "McCartney on McCartney," (1989), episode 2. Cf. Lew-isohn, "The Paul McCartney Interview" (1988), 7; Miles, *Many Years from Now* (1995), 91-92. According to Martin, he "told them what beginning and what ending to put on it," Martin, *All You Need is Ears*, 130. He also said that he demanded that they speed up the song. Irvin, "George Martin" (2007).
[36] Gambaccini, "The Rolling Stone Interview" (1973).

way out." However, then he switches to "we": "But we did this one strictly for the hit parade."[37] The following year, Lennon again ascribed this to collaboration: "We did . . . 'Please Please Me.'"[38] Paul's earliest comment on the song, in 1963, also recorded collaboration: "We wrote 'Please Please Me' but that hasn't exhausted our supply of compositions."[39] In another early statement, in 1965, Paul stated that Lennon wrote it "almost on his own"[40] — "almost" shows that there was some slight collaboration.

By 1971, John claimed "Please Please Me" as entirely his own: "I wrote all of this one. I was trying to do a Roy Orbison,"[41] and after this he continued to claim it as his song.[42] In late interviews, Paul also affirmed John's primary authorship. In 1989 he said: "John had this quite slow song called 'Please Please Me'."[43] However, his latest statement, in 2000, while restating John's main authorship, allowed for the possibility that he (Paul) made some minor contribution: "'Please Please Me' was more John than me; I didn't have such a hand in it."[44]

While this is definitely a song by John, the earliest evidence suggests that he also worked on the music with Paul.

- **Ask Me Why — (Lennon-McCartney) (lead vocal: John) (recorded on November 26, 1962)**

This was another song begun by John, and finished with collaboration, perhaps as early as 1960.[45] The evidence for authorship is flatly con-

---

[37] Alan Smith, "At a Recording Session With the Beatles" (1963).
[38] Roberts, "How to Write a Hit," 11.
[39] Smith, "You've Pleased — Pleased Us! say the Beatles."
[40] Wyndham, "Paul McCartney As Songwriter."
[41] Hennessey, "Who Wrote What."
[42] In 1971, John wrote, in a postcard to George Martin/Richard Williams, "I wrote Please Please Me alone. It was recorded in the exact sequence in which I wrote it." Davies, *The John Lennon Letters*, 197. See also in 1980, Sauter, "One John Lennon,"cf. Sheff, *The Playboy Interviews*, 179.
[43] Read, "McCartney on McCartney," episode 2. Miles, *Many Years from Now*, 91-92. See also *The Beatle's Book* 136 (Aug. 1987), 39; *Anthology* video, "This is one John had just written."
[44] *Anthology*, 94.
[45] Winn, *Way Beyond Compare*, 3.

tradictory. John, in 1971, claimed complete responsibility for the song ("I wrote all of that ... I wrote it.").[46] Paul, in 1962, apparently wrote, "John did write Ask Me Why."[47]

However, in 1995, Paul ascribed the genesis of the song to John, but also remembered a collaboration session: "It was John's original idea and we both sat down and wrote it together, just did a job on it. It was mostly John's."[48] I lean toward viewing this as John's song with minor collaboration following. In the early Beatles period, collaboration is often the norm.

"Misery / Shut The Door" single, by Kenny Lynch, March 15, 1963

o   Misery — (Lennon-McCartney)

This has historical interest, as the first cover of a Beatle song ever released. For full treatment of the song, see *Please Please Me* album, below.

o   Shut The Door (Kenny Lynch)

Please Please Me album, March 22, 1963

The first Beatles album was revolutionary in many ways. Remarkably enough, it was mostly recorded in one day. In 1965, Norman Smith, the engineer at Abbey Road, said that the recording session was "A tremendous day's recording ... an all-time record for the Beatles. We did thirteen titles in ten hours — all for the first LP. A day of musical excitement. Their voices must have been rasping."[49]

It was in essence a live album, though recorded in the studio, as the group needed an album quickly so decided to simply perform some of the best songs from their live show. Paul said, in 1989, "We could have played

[46] Unpublished section of interview with Mike Hennessey for *Record Mirror*, Oct. 2, 1971, as cited in Lewisohn, *Tune In*, extended, 2:1573n15.
[47] As cited in Lewisohn, *Tune In*, extended, 1573n15.
[48] Miles, *Many Years from Now*, 92.
[49] Goodman, "Norman Smith Continues Talking About Balancing the Beatles," 15.

that in Hamburg, or the Cavern. And we would have just done an hour's show . . . of good numbers that people liked, not numbers that everyone had recorded, because of our policy of sort of looking for offbeat things."[50]

Therefore, except for the songs from the two previous singles, all of it was recorded on February 11, 1963.

- **I Saw Her Standing There — (McCartney-Lennon) (lead vocal: Paul)**

Paul came up with the idea of this song, and its beginning, when he was driving home from a concert in Southport, about fifteen miles north of Liverpool.[51] "I did it going home in a car one night," he said in 1965.[52] Thirty years later, he said that the song "was my original, I'd started it and I had the first verse, which therefore gave me the tune, the tempo, and the key. It gave you the subject matter, a lot of the information, and then you had to fill in."[53] In 2000, he listed it as one of "my first songs."[54]

After this car ride, Paul arrived in Hurricaneville, the house of Ma Storm, mother of Rory, leader of Rory Storm and the Hurricanes, whose drummer was one Ringo Starr. Paul grabbed a guitar, and started developing the song, as Rory watched. The next day, Paul and his then girlfriend Celia Mortimer hitchhiked to London to see his friend Ivan Vaughan, and Paul was "humming it and singing it and fleshing out the words" throughout the day. At one point, according to Mortimer, Paul asked, "'What rhymes with "We danced through the night"?' and I came up with 'We held each other tight.'"[55] This is an early example of a friend who happened to be present during a Beatle song's gestation helping to supply a

---

[50] Read, "McCartney on McCartney," episode 2. Tobler and Grundy, "George Martin."

[51] McCartney, date unknown, in Badman, *The Beatles Off the Record*, 50. Paul says the concert was in Southport, but Lewisohn gives Widnes, southeast of Liverpool, and the date of first composition as October 22, 1962. Lewisohn, *Tune In*, extended, 2:1432.

[52] David Hull and Derek Taylor, "The Beatles: Let's Talk With Paul."

[53] Miles, *Many Years from Now*, 93-94.

[54] *Anthology*, 20.

[55] As quoted in Lewisohn, *Tune In*, 748.

line. Though Paul never said it explicitly, Mortimer felt the song was about them.

So he had the music, the main structure of the song, but when he sang it for John, his friend erupted in laughter at the second line of the song, "she'd never been a beauty queen."[56] So Paul and John sat down and worked out a better line. "We eventually got 'You know what I mean', which means nothing. . . . completely nothing at all," Paul said.[57] But at least, as Derek Taylor said, it wasn't embarrassing.[58] Mike McCartney has a photo of a McCartney-Lennon work session on this song.[59]

When the Beatles started arranging the song, Paul appropriated the base line from Chuck Berry's 1961 song "I'm Talking About You" for it. "I played exactly the same notes as he did and it fitted our number perfectly," he said.[60] In 1990, he described the whole song as a nick of Berry's song, another witness of Chuck Berry's influence on him.[61]

So this is basically a song by Paul, finished with collaboration. It shows John polishing the lyrics of a song mostly by Paul, an important pattern. The evidence for this picture is not too problematic, though sometimes Paul or John would emphasize the beginning by Paul, or the collaboration. Often Paul emphasized the collaboration, while John emphasized Paul's original authorship.

For example, in 1964, Paul said, "We spend a lot of time trying to write a real rocker. Something like "Long Tall Sally". . . . "I Saw Her Standing There" was the nearest we got to it."[62] "I wrote it with John in the front parlour of my house in 20 Forthlin Road, Allerton," he said about twenty-five years later. He also remembered: "We sagged off school and

[56] McCartney, date unknown, in Badman, *The Beatles Off the Record*, 50.
[57] Hull and Taylor, "The Beatles: Let's Talk With Paul" (1965).
[58] Ibid.
[59] Mike McCartney, *Remember*, 107.
[60] McCartney, in *Beat Instrumental*, (1964?) (repr. in *The Beatles Book* 2001), see Flippo, *Yesterday*, p. 197, quoted in Miles, *Many Years from Now*, 94 and in Turner, *A Hard Day's Write*, 18. Miles, *Many Years from Now*, 93-94.
[61] Flanagan, "Boy, You're Gonna Carry That Weight," 44.
[62] Ray Coleman, interview with the Beatles, in *Melody Maker*, Oct. 17, 1964 (Sandercombe, *The Beatles: Press Reports*, 94).

wrote it on guitars and a little bit on the piano that I had there."[63] And again, in 1995: "So it was co-written, my idea, and we finished it that day."[64] In 2007, he emphasized the collaboration: "I have fond flashbacks of John writing — he'd scribble it down real quick, desperate to get back to the guitar. But I knew at that moment [that the beauty queen line was replaced] that this was going to be a good collaboration."[65]

John, however, could say, in 1980, "That's Paul — doing his usual good job of producing a good, as George Martin used to call them, 'pot-boiler.'"[66] And in the same year, he asserted: "Paul's song."[67] But he did remember some collaboration: "I helped with a couple of the lyrics, a couple of lines here and there … I think he wrote the whole melody."[68] This is precisely what happened, based on Paul's 1965 memories of writing the song.

- **Misery — (collaboration)
  (lead vocals: John, Paul)**

In early 1963 the Beatles were preparing to go on tour with Helen Shapiro, a successful English pop singer, and her producer, the legendary Norrie Paramor, asked them to write a song for her.[69] Paul and John began writing "Misery" on January 26, 1963, "before a gig at the Kings Hall, Stoke-on-Trent," Staffordshire, and finished it at the McCartney home at Forthlin Road.[70] Apparently, the Hollies helped brainstorm on some of the words — an early example of Paul and John turning to whatever friends happened to be around to finish lyrics. Allan Clarke, one of the Hollies,

---

[63] Lewisohn, "The Paul McCartney Interview" (1988), 9.
[64] Miles, *Many Years from Now* (1995), 93-94.
[65] Doherty, "Pete Doherty meets Paul McCartney" (2007).
[66] Lost Lennon Tapes, Sept. 23, 1991, cf. Sheff, *The Playboy Interviews*, 203. See also Hennessey, "Who Wrote What," *Record Mirror* (1971).
[67] Peebles, *The Lennon Tapes*, 19.
[68] Lost Lennon Tapes, Sept. 23, 1991, cf. Sheff, *The Playboy Interviews*, 203.
[69] Smith, "You've Pleased-Pleased Us." The tour went from February 2 to March 3, 1963.
[70] Miles, *Many Years from Now*, 94.

said, "It was just four guys together sitting in a room. John and Paul were plunking along writing this song and we helped with a couple of words."[71]

Paramor turned down the song without even showing it to Helen Shapiro! But singer Kenny Lynch, also on the tour, recorded it, and his single (see above) appeared a week before the Beatles' version on *Please Please Me*.

Both Paul and John agree that the song was co-written, but they disagree on the extent of collaboration, as John sometimes described it as a co-written song he had dominated, while Paul sometimes saw it as a more 50-50 song.

The earliest comment on the song, in 1963, describes the two Beatles hashing it out together. Journalist Alan Smith reported that Paul and John, "were composing a song for Helen to record when she goes to Nashville shortly. Said Paul: 'We've called it 'Misery', . . . and we think Helen will make a pretty good job of it."[72] Much later, in the mid nineties, Paul said, "We wrote it for Helen Shapiro because we were going on tour with her . . . being young lads with an eye for an opportunity. . . . It was co-written. I don't think either of us dominated on that one."[73] And in 1988, he said, "John and I were a songwriting team, and what songwriting teams did in those days was wrote for everyone. . . . 'Misery' was for Helen Shapiro."[74]

John, in 1971, ascribed it to "Both of us," but then added, "this was mainly mine, though, I think."[75] However, he softened that in 1980, stating that "it was kind of a John song more than a Paul, but it was written together."[76]

So we have a clear contradiction: John says "both of us" but "mainly mine" (adding "I think"); Paul says "It was co-written. I don't think either of us dominated on that one." I believe that the evidence clearly shows ex-

---

[71] Quoted in Turner, *A Hard Day's Write*, 20. Tony Bramwell agrees, ibid.

[72] Smith, "You've Pleased-Pleased Us."

[73] Miles, *Many Years from Now* (1995), 94-95.

[74] Lewisohn, "The Paul McCartney Interview," 8-9.

[75] Hennessey, "Who Wrote What," *Record Mirror*.

[76] Lost Lennon Tapes, Sept. 9, 1991, cf. Sheff, *The Playboy Interviews*, 180.

tensive collaboration. Then you have John tentatively claiming some domination, though Paul denies this.

○ <u>Anna (Go to Him) (COVER) (Arthur Alexander)</u>
<u>(lead vocals: John)</u>

This marvelous song was a 1962 single for rhythm and blues singer Arthur Alexander, a favorite of the Beatles.[77]

○ <u>Chains (COVER) (Gerry Goffin, Carole King)</u>
<u>(lead vocals: George)</u>

This was a hit for the Cookies, a rhythm and blues girl group, in 1962. Paul said that the Beatles had a "policy of sort of looking for offbeat things. Like George did 'Chains.'"[78]

○ <u>Boys (COVER) (Luther Dixon, Wes Farrell)</u>
<u>(lead vocals: Ringo)</u>

This was a song by the Shirelles, another rhythm and blues girls group, the B-side of their famous "Will You Love Me Tomorrow" single, released in November 1960. Ringo used to sing this as far back as his years with Rory Storm and the Hurricanes.[79] Paul said, "And Ringo used to sing 'Boys,' another Shirelles number. It was so innocent. We just never even thought, 'Why is he singing about boys'? We loved the song."[80]

○ <u>Ask Me Why</u>
<u>(lead vocals: John)</u>

See "Please Please Me" single, above.

○ <u>Please Please Me</u>
<u>(lead vocals: John, Paul)</u>

See "Please Please Me" single, above.

---

[77] For Alexander, see Haglund, "The Forgotten Songwriter." Lewisohn, *Tune In*, extended, 2:1131-32, 1498-99.
[78] Read, "McCartney on McCartney," episode 2. For Goffin and King's impact on the Beatles, see my comments on the Decca Audition, above.
[79] Harry, "Cilla Black."
[80] Miles, *Many Years From Now*, 82.

SIDE TWO

- o Love Me Do
  (lead vocals: Paul, John)

See "Love Me Do" single, above.

- o P.S. I Love You
  (lead vocals: Paul)

See "Love Me Do" single, above.

- o Baby It's You (COVER) (Burt Bacharach, Luther Dixon
  (credited as Barney Williams), Mack David)
  (lead vocals: John)

Another Shirelles record, which had been released in 1961.

- **Do You Want to Know a Secret — (Lennon-McCartney)
  (lead vocals: George)**

John's mother would sing him "I'm Wishing" from Disney's *Snow White and the Seven Dwarves* when he was little, and this song led him to write "Do You Want to Know a Secret." He said the song "was from a Disney movie — [*singing*] "Want to know a secret? Promise not to tell. You're standing by a wishing well."[81] It was written very soon after John's marriage to Cynthia Powell on August 23, 1962. After he got the beginnings of the song, it was finished with collaboration.

Once again, John and Paul disagreed on the exact details of how this song was written. John claimed it in 1971: "Me — I wrote this for George." And at about the same time, he asserted, "I wrote this one."[82] Paul agreed that the song started with John, but remembered collaboration. In 1995, Miles wrote that "Based on an original idea by John, it was essentially what Paul calls a 'hack song', a 50-50 collaboration written to

[81] Lost Lennon Tapes, Oct. 21, 1991, cf. Sheff, *The Playboy Interviews* (1980), 175; Aldridge, *Beatles Illustrated Lyrics*, 220. Lennon in 1970, Connolly, *Ray Connolly Beatles Archive*, 102. George, on the other hand, felt that the song was a "nick" from "I Really Love You" a 1961 hit by the Stereos. White, "George Harrison Reconsidered" (1987), 55.
[82] Hennessey, "Who Wrote What," *Record Mirror*. Aldridge, *Beatles Illustrated Lyrics*, 220. Similar: Sheff, *The Playboy Interviews*, 175, in 1980. See also Connolly, cited above.

order."[83] Paul also described the songwriting as collaborative in 1984 and 2000.[84]

John probably wrote the beginnings of the song, then there was collaboration, a typical pattern for the early Beatles.

○ <u>A Taste of Honey (COVER) (Bobby Scott, Ric Marlow)</u> <u>(lead vocals: Paul)</u>

This song was originally used as an instrumental for the Broadway play *A Taste of Honey*, in 1960, and Bobby Scott released it on his album of the same name that year. The Beatles followed Lenny Welch's 1962 vocal version of it.[85]

• **There's a Place — (collaboration)** **(lead vocals: John and Paul)**

Just as "Do You Want to Know a Secret" came from a movie song, so did "There's a Place," according to Paul. He owned the record, *West Side Story*, that had "There's a Place for Us" on it, which inspired the title. After Paul started on the song, it was finished in a songwriting session with John at Forthlin Road.[86]

Once again, there is contradictory evidence for authorship. John claimed the song in 1971,[87] and nine years later, he even pointed to typical Lennon ideas in the lyrics: "'There's a Place' was my attempt at a sort of Motown, black thing," he said. "But it says the usual Lennon things, 'In my mind there's no sorrow' . . . It's all in your mind."[88] But according to Miles, it was "co-written, co-sung but with a bias towards being Paul's original idea."[89]

---

[83] Miles, *Many Years From Now*, 95.
[84] "Paul and Linda McCartney Interview," *Playboy*, 104. *Anthology*, 96.
[85] See on "Till There Was You," below.
[86] Miles, *Many Years From Now*, 95.
[87] Hennessey, "Who Wrote What," *Record Mirror*.
[88] Lost Lennon Tapes, Sept. 23, 1991, cf. Sheff, *The Playboy Interviews*, 203.
[89] Miles, *Many Years From Now*, 95.

Despite the contradictory evidence, I believe the collaboration pattern is typical of the early Beatles, and Paul's memories of starting the song from *West Side Story* are convincing.

o   <u>Twist and Shout (COVER) (Phil Medley, Bert Russell Berns) (credited as Medley-Russell)</u>
<u>(lead vocals: John)</u>

This was first recorded (as "Shake It Up Baby") by the Top Notes in 1961, but the Beatles followed the Isley Brothers' classic 1962 version. John's epic vocal performance for this has become legendary. After the Beatles' twelve-hour recording marathon for *Please Please Me*, Norman Smith remembers, "John suddenly thought of 'Twist and Shout' and said he wanted to do it. We felt sure his voice would never stand it. But it was done in one 'take.' No over-dubbing. Just one straight take."[90]

This is an example of a cover that John and the Beatles and George Martin took possession of so thoroughly that they virtually recreated the song. It almost raises the question of whether a major reinterpreter of a song should get co-writing credit. In addition, by including a cover on a Beatle album, the group made the song part of a long-form work of Beatle art.

---

[90] Goodman, "Norman Smith Continues Talking About Balancing the Beatles" (1965), 15. Cf. Norman Smith, in Lewisohn, *Beatles Recording Sessions*, 27.

4

"One-On-One, Eyeball To Eyeball"

WITH THE BEATLES

Following *Please Please Me*, the Beatles wrote the two great singles, "From Me to You" and "She Loves You," followed by a remarkable series of songs for other groups. "From Me to You" and "She Loves You" are examples of collaboration, *almost* from the ground up.

———————◦◦———————

"From Me To You / Thank You Girl" single, April 12, 1963

- **From Me To You — (collaboration, John emphasis) (lead vocals: John, Paul)) (recorded on March 5, 1963)**

    Both Paul and John remembered writing this in a bus as they were touring with Helen Shapiro. This would have occurred between York and Shrewsbury, in western England, on February 28, 1963.[1] According to John, in 1963, "We were having a lot of laughs the night Paul and I wrote 'From Me To You'. . . . there we were, not taking ourselves seriously. Just fooling about on the guitar. This went on for a while. Then we began to get a good melody line and we really started to work at it. Before that journey was over, we'd completed the lyric, everything."[2] They may have derived the title from a column in *New Musical Express*, "From You To Us."[3]

---

[1] Lennon in Smith, "Throat Sweets Keep Us Going" (1963) and in "From 'You To Us' Inspired 'From Me To You'" (1963). Ray Coleman, interview with the Beatles, in *Melody Maker*, Oct. 17, 1964 (Sandercombe, *The Beatles: Press Reports*, 94). Hennessey, "Who Wrote What" (1971). *Ray Connolly Beatles*, 101. Aldridge, *Beatles Illustrated Lyrics*, 166. Paul said they wrote it after hearing Roy Orbison play a new song for them, *Anthology*, 94, but they toured with Orbison in May to June, 1963, *after* "From Me to You" was released.
[2] Lennon in Smith, "Throat Sweets Keep Us Going" (1963).
[3] "'From You To Us' Inspired 'From Me To You'" (1963).

John remembered that he came up with the first line, which got the song going.[4] For him, it was a perfect example of collaboration.[5]

Paul, typically, remembered a musical aspect of the songwriting, an unexpected G minor chord at the beginning of the middle eight. This "takes you to a whole new world. It was exciting."[6] Paul regarded that well-crafted middle eight with that surprising G minor chord as a significant step forward in the Beatles' creativity, making this a "pivotal song."[7]

There are no real contradictions in the evidence of this song's authorship. In 1964, John stated, "Paul and I kicked some ideas around and came up with what we thought was a suitable melody line."[8] He put it in lists of fully collaborative songs in 1970 and 1971.[9] In the mid-eighties, Paul gave it as an example of a song written "from the ground up." "We would sit down with nothing and two guitars, which was like working with a mirror. I could see what he was doing, and he could see me. We got ideas off each other."[10]

This was nearly a complete 50-50 collaboration, but there is a Lennon emphasis because he apparently came up with the first line of the song.

• Thank You Girl — (collaboration, Paul emphasis) (lead vocals: John, Paul) (recorded on March 5, 1963)

This was close to another "pure" collaboration. In 1963, John said, "We'd already written 'Thank You Girl' as the follow-up to 'Please Please Me.'"[11] Then he asserted, in 1971, "Paul and me. This was just a silly song we knocked off."[12] Paul commented once on "Thank You Girl," in 1995,

[4] Sheff, *The Playboy Interviews* (1980), 179.

[5] Ibid., 150.

[6] Lewisohn, "The Paul McCartney Interview" (1988), 10.

[7] Miles, *Many Years From Now*, 149.

[8] As quoted in Turner, *A Hard Day's Write*, 31.

[9] Wenner, *Lennon Remembers*, 83; Hennessey, "Lennon: the Greatest Natural Songwriter," 12. Connolly, *Ray Connolly Beatles Archive*, 102. George Martin remembered it as a full collaboration also, Williams, "Produced by George Martin."

[10] Interview in Smith, *Off the Record*, 201. See also Miles, *Many Years From Now*, 149.

[11] Smith, "Throat Sweets Keep Us Going Say Beatles!" Cf. Lennon in 1970, *Ray Connolly Beatles*, 102: "We knocked that off as a B-side." Aldridge, *Beatles Illustrated Lyrics*, 166.

[12] Hennessey, "Who Wrote What," *Record Mirror*. Also Sheff, *The Playboy Interviews*, 180.

and agreed that it was a collaborative song, but added that it might have had a McCartney accent. "This was pretty much co-written but there might have been a slight leaning towards me with the 'thank you, girl' thing, it sounds a bit like me, trying to appease the mob."[13]

So this is another one that was near pure collaboration, though it may have had a "slight leaning" toward Paul.

———————◦◦◦———————

"Do You Want to Know a Secret / I'll Be On My Way" single — Billy J. Kramer with The Dakotas, April 26, 1963

○   Do You Want to Know a Secret

See the *Please Please Me* album, above.

- **I'll Be On My Way — (McCartney-Lennon) (recorded on April 4, 1963)**

This is an early song, very Buddy Holly in tone, written in Liverpool by Paul, then finished with collaboration. John attributed it entirely to Paul, and argued that the happy-go-lucky lyrics are typical of Paul's sole authorship.[14] But Paul remembered that John contributed to the song. Miles wrote that it was "co-written in early Liverpool days."[15] Lennon's arguments are not too persuasive, as many of the very early Lennon-McCartney songs were unsophisticated, hackneyed love songs. Unterberger also suggests that John co-singing the lead with Paul (in a BBC Beatles recording) is a mark of a collaborative song.[16]

This is the first of the songs that "the Beatles gave away" and never formally recorded themselves.[17] Billy J. Kramer, born William Howard Ashton, was another artist whom Brian Epstein managed, and his fairly

---

[13] Miles, *Many Years From Now*, 149.

[14] Hennessey, "Who Wrote What," *Record Mirror*. Sheff, *The Playboy Interviews*, 180. Wenner, *Lennon Remembers*, 26. Connolly, *Ray Connolly Beatles Archive*, 102.

[15] Miles, *Many Years From Now*, 180. John seems to agree in Roberts, "How To Write."

[16] Unterberger, *Unreleased Beatles*, 55.

[17] For the non-Beatles who sang Lennon-McCartney songs, see Engelhardt, *Beatles Undercover*; Unterberger, *Unreleased Beatles*, 341-54.

successful career began with this and other Lennon-McCartney songs.[18] The fact that Paul and John started sharing songs with other artists shows their seriousness as songwriters, even at this early stage of their recording career.

Some have suggested that "the songs the Beatles gave away" were lesser offerings that the Beatles happened to have on hand, early apprenticeship songs that they would never have considered recording themselves. There is some truth to this; the Beatles would always try to keep their best songs for themselves. But this is not the full story. Sometimes one of the Beatles might censor a song that was quite good. Most notoriously, John criticized George's superb "All Things Must Pass," and it first came to light on a Billy Preston album, and never appeared on a Beatles album. So some of these songs might have been good, but casualties of intra-Beatle politics.

Nevertheless, many of them are undoubtedly lesser songs. Paul said, "There were always a couple of songs that we didn't want to do because we didn't think they were very good, but other people would say, 'Well, I'll do it, I think it's quite good.'"[19] Speaking of giving "I Wanna Be You Man," to the Rolling Stones, John said, "We weren't going to give them anything great, right?"[20] But some of these "given" songs are good songs, or even, in a few cases, really good songs. Some of them are as good or better than the lesser or second-rate songs that somehow made it onto the Beatle albums. Paul and John would often be involved in producing and recording the "given away" songs, too, which shows their interest in these songs and in their careers as songwriters, not just as pop stars. There was an album of *The Songs Lennon and McCartney Gave Away* released in 1971; it deserves to be resurrected, or done again but in a fuller, better way, on CD.

The Beatles performed this song on the BBC show Side by Side on June 24, 1963, and this recording appears on the Beatles' *Live at the BBC*.

---

[18] Engelhardt, *Beatles Undercover*, 224-25.

[19] Miles, *Many Years From Now*, 182.

[20] Sheff, *The Playboy Interviews*, 181-82.

"Bad to Me / I Call Your Name" single — Billy J. Kramer and the Dakotas, July 26, 1963

- Bad to Me — (Lennon-McCartney)
  (recorded on June 27, 1963)

Brian Epstein asked Paul and John to provide another song for Billy J., and they wrote "Bad to Me" for him in the back of a van. John later called it a "commissioned song."[21] After this start, John may have worked on it while on his Spain vacation with Epstein, from late April to early May, 1963.

The evidence for this song's authorship is slightly muddled. In his earliest statement, in 1964, John remembered writing this with Paul. "We used to write a lot in the back of a coach. . . . We did 'Bad to Me' in the back of a van."[22] Paul consistently described the song as collaborative, including a statement even earlier than John's, from 1963: "John and I have written about 100 songs together, including 'Bad To Me' for Billy J. Kramer."[23] He made similar statements in 1988 and 1989.[24]

However, in his later interviews, John claimed full authorship. In the early seventies, he said, "Me. I wrote it for Billy J. Kramer."[25] Ten years later, he remembered writing it for Billy J. while on his vacation in Spain with Brian Epstein in late April and early May, 1963.[26]

In view of the early evidence for collaboration, a song started as an eyeball-to-eyeball composition in a van, I conclude that Paul and John

[21] Sheff, *The Playboy Interviews*, 180.
[22] Ray Coleman, interview with the Beatles, in *Melody Maker*, Oct. 17, 1964 (Sandercombe, *The Beatles: Press Reports*, 94).
[23] Smith, "Close-Up on Paul McCartney" (1963).
[24] Lewisohn, "The Paul McCartney Interview," (1988), 8. Read, "McCartney on McCartney," episode 2.
[25] Hennessey, "Who Wrote What," *Record Mirror*. See also Aldridge, *The Beatles Illustrated Lyrics*, 259: "I wrote this in Spain for Billy J. Kramer." *Ray Connolly Beatles Archive*, 102.
[26] Sheff, *The Playboy Interviews* (1980), 180.

started this, then John worked ton it in Spain.[27] There is a demo of Paul and John singing it, which was released on *The Beatles Bootleg Recordings 1963*, in 2013.

Both John and Paul remembered that the song was written to order — so it wasn't simply a lesser song that Paul and John had on hand. And in fact it became a number one record. In addition, "I Call Your Name," a first-rate song which the Beatles later recorded and released, is the B-side of this single.

    o   <u>I Call Your Name — (Lennon-McCartney)</u>

See the *Long Tall Sally* EP, below.

<hr/>

"Tip of My Tongue / Heaven Only Knows" single — Tommy Quickly, July 30, 1963

- **Tip of My Tongue — (McCartney)**
  (recorded by the Beatles November 26, 1962; date of recording by Quickly unknown)

Both Paul and John remembered this as a McCartney song — Paul to his horror. "Oh my God!" he said in 1995: ". . . This is pretty much mine, I'm ashamed to say."[28] "That's another piece of Paul's garbage, not my garbage," John said fifteen years earlier.[29] The Beatles performed this in the studio on November 26, 1962, but it was never released as a Beatle song.[30]

Tommy Quickly was a Liverpool friend of the Beatles who had been lead singer in the group The Challengers, and whom Brian Epstein was managing. Unlike Billy Kramer, his career did not take off with a Lennon-McCartney song, and he retired from the music business in 1965.[31]

<hr/>

[27] See also Tony Mansfield (of the Dakotas) in Giuliano, *The Beatles: A Celebration*, 44, who reflects collaboration.
[28] Miles, *Many Years From Now* (1995), 182.
[29] Sheff, *The Playboy Interviews*, 203. Also in 1971, Hennessey, "Who Wrote What," *Record Mirror*. Connolly, *Ray Connolly Beatles Archive*, 102.
[30] Winn, *Way Beyond Compare*, 19.
[31] Engelhardt, *Beatles Undercover*, 389-90.

Chapter 4

o   <u>Heaven Only Knows (Barry Rapaport, Mitch Murray)</u>

"She Loves You / I'll Get You" single, August 28, 1963

- **She Loves You — (collaboration, Paul emphasis)
(lead vocals: John, Paul) (recorded on July 1, 1963)**

The Beatles performed in Newcastle, in northeast England, on June 26, 1963, and on that night, or the following day, Paul and John started writing a song while they sat on beds at the hotel.[32] Paul had the idea to write an answering song, one group saying "she loves you," and the other group saying "yes, yes." This answering idea was dropped, but those fragments of lyrics remained.[33] It was polished the next day at the McCartney home on Forthlin Road, as Jim McCartney watched TV in the next room. When they'd finished the song, John and Paul played it for the elder McCartney. He approved of it, but suggested changing Yeah Yeah Yeah to Yes Yes Yes. "At which point," Paul said, "we collapsed in a heap and said 'No, Dad, you don't quite get it!'"[34]

George Harrison contributed the 6th chord at the end that George Martin objected so strongly to, at first.[35]

---

[32] Tate, Pop Chat interview, BBC, July 30, 1963. Beatles, Interview, Klas Burling, August 23, 1963. For the hotel location, also Read, "McCartney on McCartney," episode 2. Paul, in an interview with Klas Burling on August 23, 1963, said: "So we went to the hotel . . . and we just decided that we have to write a song very quickly. So we sat down, no ideas came for a bit. But eventually we got an idea. 'She Loves You' came, you know. It was just lucky."

[33] Beatles, Interview, Klas Burling Radio Interviews, late October 1963. "And I originally got an idea of doing one of those answering songs, where a couple of us sing about 'she loves you,' and the other one sorta says the 'yes, yes' bit. Y'know, 'yeah yeah'. . . . But we decided that was a crummy idea anyway, as it was. But that — at least we had the idea to write a song called 'She Loves You' then." Paul also said that he had Bobby Rydell's recent "Forget Him" in mind when the song was written. Miles, *Many Years From Now*, 149.

[34] Miles, *Many Years From Now*, 150.

[35] Paul, in *Anthology*, 96. Gambaccini, *Paul McCartney In His Own Words* (a 1973 interview), 19. Lewisohn, "The Paul McCartney Interview," 10. McCartney interview in JAMMING!, in two parts: No. 13 (June 1982); no. 14 (June 1983), as cited in Dowlding, *Beatlesongs*, 44. For George Martin's comments on the chord, see Davies, *The Beatles*, 280.

We can date the song composition very precisely. John, in 1963, said that it was written two days before it was recorded, and it was recorded on July 1, 1963.[36] As the Beatles performed in Newcastle on June 26, 1963, it was presumably written on June 26 and 27, 1963.[37] While Paul and John usually give two sites for the song's composition, a hotel room in Newcastle and the McCartney home, in 1964, John also stated that it was "half-written in a coach."[38]

Paul and John both remembered this as a very collaborative song. In a 1963 interview, they said, "**[John]**: We wrote that two days before we recorded it, actually. **[Paul]**: We wrote it in a hotel room in Newcastle."[39] "John and I wrote it together. . . . we just sat up in the hotel bedroom for a few hours and wrote it, y'know," Paul stated, also in 1963.[40] In one interview, Paul gave "She Loves You" as his first example of a song written collaboratively "from the ground up."[41] In 1971, John put it at the head of a list of co-written songs,[42] and offered it as the first example of songs written "eyeball to eyeball."[43] Even the "yeahs" were collaborative. "*Q: Who put the yeahs on 'She Loves You'?* John and I wrote it into the song," Paul said in the early 1970s.[44]

Nevertheless, both Paul (in 1963) and John remembered that the original idea for the song was Paul's. John said, in 1980, "I remember it was Paul's idea, where instead of singing I love you, we'd have a third party passing the message on to somebody else."[45]

---

[36] Tate, Pop Chat interview, BBC, July 30, 1963.
[37] See also Miles, *Many Years from Now*, 149.
[38] Ray Coleman, interview with the Beatles, in *Melody Maker*, Oct. 17, 1964 (Sandercombe, *The Beatles: Press Reports*, 94).
[39] Tate, Pop Chat interview, BBC, July 30, 1963.
[40] Beatles, Interview, Klas Burling Radio Interviews, late October 1963.
[41] Smith, *Off the Record* (ca 1988), 201.
[42] Hennessey, "Lennon: the Greatest Natural Songwriter," 12. See also Hennessey, "Who Wrote What," *Record Mirror*.
[43] Sheff, *The Playboy Interviews*, 150.
[44] Gambaccini, *Paul McCartney In His Own Words*, a 1973 interview, 19.
[45] Lost Lennon Tapes, Aug. 1, 1988, cf. Sheff, *The Playboy Interviews,* 179. For Paul, see Beatles, Interview, Klas Burling Radio Interviews, late October 1963, quoted above.

Of course, not to leave things too straightforward, Paul also contradicted himself, saying in the 1990s: "It was very co-written as I recall, I don't think it was either of our idea, I think we just sat down and said, 'Right!'"[46] His 1963 interview is preferable to this late memory.

I conclude that this was substantially co-written, a collaborative song. However, we can accept a Paul emphasis because the original idea came from him.

- **I'll Get You — (collaboration)**
  (lead vocals: John, Paul) (recorded on July 1, 1963)

Both John and Paul remembered equal collaboration on this song. In 1963, Paul said, "We wrote 'I'll Get You', which is the B-side, first."[47] Thirty years later, Paul described this as "very co-written." He felt that the imagery of the song, especially the word "imagine," was related to Lewis Carroll. Both Paul and John "were fascinated by his surreal world so this was a nice song to write."[48] "We wrote that together," John said in 1970.[49]

Paul, typically, remembered a musical idiosyncrasy in the song. He "nicked" an A minor chord from "All My Trials" on a Joan Baez album and put it into the middle eight. It was a harmonic change that had always fascinated him.[50]

---

46 Miles, *Many Years From Now*, 150.
47 Beatles, Interview, Klas Burling Radio Interviews, August 23, 1963.
48 Miles, *Many Years From Now* (1995), 150.
49 Connolly, *Ray Connolly Beatles Archive*, 102. See also Hennessey, "Who Wrote What" (1971), *Record Mirror*; Lost Lennon Tapes, July 18, 1988, cf. Sheff, *The Playboy Interviews*, 214.
50 Miles, *Many Years From Now*, 150.

"Hello Little Girl / Just In Case" single — The Fourmost, August 30, 1963

- Hello, Little Girl — (Lennon-McCartney) (recorded on July 3, 1963)

John wrote this when he a teen-ager, basing it on a thirties standard that his mother used to sing, Cole Porter's "It's De-Lovely."[51] When the Beatles got going, he worked on it with Paul, and it was one of the first songs he'd written that he got the Beatles to perform. It can be found on a summer 1960 Beatle rehearsal tape,[52] and the group often played it at the Cavern Club, where it was a big request number.[53] It was one of the three Lennon-McCartney songs performed at the Decca audition, on January 1, 1962.[54]

In his comments after the breakup, John claimed "Hello Little Girl" and referred to it as his first good song. In 1971, an interviewer wrote, "The first satisfactory tune he remembers writing was 'Hello Little Girl.'"[55] John said, "Me — this was another very early song of mine."[56] At about the same time, he said, "This was one of the first songs I ever finished. I was then about eighteen . . . I think it was the first song of my own that I ever attempted to do with the group."[57]

However, in John's earliest mention of the song, in 1964, he seemed to put it in a list of collaborative songs. "It [Lennon-McCartney collaboration] started in school holidays. I was about 15. . .We did 'Like Dreamers Do' . . . 'Hello Little Girl'. . . 'Love of the Loved' and 'Please Please Me.'"[58] This reference is impressively early. So "Hello Little Girl" was probably a

---

[51] Sheff, *The Playboy Interviews,* 182.
[52] Winn, *Way Beyond Compare,* 4.
[53] Paul, quoted in James, "Lennon & McCartney (Songwriters) Ltd." (1963).
[54] This version was released in *Anthology 1.*
[55] Hennessey, "Lennon: the Greatest Natural Songwriter," 12.
[56] Hennessey, "Who Wrote What," *Record Mirror.*
[57] Aldridge, *Beatles Illustrated Lyrics,* 215. Connolly, *Ray Connolly Beatles Archive,* 103 (it was the third or fourth song he wrote). Similar: Lost Lennon Tapes, June 20, 1988, cf. Sheff, *The Playboy Interviews,* 182: "That was me. That was actually my first song."
[58] Roberts, "How to Write a Hit," 11.

John song, finished up with collaboration.[59] In 1995, Miles, working with McCartney interviews, referred to "Hello Little Girl" and another song given to the Fourmost as "Lennon-McCartney compositions."[60]

The Fourmost were another Liverpool band managed by Brian Epstein, and this song was produced by George Martin.[61]

o <u>Just In Case (Boudleaux and Felice Bryant)</u>

"Love of the Loved / Shy Of Love" single — Cilla Black, September 27, 1963

- ### Love of the Loved — (McCartney-Lennon)

This was written by Paul as a teen, but was apparently polished with the help of John. According to Lewisohn, Paul wrote it on his Zenith one night as he walked home to Allerton.[62] Paul's girlfriend at the time, Dorothy "Dot" Rhone, said that Paul told her that he had written the song for her.[63] The Beatles recorded this at the Decca Audition, but it was not released in the *Beatles Anthology*, unlike the other two Lennon-McCartney Decca audition songs.

John post-breakup definitely ascribed "Love of the Loved" to Paul. In 1971, he said, "Paul. One of his very early songs, but I think he changed the words later for Cilla."[64] However, in his earliest comment on the song, in 1964, he seemed to remember collaboration.[65]

As the earlier testimony is preferable, I see this as a Paul song polished with some collaboration.

---

[59] Paul has not commented on the writing of the song, to the best of my knowledge.

[60] Miles, *Many Years from Now*, 181.

[61] Harry, "Fourmost." Engelhardt, *Beatles Undercover*, 170-72.

[62] Lewisohn, *Tune In*, extended, 516.

[63] Shea and Rodriguez, *Fab Four FAQ*, 362.

[64] Hennessey, "Who Wrote What," *Record Mirror*. Similar: Connolly, *Ray Connolly Beatles Archive*, 103. Sheff, *The Playboy Interviews*, 182. Pete Best also ascribed it to Paul. *Beatle! The Pete Best Story*, 144.

[65] Roberts, "How to Write a Hit," 11. Quoted at "Hello Little Girl," above.

Cilla Black, ironically born Priscilla Maria Veronica White, sang with a number of Liverpool groups; she worked as a cloak room attendant at the Cavern when the Beatles met her. Brian Epstein became her manager in 1963. "Love of the Loved" only reached 35 on the charts, but her second single, Bacharach and David's "Anyone Who Had a Heart," was a solid success, and she went on to a successful career as singer, actress and TV personality.[66]

o   Shy Of Love (Bobby Willis)

"I'll Keep You Satisfied / I Know" single — Billy J. Kramer and the Dakotas, November 1, 1963

- I'll Keep You Satisfied — (McCartney-Lennon) (recorded on October 14, 1963)

This was another "commissioned song." Apparently, Paul had the beginnings of it, then he and John sat down in a songwriting session and developed it into its final form. I say apparently, as Paul and John supply contradictory evidence here. John, after the breakup, ascribed it to Paul alone three times.[67] But in Paul's only description of writing this song (in the 1990s), he remembered collaboration: "It was pretty much co-written: John and I sat down and purposely wrote it for Billy J. in a couple of hours."[68]

Though Paul hated some of the "given away" songs from this period, he continued to have a fondness for "I'll Keep You Satisfied." "This is one I still like. I find myself whistling it in the garden," he said.[69]

o   I Know (George Martin, Bob Wooller)

[66] Harry, "Cilla Black"; Engelhardt, *Beatles Undercover*, 56-57.
[67] Connolly, *Ray Connolly Beatles Archive*, 102. Hennessey, "Who Wrote What," *Record Mirror*; Sheff, *The Playboy Interviews* (1980), 182, 204.
[68] Miles, *Many Years From Now*, 180.
[69] Ibid.

"I Wanna Be Your Man / Stoned" single, Rolling Stones, November 1, 1963

- I Wanna Be Your Man — (McCartney-Lennon)

See *With the Beatles* album, below.

- ○ Stoned (Nanker Phelge: a pseudonym for the Rolling Stones)

———————————◦———————————

"I'm In Love / Respectable" single — The Fourmost, November 15, 1963

- I'm In Love — (Lennon-McCartney)
(recorded a few days after October 14, 1963)

In 1970 John claimed this: "I wrote that for The Fourmost," but added, "I can hardly remember it myself."[70] By 1980, he couldn't remember anything about writing it (though the song sounded like his style, he thought).[71] In 1995, Miles, working with McCartney interviews, referred to it and "Hello Little Girl" as "Lennon-McCartney compositions," and Paul talked about the limitations of those songs.[72]

It was probably a Lennon song finished with collaboration.

Though the song was written for The Fourmost, apparently the Beatles offered it to Billy J. Kramer first, and he recorded it on October 14, 1963.[73] He decided not to release the song, so the Fourmost recorded it a few days later. A Beatles-era demo of the song, sung by John, has been released on *The Beatles Bootleg Recordings 1963*, see below.

- ○ Respectable (O'Kelly Isley, Ronald Isley, Rudolph Isley)

———————————◦———————————

---

[70] Connolly, *Ray Connolly Beatles Archive*, 103. Similar: Hennessey, "Who Wrote What," *Record Mirror*. Harry, "Fourmost."

[71] Sheff, *The Playboy Interviews*, 182.

[72] Miles, *Many Years from Now*, 181.

[73] This recording was eventually released on *The Best of Billy J. Kramer and the Dakotas* (1991).

With the Beatles album, November 22, 1963

After this remarkable series of songs written for other artists, the Beatles released their second album. This was not as revolutionary as *Please Please Me*, but like that album, it was a marvelous offering of solid Beatle originals mixed with great covers. In the live-show album tradition so typical of the early Beatles albums, it ends with a screamer, "Money (That's What I Want)."

- **It Won't Be Long — (Lennon-McCartney) (lead vocals: John) (recorded on July 30, 1963)**

This was probably a song begun by John, then developed in a song-writing session. Once again, in post-breakup interviews, John emphasizes separate authorship, while Paul emphasizes collaboration. "I wrote that for the second album," John said in 1970.[74] And in 1980, he asserted that the song was "mine. It was my attempt at writing another single."[75] But Paul remembered a writing session, possibly from an idea by John: "John mainly sang it so I expect that it was his original idea but we both sat down and wrote it together."[76]

- **All I've Got to Do — (Lennon) (lead vocals: John) (recorded on September 11, 1963)**

John claimed "All I've Got to Do." "That's me trying to do Smokey Robinson," he said in 1980.[77] Paul seems to agree — he said that he heard it first in the studio, just before it was recorded.[78]

- **All My Loving — (McCartney) (lead vocals: Paul) (recorded on July 30, 1963)**

Paul wrote the words to this one day on a tour bus during the tour with Roy Orbison (and thus in the period May 18 to June 19, 1963), then,

---

[74] *Ray Connolly Beatles Archive*, 103. Hennessey, "Who Wrote What," *Record Mirror*.
[75] Lost Lennon Tapes, Sept. 16, 1991, cf. Sheff, *The Playboy Interviews*, 181.
[76] Miles, *Many Years From Now*, 152.
[77] Lost Lennon Tapes, Feb. 6, 1989, cf. Sheff, *The Playboy Interviews*, 203. See also Hennessey, "Who Wrote What," *Record Mirror*.
[78] Miles, *Many Years From Now*, 148.

after getting off the bus, worked out the melody on a piano in a backstage area.[79] Since he wrote most of his songs with the music first, he called this "working backwards." Paul was so focused on music that getting the words for a song first was a remarkable event. "The first time I've ever worked upside down," he said in 1984.[80]

Both John and Paul agreed that Paul wrote this song. In 1965, Paul gave it as an example of a song he wrote on his own.[81] John said, in 1971: "Paul. This was one of his first biggies." And in 1980, he praised it: "'All My Loving' is Paul. I regret to say. Ha-ha-ha. *Q: Why?* Because it's a damn good piece."[82]

- **Don't Bother Me (Harrison)**
  (lead vocals: George) (recorded on September 11–12, 1963)

This was George's first Beatles song, written in August 1963, in a hotel in Bournemouth, on the south coast of England. He was sick in bed as he wrote it: "maybe that's why it turned out to be 'Don't Bother Me.'"[83] Not as much a songwriter as his two bandmates, he wrote it just to see if he could write a song.[84]

Journalist Bill Harry tells a different story, asserting that he was badgering George to write some songs, and George, annoyed, wrote "Don't Bother Me" in response.[85]

---

[79] Ibid., 148.
[80] "Paul and Linda McCartney Interview," *Playboy*, 104. Similar: Lewisohn, "The Paul McCartney Interview," 10. Hilburn, "From 'Yesterday' to Today." Miles, *Many Years From Now*, 148.
[81] Wyndham, "Paul McCartney As Songwriter." Gambaccini, "The Rolling Stone Interview," see also Gambaccini, *Paul McCartney In His Own Words*, 17.
[82] Lost Lennon Tapes, Sept. 16, 1991, cf. Sheff, *The Playboy Interviews*, 181.
[83] Harrison *I Me Mine* (1980), 84. See also Harrison, radio interview with Johnny Moran, March 11, 1970, as summarized in Winn, *That Magic Feeling*, 376; Sulpy and Schweighardt, *Get Back*, 129; Harrison, date unknown, in Badman, *The Beatles Off the Record*, 72; The Beatles, interview, Dunedin, June 26, 1964; McCartney, Lewisohn interview (1988), 12; McCartney, in *Anthology*, 96. There is a composing tape of the song, Winn, *Way Beyond Compare*, 69.
[84] Harrison, "By George" (1964).
[85] Bill Harry, "George Harrison, Songwriter."

- **Little Child — (collaboration)**
  (lead vocals: John, Paul) (recorded on September 11–12 and October 3, 1963)

Paul referred to "Little Child" as a "work job," written in a couple of hours with John to get a song for Ringo to sing. Certain songs were "inspirational" but this wasn't one of them.[86] As it turned out, John and Paul, not Ringo, sang the song. John also remembered it as a jointly-written song. "Both of us. This was a knock-off between Paul and me for Ringo," he said in 1971.[87]

Paul's contrast of "work" songs with "inspirational" songs shows how he and John had begun to master the craft of songwriting. Just as the Beatles had learned to play eight-hour sets in Germany, Paul and John were learning to produce songs quickly, on order.

- Till There Was You (COVER) (Meredith Willson)
  (lead vocals: Paul)

Paul had heard this song from *Music Man* in a 1961 Peggy Lee recording, and began playing it with the Beatles. They performed it at the Decca Audition. Paul has gone out of his way to defend the inclusion of non-rock'n'roll songs, such as this, in the Beatles' repertoire. "Rock'n'roll wasn't all I liked in music," he said.[88] He loved the old standard tunes partially as the result of his father's influence, but he also felt that the Beatles' range set them apart from more limited groups.[89]

- Please Mr. Postman (COVER) (Brian Holland, Robert Bateman, Berry Gordy)
  (lead vocals: John)

This was a hit for the Marvelettes, a Motown girls group, in 1961.

---

[86] Miles, *Many Years From Now* (1995), 153.
[87] Hennessey, "Who Wrote What." Similar: Connolly, *Ray Connolly Beatles Archive*, 103. Sheff, *The Playboy Interviews*, 181 (1980).
[88] *Anthology*, 22.
[89] Ibid., 68. See also Lewisohn interview, 8; Read, "McCartney on McCartney," episode 2; Du Noyer, *Conversations*, 15. For John, see on "Hello Little Girl."

Chapter 4

SIDE TWO

- o Roll Over Beethoven (COVER) (Chuck Berry)
  (lead vocals: George)

This was released as a single by Chuck Berry in 1956 and quickly became a rock'n'roll standard. It was a Beatle standby.[90] Live versions can be
found on *Beatles at the BBC*, volumes 1 and 2, and *Anthology 1*.

- **Hold Me Tight — (McCartney-Lennon)
  (lead vocals: Paul) (recorded on February 11, September 12,
  1963)**

Paul apparently started this song, then he and John worked on it together at Forthlin Road.[91] Paul called it a "work" song, "a bit Shirelles."[92]
This was a fairly early song that the Beatles had played at the Cavern.

Neither Paul nor John commented on it until the eighties, when their
memories were not fresh. John ascribed it to Paul, and wasn't sure if he
added anything to it.[93] It's probably the familiar pattern of a work session
after one of them started the song.

This had been recorded for *Please Please Me*, but just missed the cut, so
they recorded it again for *With the Beatles*, on September 12.

- o You Really Got A Hold On Me (COVER) (William
  "Smokey" Robinson)
  (lead vocals: John, George)

This song, a hit for the Miracles in 1962, is one of many Beatle covers
showing the deep impact Motown had on them. It can also be found in
Live at the BBC, and John gives a memorable performance of it in *Let It Be*,
the movie.

---

[90] *Anthology*, 112.
[91] Miles, *Many Years from Now* (1995), 83. Sheff, *The Playboy Interviews*, 181.
[92] Lewisohn, "The Paul McCartney Interview" (1988), 10. Miles, *Many Years from Now*
(1995), 83.
[93] Sheff, *The Playboy Interviews*, 181.

o <u>I Wanna Be Your Man (McCartney-Lennon)</u>
<u>(lead vocals: Ringo) (recorded on September 11, 12, 30, and</u>
<u>October 3, 23, 1963)</u>

As Paul and John tell the story, they had recommended the Rolling Stones to Decca, and later Mick Jagger[94] asked Paul and John for a song. Paul said, in 1984, "We met Mick and Keith in a taxi one day in Charing Cross Road and Mick said, 'Have you got any songs?' So we said, 'Well, we just happen to have one with us!'"[95] They went to a club and played this for the Stones — no more than an incomplete song by Paul which he had written for Ringo.[96] When the Stones agreed that the song was in their style, Paul and John went into another part of the room and finished it off, probably adding another verse to the lyrics. John said, in 1980, "And we came back. And that's when Mick and Keith got inspired to write, they said, "Jesus, look at that. They just went in the corner and wrote it and came back!' Right in front of their eyes we did it."[97] This probably occurred on September 10, 1963.[98]

Paul took credit for this song in 1984: "I wrote it for Ringo to do on one of the early albums."[99] However, in two subsequent interviews, he referred to it as a collaboration: "We wrote 'I Wanna Be Your Man' for Ringo," he said in 1995,[100] and five years later, he stated, "So we tried to write something else for Ringo, something *like* 'Boys,' and we came up with 'I Wanna Be Your Man' — a Bo Diddley kind of thing."[101]

Lennon, in his earliest comment on the song, in 1971, ascribed the original song to Paul but then mentioned collaboration: "Both of us, but

---

[94] Or the Stones' manager, Andrew Oldham, according to one interview with John. Badman, *Beatles Off the Record*, 66, giving the date of the interview as Nov. 1974.

[95] "Paul and Linda McCartney Interview," *Playboy* (1984), 104.

[96] Lost Lennon Tapes, Aug. 1, 1988, cf. Sheff, *The Playboy Interviews*, 181-82.

[97] Ibid. See also Paul in *Anthology*, 101. John in the *Anthology* video, said that he and Paul "virtually finished [the song] off in front of them [the Stones]."

[98] Winn, *Way Beyond Compare*, 75.

[99] "Paul and Linda McCartney Interview," *Playboy*, 104.

[100] Miles, *Many Years From Now*, 153.

[101] *Anthology*, 101.

mainly Paul . . . I helped him finish it.”[102] Ten years later, he referred to it as “a kind of lick Paul had, ‘I wanna be your lover, baby, I wanna be your man.’”[103]

Thus this is a typical early Beatles songwriting process: one of the two started the song, then the other helped finish it in songwriting sessions. So when in later interviews, Paul or John mentioned the original writing or the subsequent collaboration, the interviews can seem contradictory, but they probably are only emphasizing different stages in the songwriting process.

The Stones recorded “I Wanna Be Your Man” on October 7 and it was released as their second single on November 1, 1963; it reached 12 on the U.K. charts.

  o   <u>Devil In Her Heart (COVER) (Richard B. Drapkin)</u>
       <u>(lead vocals: George)</u>

The Donays, a girl group from Detroit, released this, their only record, in 1962.

- **Not a Second Time — (Lennon-McCartney)**
  (lead vocals: John) (recorded on September 11, 1963)

This looks like a song started by John, then finished with collaboration. Like many of the early Beatle songs, it was Motown-influenced: “To me, I was writing a Smokey Robinson or something at the time,” John said.[104]

He claimed it in a number of interviews. “Another I wrote for the second album,” he said in 1970.[105] But in a familiar pattern, Paul remembered collaboration:

---

[102] Hennessey, “Who Wrote What,” *Record Mirror*.
[103] Lost Lennon Tapes, Aug. 1, 1988, cf. Sheff, *The Playboy Interviews,* 181-82.
[104] Lennon 1972 (*Anthology*, 96). “Paul and Linda McCartney Interview,” *Playboy* (1984), 107.
[105] Connolly, *Ray Connolly Beatles Archive*, 104. Similar: Aldridge, *Beatles Illustrated Lyrics*, 245. Hennessey, “Who Wrote What,” *Record Mirror*. Lennon in 1972, *Anthology*, 96. His memories are vaguer in 1980: “That’s me trying to do something. I don’t remember. [*Laughs*].” Sheff, *The Playboy Interviews*, 203.

William Mann in the *Times* wrote of the descending "Aeolian cadence" in our song "Not a Second Time" … We hadn't been conscious of any of that. We just did our songs in hotel rooms whenever we had a spare moment; John and I, sitting on twin beds with guitars. He on one bed, me on another.[106]

- o   Money (That's What I Want) (COVER) (Berry Gordy, Janie Bradford)
  (lead vocals: John)

"Money" is the screamer that ends this "album as Cavern performance." A 1959 Barrett Strong single, it was co-written by Berry Gordy, the founder of Motown, and was in fact Motown's first hit. It gives an exclamation point to the strong Motown influence on this album.

The Beatles had also recorded "Money" in the Decca Audition, and other versions can be found on *Anthology 1*, *On Air — Live at the BBC Volume 2*, and Plastic Ono Band*'s Live Peace in Toronto 1969*.

---

[106] McCartney 2000, in *Anthology*, 96.

5

"He'd bring them in, we'd check 'em"

A HARD DAY'S NIGHT

A Hard Day's Night presents a striking contrast to the Beatles' earlier albums, as it contains all original songs. In fact, the major release that immediately preceded it, the *Long Tall Sally* EP, might have led Beatle observers to expect a predominance of covers. (And in fact, they still had a vast repertoire of covers they could have drawn on.) Instead, the Beatles released an entire album of newly-written original songs. So this album represents a watershed in the group's creative development.

On the authorship of the Lennon-McCartney songs on this album, Paul said, in a very early interview:

> John wrote some which when we got back to England I finished off with him. He sort of half wrote them, and then when I — when we both got back, you know, we talked about them, and finished them off. . . . We normally help each other. Maybe if John writes a song, I sort of say, well, that's no good, and that's very good, and that's no good, and we talk about the song together and work it out, y'know.[1]

This attests to both original authorship of many songs on the album, and collaborative work on them.

A number of the Beatles' albums were connected to movies: aside from *A Hard Day's Night,* we have *Help!, Magical Mystery Tour, Yellow Submarine* and *Let It Be.* The *Hard Day's Night* movie, however, based on the Beatles' manic daily life after they hit stardom, was probably the best.

---

[1] Paul McCartney, Interview with Klas Burling, July 29, 1964.

"I Want to Hold Your Hand / This Boy" single, November 29, 1963

- I Want to Hold Your Hand — (collaboration) (lead vocals: John, Paul) (recorded on October 17, 1963)

John and Paul wrote this together from the ground up. On October 16, 1963 they were in the basement, the music room, in the house of Paul's new girlfriend, Jane Asher,[2] and evidently, the pressure was on for them to write a new single. So they started pounding on the piano together. Then they got the "catch line," "I want to hold your hand" — "and so we started working on it from there," said Paul in an early interview. "We got our pens and paper out, and we just wrote the lyrics down. And uhh, eventually you know, we had some sort of a song."[3] John remembered Paul coming up with a striking chord, and he immediately recognized it as right: "That's it! Do that again!"[4] They recorded the song the next day.[5]

Both Paul and John remembered collaboration on this song. In 1970, John said, "I like 'I Want to Hold Your Hand,' we wrote that together — it's a beautiful melody."[6] Later he used it as an example of how they would spend "hours and hours and hours" writing together.[7]

Paul agreed, saying that he and John used to write "facing each other, eyeball to eyeball, exactly like looking in the mirror. That's how songs like 'I Want to Hold Your Hand' were written."[8]

---

[2] For more on the Asher music room, see "Interview with Peter Asher" (who remembers that "I Want to Hold Your Hand" was written there by Paul and John sitting at a piano); Miles, *Many Years from Now*, 107-8 (but Paul doesn't confirm that "I Want to Hold Your Hand" was written there). Miles lists: "And I Love Her," "Every Little Thing," "Eleanor Rigby," "I've Just Seen a Face," "You Won't See Me," and "I'm Looking Through You."
[3] Kelley, Interview with the Beatles, Paris, 1964.
[4] Sheff, *The Playboy Interviews*, 150.
[5] Kelley, Interview with the Beatles, Paris.
[6] Lennon, Rolling Stone Interview, Dec. 1970, BBC, part 4, cf. Wenner, *Lennon Remembers*, 98-99, also 26, 83. See also: Connolly, *Ray Connolly Beatles Archive*, 108 (John here seems to claim the song, oddly). Hennessey, "Lennon: the Greatest Natural Songwriter," 12. Hennessey, "Who Wrote What." McCabe and Schonfeld, *John Lennon: For the Record*, 118.
[7] Sheff, *The Playboy Interviews*, 150.
[8] *Uncut* interview, 2004, in Sawyers, *Read the Beatles*, 245. Similar: Miles, *Many Years From Now*, 108; Williams, "Produced by George Martin."

In a 1964 interview, Paul and John told a bizarre story of wandering into an abandoned house that happened to have a piano and an organ in the basement and writing the song there.[9] In fact, this was a joke cover story to hide the fact that Paul was having a relationship with Jane Asher. Paul and the eighteen-year-old Jane had met on April 18, 1963, and soon became close. He moved into the Asher house, 57 Wimpole Street, Marylebone, London, in November, and would live there for some three years. Jane and her family apparently opened up a new world of urban sophistication to Paul that he'd never known before.

- **This Boy — (collaboration, John emphasis)
  (lead vocals: John, Paul, George) (recorded on October 17, 1963)**

Paul and John had remarkably different memories of writing this song, and typically Paul remembers collaboration and John remembers individual authorship. According to Paul, the band arrived at a hotel room at one in the afternoon and had a couple hours free. So John and Paul decided to write a song. They sat on twin beds and wrote this from the ground up (per Paul). He remembered the details of the room, the beds, "the G-Plan furniture, the British hotel with olive green and orange everywhere." They eventually arranged the song in three part harmony (taking Phil Spector's "To Know Him Is to Love Him" as their model), which was a departure for them.[10] John, however, sang the middle section solo.

John's memories are contradictory. In 1970, he said, "I don't remember writing that one," which usually means that Paul wrote it.[11] But he also claimed the song for himself, starting in 1971. Ten years later, he said it was "my attempt at writing one of those black B-side records that have nice three-part-harmony and sort of Smokey Robinson songs."[12] He of-

---

[9] Kelley, Interview with the Beatles, Paris.
[10] Lewisohn, "The Paul McCartney Interview," 10 (1988); Miles, *Many Years From Now*, 155 (1995). Interview in Smith, *Off the Record* (before 1989), 201.
[11] *Ray Connolly Beatles Archive*, 103. In history, the earliest witness is usually the best.
[12] Hennessey, "Who Wrote What," *Record Mirror*. Lost Lennon Tapes, Sept. 16, 1991, cf. Sheff, *The Playboy Interviews*, 203.

fered it as an example of his interest in melody: "When I go back in my own songs — . . . early attempts at melodies — 'This Boy' or any sort of early Beatle stuff, . . . I was writing melodic "muzak" (in quotes) with the best of them."[13] John's earliest witness, contradicting this, is problematic.

Paul's vivid memories of the place of writing are convincing, and in addition, a song sung as a duet is often a sign of collaboration. Furthermore, most early Beatles songs were written with some degree of collaboration. However, John may have dominated the songwriting session, or begun the song, and his singing the middle might be evidence for this.

"A World Without Love / If I Were You" single — Peter and Gordon, February 28, 1964

- A World Without Love — (McCartney)
  (recorded on January 21, 1964)

This is a very early song by Paul, written when he was sixteen, at his home in Forthlin Road.[14] One day he introduced it to the Beatles with a jaunty introduction, "Listen to this song, fellers." However, when he sang the first line, "Please lock me away," they collapsed in laughter.[15] Though Ringo liked the song, Paul decided it wasn't Beatleworthy. He first offered it to Billy J. Kramer, who rejected it, but Peter Asher, Jane Asher's brother, leader of the duo Peter and Gordon, liked it.[16] "Oh sure," Paul said to him. "We don't want it."[17]

After Peter kept urging Paul to finish the song, he added a bridge,[18] and perhaps significantly, he didn't change the first line. The single was quite successful, reaching number one in the U.K. and U.S. (which is one

---

[13] Sheff, *The Playboy Interviews*, 149.
[14] Miles, *Many Years from Now*, 111-12. According to Lewisohn, Paul started the song "during a dark, late-night walk home." *Tune In*, extended, 516.
[15] Milwaukee Press Conference, Sept. 4, 1964.
[16] Miles, *Many Years from Now*, 111-12.
[17] Milwaukee Press Conference, Sept. 4, 1964.
[18] Peter Asher, 1995 *Goldmine* article, as cited in Unterberger, *The Unreleased Beatles*, 345.

more warning that "the songs the Beatles gave away" were not uniformly second rate.)

Both Paul and John agreed that this was a McCartney song. In 1965, he gave it as the first example of a song he had written entirely on his own.[19] Thirty years later, he said, "It was an early song of mine that we didn't use for the Beatles."[20] John, asked about the song in 1980, said that Paul had the song even before the Beatles.[21]

In 1964, Paul twice referred to it as a co-written song, but he was probably just making a nod to the "Lennon-McCartney" label.[22]

Peter and Gordon went on to a successful recording career in the U.K. and U.S., and Peter later managed artists such as Linda Ronstadt and James Taylor in the states.[23]

o If I Were You (Peter Asher, Gordon Waller)

"Can't Buy Me Love / You Can't Do That" single, March 16, 1964

- **Can't Buy Me Love — (McCartney-Lennon) (lead vocals: Paul) (recorded on January 29, 1964 in France, and February 25, 1964 in London)**

"Can't Buy Me Love" was written while the Beatles were in Paris in January 1964.[24] It's a McCartney song, but Lennon helped finish it. There are pictures of them composing or rehearsing in the George V hotel, Paul and John on piano, George with guitar.[25] Journalists Billy Shepherd and Johnny Dean reported seeing the Beatles "huddled round a piano in the

[19] Wyndham, "Paul McCartney As Songwriter."
[20] Miles, *Many Years from Now*, 111-12.
[21] Sheff, *The Playboy Interviews*, 183-84. Similar: Hennessey, "Who Wrote What," *Record Mirror*
[22] He referred to the "composers" of the song, Interview with the Beatles, *Disc Weekly*, May 9, 1964 (Sandercombe, *The Beatles: Press Reports*, 62).
[23] Engelhardt, *Beatles Undercover*, 373-74.
[24] McCartney, [1964] in Badman, *The Beatles Off the Record*, 97.
[25] Everett I, 221.

plushly-magnificent Hotel George Cinq in Paris . . . with Paul and John furiously working on last-minute songs for recording and for a film."[26]

Both Paul and John agree that this was mainly a Paul song. However, they produce contradictory testimony on whether it was a collaboration or not. Paul claimed it in 1965: "What did I write on my own? Oh, . . . 'Can't Buy Me Love.'"[27] Thirty years later, he said, "'Can't Buy Me Love' is my attempt to write a bluesy mode."[28] However, his earliest statement, apparently in 1964, mentions collaboration. "This was written really when we were in Paris. We had to have a new record ready for recording in England and we were going to record a song in Paris as well, so we wrote 'Can't Buy Me Love' there and we recorded the first track of it in Paris and we finished it off in London. It's a two-country effort."[29]

John's statements definitely attributed the song mainly to Paul, but also reflected some collaboration. "John and Paul, but mainly Paul," he said in 1971.[30] After thus pointing to definite collaboration, he referred to it in 1980 as "Paul's completely." After such a resounding attribution, he goes on to undercut himself by stating that he *might* have helped with the middle of the song. But then he retreats from *that* idea! "But I don't know. I always considered it his song."[31] Repeatedly, in dealing with the Beatle songwriting interviews, we're brought face to face with the fragility of memory.

An early statement by George Harrison also reflects collaboration: "They [Lennon and McCartney] did 'Can't Buy Me Love' in Paris."[32]

---

[26] Shepherd and Dean, "Behind the Spotlight," *The Beatles Book, Monthly* no. 31 (Feb. 1966), 21.

[27] Wyndham, "Paul McCartney As Songwriter."

[28] Miles, *Many Years from Now*, 161.

[29] McCartney, in Badman, *The Beatles Off the Record*, 97.

[30] Hennessey, "Who Wrote What," *Record Mirror.*

[31] Sheff, *The Playboy Interviews,* 182. See also Lennon in Cott, "The Rolling Stone Interview," (1968). Lennon [1964], in Badman, *The Beatles Off the Record*, 97, seems to refer to recording the song, not to songwriting.

[32] Harrison [1964] in Badman, *The Beatles Off the Record*, 97. Shepard and Dean also reported that "Can't Buy Me Love" was co-written: "He [Paul] and John had written the song ['Can't Buy Me Love'] at late-night sessions in Paris during January." Shepherd and Dean,

I conclude that this is a Paul song, finished with collaboration. It is another example of how a song can be firmly "owned" by one or the other writers, but can be finished up in a songwriting session, with music or word editing from the other member of the team.

- **You Can't Do That — (Lennon)**
  (lead vocals: John) (recorded on February 25, 1964)

George said the song was written in Miami Beach, Florida, from February 14 to 21, 1964.[33] John claimed this song in the early seventies, saying that he was trying to trying to emulate rhythm and blues star Wilson Pickett.[34] Miles, presumably reflecting Paul McCartney, also ascribed it to John.[35]

Pickett is best known for "In the Midnight Hour" (1965); his album *It's Too Late* had been released in 1963.[36]

"Ain't She Sweet / Take Out Some Insurance on Me, Baby" single, Germany, April 1964

- Ain't She Sweet (COVER) (Jack Yellen, Milton Ager) (lead vocals: John)

This is one of the 1962 Hamburg recordings, which was finally released now as Polydor sought to capitalize on every possible scrap of Beatles recordings. It is the first professionally recorded Beatles performance with vocals, but otherwise has little interest, except for completists. The recording was also released as a single in the U.K. on May 29, 1964.

"Behind the Spotlight," *The Beatles Book, Monthly* no. 32 (March 1966), 22. See also "Beatle News," *Beatles Book Monthly* 9 (April 1964), 29.
[33] Coleman, "George Harrison — Exclusive." See also Harrison [1964], in Badman, *The Beatles Off the Record*, 97.
[34] Connolly, *Ray Connolly Beatles Archive*, 104. Aldridge, *Beatles Illustrated Lyrics*, 212. See also Sheff, *The Playboy Interviews*, 204.
[35] Miles, *Many Years From Now* (1995), 164.
[36] For another song in Pickett's style, see "When I Get Home" below.

"One And One Is Two / Time and the River" single — The Strangers with Mike Shannon, May 8, 1964

- One and One is Two — (McCartney-Lennon) (recorded on March 20, 1964)

Paul wrote the beginnings of this song in the George V Hotel in Paris, then he and John worked on it together after a show at the Olympia Theater.[37] Thus it was written from late January to early February, 1964. Paul and John recorded four demos in Paris (with Paul on guitar and John adding a minor piano part), sending the final one to Billy J. Kramer.[38] When the demos were done, John remarked, "Billy J is finished when he gets this song."[39] The tune was in fact rejected by both Kramer and the Fourmost,[40] before it found a home with The Strangers, an obscure group from South Africa whom the Beatles had known in Liverpool. The song never charted.

Both Paul and John agreed that this was mainly a McCartney song. John, starting in 1970, ascribed it to Paul: "That was another one of Paul's."[41] However, journalist Michael Braun described Paul working on the lyrics with John and George — one more reminder that there may have been minor collaboration in all the songs John or Paul claimed for themselves, in the early Beatles era.[42] Bill Harry, editor of *Mersey Beat*, also records collaboration — he wrote that the song "was mainly written by Paul," but "Paul and John worked together on the number in their suite at the George V Hotel."[43]

- o Time and the River (Aaron Schroeder, Wally Gold)

c

[37] Harry, "Billy J. Kramer." Miles, *Many Years From Now* (1995), 162.
[38] Braun, *Love Me Do*, 82-83. Winn, *Way Beyond Compare*, 120.
[39] Braun, *Love Me Do*, 82-83.
[40] Engelhardt, *Beatles Undercover*, 476. Unterberger, *The Unreleased Beatles*, 86.
[41] Connolly, *Ray Connolly Beatles Archive*, 104. Hennessey, "Who Wrote What," *Record Mirror*. Sheff, *The Playboy Interviews*, 184. For Paul, Miles, *Many Years From Now* (1995), 162.
[42] Michael Braun, *Love Me Do*, 82-83; Winn, *Way Beyond Compare*, 120.
[43] Harry, "Billy J. Kramer."

"Nobody I Know / You Don't Have To Tell Me" single — Peter and Gordon, May 29, 1964

- Nobody I Know — (McCartney)
  (recorded in April 1964)

Paul wrote this specifically for Peter Asher.[44] According to Asher, when Peter and Gordon returned from their American tour, Paul met them and said, "I've written your second single, here it is, hope you like it."[45]

John, asked about the song in 1980, ascribed it to Paul.[46] It reached number ten in the U.K. and twelve in the U.S.

  o You Don't Have To Tell Me (Peter Asher, Gordon Waller)

———————•◦•———————

"Like Dreamers Do / (Boom, Boom, Boom, Boom) Everybody Fall Down" single — The Applejacks, June 5, 1964

- Like Dreamers Do — (McCartney)

In 1961, Paul felt that all the groups in Liverpool were doing the same songs, so he decided to steal a march on them by writing a song himself. He came up with "Like Dreamers Do" during a bus ride, then played it to the Beatles the next day. They weren't too enthusiastic, but learned the song, and possibly Paul and John did some work on it together to finish it off. It became quite popular at the Cavern, probably because "it had a novelty value. . . . It was our big number for week and weeks," Paul said in 1963.[47] Thus it was actually one of the earliest self-written songs that the Beatles performed.

---

44 Miles, *Many Years from Now*, 112.
45 Peter Asher, Introduction to performance of "Nobody I Know," 2015.
46 Sheff, *The Playboy Interviews,* 204. See also Hennessey, "Who Wrote What," *Record Mirror.*
47 Coleman and Roberts, "What Makes a Beatle Beat?" ("Like Dreamers Do" not named, but in other listings, it's always put first, as in Roberts, "How to Write a Hit.") Miles, *Many Years from Now*, 82. See also *Anthology,* 18, 68. Lewisohn, *Tune In*, extended, 516-17.

The Beatles included it in the Decca audition on January 1, 1962,[48] but never were interested in putting it on a Beatle album. They met the Applejacks, a group from Birmingham who had signed with Decca, at a television appearance, and Paul and John gave them this song to record. It became the Applejacks' second single, reaching number twenty in the U.K. charts.[49]

Paul and John usually ascribed "Like Dreamers Do" totally to Paul, who evaluated it with refreshing candor in the 1990s: "I did a very bad song called 'Like Dreamers Do.'"[50] John, in 1971, described it as "A very early one of Paul's,"[51] and in 1980 he said that Paul had written it as a teenager and then later revived and polished it.[52]

However, in 1964, John seemed to remember it as a collaboration: "It [the Lennon-McCartney songwriting] started in school holidays. I was about 15... At that time we did 'Like Dreamers Do'."[53] John was fifteen from October 1955 to 1956. However, he did not meet Paul until July 1957, when he was sixteen, and the songwriting sessions with Paul did not begin immediately. But even a 1958 or 1959 date for the song conflicts with Paul's 1963 statement.

I accept this as a Paul song, possibly finished with collaboration, though the evidence is sketchy.

o (Boom, Boom, Boom, Boom) Everybody Fall Down (Dello [Peter Blumson], Ray Cane [Raymond Byart])

[48] This performance can be found on *Anthology 1*.
[49] Engelhardt, *Beatles Undercover*, 24.
[50] Miles, *Many Years from Now*, 36.
[51] Hennessey, "Who Wrote What," *Record Mirror*.
[52] Sheff, *The Playboy Interviews*, 183.
[53] Roberts, "How to Write a Hit."

Long Tall Sally EP, June 19, 1964 — "Long Tall Sally / I Call Your Name / Slow Down / Matchbox"

An EP of three rousing covers and one solid Lennon-McCartney; unlike their first two albums, here the screamer came first. All four songs were recorded on June 1, 1964.

- ○ Long Tall Sally (COVER) (Enotris Johnson, Richard Penniman ("Little Richard") and Robert "Bumps" Blackwell) (lead vocals: Paul)

Little Richard released the "Long Tall Sally" single in 1956. Paul sang this song at his first stage performance, when he was about fourteen, and it became a McCartney vocal specialty.[54] "Ever since I heard Little Richard's version, I started imitating him," he said in 1973. "It was just straight imitation, really, which has gradually become my version of it as much as Richard's."[55]

John would egg him on as he performed this and other Little Richard rave-ups.[56] In 1963, when the Beatles were preparing for their performances in France, John said, "If they want things like "Sally" and "[Roll Over] Beethoven", we can do that standing on our ears."[57] They often performed this as the last song of a show. "I could never think of a better number to finish on," Paul said.[58]

Other performances of "Long Tall Sally" are on the *Live at the BBC* albums, *The Beatles At The Hollywood Bowl* (where it closes the show) and *Anthology 1* (a TV performance from 1963).

---

[54] McCartney in Gambaccini, "The Rolling Stone Interview."
[55] Ibid. Du Noyer, *Conversations*, 30.
[56] McCartney in Goodman, "Playboy Interview," 88.
[57] *Anthology*, 112.
[58] Gambaccini, "The Rolling Stone Interview".

- ## I Call Your Name (Lennon-McCartney) (lead vocals: John) (recorded on March 1, 1964)

John wrote the beginnings of this song before the Beatles, when he was about fifteen, he said. Later, he worked on it with Paul at John's house at Menlove Avenue.[59] Finally, in early 1964, he added a middle eight to it.[60]

In a familiar pattern, John claimed this as his song entirely, while Paul remembered some collaboration. John said,

> That was my song. The bulk of the "I Call Your Name" part written around the period Paul was writing "Love Me Do" when there was no Beatles and no group. And I just had it around, it was my effort at the kind of blues originally. And then I wrote the middle eight just to stick it in the album when it came out years later.[61]

Paul agreed that it was primarily John's, but in 1995 did remember some collaboration. "We worked on it together, but it was John's idea. When I look back at some of these lyrics, I think, Wait a minute. What did he mean? 'I call your name but you're not there.' Is it his mother? His father?"[62]

This was first released on the "Bad to Me" / "I Call Your Name" single by Billy J. Kramer and the Dakotas, see above.

- ○ Slow Down (COVER) (Larry Williams) (lead vocals: John)

This was the B side of the 1958 "Dizzy Miss Lizzie" single by Larry Williams, another rhythm and blues singer important to the Beatles. In an interview from 1964, John said "Slow Down" was "just an old rock and

---

[59] Miles, *Many Years from Now*, 46.

[60] Sheff, *The Playboy Interviews* (1980), 180.

[61] Lost Lennon Tapes, Sept. 16, 1991, cf. Sheff, *The Playboy Interviews*, 180. Similar: Hennessey, "Who Wrote What," *Record Mirror*. Aldridge, *Beatles Illustrated Lyrics*, 201. Lennon in 1974, cited in Google Groups: "A song that I wrote — except for the middle part — when I was sixteen. We recorded the middle-eight in Ska-style." He said he wrote the middle eight when he came to London, Connolly, *Ray Connolly Beatles Archive*, 102.

[62] Miles, *Many Years from Now*, 46.f

roll number from eight years ago. . . . And it's one we've done for a long time, and we thought we'd just stick it on the EP."[63] Another version of this is on *Live at the BBC*.

    ○ <u>Matchbox (COVER) (Carl Perkins/Blind Lemon Jefferson)</u>
        <u>(lead vocals: Ringo)</u>

The rockabilly Carl Perkins, another Beatles favorite, released this single in 1957, and it became one of his most widely-known songs. Perkins came to the Beatles recording session on June 1, which unnerved Ringo as he laid down his vocals.[64] It was partially based on the blues song "Match Box Blues" (1927) by Blind Lemon Jefferson. "Matchbox" is also on *Live at the BBC*.

A Hard Day's Night album, July 10, 1964

- **A Hard Day's Night — (Lennon-McCartney-Starkey) (lead vocals: John and Paul) (recorded on April 16, 1964)**

When the Beatles were in Paris, in January 1964, Paul had been introduced to some Dylan records at a radio station. "Paul got them off whoever they belonged to," said Lennon, "and for the rest of the three weeks in Paris we didn't stop playing them. We all went potty on Dylan."[65] This song is the first fruit of that influence.[66]

As the Beatles prepared for their first movie, producer Walter Shenson[67] needed a title for the movie and a title song, and suggested to the Beatles[68] that Ringo's phrase "Hard Day's Night" would work.[69] John thought about this, went home and came up with the song. In a 1965 in-

---

[63] The Beatles, Interview, Auckland, June 24, 1964.
[64] Ibid.
[65] Lennon, interview, in Coleman, "Beatles Say – Dylan Shows the Way" (1965), quoted below.
[66] Ibid.
[67] Or director Richard Lester. Sheff, *The Playboy Interviews*, 185.
[68] Or to Lennon and McCartney, or Lennon alone. Lost Lennon Tapes, July 9, 1990.
[69] Or the Beatles decided the phrase would work. Miles, *Many Years from Now*, 164.

terview, he said that the song was in the "Dylan vein" when he first wrote the opening bars. "But later we Beatle-ified it before we recorded it."[70]

The next morning he came into Abbey Road early and one observer described him humming the melody to the other Beatles.[71] He and Paul then developed the music and lyrics. At 8:30 a.m. Lennon called Shenson into their studio and he and Paul played it for him. Shenson said "that [John] and Paul had roughed [a song] out on scraps of paper."[72] According to Miles, the film was titled on April 13, the Beatles played the song to Shenson the next day, and recorded it on the 16th.[73]

John repeatedly and strongly claimed this song as his own, written with no collaboration. In 1971, he listed it as an example of how he would sometimes write alone: "And we'd written separately for years. . . . I wrote 'A Hard Day's Night,'" he said.[74] He remembered writing it by himself quickly, after Walter Shenson, the film's producer, asked for a title song for the movie as soon as possible. Dick Lester suggested Ringo's phrase, hard day's night, "and the next morning I brought in the song. 'Cause there was a little competition between Paul and I as to who got the 'A' sides."[75] George Martin, in 1964, remembered "everyone" liking Ringo's phrase, Hard Day's Night. Then "John went off and came back the next day with a song he'd written to go with the title."[76]

---

[70] Lennon, interview, in Coleman, "Beatles Say — Dylan Shows the Way" (1965).

[71] Maureen Cleave (as quoted in Turner, *A Hard Day's Write*, 47).

[72] Walter Shenson, article about *Hard Day's Night*, in *Disc Weekly*, July 18, 1964 (Sandercombe, *The Beatles: Press Reports*, 72). Similar: Walter Shenson, March 1966, in Lydon, "Lennon and McCartney: Songwriters," also in *Flashbacks: Eyewitness Accounts of the Rock Revolution*, 11. See also Shenson in Pritchard and Lysaght, *The Beatles: An Oral History*, 164: "At eight-thirty the next morning John and Paul called me into their dressing room at the studio. On the back of a matchbook cover they had the lyrics of 'A Hard Day's Night.' The two of them then took out their guitars and played this song."

[73] Miles, *Many Years from Now*, 164-65.

[74] McCabe and Schonfeld, *John Lennon: For the Record*, 118. Similar: Hennessey, "Who Wrote What," *Record Mirror*. Coleman, "Wish Elvis" (1965).

[75] Sheff, *The Playboy Interviews*, 185.

[76] Interview with Nigel Hunter, *Disc Weekly*, June 19, 1964 (Sandercombe, *The Beatles: Press Reports*, 62).

However, there is substantial evidence for collaboration (aside from the title coming from Ringo). In a 1964 interview, Paul said, "John and I wrote this especially for the film." He remembered Shenson asking both him and John to write a title song. "We just thought about it and I thought it seems a bit ridiculous writing a song called 'A Hard Day's Night' — because it sounded funny at the time, but after a bit, you know, we got the idea of saying that it had been a hard day's night and we'd been working all the day so we could get back to a girl and everything's fine, you know. And we sort of turned it into one of those songs."[77] In 1995, he suggested that he probably contributed to the words and the middle eight, a twenty-minute touchup to the song John had brought in.[78]

Early insiders Walter Shenson and Dick James also remembered collaboration. Shenson, in 1964, wrote that Ringo came up with the movie title, then "Late one evening, Shenson asked Lennon to write a title song. At 8:30 the following morning, John called and said that he and Paul had roughed one out on scraps of paper. They recorded it that night."[79] Dick James, the Beatles' music publisher, in 1965 spoke of John saying to him, about the song, "we've already written half of it."[80]

The early evidence is thus complex. It seems likely that this started out as a John song, but was finished with collaboration.

---

[77] Lost Lennon Tapes, July 9, 1990. *Anthology*, 129.
[78] Miles, *Many Years from Now*, 164-65.
[79] Walter Shenson, article about *Hard Day's Night*, in *Disc Weekly*, July 18, 1964 (Sandercombe, *The Beatles: Press Reports*, 72). Similar: Walter Shenson, March 1966, in Lydon, "Lennon and McCartney: Songwriters," also in *Flashbacks: Eyewitness Accounts of the Rock Revolution*, 11. See also Shenson in Pritchard and Lysaght, *The Beatles: An Oral History*, 164: "At eight-thirty the next morning John and Paul called me into their dressing room at the studio. On the back of a matchbook cover they had the lyrics of 'A Hard Day's Night.' The two of them then took out their guitars and played this song."
[80] Dick James, in Jones, "Northern Songs Ltd. for Beatle Songs Unlimited," 11.

- **I Should Have Known Better — (Lennon)
  (lead vocals: John) (recorded on February 25–26, 1964)**

  Both John and Paul agreed that John wrote this. In 1971, John included it in a list of songs he had written, and in 1980, he said, "That's me."[81]

- **If I Fell — (Lennon-McCartney)
  (lead vocals: John and Paul) (recorded on February 27, 1964)**

  John used the song to show how he could excel at what many people regard as the McCartney side of the Beatles: "That's my first attempt at a ballad proper," he said in 1980. ". . . That shows that I wrote sentimental love ballads, silly love songs, as you call them, way back when." But he said that Paul had contributed the middle eight to this.[82] Earlier, he put it on a list of John songs.[83] There is a composing tape or demo of the song, in which John sings, accompanied by guitar.[84]

  Paul remembered a songwriting session for this song, though it was a session dominated by John, and he also cited the song as an example of John's tender side. He said, in 1995, "People tend to forget that John wrote some pretty nice ballads. People tend to think of him as an acerbic wit and aggressive and abrasive, but he did have a very warm side to him really which he didn't like to show too much in case he got rejected." "We wrote 'If I Fell' together," he said; however, he agreed that "the emphasis [is] on John." But then he added, "because he sang it."[85] This increases the confusion still further, because Paul sang melodic lead on the song. (Possibly because the melody was too high for John.) Miles writes, "'If I Fell,' 'I'm Happy Just to Dance with You' and 'I'll Be Back' were all co-written with John."[86]

---

[81] Hennessey, "Who Wrote What," *Record Mirror*; Sheff, *The Playboy Interviews,* 204. For Paul, "Paul and Linda McCartney Interview," *Playboy,* (1984), 107; Miles, *Many Years from Now,* 164 (assuming that Miles reflects Paul).

[82] Lost Lennon Tapes, Sept. 23, 1991, cf. Sheff, *The Playboy Interviews,* 204.

[83] Hennessey, "Who Wrote What," *Record Mirror.*

[84] Winn, *Way Beyond Compare,* 113.

[85] Miles, *Many Years from Now,* 162.

[86] Ibid.

In a very late interview, Paul claimed the intro: "One song I wrote a little after "Please Please Me" was my best attempt at a preamble: "If I Fell." [Sings] 'If I fell in love with you, would you promise to be truuue...' Then after the line, 'just holding hands,' the song properly gets going. [Raises voice] That's it, everyone!"[87] This would make a neat parallel to Paul's "Here, There and Everywhere" intro.

- **I'm Happy Just to Dance with You — (Lennon-McCartney) (lead vocals: George) (recorded on March 1, 1964)**

John and Paul knew that George needed a song to sing in the movie and came up with this for him. It represents another example of flat contradiction in attribution. John claimed it as his song. "I wrote that for George to sing," he said in 1970.[88] But Paul, in 1995, remembered this as "a straight co-written song for George." "We wrote 'I'm Happy Just To Dance With You' for George in the film." Paul, typically, commented on the chords. He and John knew that using an E to A-flat-minor chord progression "pretty much always excited you."[89]

- **And I Love Her — (McCartney-Lennon-Harrison) (lead vocals: Paul) (recorded on February 25–27, 1964)**

Paul wrote this, and he said it became "the first ballad I impressed myself with."[90] According to Miles in 1995, the song was inspired by Jane Asher (which Paul had denied in 1984).[91] It was certainly written in the Asher home, during the Jane Asher period. Paul remembered playing the song in the upstairs drawing room of the Asher residence, soon after writing it.[92]

---

[87]"How Does It Feel to Be a Beatle," Interview with Jude Rogers, *Q Magazine*, May 2013, as cited in Beatles Bible. Paul was not claiming the entire song as his own, as his 1995 interview shows.

[88] Connolly, *Ray Connolly Beatles Archive*, 104. Hennessey, "Who Wrote What," *Record Mirror*.

[89] Miles, *Many Years from Now*, 163.

[90] Ibid., 122-23.

[91] Ibid., 122. Goodman, "Paul and Linda McCartney Interview," *Playboy*, 107.

[92] Miles, *Many Years From Now*, 122-23.

John helped with the middle eight. Dick James left an account of Paul and John writing it together at the studio. "John and Paul went to the piano and, while Mal Evans was getting tea and some sandwiches, the boys worked at the piano. Within half an hour they wrote, there before our very eyes, a very constructive middle to a very commercial song."[93]

Both Paul and John agreed that the main song was written by Paul. In fact, in 1995, Paul felt that the song might have been entirely his own: "I'm not sure if John worked on that at all."[94] John said, in 1980, "'And I Love Her' is Paul again. I consider it his first 'Yesterday.'"[95] However, there was disagreement on the middle eight. In 1971, John claimed this entire section of the song: "Both of us. The first half was Paul's and the middle eight is mine."[96] Paul flatly disagreed, in 1995: "The middle eight is mine. I would say that John probably helped with the middle eight, but he can't say 'It's mine.' I wrote this on my own."[97] And in 1980, John softened his 1971 statement, saying that he only "helped" with the middle eight.

In addition, George contributed the important guitar riff at the beginning of the song.[98]

I conclude that the main song is Paul's, but that the middle eight was collaborative, completed by Paul and John in the studio.

- **Tell Me Why — (Lennon)**
  (lead vocals: John) (recorded on February 27, 1964)

The movie men needed another upbeat song, "and I just knocked it ["Tell Me Why"] off," John said in 1980. It was in the genre of black girl group music.[99] Paul agreed that it was John's and felt that it may have been

[93] Harry, *McCartney Encyclopedia*, at "And I Love Her."
[94] Miles, *Many Years From Now*, 122-23.
[95] Sheff, *The Playboy Interviews*, 183.
[96] Hennessey, "Who Wrote What," *Record Mirror*. He put it on a list of songs that were collaborative. Hennessey, "Lennon: the Greatest Natural Songwriter," 12.
[97] Miles, *Many Years From Now*, 122-23.
[98] McCartney interview in Scorsese, *Living in the Material World*.
[99] Lost Lennon Tapes, Sept. 23, 1991, cf. Sheff, *The Playboy Interviews*, 204-5. Hennessey, "Who Wrote What," *Record Mirror*.

based on his relationship with Cynthia or with relationships he was having with other women at the time.[100]

    o   Can't Buy Me Love — (McCartney-Lennon) (lead vocals: Paul)

See the "Can't Buy Me Love / You Can't Do That" single, above.

SIDE TWO

- **Anytime at All — (Lennon-McCartney) (lead vocals: John) (recorded on June 2, 1964)**

In 1971, John claimed this, and Miles/Paul also ascribe it to him.[101] Simple enough, it would seem. However, in an undated comment by Lennon that was printed in 1972, he stated that the song was co-written. It was "Another of those songs we wrote about the time of *Hard Day's Night*."[102] This is an example of one of the individual Beatles disagreeing with himself. It's unfortunate that the second comment is undated, but it's at least as early as the first listing by John.

If Paul did collaborate, the songwriting session was probably dominated by John.

- **I'll Cry Instead — (Lennon) (lead vocals: John) (recorded on June 1, 1964)**

In 1971, John claimed this.[103] "I wrote that for *Hard Day's Night*," he said in 1980.[104] Miles/Paul agreed in 1995.[105] The only complexity in the historical record comes from a very early interview with George Martin, who in 1964 spoke of it as co-written — "the boys came up with this" — but he may have been just assuming collaboration.[106]

---

[100] Miles, *Many Years From Now*, 164.
[101] Hennessey, "Who Wrote What," *Record Mirror*. Miles, *Many Years From Now*, 164.
[102] Aldridge, *Beatles Illustrated Lyrics*, 186.
[103] Hennessey, "Who Wrote What," *Record Mirror*.
[104] Sheff, *The Playboy Interviews*, 205.
[105] Miles, *Many Years From Now*, 164.
[106] Nigel Hunter, interview with George Martin, *Disc Weekly*, June 13, 1964, as quoted in Sandercombe, *The Beatles: Press Reports*, 62.

- **Things We Said Today — (McCartney-Lennon)
(lead vocals: Paul) (recorded on June 2, 1964)**

This song was written while Paul and Jane Asher, and Ringo and Maureen Cox, were on a yacht vacation in the Virgin Islands in May 1964. McCartney separated from his friends, went below deck with a guitar, and started writing the song. However, the smell of oil was oppressive, the boat was rocking, and he started to feel queasy, so he went up to the back deck and finished the song there.[107] According to Miles, it reflected Paul's and Jane Asher's relationship — times together, then a great deal of time apart.[108] Paul described it as "a slightly nostalgic thing already, a future nostalgia."[109] He said the Beatles had a fondness for it because it was "like folk music."[110] So like the first song on the album, it was influenced by the folk renaissance.

Both Paul and John have ascribed the song directly to Paul.[111] The latter, in 1964, said, "I did a couple while I was there [the Virgin Islands], which we recorded when we got back, 'Things We Said Today' and 'Always and Only.'"[112] In 1995, he said, "I wrote 'Things We Said Today' on acoustic."[113]

We seem to have achieved an uncontroversial attribution; but as often, a stray piece of evidence breaks the symmetry. In another early interview, Paul said that he wrote the song on holiday, then he and John "finished [it] off when we got back."[114] Paul stated this quite firmly, so I accept that there was some "finishing" collaboration with John on this song.

---

[107] Miles, *Many Years From Now*, 121.
[108] Ibid., 122.
[109] Ibid.
[110] McCartney, interview with Klas Burling, July 29, 1964.
[111] For John, see Hennessey, "Who Wrote What," *Record Mirror* (a list of Paul songs); Lennon in 1980 (Lost Lennon Tapes, Episode Sept. 16, 1991; cf. Sheff, *The Playboy Interviews*, 204).
[112] Shepherd, "Beatles on Holiday," 9. "Always and Only" is a mystery. Some believe that the transcriber of the interview, or the ghost writer of the article, got the name wrong. Unterberger, *The Unreleased Beatles*, 116.
[113] Miles, *Many Years From Now*, 122.
[114] McCartney, interview with Klas Burling, July 29, 1964.

- **When I Get Home — (Lennon)**
  (lead vocals: John) (recorded on June 2, 1964)

John claimed this. "That's me again, another Wilson Pickett, Motown sound, a four-in-the-bar cowbell song."[115] Miles/Paul agreed in 1995, putting it in a list of songs written by John.[116]

  o <u>You Can't Do That — (Lennon)</u>
     <u>(lead vocals: John)</u>

See the "Can't Buy Me Love / You Can't Do That" single, above.

- **I'll Be Back — (Lennon-McCartney)**
  (lead vocals: John) (recorded on June 1, 1964)

John claimed this strongly in his three comments on the song. In 1971, he said, "Me. A nice tune, though the middle is a bit tatty."[117] At about the same time, he referred to it as "An early favorite that I wrote,"[118] and in 1980, he affirmed, "'I'll Be Back' is me completely."[119]

Paul, in the 1990s, however, stated that the song was a mixture of John's original authorship and collaboration:

> "I'll Be Back" was co-written, but it was largely John's idea. When we knew we were writing for something like an album he would write a few in his spare moments, like this batch here. He'd bring them in, we'd check 'em. I'd write a couple and we'd throw 'em at each other, and then there'd be a couple that were more co-written.[120]

It was probably a song that was begun by John, then finished with collaboration.

---

[115] Sheff, *The Playboy Interviews,* 205. Similar: Connolly, *Ray Connolly Beatles Archive*, 104. Hennessey, "Who Wrote What," *Record Mirror.*

[116] Miles, *Many Years From Now*, 164.

[117] Hennessey, "Who Wrote What," *Record Mirror.* See also Connolly, *Ray Connolly Beatles Archive*, 102.

[118] Aldridge, *Beatles Illustrated Lyrics*, 171.

[119] Lost Lennon Tapes, Sept. 16, 1991, cf. Sheff, *The Playboy Interviews*, 173.

[120] Miles, *Many Years from Now*, 163.

In other words, according to Paul, there had been two levels of collaboration on many songs. One was John or Paul writing songs, then bringing them to the other, to "throw them at each other" and "check them." This was not collaboration from the ground up, but it was collaboration, as theoretically this quality control process involved some changes. You could call it major collaboration and minor (finishing) collaboration. However, there was undoubtedly a continuum between the two types of collaboration, so we are left to wonder how much, exactly, was John, and how much, exactly, was Paul, in many of these early Beatle songs.

6

"A folk song gone pop"

BEATLES FOR SALE

Beatles for Sale marked a return to "live show" album format, part Lennon-McCartney songs, part covers. Paul said, "Recording *Beatles for Sale* didn't take long. Basically it was our stage show, with some new songs."[1]

During this time period, Paul remembers, the record company would call them up a month before the recording session, and let them know that they would have a week off scheduled for them to write songs. So Paul would go to John's new house in Weybridge every day for a week, and they would go to the music room at the top of the house and work from about one or two in the afternoon till four or five. They would write a song a day and be ready for the recording session.[2]

John had bought this new house, called Kenwood, at Weybridge, Surrey, in the London suburbs, on July 15, 1964. The music room was an attic where John kept most of his musical instruments and tape recorders. Many of the great Beatles songs were written in this house, or outside, near the swimming pool (as was the case with Paul's "Here, There and Everywhere") or in the gardens, as memorialized in John's line from "I Am the Walrus": "sitting in an English garden, waiting for the sun."

---

[1] *Anthology*, 159. Paul referred to the covers in this album as "old Cavern" things. Nigel Hunter, interview with McCartney, *Disc Weekly*, Nov. 14, 1964 (Sandercombe, *The Beatles: Press Reports*, 102).

[2] Miles, *Many Years from Now*, 171.

"From a Window / Second To None" single —
Billy J. Kramer and the Dakotas, July 17, 1964

- From a Window — (McCartney-Lennon)
  (recorded on May 29, 1964)

  Apparently, Brian Epstein came to Paul and John and said that Billy needed a new song. So Paul had the beginnings of a song, and he and John worked on it till it was good enough to "give away."

  Neither Paul nor John remembered the details of actually writing "From a Window." John ascribed it to Paul, but without any great certainty. "Paul — must be Paul's. I can't really remember it," he said in 1971.[3] And nine years later, he again credited the song to Paul, but then added, "I'm not sure."[4]

  Miles, however, refers to it as a collaboration:

  > "From a Window" was again written purposely for Billy. [Brian would ask for a song] . . . and they would write it on the spot." **Paul:** "We would just make it up. We would sit down at rehearsal . . . and just with pen and paper, scribble the lyrics down."[5]

So it was probably a Paul song finished with collaboration.

  George Martin produced this recording session, and Paul and John attended.

- o Second To None (Robin MacDonald)

---

[3] Hennessey, "Who Wrote What," *Record Mirror.*
[4] Sheff, *The Playboy Interviews*, 183.
[5] Miles, *Many Years From Now*, 181.

"It's For You / He Won't Ask Me" single — Cilla Black, July 31, 1964

- It's For You — (McCartney-Lennon)
  (recorded on July 2, 1964)

When Cilla Black recorded Burt Bacharach's "Anyone Who Had a Heart" Paul was at the recording session. He told her he liked the song and that he and John would try to write something similar for her.[6] Paul wrote "It's For You" and brought it to John for quality control. John objected to something about it, Paul said. "I'd written it basically, and John said, well, that's no good, you know." So they "talked it over together" and "eventually finished it."[7]

In Paul's earliest interview on the song, he both claimed it and acknowledged John's input. "Well it was me and sort of with a lot of help from John, y' know."[8] Later, in somewhat contradictory statements, he emphasized his own authorship. In 1988, after discussing how he and John collaborated on many of their songs for others, he said, "Cilla's 'It's For You' was something else, that was something I'd written. You sometimes would pull one out of the drawer and say, 'Maybe this would be good for you.'"[9] And in 1995, he said, "I wrote it for Cilla."[10]

Paul's earliest interview is preferable. He wrote the song at first, then it was finished with John.

George Martin produced the recording session for this song, and Paul and John attended. It rose to number seven in the U.K. charts.

  o He Won't Ask Me (Bobby Willis)

---

[6] Cilla Black, quoted in Miles, *The Beatles: A Diary*, 131.
[7] Paul McCartney, interview with Klas Burling, July 29, 1964.
[8] Ibid.
[9] Lewisohn, "The Paul McCartney Interview" (1988).
[10] Miles, *Many Years From Now*, 122. John left no known comments on the song.

"I Don't Want To See You Again / I Would Buy" single — Peter and Gordon, September 11, 1964

- I Don't Want to See You Again — (McCartney) (recorded August 1964)

Both Paul and John ascribed this to Paul. Miles wrote that it "was again written entirely by Paul."[11] In 1971 and 1980, John said that Paul alone had written it.[12] Peter and Gordon's third single, it reached number eighteen in the U.S., and became the title track of their second album.

- o   I Would Buy (Peter Asher, Gordon Waller)

"I Feel Fine / She's a Woman" single, November 23, 1964

- I Feel Fine — (Lennon) (lead vocals: John) (recorded on October 18, 1964)

When the Beatles were getting to the end of recording *Beatles for Sale*, John became completely enamored of a guitar riff, and tried to introduce it into all the songs on the album.[13] The other Beatles vetoed this idea, so he told them he'd write a song especially for it. "Yes, you go away and do that," they said, thinking he wouldn't get it done on time. But he wrote "I Feel Fine" fairly quickly, and brought it in to the studio. "I've written this song but it's lousy," he told Ringo. Actually, its energy caused it to be chosen as an A-side of a single — the holy grail for Beatle songs.[14]

Once again, there is contradictory testimony on whether there was collaboration on the song, after John brought it in. He always claimed it as

---

[11] Miles, *Many Years from Now*, 112.

[12] Hennessey, "Who Wrote What," *Record Mirror.* Sheff, *The Playboy Interviews*, 204.

[13] According to George Harrison, the guitar riff John so loved was from Bobby Parker's "Watch Your Step." Rowland, "The Quiet Wilbury" (1990), 34. This was one of his favorite records, *Anthology*, 160. Lost Lennon Tapes, July 11, 1988. Parker evidently adapted his guitar riff from an electric piano motif on Ray Charles's 1959 single, "What'd I Say." Shea and Rodriguez, *Fab Four FAQ*, 303. See also George in *Anthology*, 160.

[14] Hutchins, "Secrets of the House of Lennon," a 1964 interview.

entirely his own.[15] In 1995, however, Paul said, "The song itself was more John's than mine. We sat down and co-wrote it with John's original idea. John sang it, I'm on harmonies."[16] However, in 1965 Paul had agreed that the song was John's: "John wrote 'I Feel Fine' on his own."[17] In the same year, in an interview with Paul and Derek Taylor, Taylor said,

> I would like to say that during the time I was with the Beatles, I never ever saw any professional jealousy. . . . Paul, for instance, came up with "She's A Woman", and I thought it was an A [side], and — and other people did, and John came up with "I Feel Fine", so Paul's "She's A Woman" went on the back. Did you mind? **Paul:** I didn't mind at all.[18]

Given the conflict in Paul's testimony, and the anecdotal fullness of John's early interviews, I lean toward the earlier witnesses, including Paul's, and regard this as a song by John alone. However, you could argue the other way. In about 1971, John said, "I wrote this at a recording session."[19] This conflicts with his earlier interview, in which he wrote it at home. If he were writing at the studio, input from Paul would be more likely.

In a bizarre further divergence, George Harrison stated that he was present at the genesis of the song, and it was completely collaborative, with George contributing. The Beatles were crossing Scotland in an Austin Princess, a big luxury car, and they began singing Carl Perkins's "Matchbox" in three-part harmony. This gradually, magically morphed into "I Feel Fine." George gave this as an example of people outside John and Paul contributing to Lennon-McCartney songs.[20] This directly conflicts with John's early memory of writing the song, so must be rejected. Nevertheless, it's intriguing. Did John have a memory of that improvised Scot-

---

[15] "That's me completely," he said in 1980. Sheff, *The Playboy Interviews,* 184. See also Hennessey, "Who Wrote What," *Record Mirror.* "Me." *Ray Connolly Beatles Archive,* 104.

[16] Miles, *Many Years From Now,* 172.

[17] Wyndham, "Paul McCartney As Songwriter."

[18] McCartney, "Interview with Derek Taylor."

[19] Aldridge, *The Beatles Illustrated Lyrics,* 246.

[20] Rowland, "The Quiet Wilbury" (1990), 34.

land song in his head when he went home to write a song around the Bobby Parker riff?

- ## She's a Woman — (McCartney-Lennon) (lead vocals: Paul) (recorded on October 8, 1964)

Paul liked singing Little Richard screamers in the live shows, often as the final song, but then he started thinking: why don't I write one myself? So on the morning of October 8, 1964, he tried to write a very "bluesy" song.[21] After it was substantially done, music and the "template" of the lyrics, he walked around St John's Wood, running through it in his head.[22] Later that day, he brought it to the studio. According to a 1964 interview with Paul and John, Paul only had the first verse, then the rest of the lyrics were written at the studio. "We had to finish it off quickly," said John. "That's why they're such rubbishy lyrics."[23] Paul was happy to be able to write a song in this style. "Bluesy melody is quite hard to write so I was quite pleased to get that," he said in 1995.[24]

The earliest interviews by Paul and John reflect collaboration. "This is the first real rocker we've written," Paul explained in 1964. "It's the coloured sound."[25] But it was collaboration to finish a song Paul had substantially started. John, in 1971, emphasized Paul's contribution: "Paul. Though I helped with the middle. I think."[26] A 1980 statement is similar: "That's Paul with some contribution from me on lines, probably."[27]

In 1989, Paul claimed it. "Once I found I could sing in that high, screamy voice, I started to write songs in that vein. And 'She's a Woman' and 'I'm Down' are really the two."[28] In 1995, he limited John's contribu-

---

[21] For the date, BBC interviews, Nov. 17, 1964, as reported in Unterberger, *The Unreleased Beatles*, 114. See also Miles, *Many Years From Now*, 172-73.

[22] Miles, *Many Years From Now*, 173.

[23] BBC interviews, Nov. 17, 1964, as reported in Unterberger, *The Unreleased Beatles*, 114.

[24] Miles, *Many Years From Now*, 173.

[25] *Melody Maker*, Nov. 7, 1964, p. 3, cf. Badman, *The Beatles Off the Record*, 134. BBC interviews, Nov. 17, 1964, as reported in Unterberger, *The Unreleased Beatles*, 114.

[26] Hennessey, "Who Wrote What," *Record Mirror*.

[27] Sheff, *The Playboy Interviews*, 184.

[28] Read, "McCartney on McCartney," episode 2.

tion to "checking" the song after he brought it in.[29] The earlier evidence points to more substantive collaboration — probably Paul had all the music, and the first verse, then John worked with him on the subsequent verses at the studio.

Beatles for Sale album, December 4, 1964

- ### No Reply — (Lennon-McCartney) (lead vocals: John) (recorded on September 30, 1964)

Evidently Brian asked the Beatles to write a song for Tommy Quickly, and John shouldered the task.[30] He wrote this as a variation on "Silhouettes," a doo-wop hit by The Rays from 1957:

> Took a walk and passed your house late last night
> All the shades were pulled and drawn way down tight
> From within the dim light cast
> Two silhouettes on the shade
> Oh what a lovely couple they made.

So John was thinking of walking down the street and seeing the girl silhouetted in the window, after she hadn't answered his phone call. John brought the song to Paul and they finished it together. Lennon later remembered that when publisher Dick James heard it, he told the songwriter, "'You're getting much better now. . . that was a complete story.' Apparently, before that he thought my songs tended to sort of wander off."[31]

In a familiar pattern, John claimed this song completely (in 1971, "Me," and in 1980, "That's my song"[32]), but Paul remembered some collaboration, though it came from "a strong original idea" of John's. "I think he pretty much had that one," he said, but it apparently lacked some words

---

[29] Miles, *Many Years From Now*, 173.
[30] For Quickly, see "Tip of My Tongue," above. Lewisohn, in Booklet to *Anthology 1*, 41.
[31] Hennessey, "Who Wrote What," *Record Mirror*.
[32] Ibid. Sheff, *The Playboy Interviews*, 184.

or the middle eight.[33] When there are conflicts in testimony, I lean toward collaboration on early Beatle songs.

Quickly's June 1964 recording of this was never released, as the Beatles decided to keep the song for themselves. A Beatles demo version can be found on *Anthology 1*.

- **I'm a Loser — (Lennon-McCartney)**
  (lead vocals: John) (recorded on August 14, 1964)

John wrote this in the autobiographical mode. In 1970, he put it on a shortlist of his "personal records." "I always wrote about me," he said.[34] This and "Hide Your Love Away" were the beginning of his writing about his own emotions.[35] In 1965, he said it was influenced by Dylan, and "I could have made it even more Dylanish if I tried."[36] A songwriting session with Paul ensued, though as Paul said in a 1965 interview, "John wrote most of it."[37] In the studio, the Beatles turned it into a rock song. In a 1964 interview, Paul said, "I reckon the best way to describe this one is a folk song gone pop."[38]

John claimed this song,[39] correctly, though there was some minor collaboration. Paul, in 1996, observed, "You really didn't think about it [the "loser" theme] at the time, it's only later you'd think, God! I think it was pretty brave of John."[40]

---

[33] Miles, *Many Years From Now*, 176.

[34] Lennon, Rolling Stone Interview, Dec. 1970, BBC, part 1; Wenner, *Lennon Remembers*, 9.

[35] Ibid., 83.

[36] Coleman, "Beatles Say – Dylan Shows the Way."

[37] Hutton, "Protest palls: Says Paul," 1. Thirty years later, Paul thought he might have contributed a little to it, but now wasn't sure. Miles, *Many Years From Now*, 176.

[38] Nigel Hunter, interview with McCartney, *Disc Weekly*, Nov. 14, 1964 (Sandercombe, *The Beatles: Press Reports*, 102).

[39] Hennessey, "Who Wrote What," *Record Mirror*. Sheff, *The Playboy Interviews*, 205.

[40] Miles, *Many Years from Now*, 176.

- **Baby's In Black — (collaboration)
  (lead vocals: John and Paul) (recorded on August 11, 1964)**

This was another song written together, from the ground up.[41] Paul and John wanted to write something a little darker and more bluesy than their other songs,[42] and started writing this song in waltz time, Paul said in 1964, "but it finished as a mixture of waltz and beat."[43] Originally John sang the melody and Paul sang harmony, but then the harmony began to take on a life of its own. Finally, "the" melody became ambiguous — you could take either line as the main melody, Paul said in 1995.

  o <u>Rock and Roll Music (COVER) (Chuck Berry)</u>
     (lead vocals: John)

This Chuck Berry single had been released in 1957, and became a Beatles staple. Other versions are on *Anthology 2* and *Beatles at the BBC*.

- **I'll Follow the Sun — (McCartney-Lennon)
  (lead vocals: Paul) (recorded on October 18, 1964)**

"I'll Follow the Sun" is one of Paul's early songs, written at Forthlin Road in the late fifties, a day after Paul recovered from a bout of the flu. "I had that cigarette that's the 'cotton-wool' one. . . . I remember standing in the parlour, with my guitar, looking out through lace curtains of the window and writing that one," Paul said.[44] Pete Best remembered that Paul would busk it on the piano at the Kaiserkeller,[45] and it can be found on a summer 1960 Beatle rehearsal tape.[46] However, it was never entirely fin-

---

[41] John and Paul agree on this. Hennessey, "Lennon: the Greatest Natural Songwriter," 12; Hennessey, "Who Wrote What," *Record Mirror*. Sheff, *The Playboy Interviews*, 214. Nigel Hunter, interview with McCartney, *Disc Weekly*, Nov. 14, 1964 (Sandercombe, *The Beatles: Press Reports*, 102). Miles, *Many Years from Now*, 175. Paul in *Anthology*, 160.

[42] Miles, *Many Years from Now*, 175.

[43] Nigel Hunter, interview with McCartney, *Disc Weekly*, Nov. 14, 1964 (Sandercombe, *The Beatles: Press Reports*, 102).

[44] Lewisohn interview (1988), 12.

[45] McDonald, *Revolution in the Head*, 138.

[46] Winn, *Way Beyond Compare*, 4.

ished,[47] and Paul worked on it with John; then just before recording it they changed the middle section.[48]

Both Paul and John agree that it was a McCartney song.[49] In 1965, John said that "Paul wrote that when he was ten."[50] That would have been in 1952, but John was exaggerating, as he often did! In 1971, John said, once again: "Paul. A nice one — one of his early compositions."[51] However, a 1964 interview with Paul makes the collaboration certain: "John and I wrote this one some while ago, but we changed the middle eight bars before we actually recorded it."[52] This may parallel Paul's 1995 statement that the song had been unfinished.

o   <u>Mr. Moonlight (COVER) (Roy Lee Johnson)</u>
    <u>(lead vocals: John)</u>

This was first released in 1962, as the B-side of the "Dr. Feelgood" single by Dr. Feelgood and the Interns. Dr. Feelgood was William "Willie" Lee Perryman, also known as Piano Red, one of the early blues-rock-n-roll pioneers.

o   <u>Kansas City/Hey! Hey! Hey! Hey! (COVER) (Jerry Leiber,</u>
    <u>Mike Stoller/Richard Penniman)</u>
    <u>(lead vocals: Paul)</u>

This is another of Paul's Little Richard rave-ups. Leiber and Stoller wrote "Kansas City" in 1952, and it became a major hit for Wilbert Harrison seven years later. In the same year, Little Richard recorded it, changing some words and adding a song he had recorded in 1958, "Hey! Hey! Hey! Hey!", the B-side to his "Good Golly Miss Molly." This is the version that

---

[47] Miles, *Many Years from Now*, 38-39.
[48] Nigel Hunter, interview with McCartney, *Disc Weekly*, Nov. 14, 1964 (Sandercombe, *The Beatles: Press Reports*, 102).
[49] Lewisohn interview (1988), 12. Miles, *Many Years from Now*, 38-39.
[50] Coleman, "Life with the Lennons."
[51] Hennessey, "Who Wrote What," *Record Mirror*. Also, Connolly, *Ray Connolly Beatles Archive*, 104. Sheff, *The Playboy Interviews*, 184.
[52] Nigel Hunter, interview with McCartney, *Disc Weekly*, Nov. 14, 1964 (Sandercombe, *The Beatles: Press Reports*, 102).

Paul covered. "'Kansas City' is one of my all-time favorite records, actually," he said in 1964.[53]

Since "It requires a great deal of nerve to just jump up and scream like an idiot, you know?" as Paul said,[54] John acted as his cheerleader when he recorded this song: "Come on, Paul, knock the shit out of 'Kansas City'" or "You can do it, you've just got to scream, you can do it."[55]

Other versions are on the *Live at the BBC* albums and *Anthology 1*.

SIDE TWO

- **Eight Days a Week — (McCartney-Lennon) (lead vocals: John and Paul) (recorded on October 6, 1964)**

According to Paul, he got the idea for this song from the chance phrase of a chauffeur who drove him out to John's house at Weybridge one night. The chauffeur said the employees in his company were being worked so hard that they seemed to work "eight days a week."[56] "So when I got to John's house, I said, 'Eight Days a Week.'"[57] In 1995, Paul emphasized that he had nothing beyond the title when he and John started the songwriting session. "I didn't have any idea for it other than the title, and we just knocked it off together, just filling in from the title. So that one came quickly."[58]

---

[53] Rybaczewski, "'Kansas City/Hey-Hey-Hey-Hey!' History."

[54] Goodman, "Paul and Linda McCartney Interview," *Playboy*, 88.

[55] McCartney, in Garbarini and Baird, "Has Success Spoiled Paul McCartney?" (1985), 60. McCartney, Letter to John on John's Induction. See also O'Hare, "McCartney on McCartney."

[56] Nigel Hunter, interview with McCartney, *Disc Weekly*, Nov. 14, 1964 (Sandercombe, *The Beatles: Press Reports*, 102).

[57] Interview in Smith, *Off the Record*, 201. Linda's idea that Ringo said it, which Paul doesn't correct, is evidently wrong. Goodman, "Paul and Linda McCartney," *Playboy* (1984), 90.

[58] Miles, *Many Years From Now*, 174. Similar: *Anthology*, 159; Badman, *The Beatles Off the Record*, 135.

John, in 1970, said that this was "Mainly Paul, I think." A year later, he leans toward collaboration: "Both of us."[59] In 1980, he again emphasized Paul's contribution: "It was Paul's effort at getting a single for the movie. . . . It was his initial effort, but I think we both worked on it. I'm not sure."[60]

I conclude that it was co-written, but from Paul's title and idea.

John's statement that the song was "Paul's effort at getting a single for the movie" is questionable, from a chronological point of view. The song was recorded on October 6, 1964, during the *Beatles for Sale* sessions, while *Help!* didn't start filming till February 1965.[61] Evidently, John confused this title with *Eight Arms to Hold You*, an early working title of the *Help!* movie.[62]

o   Words of Love (COVER) (Buddy Holly)
   (lead vocals: John and Paul)

Buddy Holly released this as a single in 1957.

o   Honey Don't (COVER) (Carl Perkins)
   (lead vocals: Ringo)

This was released in 1956 as the B-side of Carl Perkins's "Blue Suede Shoes." Other Beatle versions can be found on the *Live at the BBC* albums, one of which has John singing lead.

- **Every Little Thing — (McCartney-Lennon)**
  (lead vocals: John and Paul) (recorded on September 29–30, 1964)

All the evidence on the songwriting for "Every Little Thing" is contradictory. Paul and John here seem to disagree with themselves, not just with each other. Any number of possible reconstructions of the songwriting process is possible. Following is one attempt.

---

[59] Connolly, *Ray Connolly Beatles Archive*, 104. Hennessey, "Who Wrote What," *Record Mirror*. He also put it on a list of collaborations, Hennessey, "Lennon: the Greatest Natural Songwriter," 12.

[60] Sheff, *The Playboy Interviews*, 185.

[61] Turner, *A Hard Day's Write*, 63.

[62] Article in *Melody Maker*, March 27, 1965 (Sandercombe, *The Beatles: Press Reports*, 120); Soderbergh and Lester, *Getting Away With It*, 52.

Paul started writing this in London, in the Asher residence, either in the basement music room or in the garret.[63] Then he and John worked on it in Atlantic City, when they were touring the U.S., and finished it then, in late August, 1964.[64] (The Beatles played Convention Hall in Atlantic City on August 30, 1964.)

Both Paul and John attest to collaboration on this song — Paul said, "John and I got this one written in Atlantic City during our last tour of the States." John put it on a list of jointly written songs.[65] Yet both Paul and John agree that Paul was the main songwriter for this song. Paul said: "'Every Little Thing,' like most of the stuff I did, was my attempt at the next single."[66] In 1970, John said, "Paul wrote that on tour. Yeah. That was a nice one. I was helping but I'm not taking much credit for it."[67] It was probably a Paul song, finished with collaboration.

- **I Don't Want to Spoil the Party — (Lennon-McCartney) (lead vocals: John and Paul) (recorded on September 29, 1964)**

John started writing this as another of his new "very personal" songs.[68] Then he and Paul worked on it — Paul remembered the songwriting session as them "sitting down doing a job."[69] In 1964, he said, "We went after a real country and western flavour when we wrote this one."[70] A country-western confessional song, Beatle-ified.

---

[63] *Many Years from Now*, 108, 174.
[64] Nigel Hunter, interview with McCartney, *Disc Weekly*, Nov. 14, 1964 (Sandercombe, *The Beatles: Press Reports*, 102). Hennessey, "Who Wrote What," *Record Mirror*.
[65] Nigel Hunter, interview with McCartney, *Disc Weekly*, Nov. 14, 1964 (Sandercombe, *The Beatles: Press Reports*, 102). Hennessey, "Who Wrote What," *Record Mirror*.
[66] Miles, *Many Years From Now*, 174.
[67] Connolly, *Ray Connolly Beatles Archive*, 104. Comparable: Sheff, *The Playboy Interviews*, 214.
[68] Aldridge, *Beatles Illustrated Lyrics*, 235. John claimed this: *Ray Connolly Beatles Archive*, 104. Hennessey, "Who Wrote What," *Record Mirror* (on a list of songs John wrote himself).
[69] Miles, *Many Years from Now*, 175.
[70] Nigel Hunter, interview with McCartney, *Disc Weekly*, Nov. 14, 1964 (Sandercombe, *The Beatles: Press Reports*, 102).

- **What You're Doing — (McCartney-Lennon)**
  (lead vocals: Paul) (recorded on September 29-30 and
  October 26, 1964)

This was another song that Paul and John worked on on a day off in Atlantic City, in late August 1964.[71] Again, the evidence is somewhat contradictory, but apparently the song was more Paul's than John's.[72] John, in 1970, said, "Another one Paul wrote on tour in Philadelphia or somewhere."[73]

  o Everybody's Trying To Be My Baby (COVER) (Carl
     Perkins)
     (lead vocals: George)

This song, a very weak album finale, first appeared on *Dance Album of . . . Carl Perkins* in 1957. Another Beatle performance is on *Live at the BBC*.

---

[71] Ibid. "We wrote this one in Atlantic City like 'Every Little Thing.'" See also Winn, *Way Beyond Compare*, 359.
[72] Miles, *Many Years From Now*, 175-76.
[73] Connolly, *Ray Connolly Beatles Archive*, 104. Sheff, *The Playboy Interviews*, 214. Earlier, John put this on a list of collaborative songs, Hennessey, "Who Wrote What," *Record Mirror*.

7

"I started thinking about my own emotions"

HELP!

The collaborative songwriting for this album was mostly done at John's house, Kenwood, at Weybridge.[1] In January 1965, John said, "Well, Paul has written five structures — I suppose he means tunes without words — for the film, and I've done half a song, so we aren't doing bad."[2] Paul usually wrote music first, then added words.

Help! includes twelve original Beatle songs, and two covers, Ringo's excellent country outing, "Act Naturally," and John's scorching "Dizzy Miss Lizzie," which ends the album. This is the last major Beatle album to include covers, with the exception of the forty second joke, "Maggie Mae" on *Let It Be. Help!* is thus a transitional record, with some traits of the early Beatles albums (including a "screamer" at the end of the "show"), and then "Yesterday" and "I've Just Seen a Face," which point forward to the stylistic exploration of *Rubber Soul* and *Revolver.* Elsewhere on the record, John is reaching toward the lyrical sophistication and folk balladry of Dylan, with "You've Got to Hide Your Love Away."

"Yesterday" has the most famous songwriting story in the Beatle history: Paul dreamed the main melody and wondered if it came from a song he'd heard. It's also an example of a song written entirely without collaboration. As such, it points ahead to John and Paul writing many songs entirely separately in later Beatle albums.

---

[1] McCartney, in *Anthology,* 171.
[2] Coleman, "Wish Elvis All the Best in *Aladdin."*

"Ticket to Ride / Yes It Is" single, April 9, 1965

- Ticket to Ride — (Lennon-McCartney)
  (lead vocals: John) (recorded on February 15, 1965)

Understanding the songwriting history for this song is hampered by conflicting evidence, but following is a possible reconstruction. Sometime before Christmas, 1964, Paul and John sat down for a songwriting session at Kenwood. John had the "Ticket to Ride" phrase, and probably the general idea of the lyrics[3] but they "wrote the melody together."[4] John's domination of the lyrics caused him to think of this song as one of his personal songs that meant something to him, reflecting his "moods or moments."[5]

Paul and John sang the tune of "Ticket to Ride" to Dick James during the rehearsals for the Hammersmith Odeon Christmas Show, thus December 21st to 24th, 1964. John told James that the song had "a sort of title": "She's Got a Ticket to Ride."[6]

John played it for George Martin on a skiing holiday in February 1965, then said that "he would get together with Paul as soon as he got back to London and finish it off."[7] Paul was gone on vacation when John returned, only returning on February 14th, at which time he and John finished the song, the day before they recorded it.

The evidence shows us the familiar pattern of John describing the song as his, while Paul remembered collaboration. John claimed it in 1971, and in 1980, he said "That's me," and limited Paul's contribution to "the way Ringo played the drums"![8] But Paul, in a very early statement, described writing it in collaboration. "John and I wrote it in the middle of

---

[3] Read, "McCartney on McCartney," episode 2.
[4] Miles, *Many Years from Now*, 193.
[5] Cott, "The Rolling Stone Interview with John Lennon" (1968). Some less conclusive comments on the song: Wenner, *Lennon Remembers*, 81; Sheff, *The Playboy Interviews*, 205.
[6] Nigel Hunter, interview with George Martin and Dick James, *Disc Weekly*, April 17, 1965 (Sandercombe, *The Beatles: Press Reports*, 123).
[7] Ibid.
[8] Hennessey, "Who Wrote What," *Record Mirror*. Lost Lennon Tapes, Sept. 23, 1991 and March 20, 1989, cf. Sheff, *The Playboy Interviews*, 205.

doing some other stuff at his house one afternoon," he said in 1965.[9] This is definitively confirmed by George Martin's equally early interview.[10] In 1995, Paul still had definite memories of the songwriting session. Responding to John saying Paul's contribution was the way Ringo played the drums, Paul replied, "John just didn't take the time to explain that we sat down together and worked on that song for a full three-hour songwriting session, and at the end of it all we had all the words, we had the harmonies, and we had all the little bits."[11]

John probably had the idea of this song, and dominated writing the lyrics, but the song was still written with substantial musical and lyrical collaboration.

- **Yes It Is — (Lennon-McCartney)
(lead vocals: John) (recorded on February 16, 1965)**

John began this song as a rewrite of "This Boy"[12] and then he and Paul worked on it together. "It was his inspiration that I helped him finish off," said Paul.[13] We have the familiar pattern of John claiming a song and Paul remembering some collaboration, but Paul definitely highlighted John's contribution: "'Yes It Is' is a very fine song of John's, a ballad, unusual for John."[14]

So we have a John song, another in three-part harmony, finished with collaboration.

---

[9] "Ticket to Top Spot! Beatles Crush Knockers," *Melody Maker* 40 (Apr. 17, 1965): p. 1. See also Read, "McCartney on McCartney," episode 2.
[10] Nigel Hunter, interview with George Martin and Dick James, *Disc Weekly*, April 17, 1965 (Sandercombe, *The Beatles: Press Reports*, 123).
[11] Miles, *Many Years from Now*, 193.
[12] Connolly, *Ray Connolly Beatles Archive*, 105. Lost Lennon Tapes, March 20, 1989 ("That's me, trying to rewrite 'This Boy,' but it didn't work"), cf. Sheff, *The Playboy Interviews*, 205.
[13] Miles, *Many Years From Now*, 176.
[14] Ibid.

Beatles VI, U.S. album, June 14, 1965

Although this album contained the usual stateside mangling of the canonical British versions of the Beatle albums, it also contained a great cover song never before released by the Beatles.

- o <u>Bad Boy (COVER) (Larry Williams)</u>
  <u>(lead vocals: John)</u>

This Larry Williams song had appeared in 1959. The Beatles recording was later released on the U.K. collection, *A Collection of Beatles Oldies* (December 10, 1966) and on *Past Masters, Volume One*.[15]

━━━━━◖●◗━━━━━

"Help! / I'm Down" single, July 19, 1965

- Help! — (Lennon-McCartney)
  (lead vocals: John) (recorded on April 13, 1965)

When it came time to write a title song for the new Beatle movie, after the director and producers had decided on "Help!" as the title, John went home, "thought about it [the title song] and got the basis for it,"[16] but there wasn't much of the song there yet.[17] Paul came over to work on it, and they adapted "a little bit of a song" John had written, which had been "floating around for a long time," called "Keep Your Hands Off My Babe."[18] Paul supplied a counter-melody to the verses, starting with "When I was younger, so much younger than today."[19] He also helped develop the "structure" of the song.[20] John probably dominated writing the lyrics, while Paul probably made a substantial contribution to the music.[21]

---

[15] For Larry Williams, see "Slow Down" on the *Long Tall Sally* EP, above.

[16] Miles, *Many Years from Now*, 199.

[17] Ibid.

[18] Article in *Disc Weekly*, July 31, 1965 (Sandercombe, *The Beatles: Press Reports*, 133).

[19] Miles, *Many Years from Now*, 199.

[20] *Anthology*, 171.

[21] Director Richard Lester tells the story of Paul and John writing the song in a twenty-five minute cab ride. Soderbergh and Lester, *Getting Away With It* (1999), 62. This contradicts the memories of Paul and John, so should be rejected. Possibly they worked on it during a cab ride.

In the seventies, John claimed this song as entirely his own, and even singled it out as one of his most personal songs.[22] "The only true songs I ever wrote were like 'Help' and 'Strawberry Fields,'" he said in 1970.[23] "It was just me singing 'Help' and I meant it."[24] He even mentioned it as one of the best examples of how he wrote with no collaboration: "And we'd written separately for years. I mean, in *Help*, I wrote 'Help.'"[25] And again, in 1980, he said that, "I wrote ['Help'], bam! bam! like that and got the single."[26] He continued to emphasize the song's personal nature, reflecting his insecurity at the time: "I was just writing a song — I'd been commissioned to write a song for the movie. And I came out with 'Help!' . . . I was crying for help. It was like the fat Elvis period."[27]

But John's early interviews conclusively record collaboration. In 1965, he said, "We wrote it in my house. . . when Paul came over, we decided to, sort of adapt it [the song fragment]. We wrote "Help!" after we had been told of the film title."[28] And again, in the same year, he said, "Paul and I wrote eleven and we chose seven out of the eleven. *Q: I suppose there is a title song.* Yeah, it's called 'Help!,' you know. We think it's one of the best we've written."[29]

Paul's first attribution for this song, in 1984, reflects clear memories of collaboration: "John wrote that — well, John and I wrote it at his house in Weybridge for the film."[30] Three years later, he said, "I remember sitting there doing 'Help!'[31] In 1993 Paul, in direct contrast to John in the seventies, cited it as a good example of collaboration: "But when we came to-

---

[22] Hennessey, "Who Wrote What," *Record Mirror* (on a list of songs John said he'd written alone). Wenner, *Lennon Remembers*, 9.
[23] Lennon, Rolling Stone Interview, Dec. 1970, BBC, part 1, cf. Wenner, *Lennon Remembers*, 9.
[24] Lennon, Rolling Stone Interview, Dec. 1970, BBC, part 4, cf. Wenner, *Lennon Remembers*, 98.
[25] McCabe and Schonfeld, *John Lennon: For the Record* (1971), 118.
[26] Sheff, *The Playboy Interviews*, 185.
[27] Lost Lennon Tapes, March 21, 1988, cf. Sheff, *The Playboy Interviews*, 186-87.
[28] Article in *Disc Weekly*, July 31, 1965 (Sandercombe, *The Beatles: Press Reports*, 133).
[29] Beatles, "Beatles Interview: Bahamas, Promoting 'Help' Movie - May 1965."
[30] "Paul and Linda McCartney Interview," *Playboy*, 107.
[31] deCurtis, *In Other Words*, 61.

gether on songs, then you got a different kind of song again. You got things like 'I Wanna Hold Your Hand,' 'Help!' and stuff like that."[32] Paul said that John had the tendency to start songs and leave them unfinished, but that a co-writing session would quickly get them into a finished state. "That's what I was there for; to complete it. Had John just been left on his own he might have taken weeks to do it, but just one visit and we would go right in and complete it."[33]

Despite the fact that they had collaborated on the song, Paul said, "Help" was a song characteristic of John, "really John."[34]

Given the early testimony from John, and Paul's memories, I conclude that it was a song started by John, then finished with significant collaboration. It's possible that the lyrics were entirely dominated by John (which would fit with the lyrics being personal), while Paul contributed substantially to the music.

- **I'm Down — (McCartney-Lennon)**
  (lead vocals: Paul) (recorded on June 14, 1965)

"I'm Down" is another song Paul wrote in the rave-up genre — "Me again, you see, Little Richard gone mad," he said in 1989.[35] John may have contributed a little to it, but not much. For example, in 1995, Paul said, "I'm not sure if John had any input in it, in fact I don't think he did. But not wishing to be churlish, with most of these I'll always credit him with 10 per cent just in case he fixed a word or offered a suggestion."[36]

John had two conflicting memories about the song. In 1971, he ascribed it to Paul,[37] but by 1980, he stated that he might have contributed something to it: "That's Paul, with a little help from me, I think."[38]

---

[32] McCartney, Press Conference, 1 May 1993, Georgia Dome, Atlanta. See also Miles, *Many Years from Now*, 199.
[33] Ibid., 199.
[34] In *From Rio to Liverpool* (1990), a documentary.
[35] Read, "McCartney on McCartney," episode 2. Cf. Gambaccini, *Paul McCartney In His Own Words*, 9; McCartney in October 1964, as quoted in Turner, *A Hard Day's Write*, 73. Miles, *Many Years from Now*, 201.
[36] Miles, *Many Years from Now*, 201.
[37] Hennessey, "Who Wrote What," *Record Mirror*.

"I'm Down" is thus a Paul song, but with some possible minor collaboration from John.

It was recorded on June 14, 1965, the same session in which Paul recorded "Yesterday," a remarkable fact. Beatle neophytes often think there is a continuum between the hard rock songs of Lennon, on one side, and the ballads of McCartney on the other side. Actually, both Paul and John each had individual continuums going from hard rock to tender ballads.

Help! album, August 6, 1965

    ○   <u>Help! — (Lennon-McCartney)</u>

See the "Help / I'm Down" single, above.

- **The Night Before — (McCartney)
(lead vocals: Paul) (recorded on February 17, 1965)**

In 1970 and 1971, John said that Paul had written this.[39] He also ascribed it to Paul in 1980, but with the caveat that he didn't remember the song at all![40] Paul also claimed it, though he left open the slight possibility that John might have helped with it: "I would say that's mainly mine. I don't think John had a lot to do with that."[41]

I conclude that it was a Paul song.

- **You've Got to Hide Your Love Away — (Lennon)
(lead vocals: John) (recorded on February 18, 1965)**

John wrote this at Kenwood, and it became one of his personal songs: "I started thinking about my own emotions . . . instead of projecting my-

---

[38] Sheff, *The Playboy Interviews*, 204.
[39] Connolly, *Ray Connolly Beatles Archive*, 105. Hennessey, "Who Wrote What," *Record Mirror*.
[40] Sheff, *The Playboy Interviews*, 204.
[41] Miles, *Many Years from Now*, 195.

self into a situation, I would try to express what I felt about myself."[42] It is another Dylan-influenced song.[43]

Paul agreed, most of the time. In 1974, he gave this song as the first example of Dylan's influence on the Beatles, and said, "That was John's song."[44] In fact, in 1995, he said, "I think it was 100 per cent John's song."[45] Case closed.

Or is it? In the same interview, Paul maddeningly goes on: "I might have helped him on it. I have a vague recollection of helping to fill out some verses for him." So, after saying the song was a hundred percent written by John, he lurches in a different direction and remembers "helping to fill out some verses for him." Paul's complex statement shows how important it is to look at the historical record holistically. Here he makes two conflicting statements in the same section of an interview. The two chief Beatles often contradicted themselves in separate interviews, or, as here, in the same interview.

I lean toward seeing this as a Lennon song, as Paul's earliest testimony ascribes it to John. There may have been some slight collaboration on it, however.

- **I Need You — (Harrison)**
  (lead vocals: George) (recorded on February 15 and 16, 1965)

In 1965, George said that he wrote the melody for this in twenty minutes, but it took a few days to come up with the words.[46] There is a pleasant story that George wrote it for his eventual wife, Pattie Boyd, when he was separated from her while the Beatles were filming *Help!* in the Ba-

---

[42] Wenner, *Lennon Remembers*, 83. See also Connolly, *Ray Connolly Beatles Archive*, 105; Hennessey, "Who Wrote What," *Record Mirror* (in a list of songs John wrote alone); Aldridge, *Beatles Illustrated Lyrics*, 239.

[43] Sheff, *The Playboy Interviews*, 206. Similar attributions to John influenced by Dylan: Garbarani, "Paul McCartney: Lifting the Veil," (1980), 48; Goodman, "Playboy Interview Paul and Linda McCartney" (1984), 107. Snow, "Paul McCartney."

[44] Gambaccini, "The Rolling Stone Interview."

[45] Miles, *Many Years from Now*, 195.

[46] Beatles, Interview, August 13-24, 1965, as summarized in Winn, *Way Beyond Compare*, 351.

hamas. However, the truth is that he recorded this song on February 15 and 16, 1965, a week or two before he went to the Bahamas.[47]

- **Another Girl — (McCartney)**
  (lead vocals: Paul) (recorded on February 15 and 16, 1965)

Before recording *Help!*, Paul had been on vacation with Jane for ten days in Hammamet, Tunisia, a seaside resort, and the British government had put him up in a picturesque villa there. He wrote "Another Girl" in this villa.[48] Both John and Miles/Paul agreed that this was a Paul song.[49]

- **You're Gonna Lose That Girl — (Lennon-McCartney)**
  (lead vocals: John) (recorded on February 19, 1965)

Cynthia Lennon remembered John writing 'You're Going to Lose That Girl' late one night, then calling her to listen.[50] It was finished in a songwriting session with Paul at Kenwood.[51]

John claimed this song as entirely his own. "That was me," he said in 1970.[52] However, Miles, working from interviews with Paul, wrote, in 1995,

> "You're Going to Lose That Girl" was written by John and Paul together at John's house in Weybridge . . . . It was John's original idea, estimated by Paul as about 60 per cent written by John and 40 per cent by himself.[53]

I tend to think there was usually collaboration on the early Beatle songs, so accept that this was a John song developed with collaboration.

- Ticket to Ride — (Lennon-McCartney)

See "Ticket to Ride / Yes It Is" single, above.

---

[47] McDonald, *Revolution in the Head*, 116.
[48] Miles, *Many Years from Now*, 194.
[49] Connolly, *Ray Connolly Beatles Archive*, 105. Sheff, *The Playboy Interviews*, 205. It is also on a list of "songs which John attributed directly to Paul." Hennessey, "Who Wrote What."
[50] Cynthia Lennon, *John*, 224.
[51] Miles, *Many Years from Now*, 195.
[52] Connolly, *Ray Connolly Beatles Archive*, 105. Similar: Sheff, *The Playboy Interviews*, 206.
[53] Miles, *Many Years from Now*, 195.

SIDE TWO

- ○ <u>Act Naturally (COVER) (Johnny Russell, Vonie Morrison) (lead vocals: Ringo)</u>

This song was a country hit for Buck Owens and the Buckaroos in 1963.

- **It's Only Love — (Lennon-McCartney) (lead vocals: John) (recorded on June 15, 1965)**

This song was begun by John, then developed in a songwriting session with Paul at John's house. John claimed it in 1971 ("Me. . . . Terrible lyric"[54]) but Paul described it as a collaborative song from John's "original idea."[55]

Both writers found the song distinctly subpar. "The lyrics were abysmal. I always hated that song," said John in 1980.[56] Paul described it as "album filler."[57]

I conclude that it was started by John, then finished with collaboration.

- **You Like Me Too Much (Harrison) (lead vocals: George) (recorded on February 17, 1965)**

I have found no comments by George on this song, which didn't make it into the movie.

- **Tell Me What You See — (McCartney-Lennon) (lead vocals: Paul) (recorded on February 18, 1965)**

This was a Paul song, apparently finished with collaboration. The second verse, "Big and black the clouds may be, time will pass away. / If you put your trust in me I'll make bright your day," seems to be based on a religious poem that hung in a frame in John's house: "However black the clouds may be, / In time they'll pass away. / Have faith and trust and you

[54] Hennessey, "Who Wrote What," *Record Mirror*. Also: *Ray Connolly Beatles Archive*, 105; Sheff, *The Playboy Interviews*, 187. See also Lennon in 1969, in Turner, *Hard Day's Write*, 82.
[55] Miles, *Many Years from Now*, 200.
[56] Lost Lennon Tapes, Oct. 21, 1991, cf. Sheff, *The Playboy Interviews*, 187.
[57] Miles, *Many Years from Now*, 200.

will see / God's light make bright your day." So the words to this verse may have been substantially written by John, from this "found" source.[58]

John ascribed this to Paul, in 1971 and 1980.[59]

Paul's comments on the song in 1995 are less than enlightening. He wanders, giving various possibilities for authorship. It could be entirely his ("I seem to remember it as mine. . . . it might have been totally me.") or it could have been a fairly equal collaboration ("I would claim it as a 60-40 . . . they [the early McCartney and Lennon] did a job.").[60]

One wonders, if it is possible that it was a pure Paul song, why the alternative to 100% would be 60-40, instead of 70-30 or 80-20. (Another reason these numerical attributions are usually not helpful.) In any event, Paul is the dominant writer. Since this is an early Beatle song, I lean toward the "Paul song, finished with collaboration" alternative.

- **I've Just Seen a Face — (McCartney)
  (lead vocals: Paul) (recorded on June 14, 1965)**

Paul composed this "slightly country and western" song at the Asher residence on Wimpole Street.[61] Known first as "Auntie Gin's Theme," because Paul's Aunt Gin (Jane Virginia McCartney Harris, Paul's father's sister) was especially fond of it, George Martin recorded it under that name.[62] (Auntie Gin later appeared in the lyrics of "Let Em In.")

Paul and John agreed that this was a Paul song. "I think of this as totally by me," Paul said in 1995. "It was from my point of view."[63] In 1970, John said, "Another one of Paul's."[64]

---

[58] A version of this is in *Spaniard in the Works*. Lydon, "Lennon and McCartney: Songwriters," also in Lydon, *Flashbacks: Eyewitness Accounts of the Rock Revolution*, 16-17. Lewisohn, *Tune In*, extended, 2:1196.

[59] Hennessey, "Who Wrote What," *Record Mirror*. Sheff, *The Playboy Interviews*, 205.

[60] Miles, *Many Years from Now*, 200.

[61] Ibid.

[62] Harry, *Paul McCartney Encyclopedia*, entry on the song.

[63] Miles, *Many Years from Now*, 200.

[64] Connolly, *Ray Connolly Beatles Archive*, 105. John also put it on a list of songs written by Paul alone. Hennessey, "Who Wrote What." Sheff, *The Playboy Interviews*, 205.

It was recorded on June 14, 1965, the same day that two other songs by Paul, "Yesterday" and "I'm Down," were recorded. This breadth looked forward to the astounding stylistic range of albums such as *Revolver* and the *White Album*.

- ## Yesterday — (McCartney) (lead vocals: Paul) (recorded on June 14, 17, 1965

"Yesterday" offers possibly the most famous composition story in the entire Beatle canon, as the music came to Paul in a dream. He wrote/dreamed it at the Asher home in Wimpole Street in May 1965, during the filming of *Help!* (which would have been before May 11, when filming ended).[65] Curiously, George Martin reported that he first heard "Yesterday," without lyrics, in January 1964, at the George V Hotel in Paris,[66] and Ray Coleman, who interviewed Paul extensively on this song in 1995, said that he wrote/dreamed it in late 1963.[67] But I accept the later date, as the song seems of very middle-Beatle vintage.[68]

As Paul has told the story many times, he woke up with the main melody of the song complete in his mind: "I awoke with this tune in my head. [He hums the tune: 'Da da da . . .'] I thought: what is *that*? I know *that*. I know *that*."[69] He at first thought it must have been one of the old standards his father would play, but he couldn't remember which one. He jumped out of bed, then picked out the chords and melody on a piano. "I

---

[65] Miles, *Many Years from Now*, 201. In 1982, Martin said that Paul told him that he had the tune for about a month before he had the lyric. This would also date the song's first composition to about May 1965. Tobler and Grundy, "George Martin."

[66] Lewisohn, *The Beatles Recording Sessions*, 59.

[67] Coleman, *McCartney: Yesterday . . . and Today*, 6-7. Paul also tells the story of this song in great detail in Miles, *Many Years from Now*, 201-9. It is possible that Coleman was working with the "Martin" chronology, as he quotes Martin when discussing Paul playing the song in France in early 1964, see p. 12.

[68] Richard Lester said that Paul played "Yesterday" constantly on the set of *Help!* Winn, *Way Beyond Compare*, 305. See also Coleman, *McCartney: Yesterday . . . and Today*, 15-16. The movie was filmed from February to May 11, 1965. Publisher Dick James said he first heard it on the set of the movie, in the Beatle flat with four doors. Nigel Hunter, interview with Dick James, Oct. 9, 1965 (Sandercombe, *The Beatles: Press Reports*, 143).

[69] Coleman, *McCartney: Yesterday . . . and Today*, 6-7.

got the G," he remembered in 1995, "then I got the nice F sharp minor seventh, that was the big waaaahhhh. That led very naturally to the B which led very naturally to the E minor. It just kept sort of tumbling out with those chords. I thought: well, this is very nice, but it's a nick, it's a nick [stolen from another song]. I don't know what it is."[70]

Giving the tune the sentimental working title "Scrambled Egg,"[71] he was never certain that the music was original, so began playing it for people, asking: "Is this like something? I think I've written it."[72] He played it for the singer Alma Cogan: "'Scrambled egg, oh my baby how I love you leg. da da da da' And she said, 'Well I'm not too keen on the lyric, but it's a nice tune.' And I said, 'But you've *heard* it.' 'No,' she said, 'I haven't heard it. No it's a good one.'"[73] He played it for John, for George Martin, for a number of older people, and even to experienced songwriter Lionel Bart.[74] No one recognized the tune.

Eventually, after he convinced himself that he had indeed written an original melody in his sleep, he worked out the "middle eight" for it at Wimpole Street.[75] However, when he tried to add serious lyrics, he came to a block. During the filming of *Help*, from February to May 11, 1965, the final lyrics were still not there, though Paul performed the song frequently on the set.[76]

On May 27 Paul and Jane Asher went on vacation to Albufeira, Portugal, a fishing village where one of the Shadows, Bruce Welch, had a villa. As they were being driven from the Lisbon Airport to Albufeira, Paul

---

[70] Ibid. See also Garbarini and Baird, "Has Success Spoiled Paul McCartney?" (1985), 62.

[71] "Paul McCartney and John Lennon at the Tonight Show," May 15, 1968. Discussion in Winn, *That Magic Feeling*, 166.

[72] "Paul and Linda McCartney Interview," *Playboy*, (1984), 107.

[73] Read, "McCartney on McCartney," episode 2. Or Paul played the tune to Alma, and her mother walked in and asked, "Would anyone like some scrambled eggs?" According to this tradition, Paul immediately took that as a title and added the legs line off the cuff. Coleman, *McCartney: Yesterday . . . and Today*, 9-10. However, elsewhere, Paul seems to remember the "Scrambled egg" lyric coming with the dream. Pritchard and Lysaght, *The Beatles: an Oral History*, 193.

[74] Coleman, *McCartney: Yesterday . . . and Today*, 8-9.

[75] Ibid., 10-11.

[76] Ibid., 15-16. See above.

started to work on the song, and the final lyrics suddenly came to him. On arriving at the villa, he played the new lyrics to Welch, then continued polishing them during the vacation.[77]

When he came back to London, he played the completed song for John, the other Beatles, and George Martin. Martin had reservations about the title because there was already a song called "Yesterdays," but Paul insisted on the singular "Yesterday," and told Martin the song was ready for recording.[78]

When Paul played it for the Beatles at the studio, they were reluctant to add vocals or other instruments to Paul's acoustic guitar. John said: "It's yours. It's good. Just you and an acoustic guitar would be all right."[79] So on June 14, 1965, Paul recorded "Yesterday" with guitar alone.[80]

When George Martin suggested adding strings to the song, Paul at first balked, not wanting to introduce a sugary sweet Mantovani sound into a Beatles record. But George suggested that they at least try adding a restrained string quartet, with no vibrato. Paul came to Martin's house and they worked out the string parts.[81] After the strings were recorded on June 17, Paul was pleased with the addition. The song was complete.

Given the beauty, complexity and sophistication of "Yesterday," and the fact that it has become one of the most recorded songs in history, this is a remarkable story. In fact, Paul viewed the composition of this song as something unexplainable, mysterious, almost supernatural.

Both Paul and John generally ascribed "Yesterday" entirely to Paul; in fact, none of the other Beatles even perform on the record. (Though the Beatles did perform it live as a group occasionally.) As early as 1965, Paul gave it as an example of a song he'd written entirely on his own: "What did I write on my own? Oh, 'World Without Love,' 'Yesterday,' Can't Buy Me

---

[77] Ibid. Matthew, "Interview with Paul McCartney & John Lennon," (1967).

[78] Coleman, *McCartney: Yesterday . . . and Today*, 19-20.

[79] Ibid.

[80] Ibid., 42-43.

[81] Gambaccini, "The Rolling Stone Interview," also Gambaccini, *Paul McCartney In His Own Words*, 17. Read, "McCartney on McCartney," episode 2. Williams, "Produced by George Martin" (1971). Pritchard and Lysaght, *The Beatles: an Oral History*, 192.

Love,' 'All My Loving,' and quite a few others. Mine are normally a bit soppier than John's. That's because I am a bit soppier than John."[82] In 1968, he also claimed authorship: *"Q My favourite is "Yesterday." How did you write it?* You know, I just started playing it and this tune came, 'cause that's what happens. They just sort of, they come, you know."[83] And in 1973, asked *"Do you feel stronger about that song than the others?"* he replied, "I do, actually, you know. I really reckon 'Yesterday' is probably my best."[84]

John generally agreed that Paul wrote the song. "'Yesterday' I had nothing to do with," he said in 1970.[85] He sometimes told the anecdote of a Spanish violinist playing "Yesterday" for him and asking him to sign the violin. "I didn't know what to say. I said: 'Well, OK.' I signed it and Yoko signed it. One day he's going to find out that Paul wrote it."[86]

However, there is just the slightest hint of complexity in the song's composition history. In 1967, Paul said that the actual title, "Yesterday," came from John.

> Well this is Paul taking up the story in a slight villa in Corsica [sic], strumming away on a medieval guitar. I thought, "Scrambled egg," but I never could finish it. And eventually, I took it back, and with the ancient wisdom of the east, John came out with, "Yesterday." So I thought, That's the name of the story for that one.[87]

If John did provide the title, this would be a significant impact on the song, for the rest of the lyrics sometimes would develop from the title.[88]

---

[82] Wyndham, "Paul McCartney As Songwriter."

[83] "Paul McCartney and John Lennon at the Tonight Show," May 14, 1968.

[84] Gambaccini, *Paul McCartney In His Own Words*, 17. Similar: Paul in Rowland, "The Quiet Wilbury" (1990): "I wrote 'Yesterday' singlehanded and not only do I share it—now with Yoko—but the Lennon name comes before mine."

[85] Wenner, *Lennon Remembers*, 81.

[86] Coleman, *McCartney: Yesterday . . . and Today*, 94.

[87] Matthew, "Interview with Paul McCartney & John Lennon," March 20, 1967.

[88] Coleman, *McCartney: Yesterday . . . and Today* (1995), 19-20, working from interviews with Paul, says that Paul came up with the title and final lyrics when he was on the Portugal vacation with Jane. He came back to England, and "When he told his Beatles colleagues

However, Paul's tone here is light, and he was probably simply joking around. About a year later, he said, "It was called 'Scrambled Egg' for a couple of months. . . (*laughter*) until I thought of 'Yesterday' and that's it."[89]

In 1965, John speaks of some collaborative work on the song: it "was around for months and months before we finally completed it. Paul wrote nearly all of it but we just couldn't find the right title. . . . We almost had it finished . . . Then one morning Paul woke up — and the song and the title were both there — completed."[90] (This is somewhat different from Paul's 1967 interview). In 1966, John said, "'Yesterday' is Paul completely on his own, really." This seems straightforward. But then John continued, "We just helped finishing off the ribbons 'round it, you know — tying it up."[91] So there was some help by John (and possibly George), though it was small finishing touches.

Then, in 1970, John stated flatly, "'Yesterday' I had nothing to do with."

In view of the weight of testimony for Paul's full authorship, I think we can accept it. I assume those early statements suggesting collaboration were made when it was customary for the Beatle songwriters to speak of collaboration. But if further early evidence for minor collaboration appears, we might want to see this as a McCartney song with some final edits from John, rather than completely a McCartney song.

   o   Dizzy Miss Lizzie (COVER) (Larry Williams) (lead vocals: John)

As we have seen, the Beatles used to finish live sets with screamers, and their early albums were modeled on their live shows. John continues the tradition here, with a song that Larry Williams had released as a single in 1958. Other Beatle versions of this song appear on *Live at the BBC*, and the Plastic Ono Band's *Live Peace in Toronto 1969*.

---

that he had re-named 'Scrambled Eggs' as 'Yesterday' and completed the lyric, there was little response."

89 "Paul McCartney and John Lennon at the Tonight Show," May 14, 1968.
90 Dawson, "Lennon's Eye View," p. 13.
91 Robbins, "Interview with John Lennon."

8

"He'd say, 'Nowhere land,' and I'd say, 'For nobody.' It was a two-way thing"

RUBBER SOUL

T his album marked a major watershed for the Beatles. Though their previous albums and songs had been generally superb, and showed signs of the songwriting ambitions of the two lead songwriters, *Rubber Soul* seemed a quantum leap forward, both in its unique and personal lyrics and in its musical depth and creativity. Instead of producing standard boiler-plate love lyrics, Paul and John started to write songs that were enigmatic and unsentimental. Some of the love songs that were on the album, such as "In My Life," "Girl," and "Michelle," were unique and deeply felt. There are hints of the innocent, exuberant early Beatles on *Rubber Soul*, and suggestions of the mature Beatles that were to come.

With *Rubber Soul* the Beatles made a conscious effort to shed their "teen-age" image. "*Rubber Soul* for me is the beginning of my adult life," Paul said, in 1966.[1] "You don't know us if you don't know *Rubber Soul*," John said in the same year. "All our ideas are different now."[2] In fact, the songs on this album are generally more mature, more complex, and simply better than most of the songs on the previous albums. Perhaps as a result, song attribution in later interviews became more conflicted. One of the most disputed songs in the Beatles canon is *Rubber Soul*'s "In My Life."

---

[1] Lydon, "Lennon and McCartney: Songwriters," also in Lydon, *Flashbacks: Eyewitness Accounts*, 12.
[2] Ibid. For the album's title, Winn, *Way Beyond Compare*, 324.

"That Means A Lot / My Prayer" single — P. J. Proby, September 17, 1965

- That Means a Lot — (McCartney-Lennon) (recorded on April 7, 1965)

Paul and John wrote this for *Help!*. "The song is a ballad which Paul and I wrote for the film," John said in 1965.[3] Though this early evidence points to collaboration, John later ascribed the song to Paul, so the collaboration probably came from a song Paul had started, or he dominated the writing session.[4]

The Beatles did record this, on February 20 and March 30, 1965, but it didn't make it into the *Help!* movie or album. John's story was that he and Paul didn't sing it very well. Paul said they just weren't that keen on the song.[5] It never appeared on a Beatles album until it was released on *Anthology 2*.

Then John ran into one P. J. Proby at a nightclub one night. Proby (an American, born James Marcus Smith) had a moderately successful singing career in England from 1964 to 1966, and was a friend of the Beatles, especially John. Proby asked John to write him a song, and John agreed. They met a week later and John gave him "That Means a Lot."[6] Proby's recording of it went to number 24 in England.

Working from the available evidence, one could view this as a pure Paul song (based on John's later evidence), as a collaboration dominated by Paul (based on John's early evidence), or as a John song (which seems to be Proby's view). My vote goes for option two, as major or minor collaboration was characteristic of early Beatles songs. In addition, this is the earliest evidence.

---

[3] John in *New Musical Express*, 1965, as quoted in the *Beatles Bible* website, at "That Means a Lot"; also in Harry, *The Paul McCartney Encyclopedia*, at the entry, "That Means a Lot"; Lewisohn, *The Beatles Recording Sessions*, 56–57.

[4] *Ray Connolly Beatles*, 105. Hennessey, "Who Wrote What." Sheff, *Playboy Interviews*, 205.

[5] John in *New Musical Express*, 1965, as quoted in the *Beatles Bible* website, at "That Means a Lot"; also in Harry, *The Paul McCartney Encyclopedia*, at the entry, "That Means a Lot"). Paul, 1988 interview, Lewisohn, *The Beatles Recording Sessions*, 12.

[6] As quoted in Engelhardt, *Beatles Undercover*, 388.

o   <u>My Prayer (Georges Boulanger, Jimmy Kennedy)</u>

Rubber Soul album, December 3, 1965

- **Drive My Car — (McCartney-Lennon)**
  (lead vocals: Paul and John) (recorded on October 13, 1965)

As Paul tells the story, he worked out the melody to this — "the tune was there, I'd done the melody"[7] — and had a basic idea of a "bitchy girl" talking to the narrator about gold rings. He took the song to John, but he didn't like the ring idea — "Crap!"[8] — and Paul realized that the lyrics were "disastrous." So they spent hours trying fruitlessly to get something better. It seemed like they were going to have to admit defeat and end up with a "dry" writing session (a rarity for them), when they came up with "'Baby, you can drive my car." Then the lyrics and the story fell into place. For Paul, it was a perfect example of how he and John could work together successfully.[9]

In 1971, John described the song as collaborative.[10] But in 1980, he ascribed it to Paul, and couldn't remember if he'd added anything to it. "His song, with contributions from the . . . eeahhh, don't know if I put anything in."[11]

This is mostly Paul's song, but both Paul and the earliest evidence from John show that it was finished with collaboration. John's editing and feedback were crucial for the lyrics. It's another example of the new Beatle songs whose lyrics weren't hackneyed romantic clichés. In fact, these new lyrics were often enigmatic, as the next song would show.

---

[7] Miles, *Many Years From Now*, 269-70.
[8] Lydon, "Lennon and McCartney: Songwriters," also in Lydon, *Flashbacks: Eyewitness Accounts of the Rock Revolution*, 16.
[9] Ibid.
[10] Hennessey, "Who Wrote What," *Record Mirror* (in a list of co-written songs).
[11] Sauter, "One John Lennon"; cf. Sheff, *The Playboy Interviews*, 215.

- ## Norwegian Wood — (Lennon-McCartney) (lead vocals: John) (recorded on October 21, 1965)

Apparently John had the opening lines to this song — "I once had a girl, or should I say, she once had me" — in 1964.[12] He started to put music to the words while he was on a skiing holiday in Switzerland with Cynthia, and George Martin and his wife, from January to February, 1965. He filled out the first verse, developing lyrics reflecting an affair he was having. So he had to be careful to make sure that the relationship would not be explicit.[13]

According to Paul, when John came back in England, he and Paul had a work session on the song at Kenwood. John played the first stanza, and they developed the song from there.[14] Paul added the middle eight, then had the idea to burn down the flat at the end.[15] The song was finished.

In some interviews John claimed this song, denying collaboration. In 1980, he described it as "my song completely."[16] In 1968, he had put it in the list of personal songs "that really meant something to me."[17] In other interviews, he affirmed Paul's contributions. In 1970, he said that Paul helped with the middle eight,[18] and the following year he said "Me, but Paul helped me on the lyric."[19]

Paul never denied that John was the main songwriter for the song, but always stated that the song was finished with collaboration. For example, in 1973, he said that "Norwegian Wood" was "mainly John's," but was nevertheless co-written, and one of the co-written songs he really liked.[20]

---

[12] Everett I, 313.
[13] Lost Lennon Tapes, Jan. 9, 1989, cf. Sheff, *The Playboy Interviews*, 188.
[14] Miles, *Many Years From Now*, 270. George Martin before 1999, in Pritchard and Lysaght, *Beatles: an Oral History*, 200.
[15] Miles, *Many Years From Now*, 270-71. Paul "had the idea to set the place on fire, so I take some sort of credit. And the middle was mine, those middle eights, John never had his middle eights."
[16] Lost Lennon Tapes, Jan. 9, 1989, cf. Sheff, *The Playboy Interviews*, 188.
[17] Cott, "The Rolling Stone Interview."
[18] Wenner, *Lennon Remembers*, 85.
[19] Hennessey, "Who Wrote What," *Record Mirror*.
[20] Gambaccini, *Paul McCartney, In His Own Words*, 19.

Six years later he explained that it was one of "certain ones John wrote and I just helped a little bit."[21] In some interviews, he emphasized the collaboration more.[22]

I conclude that this was a song started by John, but finished with substantial collaboration, including Paul contributing much of the middle section.

The sitar is a remarkable feature of the recorded song. According to Lennon, he asked George to play it, and in one interview, George agrees. In another, he said that he picked the sitar up and tried it when they were looking for a new, unique sound. Indian culture had entered the Beatles' music for the first time.[23]

- **You Won't See Me — (McCartney)**
  (lead vocals: Paul) (recorded on November 11, 1965)

Paul remembered writing the tune for this song against a descending chromatic scale. "I changed it but it was still a two-note thing but instead of it going down I pushed it up and then came down again; just a slight variation."[24] It was very Motown-influenced, with its James Jameson bass lines.[25] According to Merseybeat journalist Bill Harry, the lyrics reflect that Paul wrote this at a time when Jane Asher wouldn't answer his calls.[26]

Both Paul and John agree that this song was written by Paul.[27]

- **Nowhere Man — (Lennon-McCartney)**
  (lead vocals: John) (recorded on October 21 and 22, 1965)

One day John was at his house, trying to write a song, and nothing would come. So he gave up, frustrated, and went to lie down. He thought

[21] Gambaccini, "A Conversation with Paul McCartney."

[22] McCartney, undated interview, in Badman, *Beatles Off the Record*, 189. Miles, *Many Years From Now*, 270-71.

[23] Wenner, *Lennon Remembers*, 84. Brown, "A Conversation with George Harrison" (1979); Harrison, *Anthology*, 196. Lost Lennon Tapes, Jan. 9, 1989.

[24] Miles, *Many Years From Now*, 271.

[25] Ibid.

[26] Harry," Jane & Paul: A Love Story."

[27] Hennessey, "Who Wrote What," *Record Mirror*. Sheff, *The Playboy Interviews* (1980), 205. Miles, *Many Years From Now*, 271.

of himself doing nothing and going nowhere — the nowhere man. Then the words started to come.[28]

In 1984, Paul said, "That was John after a night out, with dawn coming up. I think at that point in his life, he was a bit wondering where he was going."[29] He thought it reflected John's dissatisfaction with his marriage, living in the suburbs.[30]

John claimed this song, and Paul generally agreed.[31] However, in two late interviews he described contributing to it. In 2000, he said that it "was one of John's" and that "he'd already got most of it." But "I maybe helped him with a word here or there." One of the characteristics of their collaboration was that they liked each other, Paul said. "He'd sing something and I'd say, 'Yeah,' and trade off on that. He'd say, 'Nowhere land,' and I'd say, 'For nobody.' It was a two-way thing."[32]

And in a 2005 interview, after describing how he and John wrote together, face to face, with acoustic guitars, he said,

> If he was in C, I'd go to C, and maybe a little idea would come though that one of us had, or something might pop in to your head to the chords. Sings, "He's a real nowhere man / Living in. . . dah dah dah." Write it down, write it down! And, it'd start flowing. Middle eight. Hey! Now we go somewhere . . . and y'know, that just became the system.[33]

I conclude that this is a song by John, finished with collaboration from Paul.

---

[28] Davies, *The Beatles*, 274-75.
[29] Goodman, "Paul and Linda McCartney Interview," 107.
[30] Miles, *Many Years From Now*, 272. Snow, "Paul McCartney."
[31] Davies, *The Beatles*, 274-75. Wenner, *Lennon Remembers*, 82. Hennessey, "Who Wrote What," *Record Mirror*. Sheff, *The Playboy Interviews*, 203.
[32] *Anthology*, 196.
[33] "Interview, Observer Music Monthly."

Chapter 8

- **Think For Yourself (Harrison)**
  (lead vocals: George) (recorded on November 8, 1965)

This is George's best song yet, but he couldn't recall much about writing it, or even what it was about, beyond, possibly the Government.[34]

- **The Word — (collaboration, John emphasis)**
  (lead vocals: John, Paul and George) (recorded on November 10, 1965)

John and Paul wrote this at Kenwood. Though they usually didn't use drugs during songwriting sessions, this time they smoked some pot, said Paul, "then we wrote out a multicoloured lyric sheet, the first time we'd ever done that."[35]

In 1971 John remembered working with Paul on this and put it on a list of collaborative songs.[36] But in 1980, while not denying that collaboration was there, he claimed it as mostly his own: "'The Word' was written together, but from my — mainly mine, let's put it that way."[37] In his last interview, John emphasized that the song came from his realization: "It sort of dawned on me that love was the answer, when I was younger, on the Beatles' *Rubber Soul* album. My first expression of it was a song called 'The Word.' The word is 'love.'. . . [this] seemed like the underlying meaning to the Universe."[38]

Paul, however, always seemed to remember substantial collaboration in this song's creation. In 1965, he said, "To write a *good* song with just one note in it — like 'Long Tall Sally' — is really very hard. It's the kind of thing we've wanted to do for some time. We get near it in 'The Word.'" And thirty years later, Miles wrote, "It was a song that John and Paul wrote together at Kenwood."[39]

I conclude that the song was a collaboration with John emphasis.

---

[34] *I Me Mine*, 88.
[35] Miles, *Many Years From Now*, 272.
[36] Hennessey, "Who Wrote What," *Record Mirror*.
[37] Lost Lennon Tapes, Oct. 21, 1991, cf. Sheff, *The Playboy Interviews*, 215.
[38] Sholin and Kaye, "John Lennon's last interview" (1980).
[39] Wyndham, "Paul McCartney As Songwriter"; Miles, *Many Years From Now*, 272.

- ## Michelle — (McCartney-Lennon-Vaughan) (lead vocals: Paul) (recorded on November 3, 1965)

In its musical form "Michelle" was one of Paul's older songs; it dates back to his years at the Liverpool Institute grammar school (from 1953 to 1960).[40] He would play it as a joke song at "arty, bohemian" parties. "We'd be hanging out and being very far out," Paul said. "So there'd always be a guy in the corner with a guitar. So I used to pretend I was French."[41] It became his "French joke, on guitar."[42] He played it for years, as an instrumental, as a country-western tune in "Chet Atkins' finger-pickin' style. . . . based on Atkins' 'Trambone.'"[43] It was recorded in a Beatle rehearsal tape in summer 1963, without the later middle eight.[44]

But as the Beatles were preparing songs for *Rubber Soul*, John suggested that Paul resurrect this. "John said, 'D'you remember that French thing you used to do at Mitchell's parties?' I said yes. He said, 'Well, that's a good tune. You should do something with that.'. . . So I did."[45] Without John's encouragement, this song may have never been developed. The joke tune became a haunting ballad.

Paul worked on "Michelle" and came to a songwriting session with the beginnings of the song. In 1966, John said, "he just sort of had a bit of a verse, and a couple of words, and the idea. . . . He just brought it along and just sort of started fiddling around trying to get a middle-eight."[46] John thought of Nina Simone's version of "I Put a Spell on You,"[47] in which

---

[40] Miles, *Many Years From Now*, 272. See also *Anthology*, 20.

[41] McCartney from 1985-1989, in Somach et al., *Ticket to Ride*, 144.

[42] Read, "McCartney on McCartney," episode 2. Doherty, "Pete Doherty meets Paul McCartney."

[43] Miles, *Many Years From Now*, 273. "Trambone," one of Atkins's signature songs, appeared on his 1962 LP *Down Home*.

[44] Winn, *Way Beyond Compare*, 56.

[45] Miles, *Many Years From Now*, 273. Austin Mitchell was one of Paul's tutors.

[46] Robbins, "Interview with John Lennon." In later interviews, Paul seems to reflect that the song was more developed than this when he brought it to John.

[47] This song, written by Screamin' Jay Hawkins in 1956, received a remarkably different interpretation on jazz singer Nina Simone's 1965 album, of the same title.

she repeats, "I love you" four times, and they developed a version of that for the middle section.[48]

Paul and John often added to the lyrics of a song in informal sessions with friends, and in this case, Paul worked out the French lyrics with Jan Vaughan, a French teacher, the wife of his friend Ian Vaughan, who had introduced Paul to John on that fateful day in July 1957.[49]

> I said, "I like the name Michelle. Can you think of anything that rhymes with Michelle, in French?" And she said, "*Ma belle.*" I said, "What's that mean?" "My beauty." I said, "That's good, a love song, great." We just started talking, and I said, "Well, those words go together well, what's French for that? Go together well." "*Sont les mots qui vont très bien ensemble.*" I said, "All right, that would fit." And she told me a bit how to pronounce it, so that was it. I got that off Jan, and years later I sent her a cheque around. I thought I better had because she's virtually a co-writer on that.[50]

George Martin wrote the guitar solo, which was played by George Harrison.[51] And the song was finished.

Paul often claimed this. "Most of the ballady stuff I wrote on my own. 'Yesterday,' 'Michelle,' 'The Long and Winding Road,' 'Let It Be,' 'Eleanor Rigby,'" he said, before 1989.[52] In the same year, he said, "'Yesterday,' 'Michelle' and some of those very McCartney ones I'd written on my own because they'd come quickly and I hadn't had time to take them to John. I just started on my own at home and it had all happened. Like premature ejaculation. By the time I'd taken them to John it might just be one little

---

[48] Matthew, "Interview with Paul McCartney & John Lennon." See also Sheff, *The Playboy Interviews*, 148.
[49] For Jan Vaughan, see also Badman, *Beatles Off the Record*, 192; Turner, *A Hard Day's Write*, 94.
[50] Miles, *Many Years From Now*, 274.
[51] Pritchard and Lysaght, *Beatles: an Oral History*, 200.
[52] Interview in Smith, *Off the Record*, 201. See also Miles, *Many Years From Now*, 273.

word he'd want to change."[53] He remembered bringing the song in and "showing the guys how it went."[54]

John readily agreed that the main song was by Paul, but he always mentioned that he contributed to the middle section, with the Nina Simone "nick." "I wrote the middle with him," he said in 1971.[55] In 1967, John had said, "I think Paul wrote that one. I remember saying, Why don't you pinch that bit from so and so's song, and he said, Right."[56]

The main song was written by Paul, then, and the chorus was collaborative, with John. In addition, there were important additions from Jan Vaughan and George Martin.

SIDE TWO

• **What Goes On — (Lennon-McCartney-Starkey)**
   (lead vocals: Ringo) (recorded on November 4, 1965)

This country-western ditty apparently started off as a very early song by John, which he then worked on with Paul in Liverpool, perhaps at 20 Forthlin Road. As he considered using it for *Rubber Soul*, it was unfinished, lacking a middle eight, and Paul supplied that (with a minimal contribution from Ringo, according to Ringo: "About five words."[57]).

John correctly attributed this to Lennon-McCartney-Starkey. "Me," John said in 1971. "A very early song of mine. Ringo and Paul wrote a new middle eight together when we recorded it."[58] Neil Aspinall, in 1966, stated that it was a co-written song, and that Paul made a demo of it for Ringo. "John and Paul wrote it years ago in Liverpool. Then Ringo added things, including some new lyrics, when he'd heard Paul's special tape."[59] An early

---

[53] *The Paul McCartney World Tour*, 82.

[54] Snow, "Paul McCartney."

[55] Hennessey, "Who Wrote What," *Record Mirror*. A year later, he claimed the middle eight entirely: "I wrote the middle eight on that one." Garcia, "The Ballad of Paul and Yoko." The earlier statement is more convincing.

[56] Matthew, "Interview with Paul McCartney & John Lennon."

[57] Ringo, 1966, in an Interview with the Beatles, Aug. 28, 1966, as found in Giuliano, *The Lost Beatles Interviews*, 87.

[58] Hennessey, "Who Wrote What," *Record Mirror*. Similar: Sheff, *The Playboy Interviews*, 188.

[59] "Neil's Column." *The Beatles Monthly Book* no. 33 (April 1966): 6.

press report said that Paul wrote it, "a five-year-old country and western song," but this is not first hand.[60]

This is a Lennon song, but Paul contributed the middle section, with a few words from Ringo.

- ## Girl — (Lennon-McCartney)
  ## (lead vocals: John) (recorded on November 11, 1965)

John wrote the beginnings of this as a love song, the search for the "dream girl"[61] who later, for him, turned out to be Yoko.[62] Then he worked on it with Paul.

A book on Christianity, which John was reading, was the unlikely source for the last verse of this song. It described the Catholic idea that pain would lead to pleasure, torture of the body would lead to salvation. As he and John talked about that idea, Paul put the phrases "pain would lead to pleasure" and "a man must break his back" into the song, as a kind of protest against this idea.[63] Thus the song ends on a remarkable philosophical note.[64]

The evidence for the authorship of "Girl" shows the familiar pattern of John claiming the song, and Paul (in both early and late statements) remembering substantial collaboration. In 1968, John put it on a list of personal songs he'd written.[65] Two years later, he said, "They're sort of philosophy quotes. . . . I was thinking about it when I wrote it."[66] In 1971, he put it on the list of songs he'd written by himself, and at about the same time, he described it as, "one of my best."[67]

---

[60] Article in *Disc Weekly*, Nov. 20, 1965 (Sandercombe, *The Beatles*, 146).

[61] Sheff, *The Playboy Interviews*, 206.

[62] Wenner, *Lennon Remembers*, 99, see also 85-86.

[63] Wyndham, "Paul McCartney As Songwriter." Almost the same words in Lydon, "Lennon and McCartney: Songwriters" (1966). John also claimed those sentiments, Wenner, *Lennon Remembers*, 99, see also 85-86.

[64] Miles, *Many Years From Now*, 275-76.

[65] Cott, "The Rolling Stone Interview."

[66] Lennon, Rolling Stone Interview, Dec. 1970, BBC, part 1; Wenner, *Lennon Remembers*, 99, see also 85-86. Also in 1970, Connolly, *Ray Connolly Beatles Archive*, 106.

[67] Hennessey, "Who Wrote What," *Record Mirror*. Aldridge, *Beatles Illustrated Lyrics*, 175. See also Sheff, *The Playboy Interviews*, 206.

Paul, on the other hand, described collaboration on this song as early as 1965. After mentioning the pleasure/pain principle in the book on Christianity, he said, "So we've written a song about it."[68] Thirty years later, he said, "It was John's original idea, but it was very much co-written. . . . I credit that [song] as being towards John but I put quite a bit in. It wasn't one that he came in with fully finished at all."[69]

Paul also remembered writing the tuneful Greek theme at the end of the song when he was on a holiday in Greece in September 1963.[70]

Based on Paul's very early testimony, I accept this as a song begun by John, but finished with collaboration.

- **I'm Looking Through You — (McCartney) (lead vocals: Paul) (recorded on November 11, 1965)**

In 1968, Hunter Davies, during an interview with Paul, reported that this song resulted from a bitter parting he'd had with Jane Asher. Paul said, to Davies:

> "Another problem was that my whole existence for so long centered round a bachelor life. . . . My life generally has always been very lax, and not normal. I knew it was selfish. It caused a few rows. Jane left me once and went off to Bristol to act. I said okay, then leave; I'll find someone else. It was shattering to be without her." This was when he wrote "I'm Looking Through You."[71]

Both Paul and John ascribe this completely to Paul. "I think it's totally my song. I don't remember any of John's assistance," Paul said in 1995.[72]

---

[68] Wyndham, "Paul McCartney As Songwriter." Almost the same words in Lydon, "Lennon and McCartney: Songwriters" (1966).
[69] Miles, *Many Years From Now*, 275-76.
[70] Ibid., 120. Snow, "Paul McCartney."
[71] Davies, *The Beatles*, 309. Snow, "Paul McCartney." See also Miles, *Many Years From Now*, 276.
[72] Miles, *Many Years From Now*, 276. Hennessey, "Who Wrote What," *Record Mirror.* Sheff, *The Playboy Interviews*, 206.

Chapter 8

- **In My Life — (collaboration)**
  (lead vocals: John) (recorded on October 18, 1965)

This song began in a chance remark that journalist Kenneth Allsop made to John, just before an interview about *In His Own Write* (published in March 1964). Allsop asked, "Why don't you put some of your life, about your childhood into the songs?"[73] So one day John began writing a song lyric about Liverpool places, a "bus journey" in which he mentioned every place he could remember between his house at 251 Menlove Avenue and downtown Liverpool. This didn't work at all; it was "ridiculous," John felt, and instead he began writing the beginnings of "In My Life."[74]

As Paul tells the story, he came over to John's house one day and found the opening stanza or stanzas of the song written out, with no music.[75] So he said, "Well, you haven't got a tune, let me just go and work on it."[76] He sat down at John's Mellotron[77] and worked out a tune in the style of Smokey Robinson. "So I recall writing the whole melody. And it actually does sound very like me, if you analyse it."[78] So he took the tune up to John, and said, "Got it, great! Good tune, I think. What d'you think?" John said, "Nice." They continued from there, working on the lyrics, filling out the verses.[79]

---

[73] Lost Lennon Tapes, March 14, 1988, cf. Sheff, *The Playboy Interviews*, 162-63.

[74] Lost Lennon Tapes, March 14, 1988, cf. Sheff, *The Playboy Interviews*, 164. See also pp. 188-89, and 203.

[75] Miles, *Many Years From Now*, 277-78. Paul went back and forth on whether John had one verse or multiple verses written out. For example, see later in this same passage (single verse), and deCurtis, *In Other Words* (1987), 61: "I know he brought in 'In My Life' and he had the first verse and the rest of it wasn't written." In a 1984 interview, however, Paul seems to suggest that John had all the lyrics. "I remember he had the words, like a poem—sort of about faces he remembered." Goodman, "Paul and Linda McCartney Interview," *Playboy*, 107. Du Noyer, *Conversations*, 185: "The words to 'In My Life' were done without me."

[76] Miles, *Many Years From Now*, 277-78.

[77] A forerunner of the Moog synthesizer, which had sampled sounds on tapes. This is a convincing detail, as John had acquired a Mellotron on August 16, 1965. Babuk et al., *Beatles Gear*, 165.

[78] Miles, *Many Years From Now*, 277-78.

[79] Ibid. However, in some interviews, Paul said John had all the lyrics, see above.

George Martin wrote and performed the "harpsichord" solo, which raises the issue of whether he should get songwriting credit for such substantial contributions.[80] Where does arranging end and composing begin?

Paul's story, with its fullness of details, is quite anecdotally convincing. In many interviews, Paul tells the same story. In 1973, he said, "Those were words that John wrote and I wrote the tune to it. That was a great one."[81] In the "angry interview" published in the second edition of Hunter Davies's Beatles biography, Paul said, "He [John] also forgot completely that I wrote the tune for 'In My Life.' That was my tune. But perhaps he just made a mistake on that. Forgot."[82] And in 1984, he said, "John either forgot or didn't think I wrote the tune. I remember he had the words, like a poem — sort of about faces he remembered . . . I recall going off for half an hour and sitting with a Mellotron he had, writing the tune."[83]

On the other hand, John often claimed this song as entirely his own composition. For example, in 1980, he gave the song as an example of how, in some of his songs, "I was writing melodic 'muzak' (in quotes) with the best of them."[84] In 1971, he said, "Me. I think I was trying to write about Penny Lane when I wrote it. It was about places I remembered."[85] In 1980, he said, "I think 'In My Life' was the first song that I wrote that was really, consciously about my life."[86]

However, Lennon, in other interviews, is all over the map. In 1970 he described the song as his own, but remembered some collaboration from Paul. "I wrote that in Kenwood. . . . I wrote it upstairs, that was one where

---

[80] Pritchard and Lysaght, *Beatles: an Oral History*, 199-200. For further on George Martin's solo, see Lewisohn, *The Beatles Recording Sessions*, 65; Everett I, 31.

[81] Gambaccini, *Paul McCartney, In His Own Words*, 19.

[82] Davies, *The Beatles*, 371.

[83] Goodman, "Paul and Linda McCartney Interview," *Playboy*, 107. Similar: *Paul McCartney World Tour*, 82; *Anthology*, 194, 197.

[84] Lost Lennon Tapes, Sept. 16, 1991, cf. Sheff, *The Playboy Interviews*, 149.

[85] Hennessey, "Who Wrote What," *Record Mirror*. The first draft is extant, and has verses about places. Spitz, *The Beatles*, 587. Doggett, *The Art and Music of John Lennon*, at Oct. 12 to Nov. 11, 1965.

[86] Lost Lennon Tapes, March 14, 1988, cf. Sheff, *The Playboy Interviews*, 149.

I wrote the lyrics first and then sang it. . . . I think on . . . 'In My Life' Paul helped with the middle eight, to give credit where it's due."[87]

In 1980, he again remembered collaboration on the middle eight, and, in addition, Paul contributing "melodically" to the harmony of the song: "The whole lyrics were already written before Paul even heard it.[88] . . . his contribution melodically was the harmony and the middle eight itself — not the whole middle eight . . . his input was with me there on the chord changes."[89]

Given the convincing unity and anecdotal fullness of Paul's memories, I accept that he wrote the music to "In My Life."

If we accept Paul's version of this song's genesis, how do we view such an equally co-written song, then, with Lennon's words (mostly or completely) and McCartney's music (completely)? If we are interested in lyrics in a rock song, it is a Lennon-McCartney; but if we are focused on music, then it is a McCartney-Lennon.

So I call this song "collaboration," and leave it to the reader to call it "collaboration John emphasis" (if you're more interested in lyrics) or "collaboration Paul emphasis" (if you're focused more on music).

Of course, it's entirely possible to view the conflict in McCartney-Lennon testimonies here as a he-said / he-said situation, in which we might have to accept the testimony of either Paul or John. If we reject Paul entirely, however, then we are still left with the variations in John's testimony. The ambiguities involved in assessing the authorship of the Beatle songs are seemingly infinite.

---

[87] Wenner, *Lennon Remembers*, 85. In the same interview, he describes it as one of his "personal" songs, 9. As is consistent with Beatles usage, Lennon was using "middle eight" to mean a contrasting middle section, not a minor link between major musical sections, see Chapter Two, at "Love Me Do."

[88] This is a point of conflict, as Paul sometimes said that John had only the first verse, and they collaborated on the other verses (though Paul varies on this point, see footnote above). However, if there was collaboration on the second and third verses, John still had had the "template" for the song's lyrics, and probably dominated the collaborative session, from the standpoint of lyrics.

[89] Lost Lennon Tapes, March 14, 1988, cf. Sheff, *The Playboy Interviews*, 164. See also pp. 188-89, and 203.

- **Wait — (McCartney)**
  (lead vocals: John and Paul) (recorded on June 17 and November 11, 1965)

Paul wrote this on the set of *Help!* as American actor Brandon De Wilde watched. In 1995, McCartney remembered that Brandon "was a nice guy who was fascinated by what we did. A sort of Brat Pack actor. We chatted endlessly, and I seem to remember writing 'Wait' in front of him, and him being interested to see it being written."[90]

As it turned out, the song was not used for *Help!*, but was resurrected to fill up side two of *Rubber Soul.*[91]

"I think it was my song," Paul said in 1995. "I don't remember John collaborating too much on it, although he could have."[92] "That must be one of Paul's," John stated in 1970. "I can't remember it."[93] So this is another example of John singing lead on a song Paul wrote. Or perhaps, more exactly, John and Paul singing the lead together, though John sings the actual main melody. Paul sings the middle eight alone.

- **If I Needed Someone — (Harrison)**
  (lead vocals: George) (recorded on October 16, 1965)

George's second outing for *Rubber Soul* was based partly on a Byrds song, "The Bells of Rhymney." Roger McGuinn, when asked, *"The prevailing riff from the song sounds a lot like a riff you had in "The Bells of Rhymney." In fact, didn't George write to Derek Taylor and tell him that?"* said,

> Derek delivered the message and said, "George wants you to know that the song 'If I Needed Someone' was inspired by the lick in 'The Bells of Rhymney.'" In fact, George later told me himself. And even if he hadn't told me, I would have known it anyway, because it was the same lick. But I was very honored

---

[90] Miles, *Many Years From Now*, 278.
[91] Lewisohn, *Complete Beatles Chronicle*, 196.
[92] Miles, *Many Years From Now*, 278.
[93] Connolly, *Ray Connolly Beatles Archive*, 105.

to see that. . . . And "If I Needed Someone" is one of my favorite songs by them![94]

Many Beatle songs were inspired by previous songs, Motown, country western, folk music, pop standards. Here we begin to see the impact the American groups such as the Byrds and the Beach Boys had
on the Beatles.

- **Run For Your Life — (Lennon)**
  (lead vocals: John) (recorded on October 12, 1965)

John was often fascinated by isolated lines in songs. Under pressure to
produce another song for *Rubber Soul,* he wrote "Run For Your Life"
around a line from the 1955 Elvis single, "Baby Let's Play House:"[95] "I'd
rather see you dead little girl than to be with another man."[96]

John claims this song, though he said he never liked it. In 1970, he
said that "it was one of them I knocked off just to write a song. And it was
phony."[97] Paul stated that it was "largely John's."[98]

A disappointing conclusion for a great album.

---

[94] Somach et al, *Ticket to Ride,* 212. See also Harrison, *I Me Mine,* 90.

[95] Written and first released by Arthur Gunter the previous year.

[96] Wenner, *Lennon Remembers,* 85. Similar: Hennessey, "Who Wrote What," *Record Mirror;*
Sheff, *The Playboy Interviews,* 189.

[97] Lennon, Rolling Stone Interview, Dec. 1970, BBC, part 4; Wenner, *Lennon Remembers,*
99.

[98] Miles, *Many Years From Now,* 279.

9

"One day I led the dance . . . and another day John would lead the dance"

REVOLVER

Remarkable as the sea change from the early Beatle albums to *Rubber Soul* was, the further step forward to *Revolver* was just as extraordinary. Here the *style* of the early Beatles was almost forgotten. *Rubber Soul*, filled with magnificent songs, nevertheless had three or four filler or even subpar songs; and it ended with the song that John hated so much, "Run for Your Life," which caused the whole album to collapse in a disappointing fizzle. But all of the Lennon-McCartney songs on *Revolver* range from superior to great — both Paul and John contributed about four songs each that would become pop standards. Two of George's three songs are solid, but his "Taxman" is a step forward, for him, and is highlighted by its position starting off the album. Added to the high quality of the songwriting on this album was continued aural experimentation that was prefigured by "Rain" and certain songs on *Rubber Soul*, such as "Norwegian Wood" and "In My Life." But "Tomorrow Never Knows" took this to an entirely new level, and provided the album with a stunning, aesthetically powerful ending.

In 1966, John highlighted the experimental aspects of *Revolver*:

> *Q: What's going to come out of the next recording sessions?* Literally anything. Electronic music, jokes. . . One thing's for sure — the next LP is going to be very different. . . . Paul and I are very keen on this electronic music. You make it clinking a couple of glasses together or with bleeps from the radio, then

you loop the tape to repeat the noises at intervals. Some people build up whole symphonies from it.[1]

Paul said, at the time of *Revolver*'s recording, "It's sort of verging on the electronic." The songs were "purposely composed to sound unusual. They are sounds that nobody else has done yet — I mean nobody . . . ever."[2]

While the electronic experimentation added a third dimension to this album, it would not have been successful without the consistently inspired and well-crafted songwriting that the Beatles had come to master.

"Day Tripper / We Can Work It Out" single, December 3, 1965 (double A side)

- Day Tripper — (Lennon-McCartney)
  (lead vocals: Paul and John) (recorded October 16, 1965)

According to Paul, "John met quite a few girls who thought they were it and he was a bit up in arms about that kind of thing." As he and Paul worked on "Day Tripper," it became a tongue-in-cheek description of a girl who was only a "weekend hippie," a Sunday painter, Sunday driver, not fully committed.[3]

In both early and late interviews Paul remembered this as a fully collaborative song with a slight edge toward John. In August 1966, he used "Day Tripper" as an example of a collaborative song, one that would have been very different if it had been pure John or pure Paul. "We can write a song, say like 'Day Tripper' . . . we can write it thinking the same thing about it, but if we each wrote it individually, it'd be a completely different song."[4] Thirty years later, he remembered a very "co-written" song, from

---

[1] In Hutchins, "John Lennon Interview".
[2] "Beatlemania strikes again."
[3] Lost Lennon Tapes, Oct. 21, 1991, cf. Sheff, *The Playboy Interviews*, 187-88. Miles, *Many Years from Now*, 209.
[4] Paul and John, radio interview with Keith Fordyce, August 29, 1966, summarized in Winn, *That Magic Feeling*, 39.

an idea by John. "We were both making it all up but I would give John the main credit. Probably the idea came from John because he sang the lead, but it was a close thing. We both put a lot of work in on it."[5]

In some interviews, John agreed that there was collaboration ("Me. But I think Paul helped with the verse"[6]), but generally he claimed this as his own song. In 1968, he put it on a list of personal songs that "really meant something" to him.[7] The following year, he made the curious statement that it was "based on an old folk song I wrote about a month previous."[8] However, nine years later, John simply said: "That's mine. Including the lick, the guitar break and the whole bit."[9]

Based on Paul's impressively early testimony, I accept that the song was John's idea, but developed with significant collaboration.

- **We Can Work It Out — (McCartney-Lennon-Harrison) (lead vocals: Paul) (recorded October 20 and 29, 1965)**

Paul wrote this at Rembrandt, a house he bought for his father in the town of Heswall, Merseyside County (then Cheshire County), near Liverpool. There was a piano in the dining room that Paul would use, but if he wanted to do guitar work, he'd go to the back bedroom.[10] He had most of the song written, then took it to John for finishing off, "and we wrote the middle together," Paul said.[11] George Harrison thought of putting the middle in 3/4, like a waltz.[12] There is a demo of Paul playing the song.[13]

Paul, in 1995, said that he wrote most of this himself, then finished it with John.[14] John, however, consistently said that Paul wrote the main song, and he wrote the middle: "Paul wrote that chorus, you know, I wrote

---

[5] Miles, *Many Years from Now*, 209.
[6] Hennessey, "Who Wrote What." *Ray Connolly Beatles Archive*, 108 ("we wrote").
[7] Cott, "The Rolling Stone Interview."
[8] *Anthology*, 199.
[9] Sheff, *The Playboy Interviews*, 187-88.
[10] Miles, *Many Years from Now*, 210.
[11] Ibid.
[12] Ibid.
[13] Winn, *Way Beyond Compare*, 361.
[14] Miles, *Many Years from Now*, 210.

the middle bit about 'Life is very short, there is no time for fussing and fighting' all that bit," he said in 1970.[15] And the following year, he asserted, "Paul, but the middle was mine."[16] In 1980, John characterized the two sections as McCartney-esque optimism vs. Lennon's impatience.[17]

The main conflict in testimony, then, is whether the middle part was co-written with Paul or entirely written by John. But both writers agreed that it was mainly a Paul song, finished with collaboration. The 3/4 sections that George suggested are significant enough to mention him as a co-writer.

"Woman / Wrong From The Start" single — Peter and Gordon, February 11, 1966

- Woman — (McCartney) (recorded December 1965)

Paul wrote this for Peter and Gordon, but had it released under a pseudonym, Bernard Webb, to see if the song would do well without the Lennon-McCartney label. It was only moderately successful, reaching 14 in the U.S. and 28 in the U.K. Paul said, in 1989, "It wasn't a very big hit, I probably should have stuck my name on it, it might have been bigger."[18]

  o Wrong From The Start (Peter Asher, Gordon Waller)

---

[15] Lennon, Rolling Stone Interview, Dec. 1970, BBC, part 3; Wenner, *Lennon Remembers*, 58.
[16] Hennessey, "Who Wrote What," *Record Mirror*.
[17] Sheff, *The Playboy Interviews*, 188.
[18] Read, "McCartney on McCartney," episode 2. John put this on a list of songs written by Paul alone. Hennessey, "Who Wrote What," *Record Mirror*.

"Paperback Writer / Rain" single, May 30, 1966

- Paperback Writer — (McCartney-Lennon)
  (lead vocals: Paul) (recorded April 13 and 14, 1966)

One day Paul's aunt Lil nudged him to start writing about non-love themes — a horse perhaps — or a summit conference![19] Then one day, according to DJ Jimmy Davile, the Beatles were backstage after a show and since it had been decided that Paul would write the next single, John asked him what it would be about. Remembering Aunt Lil's challenge, Paul looked around the room and saw Ringo reading a book, so he announced that the next single would be about a book.[20]

He had always liked the word "paperback,"[21] so began thinking about using that in the title. On the way out to John's house one day, he had the idea of writing a song in the form of a letter — a paperback writer writing a letter to a publisher. He came up with the beginnings of the tune in the car,[22] and when he got to Kenwood, he and John sat down and, Paul said in 1966, "we wrote the words down like we were writing a letter."[23] In later interviews Paul described himself as the active writer, so he probably dominated.[24]

Then they went upstairs and apparently developed the tune fragment Paul had into a complete song.[25] "John and I sat down and finished it all up," said Paul, "but it was tilted towards me, the original idea was mine."[26]

---

[19] "Beatlemania Strikes Again" (1966).
[20] Turner, *A Hard Day's Write*, 101.
[21] Alan Smith, "My Broken Tooth."
[22] "In The Beatles' Song Writing Factory." Paul began this song with "a musical phrase or part of a tune," John said. "He thought that out in the car on his way to my house."
[23] Alan Smith, "My Broken Tooth."
[24] Read, "McCartney on McCartney," episode 3. Miles, *Many Years from Now*, 279. *Anthology*, 212. In these interviews, he seems to present himself as the only writer, but his early interview is preferable evidence.
[25] In 1995, Paul said they had no music until they went upstairs (Miles, *Many Years from Now*, 279), but John's testimony thirty years earlier is preferable. "In The Beatles' Song Writing Factory."
[26] *Many Years from Now*, 279.

In 2004, Paul gave it as an example of an important song in the on-going Paul-John creative tug of war: "For those early years, the competition was great ... I'd come up with 'Paperback Writer' and John would come back with 'I'm Only Sleeping.'"[27]

In 1968, Lennon put it on the list of personal songs that really meant something to him.[28] However, in 1971, he remembered the song as mainly Paul's, though he contributed to the lyrics. "Paul. I think I might have helped with some of the lyrics. Yes, I did. But it was mainly Paul's tune."[29] John's 1980 attribution mentions no contribution from himself. "'Paperback Writer' is son of 'Day Tripper,' ... Paul's song."[30]

I conclude that in this song, Paul had the beginnings of the music, then wrote most of the lyrics. Following this, he and John collaborated to finish it up.[31]

One musical factor that is emphasized on this song is Paul's bass. He developed a melodic bass style that added a level of musical complexity to all the Beatle songs, not just his own. According to Lewisohn, before 1966, Paul's bass was hardly heard because of English recording techniques, but on "Paperback Writer," specifically, that changed, as the bass was recorded clearly and mixed up.[32]

- **Rain — (Lennon-McCartney)**
  (lead vocals: John) (recorded on April 14, 1966)

John claimed this song[33] but Paul remembers collaboration: "a co-effort with the leaning slightly towards John," he said in 1995. He remembered that John had no pre-written elements for "Rain," but he started off

---

[27] *Uncut* interview, in Sawyer, *Read the Beatles*, 246.
[28] Cott, "The Rolling Stone Interview."
[29] Hennessey, "Who Wrote What," *Record Mirror*.
[30] Lost Lennon Tapes, July 18, 1988, cf. Sheff, *The Playboy Interviews*, 189.
[31] George Harrison also described the song as a McCartney-dominated collaboration. Harry, *The Paul McCartney Encyclopedia*, at "Paperback Writer."
[32] *Beatles Recording Sessions*, 74. George Martin, *With a Little Help*, 85.
[33] In 1971, he put "Rain" on a list of songs he wrote alone (Hennessey, "Who Wrote What," *Record Mirror*), and in 1980, he said, "That's me again." Lost Lennon Tapes, July 18, 1988, cf. Sheff, *The Playboy Interviews*, 207.

the songwriting session — "when we sat down to write, he kicked it off." What gave the song "its character was collaboration."[34] He described it as written 70-30 toward John, which obviously conflicts with the "leaning *slightly* towards John." I accept that there was collaboration, but with a pronounced leaning toward John.

John specifically claimed the backwards tape section. He brought the recording home, and high on marijuana, inadvertently put the tape in backwards. "I sat there, transfixed, with the earphones on, with a big hash joint. . . . And I ran in the next day and said, 'I know what to do with it, I know, listen to this!'"[35]

Just to confuse the issue, in 1966, George Martin claimed that he had created the backward tape section at the end of the song, which led to all subsequent backward tape playing in later Beatle albums. "The Beatles weren't quite sure what to do at that point, so I took out a bit of John's voice from earlier on and played it backwards. They all thought it was marvellous . . . it had a sort of unexpectedly Eastern sound. So we kept it in."[36] Despite Martin's quite believable and very early testimony, Lennon's memories of the backwards tape incident (also attested very early) are anecdotally convincing. Lennon, as the main songwriter, should be accepted here.

[34] Miles, *Many Years from Now*, 280.
[35] Lost Lennon Tapes, July 18, 1988, cf. Sheff, *The Playboy Interviews,* 207; Lennon in Alterman, "The Beatles: Four Smiling, Tired Guys" (1966); Lennon, in Beatles, "Press Conference in New York City (August 22, 1966)"; Lennon in Cott, "The Rolling Stone Interview" (1968).
[36] Smith, "The Beatles: Ringo Played Cards." Similar: Martin, *With a Little Help*, 78-79.

Revolver album, August 5, 1966

- Taxman — (Harrison-Lennon)
  (lead vocals: George) (recorded on April 20–22, May 16, and June 21, 1966)

This is George's best song yet; the lyrics came from his realization that he was giving away most of his Beatle earnings to the government.[37] In 1980, George published his book *I Me Mine*, and when John read it, he was angry that George had not given him credit for his help over the years, and affirmed that he contributed to the lyrics of this song. He said that one day George showed up to ask for help with "Taxman." John felt that he was already stretched thin with Lennon-McCartney work, but bit his tongue and "threw in a few one-liners to help the song along."[38]

In fact, George said, in 1988, "Once in a while I got a line from John when I was stuck."[39] So I accept John's memories here.

- Eleanor Rigby — (McCartney-Lennon-Harrison)
  (lead vocals: Paul) (recorded on April 28–29 and June 6, 1966)

Paul began writing this at the piano in the Asher music room one day.[40] It developed from an E minor chord. "I can hear a whole song in one chord," he said in 1966 while discussing this song. "In fact, I think you can hear a whole song in one note, if you listen hard enough. But nobody ever listens hard enough."[41] As he vamped on the E minor, he got the main melody. Soon some words started to come: "'picks up the rice in the

---

[37] Harrison, *I Me Mine*, 94; *Anthology*, 206.

[38] Sheff, *The Playboy Interviews*, 161.

[39] Smith, *Off the Record*, 261. Paul on the song: Goodman, "Paul and Linda McCartney," 107. *Anthology*, 207.

[40] Miles, *Many Years from Now*, 281-84.

[41] Davies, "All Paul." For another early account of writing the song, Alterman, "The Beatles: Four Smiling, Tired Guys" (1966). "When I started doing the melody I developed the lyric. It all came from the first line. I wonder if there are girls called Eleanor Rigby? Originally I called her Miss Daisy Hawkins. Father MacKenzie was Father McCartney originally."

church where a wedding has been.' Those are the words that arrived. Then the rest of it was work to try and explain what those words were."[42]

He began to develop the characters in the lyrics, and came up with Father McCartney, the lonely old man, and Daisy Hawkins. He became dissatisfied with these names — his own father would be viewed as the song's "Father McCartney," and Jim McCartney as not like that at all. Then one day in Bristol, while he was waiting for one of Jane's performances to end, he saw the name Rigby in a shop window, and it seemed right for the song.[43] "Eleanor" came from Eleanor Bron, an actress in *Help!*.[44] This name, Eleanor Rigby, sounded right to him. When he got that name, he remembered, he felt great. "I'd got it! I pieced all the ideas together, got the melody and the chords."[45] But the lyrics were still not finished.[46]

A collaborative songwriting session at John's house followed. "Then I took it down to John's house in Weybridge," Paul said in 1966. "We sat around, laughing, got stoned and finished it off."[47] Now they consulted a phone book and replaced Father McCartney with Father McKenzie.[48]

---

[42] Read, "McCartney on McCartney," episode 3. Davies, "All Paul" (1966). Donovan remembered hearing the song when it had lyrics "Ola Na Tungee. Blowing his mind in the dark with a pipeful of clay. No one can say." Leitch, *The Autobiography of Donovan*, 152. Miles, *Many Years from Now*, 282. Pritchard and Lysaght, *The Beatles: an Oral History*, 208. This seems to conflict with Paul's memories of getting the beginnings of the final lyrics when he got the melody. Maybe "Ola Na Tungee" was a second verse lyric that was later rejected.
[43] Davies, "All Paul" (1966); Goodman, "Paul and Linda McCartney Interview" (1984), 107. Snow, "Paul McCartney."
[44] Aldridge, "Beatles Not All That Turned On," 139. Goodman, "Paul and Linda McCartney Interview" (1984), 107. Garbarini and Baird, "Has Success Spoiled Paul McCartney?" (1985), 62.
[45] Miles, *Many Years from Now*, 281-84. There is a demo by Paul recorded about late March 1966. Winn, *That Magic Feeling*, 7.
[46] It is unclear how much of the lyrics were done at this time. Possibly two verses, Interview in Smith, *Off the Record*, 201, but this seems to conflict with the report that the last verse was written in the studio.
[47] Davies, "All Paul" (1966). Aldridge, "Beatles Not All That Turned On," 139. Miles, *Many Years from Now*, 281-84.
[48] Aldridge, "Beatles Not All That Turned On," 139. Read, "McCartney on McCartney," (1989), episode 3. However, in the earliest interviews, Paul said that he looked it up himself. Davies, "All Paul" (1966).

But apparently Paul and John had not completely finished it, and Paul took it to the recording studio still missing a verse. As Paul and John were sitting with road manager Mal Evans and Beatles assistant Neil Aspinall, Paul suddenly said to the three, "Hey, you guys, finish up the lyrics." John was offended that Paul would turn to non-musicians like Mal and Neil for help. As John tells the story, he and Paul went into a room and finished the song. According to Lennon, not a line from Mal or Neil ended up in "Rigby."[49]

However, John also attested that Paul was working on "Ah, look at all the lonely people" section with George. He and George were "settling on that as I left the room," said John, ". . . and I turned around and said, 'That's *it!*"[50]

George Martin also remembered that Paul was asking for help with the lyrics of the last verse in the studio. "At the recording Paul was missing a few lyrics, and wanting them, and going round asking people 'What can we put in here?' and Neil and Mal and I were coming up with suggestions."[51] Journalist Hunter Davies, who was present at the studio, reported that these suggestions were used: "The last verse was thought of by all of them, making suggestions at the last minutes in the studio."[52]

If we turn to Beatle insiders (and I consider their statements as secondary to first-hand statements by Paul and John), it is possible that Ringo, George Martin, Neil Aspinall, Mal Evans, and Pete Shotton contributed to the song. Shotton, a close personal friend of John, wrote, "My own recollection is that 'Eleanor Rigby' was one 'Lennon-McCartney' classic in which John's contribution was virtually nil." Ringo was the source of "darning his socks in the night." Shotton said that he advised against, "Father McCartney" and consulted the phone book, suggesting "McKenzie." "Fully caught up in the creative process, I was seized by a brainwave. 'Why don't you have Eleanor Rigby dying,' I said, 'and have Father McKenzie

[49] Lost Lennon Tapes, Jan. 7, 1991, cf. Sheff, *The Playboy Interviews,* 151-52.
[50] Sheff, "All We Are Saying: Three Weeks With John Lennon," interview with David Sheff, cf. Sheff, *The Playboy Interviews,* 151-52.
[51] Williams, "Produced by George Martin" (1971).
[52] Davies, *The Beatles,* 274.

doing the burial service for her? That way you'd have two lonely people coming together in the end — but too late.'" John responded, "I don't think you understand what we're trying to get at, Pete.'" To which Pete responded with an expletive. He was pleased when McCartney used the idea.[53] As always, it is difficult to judge how much of the testimony of non-Beatles to accept, especially when it conflicts with the memories of John and Paul. However, Shotton was an insider, and sympathetic to John.

While I ascribe the song to "McCartney-Lennon-Harrison," it could also be ascribed it to "McCartney-Lennon-Harrison-Starkey-Martin-Evans-Aspinall-Shotton."

Paul had the idea of using strings to accompany this unique song, and Martin thought of the percussive strings in film composer Bernard Herrman's work.[54] "I thought of the backing, but it was George Martin who finished it off," Paul said in 1966.[55] Paul at first was wary of the double string quartet concept, but agreed to give it a try. "Okay, but I want the strings to sound really biting," Paul warned Martin as he agreed to the plan.[56]

"Eleanor Rigby" represents an important divergence in Lennon and McCartney's testimony. It seems clear that Paul wrote the melody, the title, and the first verse of the lyrics.[57] It also seems clear that Lennon helped finish up the lyrics. Beyond that, the extent of Lennon's contribution to the rest of the song is uncertain. In 1970, Lennon said that he'd written half or more of the lyrics.[58] A year later, he said that he much more than half of the lyrics. "Both of us. I wrote a good lot of the lyrics, about 70 per

---

[53] Shotton and Schaffner, *The Beatles, Lennon and Me,* 214-17.
[54] Everett II, 51. Martin said *Fahrenheit 451* was the immediate influence, but he was apparently mistaken, as *Fahrenheit 451* was not released in the U.K. till September 16, 1966, long after "Eleanor Rigby" was recorded.
[55] Davies, "All Paul." Tobler and Grundy, "George Martin."
[56] Emerick, *Here, There and Everywhere,* 127.
[57] In a 1966 interview, George Harrison simply called it "Paul's." Alan Walsh, "George— More to Life."
[58] Wenner, *Lennon Remembers,* 82. Similar: Letter to George Martin/Richard Williams, Sept. 1971, in Davies, *The John Lennon Letters,* 213. "At least 50% of the lyrics of Eleanor Rigby was written by me in the studio and at Paul's place."

cent."[59] In 1980, he stated that Paul had contributed only the first verse of the lyrics, and he wrote the rest: "Yeah, 'Rigby.' His first verse and the rest of the verses are basically mine."[60]

However, in the 1980 interview, John went on to describe finishing the song as a collaboration on the lyrics, not as him writing them alone. "Oh he had the whole thing about [sings first lines of song] . . . and he had the story and knew where it was going. So then we had to work out, 'Well is there anybody else in this?'"[61] John even remembers Paul working out the chorus with both him and George Harrison. George also remembers contributing to the lyrics. "I gave them lyrics. I helped out on 'Eleanor Rigby,'" he said.[62]

Paul, on the other hand, in his "angry" interview with Davies in 1985, curtly described Lennon as contributing "about half a line" to the song.[63] In a 1966 interview, he also described finishing the lyrics at Lennon's house, not at the studio, as Lennon remembered in 1980.[64] In 1988, he said he brought the song to John for help with the third verse only.[65] His memories are no different in 1995: John only helped with "a few words."[66] In 1973, however, Paul seemed to view the song as more collaborative, when he included it in a short list of favorite songs he wrote with John. "*Do you have any favourites that you wrote with John?* [He mentioned 'In My Life,' and 'Norwegian Wood.'] . . . I like 'Eleanor Rigby' too, I thought that was a fair one."[67]

It seems probable that both Beatles were swayed by emotion in their conflicting accounts; John tells the story of the song's completion with

---

[59] Hennessey, "Who Wrote What," *Record Mirror*.
[60] Lost Lennon Tapes, Jan. 7, 1991; cf. Sheff, *The Playboy Interviews*, 151-52.
[61] Lost Lennon Tapes, Jan. 7, 1991.
[62] Smith, *Off the Record* (1988), 261.
[63] Davies, *The Beatles*, 371.
[64] Davies, "All Paul." In the 1971 letter, Lennon remembered two finishing sessions, one at Paul's house, one at the studio.
[65] Interview in Smith, *Off the Record*, 201.
[66] Miles, *Many Years from Now*, 281-84.
[67] Gambaccini, *Paul McCartney In His Own Words*, 19. In Lost Lennon Tapes, Jan. 7, 1991, Paul seems to claim the song as entirely his own, then firmly remembered collaboration.

some bitterness (for Paul had not come to him to finish the last verse of the song), and Paul reacts in a similar fashion. The truth of John's contribution probably lies somewhere between "half a line" and "70 per cent." A likely scenario would be, Paul comes in with the music and first verse and ideas for the rest; he then collaborates with John on all the lyrics except the last verse. Then he took it into the studio and opened it up to everyone there (though John reports that he then took Paul aside to do the serious finishing of the song).

We should emphasize: all of this collaboration took place on lyrics, not on music. This is generally true of Beatle collaboration with "outsiders." Paul would never come to Ringo, Neal or Mal and say, could you help me write the melody for a chorus? But he often did that with lyrics.

I see this as a Paul song finished in collaboration with John, and to a lesser extent, with George and Ringo. Minor contributions from other Beatle insiders apparently occurred.

- **I'm Only Sleeping — (Lennon-McCartney) (lead vocals: John) (recorded on April 27-29, and May 5-6, 1966)**

Paul used to come over to John's house at noon or the early afternoon and wake him up. One day this gave John the idea for a song on sleeping, and the idea was taken up in a songwriting session with Paul. According to McCartney, the song was begun and finished in one multi-hour session.[68]

John claimed the song in 1971 and 1980: "That's me — dreaming my life away."[69] Unfortunately, he didn't comment much on it. In 1995, Paul described it as a song that started out as a John idea, but then there was collaboration — it was "co-written." And in the same interview, according to Paul, "One day I led the dance, like 'Paperback Writer,' and another day John would lead the dance, like 'I'm Only Sleeping.' It was nice, it wasn't

---

[68] Miles, *Many Years from Now*, 285.
[69] Hennessey, "Who Wrote What"; Lost Lennon Tapes, July 18, 1988, cf. Sheff, *The Playboy Interviews*, 208.

really competitive as to who started the song."[70] In 2004, Paul emphasized John's "ownership" of the song, saying, "For those early years, the competition was great . . . I'd come up with 'Paperback Writer' and John would come back with 'I'm Only Sleeping.'"[71]

Paul definitely regarded it as a John song, despite his input in finishing it. I accept it as a Lennon song, finished with Paul, in Lennon-dominated collaboration.

- **Love You To (Harrison)**
  (lead vocals: George) (recorded on April 11, 1966)

While the Beatles were filming *Help!*, one of the Hindu cast members gave each of the Beatles a book on reincarnation. During a break in the Beatles' 1965 American tour, from August 23 to 27, they rented a luxurious house in Benedict Canyon, near Los Angeles, owned by Zsa Zsa Gabor, and invited friends to visit, among whom were the Byrds, Joan Baez, and Peter Fonda, not yet a star. There Byrd member Roger McGuinn introduced George to the sitar style of Ravi Shankar. As we have seen, in October 1965, the Beatles recorded "Norwegian Wood" with sitar. In just a few months, in June 1966, George would meet Shankar in London and start taking lessons from him.

George said that this, the first major Indian song in the Beatles' canon, was one of the first songs he wrote for sitar. [72] In 1966, he explained, "On the new album I developed it [sitar music] a little bit. But I'm far from the goal I want to achieve. It will take me 40 years to get there. I'd like to be able to play Indian music as Indian music instead of using Indian music in pop." Asked how an Englishman got so involved in Indian music, he replied: "A whole lot of things got me interested. The more I heard it, the more I liked it. It's very involved music. . . . Indian music is hip, yet 8,000 years old."[73]

---

[70] Miles, *Many Years from Now*, 285, 284.
[71] *Uncut* interview, in Sawyer, *Read the Beatles*, 246. The "backwards" guitar was George Harrison's idea. Lewisohn, *Beatles Recording Sessions*, 78.
[72] *I Me Mine*, 102.
[73] Alterman, "The Beatles: Four Smiling, Tired Guys."

- ## Here, There and Everywhere — (McCartney-Lennon) (lead vocals: Paul) (recorded on June 14, 16-17, 1966)

Paul came to John's house one early afternoon and found him asleep. So he took a guitar and went to sit outside, by the pool. He started strumming in E and soon had a few chords, then a tune, and most of the lyrics. John eventually showed up, and they "took it indoors and finished it up. . . . John might have helped with a few last words."[74]

A number of influences came together as they were writing this. First, John's mother Julia had taught them old standards, such as "Ramona" and "Wedding Bells are Breaking Up That Old Gang of Mine." Paul said that he and John "often tried to write songs with that same feeling to them. 'Here, There and Everywhere' was one we wrote along those lines."[75]

This song also reflects a new major influence on Paul: Brian Wilson of the Beach Boys. "'Here, There and Everywhere' was supposed to be a Beach Boys song, but you wouldn't have known," Paul said in 1973.[76] *Pet Sounds*, Paul's favorite rock album, which included "God Only Knows," Paul's favorite song, had been released just two months earlier, on May 16, 1966.

John ascribed this song to Paul in 1971: "Paul. This was a great one of his."[77] In 1980 he said, "Paul's song completely, I believe. And one of my favorite songs of Beatles."[78] John could be generous in his appraisal of selected Paul songs.

Paul claimed the song in 1984: "I wrote that by John's pool one day."[79] In 1995, he gave it as an example of a song he'd written in the tradition of old melodic standards: "And I continued to write those tunes with things like 'Let It Be,' 'Here There and Everywhere,' 'The Long and Wind-

[74] Miles, *Many Years from Now*, 285-86.
[75] Baird, *John Lennon, My Brother*, 38. Paul said it was written "in the tradition of old melodic standards." Coleman, *Yesterday . . . and Today*, 38-39.
[76] Gambaccini, "The Rolling Stone Interview," also Gambaccini, *Paul McCartney In His Own Words*, 66.
[77] Hennessey, "Who Wrote What," *Record Mirror*.
[78] Lost Lennon Tapes, Sept. 23, 1991, cf. Sheff, *The Playboy Interviews*, 189.
[79] Goodman, "Paul and Linda McCartney Interview," *Playboy*, 107.

ing Road."[80] However, as we have seen, in two interviews, in 1988 and 1995, Paul spoke of collaborating with John to finish the song.

If we turn to non-Beatles, roadie Mal Evans claimed that he contributed a phrase to "Here, There." One day Paul showed up at Neil and Mal's house in the morning, said he was stuck for a line in one of his songs, and played this, with the blank. Mal said he suggested, "'Watching her eyes, hoping I'm always there.' I'm very eye conscious."[81] As always, such statements by Beatles insiders are hard to assess without further support.

So this is a Paul song, with minor collaboration from John.

- **Yellow Submarine — (McCartney-Lennon-Donovan) (lead vocals: Ringo) (recorded on May 26 and June 1, 1966)**

Paul wrote the beginning of this as he faded away into sleep one night in the Asher house. He was trying to write a children's song, so made the lyrics extremely simple. He thought of colored submarines, blue, green and yellow ones, but finally narrowed it down to a yellow submarine.

Some collaboration followed. Either John helped with the lyrics, or he contributed a song fragment, words and music, to help create the verse.

At some point, when the song was still missing some lines, Paul visited the apartment of folk-pop songwriter, Donovan, and asked for help. Donovan went into a different room and came up with "Sky of blue and sea of green." "They had always asked people for help with a line or two, so I helped with that line," said Donovan. "He knew that I was into kids songs and he knew that I could help."[82] Donovan's claim to those lines is supported by John.[83]

According to Neil Aspinall, Paul and John added the last lyrics just before the song was recorded.[84]

---

[80] Coleman, *Yesterday . . . and Today*, 38-39.
[81] Lost Lennon Tapes, Jan. 21, 1991; Badman, *The Beatles Off the Record*, 223.
[82] Donovan 1985-89, in Somach et al., *Ticket to Ride*, 156. See also Turner, *A Hard Day's Write*, 108-9; Pritchard and Lysaght, *The Beatles: an Oral History*, 208; Leitch, *The Autobiography of Donovan*, 153. Miles, *Many Years from Now*, 287.
[83] Sheff, *The Playboy Interviews*, 189-90.
[84] Aspinall, "Neil's Column," *The Beatles Monthly Book* no. 38 (Sept. 1966), 25.

John also contributed in a major way to the song's recording (including the voice in the funnel), which is unique enough to be regarded as experimental music. "We virtually made the track come alive in the studio," he said.[85] George Harrison said, "every time we'd all get around the piano with guitars and start listening to it and arranging it into a record, we'd all fool about."[86] Which is one way of composing experimental music. George Martin remembered that they used chains and bowls of water. They would blow through straws into bottles of water to replicate the sound of submarines surfacing. "It was nice to do because it, we were all being very inventive. And it was fun, it was like a party almost."[87] He also said, "It must have been one of the most unusual Beatles sessions ever. It was more like the things I've done with The Goons and Peter Sellers."[88] Sometimes we think of the fantasy-Lewis Carroll side of the Beatles as coming from Lennon, but this song shows that Paul had leanings toward surrealism also.

A major problem in assessing the songwriting for this song is that the earliest interview contradicts all other interviews. In a March 1967 interview with Paul and John, Brian Mathew said, "John, earlier before we started recording, you said it was in effect written as two separate songs." John responded:

> Yeah. I seem to remember, like, the submarine . . . the chorus bit, you coming in with it. *Paul:* Yeah. *John:* And wasn't the other bit something that I had already going, and we put them together? *Paul:* Well, yeah. Right. Yeah. *John:* And it made sense to make it into . . . *Paul:* Yeah, the bit . . . [*sings melody to verse*] 'Dut-ta-da, da-dut-ta-da.'[89]

[85] Sheff, *The Playboy Interviews*, 189-90. See also George Harrison in White, "Billboard Interview" (1999).
[86] White, "Billboard Interview" (1999).
[87] Hieronimus, Interview with George Martin, 1995.
[88] Badman, *The Beatles Off the Record*, 207.
[89] Matthew, "Interview with Paul McCartney & John Lennon," March 20, 1967. In the same interview, Paul said, "I suppose I thought of the idea and then John and I wrote it . . . We just sort of thought, we have to have a song. That it was. Sort of bit of fantasy in

So, by this account, it was a song like "A Day in the Life," "Baby I'm a Rich Man," or "I've Got a Feeling," in which two entirely separate songs were combined. Paul wrote the chorus, while John wrote the verse.

However, unlike the situation with "A Day in the Life," "Baby I'm a Rich Man," or "I've Got a Feeling," in subsequent interviews, neither Beatle remembered it that way. Did they forget? Or was that 1967 interview somehow mistaken? For example, in 1995, Paul remembered writing the story of the verse in that initial half-waking composing session: "I just made up a little tune in my head, then started making a story, sort of an ancient mariner, telling the young kids where he'd lived and how there'd been a place where he had a yellow submarine. It's pretty much my song as I recall." [90]

There was definitely collaboration on it. In 1966, Paul said: "We were trying to write a children's song."[91] In the same year, he remembered, "Originally we intended it to be 'Sparky' a children's record. But now it's the idea of a yellow submarine where all the kids went to have fun." This represents the song as a joint effort. However, Paul continued, "I was just going to sleep one night and thinking if we had a children's song, it would be nice to be on a yellow submarine where all your friends are with a band."[92]

Thirty years later, he stated, "I think John helped out; the lyrics got more and more obscure as it goes on." Nevertheless, Paul explicitly claimed the verse and chorus, and the story of the lyrics: "the chorus, melody and verses are mine."[93]

This is written from Paul's perspective, and it reflects memories some thirty years after the time of composition. However, John, though he always claimed that he helped with the song, sometimes described the song as mainly Paul's. For example, in 1980, he remembered, "'Yellow Subma-

---

it, you know. And the only way to do that would be to have it so kids could understand it, and anyone could take it on any level. Multi-level song."

[90] Miles, *Many Years from Now*, 286-87.

[91] Beatles, "Press Conference in New York City (August 22, 1966)."

[92] Alterman, "The Beatles: Four Smiling, Tired Guys."

[93] Miles, *Many Years from Now*, 286-87.

rine' is Paul's baby. Donovan helped with the lyrics. I helped with the lyrics, too. . . . but based on Paul's inspiration. Paul's idea, Paul's title. So I count it as a 'Paul' song."[94] Here John seems to be limiting his contribution to the lyrics. Paul also sometimes seems to limit John's contribution to the lyrics.[95] This would fit with the standard pattern of one of the Beatles having the music, verse and middle (AB), of a song, and the beginning of lyrics, then finishing it off with the other Beatle (or with the Beatles and insiders).

In 1984, Paul seems to describe writing the song outright ("I wrote that in bed one night"[96]), and he often described it as his song. "I told them we'd just got a song, Yellow Submarine, which I'd written for Ringo, very childrensy, but it could be great," he said in 1989.[97] But in the same year he again describes collaboration, developing his original idea: "You see with John and I, certain songs would nearly always be the idea of one of us. One of us had actually said, 'Ooh, Yellow Submarine would be good.' The other one would say, 'Ok, that's what we'll write today.'"[98]

John usually ascribed the song mainly to Paul, but with some collaboration added. "Both of us. Paul wrote the catchy chorus. I helped with the blunderbuss bit," he stated in 1971.[99] (No one has yet explained what he meant by "blunderbuss," an archaic gun, in this context. Perhaps he meant the funnel, or perhaps the transcriber got the word wrong.)

It is possible that John applied lyrics that he had written before to Paul's melody in the verse.

To sum up: the evidence for the writing of this song is quite ambiguous. If we look at the 1967 dual interview as the earliest substantial record of the song's composition, one might ascribe the chorus to Paul, and the

---

[94] Sheff, *The Playboy Interviews*, 189-90.
[95] Miles, *Many Years from Now*, 286-87, quoted above.
[96] Goodman, "Paul and Linda McCartney Interview," 107.
[97] *The Paul McCartney World Tour*, 55. See also an undated interview with Paul in Badman, *The Beatles Off the Record*, 228. "Just before I went to sleep I had this idea about a yellow submarine. It just came into my mind, so, the next day I started writing it, and finished it up."
[98] Read, "McCartney on McCartney," episode 2.
[99] Hennessey, "Who Wrote What," *Record Mirror*.

music and lyrics of the first verse to John. However, if that were the case, it is odd that this view was never repeated, either by John or Paul. The other possibility is that this song was substantially begun by Paul, with the music of both chorus and verse, and perhaps the words of the first verse, then John and others helped fill in the words of the subsequent verses. All the evidence outside of the 1967 interview supports this perspective, and it is a very common pattern in Paul and John's collaboration during this period. This is supported by a George Harrison statement: "'Yellow Submarine' was written by Paul and John, but even in the early days they were writing large portions on their own. Then one would help the other one finish it off; but that became more apparent later on."[100]

It was certainly finished with collaboration on the lyrics from John and Harrison and Donovan. The rest of the Beatles, with George Martin, were major contributors to the experimental sections of the song.[101]

- **She Said She Said — (Lennon-Harrison)**
  (lead vocals: John) (recorded on June 21, 1966)

At the house in Benedict Canyon, on August 24, 1965,[102] the sun was shining, girls were dancing, and John was high on acid. As John tells the story, Peter Fonda, wearing sunglasses, sat next to him and said "I know what it's like to be dead." This was not what John wanted to hear, but Peter kept repeating this unnerving message to him.[103] As Fonda recalls the incident, he simply told the Beatles about surviving an operation in which he had been declared legally dead. "'I know what it's like to be dead,' I

---

[100] *Anthology*, 208.

[101] Harrison in White, "Billboard Interview." Hieronimus, Interview with George Martin, 1995. Aspinall, "Neil's Column," *The Beatles Monthly Book* no. 38 (Sept. 1966), 25. Guests in the studio, people like Brian Jones, Marianne Faithfull and Pattie Harrison, also contributed special effects, Winn, *That Magic Feeling*, 22.

[102] See on "Love You To," above. George, in *Anthology*, 190. Miles, *Many Years from Now*, 288. Peter Fonda and Roger McGuinn also tell the story, Turner, *A Hard Day's Write*, 111. For the date, Everett II, 62.

[103] Lost Lennon Tapes, Dec. 5, 1988, cf. Sheff, *The Playboy Interviews*, 190.

said, and just then John walked past and said, 'Who put all that shit in your head?'"[104]

Later, in London, John took this experience, changed Fonda into a fictional female, and wrote "She Said She Said." There are some striking contrasts in tempo in this song; as John remembered it, the "middle eight" came when he just "wrote the first thing that came into my head and it was 'When I was a boy,' in a different beat."[105] However, according to George Harrison, he helped John "weld" three different unfinished songs together to create this song: "'I was at John's house one day, and he was struggling with some tunes,' recalled Harrison, 'loads of bits. . . . The middle part was a different song — 'I said no, no, no, you're wrong' — then it goes into the other one, 'When I was a boy.' That was a real weld!'"[106]

John and Paul agree that Paul did not collaborate on this. In 1968, John put it on a list of his personal songs.[107] Paul said the song was "Very much John. It's a nice one. . . . John brought it in pretty much finished, I think."[108]

SIDE TWO

- ### Good Day Sunshine — (McCartney-Lennon) (lead vocals: Paul) (recorded on June 8, 1966)

Paul wrote this at Kenwood on a bright sunny day,[109] modeling it on "Daydream" by the Lovin' Spoonful, which had the line, "I'm blowin' the day to take a walk in the sun."[110] John did help to finish this up: "John and

---

[104] Peter Fonda, before 1982 (in Cott and Doudna, *The Ballad of John and Yoko*, 217-18).

[105] Cott, "The Rolling Stone Interview" (1968).

[106] *Anthology*, 97.

[107] Cott, "The Rolling Stone Interview" (1968). See also Lennon in 1970 (*Anthology* 190); Hennessey, "Who Wrote What," *Record Mirror*; Lennon before 1972 (Aldridge, *Beatles Illustrated Lyrics*, 210); Lennon before 1979 (Cowan, *Behind the Beatles Songs*, 42); Wenner, *Lennon Remembers*, 55; Sheff, *The Playboy Interviews*, 190. Composing tapes, Lost Lennon Tapes, June 25,1990.

[108] Miles, *Many Years from Now*, 288.

[109] Goodman, "Paul and Linda McCartney Interview," 107 (1984). Similar: Read, "McCartney on McCartney," episode 3.

[110] Du Noyer, *Conversations*, 55; Miles, *Many Years from Now*, 288.

I wrote it together at Kenwood, but it was basically mine and he helped me with it," said Paul.[111] John also ascribed this song to Paul, but remembered some possible collaboration. "Paul. But I think maybe I helped him with some of the lyric," he said in 1971.[112]

While the Beatles were enormously influenced by Motown, soul, girl groups, early rock such as Elvis, Little Richard and Buddy Holly, early duos like the Everly Brothers, and Brill Building songwriters like Goffin and King, they were also significantly influenced by American rock that was contemporary to them — the Byrds, the Mamas and Papas, the Lovin' Spoonful, the Beach Boys, and Dylan.

- **And Your Bird Can Sing — (Lennon-McCartney-Harrison) (lead vocals: John) (recorded on April 26, 1966)**

John claimed this exuberant rock song, though for some unaccountable reason he didn't like it much. "Me. Another horror," he said in 1971.[113] And nine years later, he described it as one of his "throwaways."[114] Paul agreed that it was written by John, but remembered some collaboration: "'And Your Bird Can Sing' was John's song. I suspect that I helped with the verses because the songs were nearly always written without second and third verses. I seem to remember working on that middle-eight with him but it's John's song, 80-20 to John."[115]

Paul and George wrote the melodic guitar duet that begins the song, a significant contribution. "We wrote it [the duet] at the session and learned it on the spot — . . . then we sat and played it," Paul said.[116]

---

[111] Ibid.

[112] Hennessey, "Who Wrote What," *Record Mirror*. Nine years later, his memories of collaboration are even more vague: "'Good Day Sunshine' is Paul's. Maybe I threw a line in or something. I don't know." Sheff, *The Playboy Interviews*, 190.

[113] Hennessey, "Who Wrote What," *Record Mirror*.

[114] Sheff, *The Playboy Interviews*, 190.

[115] Miles, *Many Years from Now*, 288.

[116] Flanagan, "Boy, You're Gonna Carry That Weight," 44 (1990).

- **For No One — (McCartney)**
  (lead vocals: Paul) (recorded on May 9, 16 and 19, 1966)

Paul wrote this in March 1966 while he was on a skiing vacation with Jane Asher in the Swiss Alps, near Kloster, in a little bathroom in a chalet.[117] It took him about a week to finish the song.[118] In 1989, he explained how he liked songs about the daily life of working girls, such as his early solo single, "Another Day."[119] In 1995, he commented on another theme in the song: "I suspect it was about another argument. I don't have easy relationships with women, I never have."[120] So this may reflect problems in his relationship with Jane. He later rerecorded the song for his ill-fated movie, *Give My Regards To Broad Street*, and explained, "I'd written the song, took it to the studio, one day recorded it, end of story. It's just a record, a museum piece. And I hated the idea of them staying as museum pieces."[121]

Alan Civil, distinguished classical hornist, played the remarkable French horn solo. But who wrote it? Even the solos of Beatle songs are disputed territory. Civil says that he made up his solo entirely, with no help at all from George Martin or Paul McCartney. "McCartney sang nothing," he said. "Nobody seemed to know what they wanted at all, even George Martin. . . . I was entirely responsible for inventing the motive."[122] Paul's memories flatly contradict this: "George asked me, 'Now, what do you want him to play?' I said, 'Something like this,' and sang the solo to him, and he wrote it down. Towards the end of the session, when we were getting the piece down for Alan to play, George explained to me the range of the instrument: 'Well, it goes from here to this top E,' and I said, 'What if

---

[117] Goodman, "Paul and Linda McCartney Interview," 107 (1984).

[118] Elson, *McCartney — Songwriter*, 163.

[119] Read, "McCartney on McCartney," episode 3.

[120] Miles, *Many Years from Now*, 288-89. Similar: *Anthology*, 207; Snow, "Paul McCartney": "I was going out with Jane Asher at the time, and I was . . . commenting on the relationship, perhaps."

[121] Garbarini and Baird, "Has Success Spoiled Paul McCartney?" 62.

[122] As quoted in Everett II, 54.

we ask him to play an F?"'[123] Both Civil and McCartney are quite anecdotally convincing, but I lean toward the songwriter.

Paul and John agree that this is a Paul song. John not only attributed this to Paul, but was generous in his praise for it. "Paul. Another of his I really liked," he said in 1971.[124] And in 1980 he enthused: "Paul's. One of my favorites of his, too. . . . A nice piece of work, I think."[125]

- ## Dr. Robert — (Lennon-McCartney) (lead vocals: John) (recorded on April 17 and 19, 1966)

Much of the commentary on "Dr. Robert" revolves around the identity of the pill-dispensing doctor in the song's title. John said that he himself was the doctor. "Another of mine," he said in 1980. "It's mainly about drugs and pills. It was about myself, I was the one that carried all the pills on tour."[126]

Pete Shotton, on the other hand, said that the doctor of the song's title was "Charles Roberts," who was part of the Andy Warhol entourage.[127] However, according to Miles/McCartney, the song was based on Dr. Robert Freymann, a New York physician.[128] Paul gave one more option for interpreting the doctor in 1995, as he described the song as a fantasy and parody, rather than a realistic portrait.[129]

John claimed the song as his own in 1980 ("Another of mine"), but in 1971 he thought some collaboration was possible: "Me — I think Paul helped with the middle."[130] In 1995, Paul seemed to regard it as a collaboration: "John and I thought it was a funny idea: the fantasy doctor who would fix you up by giving you drugs, it was a parody on that idea. It's just

---

[123] *Anthology*, 207.

[124] Hennessey, "Who Wrote What," *Record Mirror*. Also, Connolly, *Ray Connolly Beatles Archive*, 106.

[125] Lost Lennon Tapes, Sept. 23, 1991, cf. Sheff, *The Playboy Interviews*, 190.

[126] Lost Lennon Tapes, Sept. 23, 1991, cf. Sheff, *Playboy Interviews.*, 190-91.

[127] Shotton and Schaffner, *The Beatles, Lennon and Me*, 213-14.

[128] Miles, *Many Years from Now*, 289; Turner, *A Hard Day's Write*, 114.

[129] Miles, *Many Years from Now*, 290.

[130] Hennessey, "Who Wrote What," *Record Mirror*.

a piss-take. As far as I know, neither of us ever went to a doctor for those kind of things."[131]

It is probably the familiar pattern of a song started by John, and finished with collaboration.

- **I Want To Tell You — (Harrison)**
  (lead vocals: George) (recorded on June 2, 1966)

George said that this song "is about the avalanche of thoughts that are so hard to write down or say or transmit."[132]

- **Got To Get You Into My Life — (McCartney)**
  (lead vocals: Paul) (recorded on April 7 and June 17, 1966)

This Motown-influenced rhythm and blues song with brass appears to be a straight love song, but it had a drug-related secondary meaning — it was "an ode to pot," Paul said, written not long after he had first been introduced to marijuana. "I didn't have a hard time with it [marijuana] and to me it seemed it was mind-expanding, literally mind-expanding."[133] However, the song also works as a love song; it is one of many cases of lyrical double meanings in the Beatles' oeuvre.

In his interviews Paul has acknowledged no contribution from Lennon to this song. "That's mine; I wrote it," he said in 1984.[134] In 1980, John agreed that this was Paul's, saying that he didn't even help with the lyrics: "Paul's again. I think that was one of his best songs, too, because the lyrics are good and I didn't write 'em." John thought the song was about LSD, not marijuana.[135] However, nine years earlier, Lennon thought that he (and George) *might* have helped with the lyrics: "Paul. I think George and I helped with some of the lyric. I'm not sure."[136]

---

[131] Miles, *Many Years from Now*, 289-90. See also Aldridge, "Beatles Not All That Turned On," 139-40.

[132] Harrison, *I Me Mine*, 96.

[133] Miles, *Many Years from Now*, 190.

[134] Goodman, "Paul and Linda McCartney Interview," 107.

[135] Lost Lennon Tapes, Sept. 23, 1991, cf. Sheff, *The Playboy Interviews*, 191.

[136] Hennessey, "Who Wrote What," *Record Mirror*.

Granted John's strong statement in 1980 that the lyrics were written by Paul, it seems likely that the song is wholly by McCartney.

- **Tomorrow Never Knows — (Lennon-*Tibetan Book of the Dead*-McCartney-Starkey) (lead vocals: John) (recorded on April 6, 7, and 22, 1966)**

Timothy Leary, Ralph Metzner and Richard Alpert wrote *The Psychedelic Experience: A Manual Based on the Tibetan Book of the Dead* in 1964. John Lennon bought a copy in March 1966, and followed Leary's invitation to take a trip with LSD: "I did it just like he said in the book."[137] In the introduction to the book is the sentence, "When in doubt, relax, turn off your mind, float downstream."[138] That turned into the first line of "Tomorrow Never Knows." John apparently wrote music to the song that was like a chant, and used only one chord, C, as in much Indian music. (However, in the second half of the verse, the Beatles added a B flat overlay over the C that in effect gives the song two chords.[139])

John premiered it to the other Beatles and George Martin at Brian Epstein's house in Chapel Street in Belgravia. Paul said:

> We were there for a meeting. George Martin was there so it may have been to show George some new songs or talk about the new album. John got his guitar out and started doing "Tomorrow Never Knows" and it was all on one chord. This was because of our interest in Indian music.[140]

Paul was worried about how George Martin would react to a heavy philosophical song all on one chord, but, wise producer that he was, Martin said, "Rather interesting, John. Jolly interesting!"[141] The song was scheduled for recording.

---

[137] John in *Anthology*, 209.

[138] Miles, *Many Years from Now*, 229-30.

[139] George Harrison, in *Anthology*, 210. Pollack, "Notes on … Series."

[140] Miles, *Many Years from Now*, 290-91. Also, *Anthology*, 210.

[141] *Anthology*, 210. Also, Read, "McCartney on McCartney," (1989), episode 3.

It was originally called "The Void," but John decided to use one of Ringo Starr's homely sayings, "Tomorrow Never Knows," for the song's title "sort of to take the edge off the heavy philosophical lyrics."[142] Ringo did indeed use the phrase. In a 1964 Beatles press conference, he told how someone had cut some of his hair unexpectedly at a public occasion. "I was talking away and I looked 'round, and there was about 400 people just smiling. So, you know — what can you say! *John:* What can you say! ***Ringo:*** Tomorrow never knows." John laughed.[143]

Apparently John just had the first "verse" so he and Paul had a songwriting session with the song. They managed to fill out two "verses," but couldn't stretch it to three.[144] "We racked our brains but couldn't come up with any more words, because we felt it already said everything we wanted to say in the two verses," said Paul.[145]

But something needed to be done for that third verse. Then Paul had the idea to use experimental music he'd been toying with at home to fill the gap. He'd been playing with a tape recorder, taking the erase head off and recording a sound over and over again on a tape until it was "saturated." He called these tape loops.[146] They had "funny, distorted, dense little noises on them," said George Martin.[147] Paul's immediate inspiration for this experimental music was the experimental "classical" composer Karlheinz Stockhausen — "these saturated loops were inspired by his work,"

---

[142] Lost Lennon Tapes, July 18, 1988, cf. Sheff, *The Playboy Interviews*, 191. Read, "McCartney on McCartney," episode 3. Lewisohn, *The Beatles Recording Sessions*, 70, cites Neil Aspinall on the title "The Void," but evidently thinks Aspinall was wrong.

[143] Beatles Interview, February 22, 1964; also in Badman, *The Beatles Off the Record*, 88.

[144] Paul is probably talking about the two sections of the song; the first part seems to have three verses, the second part four verses.

[145] In Pritchard and Lysaght, *The Beatles: an Oral History*, 209.

[146] Paul and tape loops: McCartney in Pritchard and Lysaght, *The Beatles: an Oral History*, 209. Miles, *Many Years from Now*, 291. Beatle interview, with Ken Douglas, August 12, 1966, as summarized in Winn, *That Magic Feeling*, 43. Beatles interview, August 11-29, 1964 (both Paul and John), as cited in Winn, *That Magic Feeling*, 63. Williams, "Produced by George Martin." George Martin before 1995, in *With a Little Help*, 79-80. See also Martin quoted in Turner, *A Hard Day's Write*, 116.

[147] George Martin before 1995, in *With a Little Help*, 79-80. See also Martin quoted in Turner, *A Hard Day's Write*, 116.

he said.[148] This idea for the song was accepted. George Martin remembered that Paul "told the others, and they, too, took the wipe heads off their recorders and started constructing loops of taped gibberish."[149] The Beatles brought in some thirty tapes and George Martin selected sixteen of them for "Tomorrow Never Knows."[150]

So just as John added significantly to performance-composition in Paul's "Yellow Submarine," Paul added significant performance-composition to John's song here.

John had originally envisioned the song as sung by thousands of monks chanting. "That was impractical, of course," he said in about 1970, "and we did something different."[151] As George Martin remembered, John wanted his voice "to sound like the Dalai Lama, singing from a Tibetan hill top." So Martin put his voice through a Leslie speaker. A tambour was added, and tape loop noises that sounded like seagulls. This didn't approximate John's original mystical vision. "It was a bit of a drag," he said, "and I didn't really like it. I should have tried to get near my original idea, the monks singing."[152] Nevertheless, this is how the finished product was created.

John claimed this song in a number of interviews. In 1971, he said, "Me — this was my first psychedelic song."[153] Paul, in 1966, agreed: "Every track on the LP has something special. . . . George wanted to get his Indian stuff on the record, I wanted to do some new electronic things, and John even had a song in which his inspiration was *The Tibetan Book of the Dead*."[154] But a year later, still very early, Paul said, "The song was John's idea but we all had a bash at it."[155] In this song, the experimentalism of the

---

[148] McCartney in Pritchard and Lysaght, *The Beatles: an Oral History*, 209.

[149] George Martin before 1995, in *With a Little Help*, 79-80. See also Martin quoted in Turner, *A Hard Day's Write*, 116.

[150] Martin, *With a Little Help*, 79-80.

[151] Aldridge, *Beatles Illustrated Lyrics*, 12.

[152] Ibid.

[153] Hennessey, "Who Wrote What." See also McCabe and Schonfeld, "John & Yoko." Sheff, *The Playboy Interviews*, 191.

[154] June 1966 interview, in Badman, *Beatles Off the Record*, 207.

[155] James, "Beatles Talk," Jan. 1967.

recording is part of the composition, and Paul claimed much of this. In 1966, he said, "we've got this track (Tomorrow Never Knows) with electronic effects I worked out myself."[156]

Beatle insider Neil Aspinall said in 1966 that Lennon brought only the words to the studio, and the Beatles came up with the "tune" there:

> The words were written before the tune and there was no getting away from the fact that the words were very powerful. So all four boys were anxious to build a tune and a backing which would be as strong as the actual lyrics. The basic tune was written during the first hours of the recording session.[157]

This statement is impressively early, and Aspinall was apparently a first-hand witness; if this is true, then the melody of the song was truly collaborative, with all the Beatles contributing. However, this conflicts with Paul's statements that when he first heard the song John was playing it on one chord. In other words, it sounds like there was a song with words (at least the first section) and tune when Paul first heard it.

Unless John was singing it on one note before they showed up at Abbey Road to record it. It's an interesting theory, but I tend to think that John came up with the first section of the lyrics and the tune long before the recording studio. Perhaps John and Paul and George worked on the melody when they got to the studio.

In any event, the end result was a song that had come a long way from "Love Me Do." It became an overwhelming climactic ending to an album that was amazingly different from *Please Please Me*, which had been released just a few years before.

While *Sgt. Pepper* has generally been ranked highest of the Beatle albums in music polls and in collective critical taste, *Revolver* has sometimes been regarded as the Beatles' finest achievement.[158]

---

[156] Smith, "My Broken Tooth."
[157] Aspinall, "Neil's Column," *The Beatles Monthly Book* no. 38 (Sept. 1966), 25.
[158] For example, in a *Rolling Stone* readers poll in 2002, *Revolver* is 1 (*Sgt. Pepper* is 3, the White Album is 5, and *Abbey Road* is 6). Tim Riley, an important Beatles critic, agrees. *Tell Me Why*, 181, 203.

10

"We were often answering each other's songs"

SGT. PEPPER'S LONELY HEARTS CLUB BAND

In this period, John and Paul wrote "answering songs," as Paul's "Penny Lane" responded to John's "Strawberry Fields Forever." This paradoxically shows both their growing independence as writers and their mutual influence. Paul contributed the structural idea and title songs for both *Sgt. Pepper* and *Magical Mystery Tour;* he also was the "lead" writer on many of the songs for these albums. So he was a dominant force behind *Sgt. Pepper*, often regarded as the finest album in the popular music canon, and a central "countercultural" work of art (though the album was much more than a simple psychedelic document, as it included such typical McCartney and Lennon themes as loneliness and loss, and love sometimes bridging human divides). John later perceived himself "lying fallow" as a songwriter during this period,[1] though this concept is belied by such Lennon-dominated masterpieces as "Strawberry Fields Forever," "Lucy in the Sky with Diamonds," "A Day in the Life," "I Am the Walrus," and "All You Need is Love." The transcendent climax of *Pepper*, "A Day in the Life," was a Lennon-McCartney collaboration in which John wrote the main song, and Paul contributed the "middle song." Both contributed to the experimental, orchestral "freakout" sections of the song. The two songwriters usually had clear possession of the songs in this period, but their opposite number often added significantly to them, as was the case in "Lucy in the Sky with Diamonds" and "For the Benefit of Mr. Kite!" (mainly by John) or "With a Little Help for My Friends" and "She's Leaving Home" (mainly by Paul). A surprising contributor to the lyrics of "Sgt. Pepper" and possibly "Fixing a Hole" is the Beatles' assistant, Mal Evans — anoth-

---

[1] See on the White Album, below.

er example of the familiar pattern of songwriting help by whoever is hanging around — but such contributions, as always, were limited to words,
filling in small gaps in the lyrics.

The Family Way soundtrack album, January 6, 1967

The original idea for *The Family Way* was for Paul to work with John
on the project, as an interview with John in 1966 shows: "I know we got
music to write, soon as we get back. And Paul's just signed us up to write
the music for a film."[2] However, Paul ended up doing the soundtrack
alone. John was reportedly offended that Paul had written the music without him, but Paul said that he thought both he and John were doing many
separate things at the time, such as John's books, and his acting in Lester's
How I Won the War.[3]

Paul worked with George Martin on arranging the music. He said, in
an undated interview:

> I just made up the themes. I just wrote the tunes and said,
> 'Here's how it goes, George,' and then explained to him how I
> wanted it orchestrated because I can't write music to this
> day. . . . I wasn't trying to write hits. I was just trying to write
> something that would suit the film, which was actually harder
> to do than something commercial.[4]

This album is based on only two melodies, the main theme (cut one),
and "Love in the Open Air" (cut seven). There were thirteen cuts in all,
and only twenty-two minutes of music in the soundtrack! However, the
two tunes are first-rate.

---

[2] Robbins, "Interview with John Lennon."

[3] Coleman, *McCartney: Yesterday & Today*, ch. 5. See also Badman, *Beatles off the Record*, 257.

[4] Interview with Nicholas Jackson, cited in Elson, *McCartney: Songwriter*, 156. See also
McCartney, interview with Sunday Times, as cited in Madinger, Liner Notes to the *Family
Way* album. John once noted that Paul wrote the soundtrack but he (John) got royalties
from it, and offered to give them back to Paul. Paul said, "Don't be soft." Fallon, "Will
the Real John Lennon" (1969).

- **"The Family Way," main theme — (McCartney) (recorded in November and December 1966)**

Paul has always loved brass band music, very typical of northern England, as his father had played trumpet and his grandfather had played in bands. He thought this kind of music wouldn't fit with the Beatles, but it would fit with *The Family Way*, set in northern England. "For the film I got something together that was sort of 'brassy band,' to echo the Northernness of the story, and I had a great time," he said.[5]

- **"Love in the Open Air" — (McCartney) (recorded in November and December 1966)**

Paul had written the main theme for the movie, but George Martin realized they needed a theme for the love story in the movie, "something wistful." He told Paul, then waited, but no love theme was forthcoming. Finally, as he tells the story, he had to come to Paul's house "and literally stand there until he'd composed something. John was visiting and advised a bit, but Paul created the tune and played it to me on guitar." Martin wrote it down, then arranged it for woodwinds and strings. "It is a fragile, yet compelling, melody," he said. "We called it Love in the Open Air. It's quite haunting."[6]

Paul tells the story a bit differently. He agreed that George requested the theme, and quickly. "I said, 'I'll tell you what, George, come on over and see me (he lived about half an hour away) and I'll try to knock up something by the time you get there.'" Paul had the tune by the time George walked in the door.[7]

I tend to think that Paul would more easily come up with a tune this sophisticated without someone standing over him, so I lean toward the lat-

---

[5] *Anthology*, 223. See also McCartney 1995 (Oobu Joobu, Show 7); George Martin in 1979 (*All You Need is Ears*, 223).

[6] George Martin, *New Musical Express*, #1941, December 24, 1966, as cited in "The Family Way (Original Motion Picture Soundtrack)," in the Beatles Bible. See also Martin, *All You Need is Ears*, 223.

[7] McCartney in 1995 (Oobu Joobu, Show 7).

ter story. Whichever is correct, the finished tune was a solid success, and went on to win the Ivor Novello award.

━━━━━●○●━━━━━

"Strawberry Fields Forever / Penny Lane" single, February 17, 1967 (double A-side)

This, one of the great singles in the history of popular music, marked an advance even from *Revolver*.

- **Strawberry Fields Forever — (Lennon-McCartney) (lead vocals: John) (recorded on November 24, 28-29, December 8-9, 15, 21-22, 1966)**

As a boy, John lived next door to Strawberry Fields, a Salvation Army orphanage, on Beaconsfield Road in Woolton, Liverpool. He and his aunt would attend fêtes there, which John always looked forward to. Much later, nudged by a journalist to write more about his life in his songs,[8] he began to think of places in his childhood, such as Strawberry Fields. "We were trying to write about Liverpool, and I just listed all the nice-sounding names, just arbitrarily. . . . But Strawberry Fields — I mean, I have visions of Strawberry Fields. . . . Because Strawberry Fields is anywhere you want to go."[9] So a song devoted entirely to the place resulted.

John began writing the song in September and October 1966, when he was acting in Dick Lester's *How I Won The War* in Almeria, Spain.[10] In 1967, he stated, "it was written in this big Spanish house, part of it, and then finished on the beach."[11] John's roommate, actor Michael Crawford, was the first to hear the song (according to Crawford).[12] John referred to "Strawberry Fields" as "psychoanalysis set to music really."[13]

---

[8] Sheff, *The Playboy Interviews*, 162-63. See on "In My Life" above.

[9] Cott, "The Rolling Stone Interview." See also *Anthology*, 237. On the place, Strawberry Fields, see McCartney in Miles, *Many Years from Now*, 307-8.

[10] James, "Beatles Talk," March 1967.

[11] Cott, "The Rolling Stone Interview." See also Sheff, *The Playboy Interviews*, 165, 166-69. McLean, "Stories Behind the Song: 'Strawberry Fields Forever'."

[12] McLean, "Stories Behind the Song: 'Strawberry Fields Forever.'"

[13] Howard Smith, "Interview with John Lennon and Yoko Ono," Dec. 12, 1970.

He did not write the first verse first. He wrote the second verse and chorus in Spain, and added the third verse when he returned to London in November. George Martin remembered John playing the new song for him, "sitting on a stool in front of me strumming an acoustic guitar."[14] By the time the Beatles began recording the song, on November 24, the first verse was present.[15]

Paul helped finish the song. John said, in 1967, "But we don't often write entirely on our own — I mean I did bits for 'Penny Lane' and Paul wrote some of 'Strawberry Fields.'"[16] Paul played the intro on a Mellotron, in flute music, and played Mellotron in strings in the early part of the song; the intro was Paul's melody from John's harmony, an example of musical collaboration. George Martin called it a "simple but inspired piece of composition."[17]

In a stark contrast to early Beatles practice, this song took some four weeks to record. It was done first in bare style; then John had George Martin help with a "heavier" orchestrated version. When John asked Martin to combine the two versions, with the first version morphing into the second, the producer and engineer Geoff Emerick were able to link the two versions together only with great difficulty.[18]

"Strawberry Fields" is definitely a John composition, and John claimed it in many interviews. In 1968, he discussed what he meant when he wrote it.[19] And in 1970, he said, "The only true songs I ever wrote were like 'Help' and 'Strawberry Fields.'"[20] Paul also referred to "Strawberry Fields" as a John song. In 2004, he affirmed, "For those early years, the

---

14 Tobler and Grundy, "George Martin."
15 Unterberger, *The Unreleased Beatles*, 153-58; Turner, *A Hard Day's Write*, 119.
16 James, "Beatles Talk," March 1967.
17 Martin, *With a Little Help from My Friends*, 17-18. Emerick, *Here, There and Everywhere*, 136.
18 Hugh Nolan, Interview with Geoffrey Emerick, *Disc and Music Echo*, March 30, 1968, in Sandercombe, *The Beatles*, 236. Lewisohn, *The Beatles Recording Sessions*, 87-90.
19 John Lennon, interview with Kenny Everett, Feb. 4, 1968; Winn, *That Magic Feeling*, 150. Hennessey, "Who Wrote What," *Record Mirror*.
20 Lennon, Rolling Stone Interview, Dec. 1970, BBC, part 1; Wenner, *Lennon Remembers*, 9. Here he also refers to it as one of his "personal" songs. See also Connolly, *Ray Connolly Beatles Archive*, 109 ("I was having a hard time"). Sheff, *The Playboy Interviews*, 165.

competition was great . . . If he wrote 'Strawberry Fields,' it was like he'd upped the ante, so I had to come up with something as good as 'Penny Lane.'"[21]

Despite these statements, in other places, both John and Paul stated that Paul made a contribution to the song, if a limited one.[22] In 1973, Paul said, "We'd kind of write 80% together and the other 20% for me were things like 'Yesterday' and for John things like 'Strawberry Fields' that he'd write mainly on his own."[23] While Paul definitely refers to "Strawberry Fields" as John's individual song here, he does temper that with "mainly." As late as 2007, Paul mentioned that he and John were starting to write separately, in songs like "Penny Lane" and "Strawberry Fields," but "We'd get together and polish them."[24]

Thus this is a song substantially written by John, but finished off with some minor collaboration from Paul.

"Strawberry Fields" was intended to be the first song on the next album, which ended up being titled *Sgt. Pepper's Lonely Hearts Club Band*. However, because it was decided to make this and "Penny Lane" a single, and the Beatles sometimes kept songs on singles separate from albums, it was not included on *Sgt. Pepper*. It later ended up on the U.S. *Magical Mystery Tour* album, which became the "canonical" album home for it. Three versions of the song can be found on *Anthology 2*.

- **Penny Lane — (McCartney-Lennon)**
  (lead vocals: Paul) (recorded December 29, 1966 to January 17, 1967)

In 1966, Paul, perhaps influenced by John, was thinking about writing a song about his childhood. "I still want to write a song about the places in Liverpool where I was brought up," he said. "Places like The Docker's

---

[21] *Uncut* interview, in Sawyer, *Read the Beatles*, 246. Similar: Davies, *The Beatles*, 368.

[22] For John see James, "Beatles Talk," March 1967, quoted above.

[23] Gambaccini, *Paul McCartney In His Own Words*, 17. "'Strawberry Fields' is a song that John had because he used to lived next door to this place called Strawberry Fields . . . and he used to bunk over and it was his little magic garden." Paul in *Anthology* video.

[24] Doherty, "Pete Doherty meets Paul McCartney."

Umbrella which is a long tunnel through which the dockers go to work on Merseyside, and Penny Lane near my old home."[25] Penny Lane is a road, but Paul was specifically thinking of the "bus roundabout" (a circular traffic exchange) and terminus that was sometimes called the Penny Lane Roundabout or simply Penny Lane. This terminus indeed has a barber shop and a "shelter in the middle of the roundabout."[26] Paul and John often caught buses there.

Paul and Jane Asher moved into a new home at 7 Cavendish Avenue, in St. John's Wood, near Abbey Road, in March 1966, and he wrote "Penny Lane" here in December, in the music room at the top of the house, on a piano which had recently been painted with a psychedelic rainbow.[27]

"Strawberry Fields" and "Penny Lane," both about childhood places in Liverpool, seemed linked together. In 1985, Paul thought the songs influenced each other, but was not sure how: "We were often answering each other's songs so it might well have been my version of a memory song," he said. It seems likely that John's "Strawberry Fields," written first, inspired Paul to write his own "memory song," though it was entirely unlike John's.[28]

This was substantially Paul's song, as both Paul and John stated. John, when talking about the journalist who suggested he write about his childhood, said, "Which manifests later as 'Penny Lane' from Paul — although it was actually me who lived in Penny Lane — and 'Strawberry Fields.'"[29] In 1985, Paul said, "We were always in competition. I wrote 'Penny Lane,' so he wrote 'Strawberry Fields.'"[30]

---

[25] John Lennon and Paul McCartney Interview, *Flip Magazine*.

[26] Aldridge, *Beatles Illustrated Lyrics*, 140. Miles, *Many Years From Now*, 307.

[27] Miles, *Many Years from Now*, 307-8.

[28] Ibid.

[29] Lost Lennon Tapes, March 14, 1988, cf. Sheff, *The Playboy Interviews,* 162-63. Lennon did live the first five years of his life near Penny Lane Roundabout, but then he moved to live with his Aunt Mimi at Mendips, as far away from the roundabout as Paul's 20 Forthlin Road.

[30] Davies, *The Beatles*, 368. Paul probably gets the order of writing wrong here. Similar: the Uncut interview, quoted in the "Strawberry Fields" section above.

Nevertheless, there was some limited collaboration with John to finish the song. In 1995, Paul said that "When I came to write it, John came over and helped me with the third verse, as often was the case. We were writing childhood memories."[31] And again, in 2007, Paul remembered, "I had kind of done 'Penny Lane' and 'Yesterday', when he'd done 'Strawberry Fields' at his place. We'd get together and polish them."[32] Much earlier, in 1967, John said, "I did bits for 'Penny Lane'."[33]

And we see how even a Beatles insider can be wrong. In 2004, George Martin said, "'Penny Lane' was entirely a Paul composition; 'Strawberry Fields' was entirely a John composition."[34] Actually, there was slight collaboration for each.[35]

Sgt. Pepper's Lonely Hearts Club Band, album, June 1, 1967

After the quantum stylistic leaps of *Rubber Soul* and *Revolver*, what? The album that is often regarded as the greatest rock album ever.[36] It would combine John's increasingly surreal lyrics, George's Indian leanings, Paul's interest in experimental and classical music, the Beatles' encyclopedic knowledge of the styles of rock and popular music, and create something that was acclaimed as uniquely unified and powerful. Unlike much experimental music, the body of the work is based on solid musical craftsmanship, Paul and John's mastery of melody, harmony, striking lyrics, superb performance musicianship, and the popular idioms of rock, music-hall song and ballad. George Martin, was, as always, the irreplaceable fifth

---

[31] Miles, *Many Years from Now*, 307-8.
[32] Doherty, "Pete Doherty meets Paul McCartney."
[33] Lennon and McCartney 1967 (James, "Beatles Talk," March 1967).
[34] George Martin, audio, transcribed from Sold on Song website.
[35] Paul wrote the piccolo trumpet solo, Tannenbaum, "Paul McCartney Reveals."
[36] See chapter 16. In a survey of forty-three album polls I made at one point, *Sgt. Pepper's* was number one in eight polls; its closest competitors were *Revolver* (4), *Pet Sounds* (4), *The Velvet Underground & Nico* (3) and *OK Computer* (3). No poll is authoritative, of course, but such polls record snapshots of collective taste and impact.

Beatle in this album, serving as the mediator between Paul, John, George and the world of orchestral, classical, and experimental sound.

This album reflects the Beatles' growing artistic maturity. Nevertheless, it is also a record of changing dynamics within the group. Paul and John, who had started as a self-conscious songwriting duo, were writing increasingly apart, and so this brought additional tension and competition. Paul, as songwriter, was becoming more and more productive, while John had a tendency to write fewer songs, and polish them over a length of time, as he had done with "Strawberry Fields." John would either have to equal Paul's productivity or contribute fewer songs to an album, and the latter eventuality is what happened during this period. John said, in 1971,

> And then Paul started doing that — "Now we're going to make a movie," or "Now we're going to make a record.". . . He'd come in with about 20 good songs and say "We're recording." And I had to suddenly write a fucking stack of songs. *Pepper* was like that. *Magical Mystery Tour* was another. So I hastily did my bits for it.[37]

And so John, though he made significant contributions to both *Sgt. Pepper* and *Magical Mystery Tour*, felt ambivalent about these albums. "I always kept saying I prefer the double album, cause *my* music is better on the double album," he said in 1970. "I don't care about the whole concept of *Pepper*."[38]

Paul was becoming increasingly prolific as a songwriter, but he was also increasingly acting as a producer and arranger in the recording studio. Journalist Hunter Davies, who witnessed the *Sgt. Pepper* studio sessions, said:

> They knew at the time that *Sgt. Pepper* was going to be bigger and better and different, with a new concept of the "album," all together and connected. Paul was definitely in charge of *Sgt.*

[37] Interview with Peter McCabe and Robert Schonfeld, Sept. 5, 1971. Similar: Wenner, *Lennon Remembers*, 26.
[38] Wenner, *Lennon Remembers*, 116.

Pepper. . . . It seemed to be all coming from Paul's house, and he seemed to be the total inspiration and the main motivator. John was becoming bored by the Beatles by then and was getting lazy and thinking of ideas and half-songs and not finishing them. So Paul forced him to finish things off, or to bring them to Paul half-done and they'd knock them out together. There was no resentment, though. He was just waiting for Yoko or something else to come along in his life.[39]

The other Beatles both relied on Paul's increasing presence as producer, manager, and creative nagger, and were deeply annoyed by it. Davies's generalization that "there was no resentment" has been contradicted by many statements from the other Beatles.

Paul came up with the idea of the album as concept, the St. Pepper framework band. When asked if the album had originated as a "fantasy thing," Paul replied, "Yeah, I had this idea that it was going to be an album of another band that wasn't us — we'd just imagine all the time that it wasn't us playing. It was just a nice little device to give us some distance on the album."[40]

So, in the same way that the early Beatle albums were recorded like the early live shows, with covers, and a screamer at the end, this album was also set up as a "live" show.

Earlier, songs such as "If I Needed Someone," "Good Day Sunshine" and "Here There Everywhere" had been influenced by American folk, rock and pop (Dylan, the Byrds, the Lovin' Spoonful and the Beach Boys). *Sgt. Pepper* was influenced by America also. When Paul was asked in 1980 how the album came about, he answered:

I think the big influence was *Pet Sounds* [released May 1966] by the Beach Boys. That album just flipped me. Still is one of my favorite albums — the musical invention on that is just amaz-

---

[39] Gass, "Interview with Hunter Davies."
[40] Garbarini, "Paul McCartney: Lifting the Veil Off the Beatles," (1980), 48. See on the "Sgt. Pepper's" song, below.

ing . . . When I heard it I thought, "Oh dear, this is the album of all time. What the hell are we going to do?" My ideas took off from that standard.[41]

- **Sgt. Pepper's Lonely Hearts Club Band — (McCartney) (lead vocals: Paul) (recorded on February 1, 1967)**

The first big surprise about the songwriting on the *Sgt. Pepper* album is not discovering how much of the title cut was written by Paul and how much by John; it is that we have to judge whether the lyrics of some songs were co-written by the bearlike roadie, assistant and friend Mal Evans.

Paul remembers the genesis of "Sgt. Pepper's" taking place when he had an epiphany while flying home to London from Nairobi, Kenya, on November 9, 1966, after a vacation he took with Evans.[42] Paul thought, for the Beatles' next album, they would become another group, with another name:

> It was an idea I had, I think, when I was flying from L.A. [sic] to somewhere. I thought it would be nice to lose our identities, to submerge ourselves in the persona of a fake group. We would make up all the culture around it and collect all our heroes in one place. So I thought, a typical stupid-sounding name for a Dr. Hook's Medicine Show and Traveling Circus kind of thing would be Sgt. Pepper's Lonely Hearts Club Band. Just a word game, really.[43]

And in 1995, he said:

---

[41] Garbarini, "Paul McCartney: Lifting the Veil Off the Beatles," 48. Also, Snow, "Paul McCartney."

[42] Miles, *Many Years from Now*, 302-4. Elsewhere, Paul and John often talked about this epiphany occurring on a plane trip from L.A. to London. However, the only such possible flight from L.A. to London would have been on August 30, 1966, after the Beatles' last U.S. tour ended in California. But, in Paul's recounting, he seems to be separated from the Beatles on the plane. Therefore, the clear memories of Miles/McCartney are preferable.

[43] "Paul and Linda McCartney Interview," *Playboy* (1984), 107.

We were fed up with being Beatles. We really hated that fucking four little mop-top boys approach. We were not boys, we were men. It was all gone, all that boy shit, all that screaming, and we didn't want anymore, plus, we'd now got turned on to pot and thought of ourselves as artists rather than just performers. . . . Then suddenly on the plane I got this idea. I thought, Let's not be ourselves. Let's develop alter egos so we're not having to project an image which we know. It would be much more free.[44]

He immediately began to work on a song, and in a brainstorming session with Evans, came up with the name of the group, as Miles reported in 1995. Paul got the title while "bantering words" with Mal Evans, as they talked about salt and pepper shakers. He believes he came up with "Sergeant Pepper" not Mal. "I started writing the song: 'It was twenty years ago today, Sergeant Pepper taught the band to play.'"[45] (If this took place on the plane ride from Nairobi, then apparently the original brainstorming session with Evans took place on the plane.)

The obvious inspiration for the name was surrealistic west coast band names in America.[46] A less obvious influence was the marching band tradition in northern England. "I started writing the song: 'It was twenty years ago today, Sergeant Pepper taught the band to play,'" Paul said, in 1995. "Okay, so I was leading myself into a story. What was this about? Well, he's some guy, then, and I always imagined him as associated with a brass band; we've always liked brass bands. So again it was northern memories."[47] The marching brass band is one of the persistent influences on Paul's musical style, from "Sgt. Pepper" to "Family Way," "Thingumybob," "Let 'Em In," and other solo songs.

---

[44] Miles, *Many Years from Now*, 303-4. Snow, "Paul McCartney."
[45] Miles, *Many Years from Now*, 303, 310.
[46] Sheff, *The Playboy Interviews*, 206-7.
[47] Miles, *Many Years from Now*, 309-10.

Chapter 10

When he got back to London, Paul introduced the alter ego idea to the rest of the Beatles who willingly agreed to the Sgt. Pepper personae for the record. Paul in 1989, said:

> I remember hitting upon this idea and saying to the group, "OK, for this one album we won't be the Beatles. This is going to be our safety valve. We're going to think of a new name for ourselves, a new way of being, a new way of recording, everything fresh, and by the way, I've written a song about something called 'Sgt. Pepper's Lonely Hearts Club Band.'" And we agreed that we weren't the Beatles anymore.[48]

Both Paul and John ascribed this song to Paul alone. "'Sgt. Pepper' was Paul's song, with little or no input from John," wrote Miles.[49] "See *Paul* said, 'Come and see the show,' I didn't," John said wryly, in 1970.[50]

The contribution of Mal Evans to this song is more interesting. We have a bit of evidence from Miles, but it is also supported by Paul, Ringo, and other Beatles insiders. Paul/Miles described Paul coming up with the title while brainstorming with Mal. Ringo, in an undated interview, remembered Mal as an actual collaborator: "Paul wrote a song with Mal Evans called 'Sgt Pepper.' I think Mal thought of the title. Big Mal, super roadie!"[51] George Martin also mentioned that some gave Mal credit for the name "Sgt. Pepper."[52]

There are interviews by Mal Evans claiming his contribution to the song, and this supporting evidence makes his claims more credible. Evans

---

[48] Interview in Smith, *Off the Record*, (published in 1989), 201. See also *Anthology*, 241. Miles, *Many Years from Now*, 303-4 ("Let's develop alter egos so we're not having to project an image which we know. It would be much more free.")

[49] Miles, *Many Years from Now*, 310.

[50] Lennon, Rolling Stone Interview, Dec. 1970, BBC, part 1. Wenner, *Lennon Remembers*, 17. Also: Hennessey, "Who Wrote What," *Record Mirror* (John put it on a list of songs written by Paul alone). Sheff, *The Playboy Interviews*, 206-7.

[51] Badman, *Beatles Off the Record*, 280.

[52] *With a Little Help*, 63-64. Other comments by Martin on the song: *All You Need is Ears*, 202; *Anthology*, 241; Pritchard and Lysaght, *The Beatles: an Oral History*, 237. A very early press report states that the title "came from Paul and Mal Evans." Ray Coleman, interview with the Beatles, *Disc and Music Echo* (May 27, 1967) (Sandercombe, *The Beatles*, 192).

stated that he was a full collaborator on this song, and that Paul promised him royalties, though the Beatle later told him the song had to be published with the sacrosanct "Lennon-McCartney" attribution.[53] "The first song I ever wrote that got published was 'Sgt Pepper,'" he said in an undated interview. "At the time I was staying with Paul as his housekeeper."[54] In another interview, he said, "I stayed with him for four months and he has a music room at the top of his house with his multi-coloured piano and we were up there a lot of the time. We wrote 'Sgt Pepper.'"[55]

There is a diary written by Evans, which would support his interviews. Unfortunately, this document's authenticity has been disputed.[56]

It is possible that Mal overemphasized his contribution to the song. Paul was the only other person present and he remembered "bantering" with Mal to arrive at "Sgt. Pepper," not actual collaboration. The Ringo statement shows that one of the Beatles regarded the process as collaboration, though Ringo was not a firsthand witness.

If Mal did contribute significantly, this is close to the familiar pattern we have seen: Paul has the beginnings of a song, then turns to someone (usually John, but sometimes friends and acquaintances) to fill out the rest of the lyrics. Perhaps this time he turned to Mal, who happened to be there, to help fill in the blanks.

Neil Aspinall also mentioned being present on one occasion when Paul was writing the song (as was Mal). He said that he suggested that Sgt. Pepper should introduce the band and close it at the end, an idea that was later accepted.[57]

---

[53] Harry, *The Paul McCartney Encyclopedia*, "Sgt Pepper's Lonely Hearts Club Band (song)." Also in Badman, *Beatles Off the Record*, 280.

[54] Badman, *Beatles Off the Record*, 280.

[55] Harry, *The Paul McCartney Encyclopedia*, "Sgt Pepper's Lonely Hearts Club Band (song)." Also in Badman, *Beatles Off the Record*, 280.

[56] Evans, "Diary Extracts." For example, on January 27, 1967, Evans purportedly wrote, "Sgt Pepper: Started writing song with Paul upstairs in his room, he on piano. What can one say about today — ah yes!" On February 1, he purportedly wrote, "'Sergeant Pepper' sounds good. Paul tells me that I will get royalties on the song — great news, now perhaps a new home."

[57] *Anthology*, 241.

Chapter 10

• With a Little Help From My Friends (McCartney-Lennon) (lead vocals: Ringo) (recorded on March 29–30, 1967)

After the fictional band is introduced in the first song of the *Pepper* album, the next cut continues without a break, with Ringo singing as the fictional "Billy Shears."[58] Shears was to be "a character in this operetta, this whole thing that we were doing," said Paul.[59]

The songwriting for this song was dominated by Paul, but Paul and John both contributed to it. Hunter Davies, in an extraordinary passage, recorded a "work" session on this song at Paul's house, Paul and John playing together as if in a trance, but stopping now and then to write something down. He described thoroughgoing collaboration:

> John started playing his guitar and Paul started banging on his piano. For a couple of hours they both banged away. Each seemed to be in a trance until the other came up with something good, then he would pluck it out of a mass of noises and try it himself. They'd already established the tune the previous afternoon, a gentle lilting tune, and its name, "A Little Help From My Friends." Now they were trying to polish up the melody and think of some words to go with it.[60]

Davies describes them working out a verse. They finally got four lines and wrote them down. They now had a verse and the chorus.

It was written during multiple songwriting sessions, partially at John's house at Weybridge (per Paul), and partially at Paul's St. John's Wood house (Davies describes this session).[61]

How much John helped write this song varies in three interview statements he made. In 1970, he reported it as an equal collaboration, based on Paul's idea and some structure: "Paul had the line about 'little help from my friends.' I'm not sure, he had some kind of structure for it

---

[58] For Shears, see Gambaccini, "The Rolling Stone Interview" (1974).
[59] Miles, *Many Years from Now*, 310-11.
[60] Davies, *The Beatles*, 263-67.
[61] Miles, *Many Years from Now*, 310-11.

and — we wrote it pretty well fifty-fifty but it was based on his original idea."[62] The following year John said it was Paul's song, but stated that he helped with "some" of the words. "Paul. It was Paul's idea. I think I helped with some of the words. In fact, I did. Hunter Davies was there when we did it and mentioned it in the book. "What do you see when you turn out the light. I can't tell you but I know it's mine." That was mine."[63] In 1980, he remembered, "That's Paul with a little help from me."[64]

Paul's only comment on writing the song is late, 1995, but he described equal collaboration: "I think that was probably the best of the songs we wrote for Ringo actually. . . . It was pretty much co-written, John and I doing a work song for Ringo, a little craft job."[65]

George Martin described "With a Little Help" as a Paul song, in an undated interview. "Paul wrote that and wrote it beautifully simple with just five notes. Terribly simple and terribly effective."[66] Once again, Martin is off slightly, not understanding that there was collaboration, but he did pick up that the song leaned toward Paul.

Despite Paul's late memories, I accept John's statements that Paul brought the idea of the song and the beginning of the music to the work session; after which I accept Paul's and John's (and Hunter Davies') description of thorough collaboration.

- ## Lucy in the Sky with Diamonds — (Lennon-McCartney) (lead vocals: John) (recorded on March 1-2, 1967)

This song started from one of John Lennon's most brilliant "found" titles. His son Julian came home one day with a picture and John asked what it was. The boy answered, "Lucy" (one of Julian's school friends) "in the sky with diamonds." John thought "That's beautiful," and recognized

---

[62] Wenner, *Lennon Remembers*, 87.

[63] Hennessey, "Who Wrote What," *Record Mirror*.

[64] Sheff, *The Playboy Interviews*, 191.

[65] Miles, *Many Years from Now*, 310-11.

[66] Badman, *Beatles Off the Record*, 46.

that this would make a good song title. "I immediately wrote a song about it."[67] So he came up with the beginnings of the song at this point.

Soon Paul visited, and John told him about the new song. They went upstairs to the music attic and, Paul said, "he played me the idea he had for it," starting with "Picture yourself." They discussed Alice in Wonderland and mentioned how the title "would make a great psychedelic song." So even if John denied that the title "meant" LSD, he and Paul saw the images of the song as relating to psychedelic experiences. They began to trade images: Paul came up with "cellophane flowers" and "newspaper taxis," which John approved of, then John replied with "girl with the kaleidoscope eyes." [68]

In the studio, on March 1 and 2, 1967, Paul played Hammond organ on this song, stopped to sound like a celesta. George Martin comments:

> The beginning of "Lucy," that hesitant, lilting introductory phrase, is crucial to the staying power of the song. It is also a marvelous piece of composition, based around five notes only.... Curiously, this introductory fragment was not formally composed; it evolved from the chords that John originated for the song, and in a similar way to "Strawberry Fields Forever," Paul improvised in his favourite arpeggio style until the magic phrase arrived.[69]

Clearly Paul sometimes arrived at melody by improvising from chords. John often claimed the song.[70] However, he sometimes mentioned contributions from Paul. When asked about the phrase "newspaper taxis"

---

[67] *Anthology*, 242 (1971). Similar: Sheff, *The Playboy Interviews*, 191-92. And from Paul: Aldridge, "Beatles Not All That Turned On," 142-43; Read, "McCartney on McCartney," episode 3; "Paul and Linda McCartney Interview," *Playboy*, 107; Paul, quoted in Martin, *With a Little Help*, 103-4; Coleman, *McCartney: Yesterday & Today*, ch. 1; Miles, *Many Years from Now*, 311-12; *Anthology*, 242. From Ringo, *Anthology*, 242. From Pete Shotton, Shotton and Schaffner, *The Beatles, Lennon and Me*, 245.
[68] Paul, quoted in Martin, *With a Little Help*, 103-4. Also, *Anthology*, 242.
[69] Martin, *With a Little Help*, 102.
[70] *Anthology*, 242 (1971). Sheff, *The Playboy Interviews*, 195 is another example.

in 1968, he said, "That was a Paul line, I think."[71] In 1971 he stated "Me — and once again, folks, this was Julian's title. It was nothing to do with LSD. I think Paul helped with the last verse."[72] Helping with the lyrics of the last verse is a typical occurrence for "finishing" collaboration on a Beatle song.

Paul remembers thoroughgoing collaboration following John's idea, his title and beginning. In an early interview, he said:

> So we had a nice title. We did the whole thing like an *Alice in Wonderland* idea, being in a boat on a river, slowly drifting downstream and those great cellophane flowers towering over your head. Every so often it broke off and you saw Lucy in the sky with diamonds all over the sky. This Lucy was God, the big figure, the white rabbit. You can just write a song with imagination on words and that's what we did."[73]

In 1974, Paul said, "I don't knock it [the song] because I helped write it."[74] And ten years later, he remembered, "And we said, 'That's a great title,' and we wrote the psychedelic song based on it."[75] A decade later, Paul again described collaborating on the song from the ground up after John got the title and the beginning melody: "So we went upstairs and started writing it."[76]

Though this song came from John's idea and beginning, I accept that there was a substantial amount of collaboration on it. Paul's opening melody alone is a major musical contribution. He also made contributions to the lyrics.

- **Getting Better — (McCartney-Lennon)**
  (lead vocals: Paul) (recorded on March 9, 1967)

According to Hunter Davies, he and Paul were walking Primrose Hill near St. John's Wood during the first day of spring, and Davies, or Paul,

---

[71] Cott, "The Rolling Stone Interview."
[72] Hennessey, "Who Wrote What," *Record Mirror*.
[73] Aldridge, "Beatles Not All That Turned On," 142-43.
[74] Brown, "McCartney: Life after Death," 63.
[75] "Paul and Linda McCartney Interview," *Playboy*, 107.
[76] Miles, *Many Years from Now*, 311-12.

said, "It's getting better," then Paul starting to laugh, remembering how in Australia, on tour, Ringo had been ill and another drummer, Jimmy Nicol, filled in for him. Every night after a performance, they would ask him how things were going, and Jimmy would say, "It's getting better." Paul laughed and began to sing, "It's getting better, It's getting better all the time."[77] Then Paul went home and began to write the song. "I went home with him and he then worked on four bars of it," wrote Davies.[78]

Later, John came in and they had a typical collaborative session, searching for rhymes and phrases that would fit the music.

> When John came around, Paul said, "Let's do a song called 'It's Getting Better.'" So they got going, both playing, singing, improvising, and messing around. When the tune was at last taking shape, Paul said, "You've got to admit it's getting better." [John said] "Did you say 'You've got to admit it's getting better'"? Then John sang that as well.[79]

In 1995, Paul said he didn't remember the genesis of the idea for the lyrics, but did remember discovering the music. "He had the music for the song title when John arrived." [80] He remembered, "The 'angry young men' and all that was John and I filling in the verses about schoolteachers. We shared a lot of feelings against teachers who had punished you too much. . . or who had just been bastards generally."[81]

Paul claimed this song, beginning in 1984, but always mentioned contributions from John:

> Wrote that at my house in St. John's Wood. All I remember is that I said, "It's getting better all the time," and John contributed the legendary line "It couldn't get much worse." Which I thought was very good. Against the spirit of that song, which

---

[77] Brightwell, "Hunter hits the mark with talk on his memoirs" (2007). Davies, *The Beatles* (1968), 268.
[78] Glenn Gass, "Interview with Hunter Davies" (2002).
[79] Davies, *The Beatles*, 268.
[80] Miles, *Many Years from Now*, 313-14.
[81] Ibid., 313-14.

was all super-optimistic... then there's that lovely little sardonic line. Typical John.[82]

John also ascribed this song to Paul, but mentioned his contributions to the lyrics. "Paul — I think I helped with some of the words in the middle," he said in 1971.[83] Nine years later, he said it was "Paul and me," from "Paul's main lick." The line about being cruel to his woman and beating her, was John, "I am a violent man who has learned not to be violent and regrets his violence."[84]

George Martin mistakenly stated that Paul and John had not collaborated on the song, though he recognized that "It couldn't get much worse" came from John.[85]

- ### Fixing A Hole — (McCartney) (lead vocals: Paul) (recorded on February 9 and 21, 1967)

This is another song attributed to Paul by both Paul and John.[86] In 1973, Paul described a tape he had of him writing the song: "It's great because on the tape I'm writing 'Fixing a Hole,' and I'm going through all these words and it goes on for hours, gradually getting the tune."[87]

In the year he wrote it, Paul explicated the lyrics, which were about:

> the hole in your make-up which lets the rain in and stops your mind from going where it will. It's you interfering with things as when someone walks up to you and says, 'I am the Son of God.' And you say, 'No you're not; I'll crucify you,' and you crucify him. Well that's life, but it is not fixing a hole ... when

---

[82] "Paul and Linda McCartney Interview," *Playboy* (1984), 110. See also Lost Lennon Tapes, Jan. 7, 1991.

[83] Hennessey, "Who Wrote What," *Record Mirror.*

[84] Lost Lennon Tapes, Jan. 7, 1991, cf. Sheff, *The Playboy Interviews*, 192.

[85] Martin, *With a Little Help*, 112.

[86] For Paul, Goodman, "Playboy Interview: Paul and Linda McCartney," 110. For John, see below.

[87] Gambaccini, *Paul McCartney In His Own Words*, 69.

I wrote it, I meant if there's a crack or if the room is uncolorful, then I'll paint it.[88]

In 1995, he turned to the lyrics again:

"Fixing a Hole" was about all those pissy people who told you, 'Don't daydream, don't do this, don't do that.' It seemed to me that that was all wrong and that it was now time to fix all of that. Mending was my meaning. Wanting to be free enough to let my mind wander, let myself be artistic, let myself not sneer at avant-garde things. . . . It's pretty much my song, as I recall.[89]

In 1980, John said, "That's Paul, *again* writing a good lyric."[90]

And so we have a song whose writing is non-controversial. Or so it seems. Once again, there is a new question: how much did Mal Evans help with the song? Mal strongly claimed contributing to it. "I stayed with him for four months," he said, "and . . . We wrote 'Sgt Pepper' and also another song on the album, 'Fixing a hole.'"[91] In addition, as we have seen with the "Sgt. Pepper" song, both Paul and Ringo reflect that Mal was involved in Paul's songwriting at this time. So we should at least consider the possibility that Evans helped Paul fill up gaps in the lyrics of "Fixing a Hole." Without support from Paul or other insiders, however, I don't accept it as certain.

Another theory about the beginnings of the song is that Paul wrote it after repairing the roof of his farmhouse in Scotland.[92] Paul, in *Many Years*

---

[88] Aldridge, "Beatles Not All That Turned On," 143.

[89] Miles, *Many Years from Now*, 314-15.

[90] Sheff, *The Playboy Interviews*, 206. See also Hennessey, "Who Wrote What," *Record Mirror* (1971).

[91] Evans, in Lost Lennon Tapes, Jan. 21,1991; cf. Harry, *The Paul McCartney Encyclopedia*, "Sgt Pepper's Lonely Hearts Club Band (song)." In the purported diary, on January 27, 1967, Evans wrote, "Sgt Pepper: Started writing song with Paul upstairs in his room, he on piano. . . . Did a lot more of "where the rain comes in". ["Fixing a Hole"] Hope people like it." Evans, "Diary Extracts."

[92] Salewicz, *McCartney*, 190. MacDonald, *Revolution*, 187.

from Now, convincingly refutes this theory, and the idea that it refers to drug needles.[93]

• She's Leaving Home — (McCartney-Lennon) (lead vocals: Paul; John counter-melody in chorus) (recorded on March 17, 1967)

Like other songs on *Sgt. Pepper,* notably "A Day in the Life," this song came from a newspaper story. In this case, a seventeen-year-old girl, Melanie Coe, disappeared from her home. "That was a *Daily Mirror* story again," Paul said in an early interview. "This girl left home and her father said, We gave her everything, I don't know why she left home. But he didn't give her that much, not what she wanted when she left home."[94] Paul wrote this moving ballad from that beginning.

He brought it to John to work on and John added some lyrics, but unusually, music too. John added the "counter-melody," "long sustained notes" and its answering words, which functioned like the commentary of a Greek chorus.[95] John said that he wrote the lines "We gave her everything money could buy" and "We never thought of ourselves." That was easy to write, he said, as those were things that Aunt Mimi would say.[96] John also sings those lines.

The lyrics of the two middle sections are as follows:

She
(We gave her most of our lives)
Is leaving
(Sacrificed most of our lives)
Home
(We gave her everything money could buy)
She's leaving home after living alone for

---

[93] Miles, *Many Years from Now,* 314-15.
[94] Aldridge, "Beatles Not All That Turned On," 143-44. For an interview with Coe, see Turner, *A Hard Day's Write,* 126.
[95] Miles, *Many Years from Now,* 314, 316
[96] Hennessey, "Lennon: the Greatest Natural Songwriter," 12; Hennessey, "Who Wrote What," *Record Mirror.*

(Bye bye)
So many years

She
(We never thought of ourselves)
Is leaving
(Never a thought for ourselves)
Home
(We struggled hard all our lives to get by)
She's leaving home after living alone for
(Bye bye)
So many years

One might conclude that Paul wrote the verses to this song, and John wrote the entire middle section. However, Paul's use of the descriptive word "counter-melody" is unique here. Usually a countermelody comes in on top of the main melody. In addition, the "long sustained notes" would be "She . . . is leaving . . . home."

John, for his part, claimed that he wrote lyrics on this song, not music, though this may reflect his artistic focus on lyrics. The music might have come with the lyrics.

Paul claimed this song in 1984: "I wrote that. My kind of ballad from that period."[97] But in 1995, he described it as a collaboration: "It was largely mine, with help from John."[98] John put it on a list of collaborative songs in 1971, and said, "Both of us. Paul had the basic theme," then John added those lines mentioned above.

I accept this as mainly Paul's song, but the middle section was a collaboration with John. It is a major example of John adding important material to a song by Paul.

This is, like "Eleanor Rigby," a study in feminine loneliness. "It's a much younger girl, but the same sort of loneliness," Paul said in an early interview.[99] The view of Paul as merely a purveyor of mindless optimism is

---

[97] "Paul and Linda McCartney Interview," *Playboy*, 110.
[98] Miles, *Many Years from Now*, 316.
[99] Aldridge, "Beatles Not All That Turned On," 143-44.

obviously flawed. He certainly has an optimistic side (as was seen in "It's Getting Better") but he also has a focus that is deeply concerned with tragedy, loneliness, human isolation.

Though some assume that George Martin arranged the strings, Paul actually worked with producer-arranger Mike Leander on this song. The Beatle had originally planned on recording with Martin, but when the producer had commitments for the near future, Paul went ahead and did the arrangement with Leander. Martin was deeply offended. "He [Martin] was busy and I was itching to get on with it; I was inspired," said Paul in 1984. "I think George had a lot of difficulty forgiving me for that. It hurt him; I didn't mean to."[100]

- **Being for the Benefit of Mr. Kite! — (Lennon-McCartney) (lead vocals: John) (recorded from February 17 to March 31, 1967)**

This is a "found" song, with lyrics taken directly from a poster. John was searching for a new song one day, when he saw a circus poster he'd bought, hanging in his front room. And the lyrics were all there, waiting to be inserted into a song. Paul happened to be visiting and they began inserting names and phrases from the poster into a verse structure, and at some point came up with suitable quirky music.

John often claimed this song, but Paul's anecdotal memories of being part of that original songwriting session are quite convincing. I believe it is another case of John claiming a song that was his idea, and in which he had dominated the songwriting session.

He said, in 1967,

> "Mr. Kite" was a straight lift. I had all the words staring me in the face one day when I was looking for a song . . . I wasn't very proud of that. There was no real work. I was just going

---

through the motions because we needed a new song for Sergeant Pepper at that moment.[101]

In the same year, he said that, in writing the song, he "just did it. I shoved a lot of words together, then shoved some noise on." When people asked him what the inner meaning of "Mr. Kite" was, he responded, "There wasn't any . . . I didn't believe in it when I was doing it. But nobody will believe it. They don't want to. They want it to be important."[102]

Paul, in 1984, said the words came off the circus poster, but "We stretched it a bit."[103] He explained, in 1989, "So we'd do stuff like that, pulling something that attracted us like that."[104] Then in 1995, Paul remembered:

> We just sat down and wrote it. We pretty much took it down word for word and then just made up some little bits and pieces to glue it together. It was more John's because it was his poster so he ended up singing it, but it was quite a co-written song. We were both sitting there to write it at his house, just looking at it on the wall in the living room. But that was nice, it wrote itself very easily.[105]

In 2013, Paul started playing "Mr. Kite" in his live show. Asked why he included it, he said that he thought that this "crazy, oddball song . . . would freshen up the set." Then he continued:

> And I have great memories of writing it with John. I read, occasionally, people say, "Oh, John wrote that one." I say, "Wait

[101] Davies, *The Beatles*, 275. See also Aldridge, "Beatles Not All That Turned On," 142; Miles, *Many Years from Now*, 318; George Harrison (Badman, *Beatles Off the Record*, 284); George Martin in 1979 (*All You Need is Ears*, 199); Shotton and Schaffner, *The Beatles, Lennon and Me*, 245.
[102] Davies, *The Beatles*, 284. John also claimed the song in the following sources: Wenner, *Lennon Remembers*, 17; Hennessey, "Who Wrote What," *Record Mirror*; Miles, *Beatles in their Own Words*, 75; Sheff, *The Playboy Interviews*, 193.
[103] "Paul and Linda McCartney Interview," *Playboy*, 110.
[104] Read, "McCartney on McCartney," episode 3.
[105] Miles, *Many Years from Now*, 318. Also, Grow, "Secret."

a minute, what was that afternoon I spent with him, then, looking at this poster?" He happened to have a poster in his living room at home. I was out at his house, and we just got this idea, because the poster said "Being for the Benefit of Mr Kite" — and then we put in, you know, "there will be a show tonight," and then it was like, "of course," then it had "Henry the Horse dances the waltz." You know, whatever. "The Hendersons, Pablo Fanques, somersets…" We said, "What was 'somersets'? It must have been an old-fashioned way of saying somersaults." The song just wrote itself. So, yeah, I was happy to kind of reclaim it as partially mine.[106]

So this is a clear divergence in testimony. I accept that it was John's idea to use the language from the poster as a song — it was typical of him to use "found poetry" like this — but then the song was developed and finished with collaboration. Possibly Paul made a contribution to the music.

When John was asked if Henry the Horse was a code word for heroin, he denied that he had even been introduced to heroin at that time, and said the song came completely from the poster, "like a painting, a pure watercolor."[107]

George Martin's contribution to the experimental, fairground atmosphere of the song was substantial. He said that John wanted to give the impression of

> sawdust in the ring, to give the idea of a fairground and a circus. So I started working out my electronic sounds to make it just that. I got lots and lots of steam-organ sounds, genuine calliope noises, which are tapes of 'Liberty Bell,' Sousa marches, that kind of thing.[108]

---

[106] Vozick-Levinson, "Q&A: Paul McCartney Looks Back," July 25, 2013.
[107] Sheff, *The Playboy Interviews*, 193.
[108] George Martin in 1971 (Williams, "Produced by George Martin").

These were recorded onto a master tape, which was cut into 15-second pieces and these cuttings were played at random in the background, while John and Martin played organs, Martin adding "swooping" chromatic runs. This achieved the effect Martin wanted: "a kind of miasma of sound, a background whirly-hurly-burly."[109]

SIDE 2

- **Within You Without You — (Harrison-Shankar) (recorded on March 15 and 22, and April 3, 1967)**

The first song George contributed to *Sgt. Pepper*, "Only a Northern Song," was apparently rejected by George Martin or Paul and John, and later ended up on the *Yellow Submarine* album. George's great Indian song, "Within You Without You," was his second offering. He began writing it at the house of Klaus Voorman (the Beatles' German friend from Hamburg days who had done the artwork for *Revolver*) in Hampstead, on a harmonium. "I was doodling on it, playing to amuse myself," he said in 1968, "when 'Within You' started to come. The tune came first then I got the first sentence. It came out of what we'd been doing that evening — 'We were talking.' That's as far as I got that night. I finished the rest of the words later at home."[110]

According to George, the music derived directly from a composition by Ravi Shankar:

> "Within You Without You" was a song that I wrote based upon a piece of music of Ravi's that he'd recorded for All-India Radio. It was a very long piece — maybe thirty or forty minutes — and was written in different parts, with a progression in each. I wrote a mini version of it, using sounds similar to those I'd discovered in his piece.[111]

---

[109] Tobler and Grundy, "George Martin."
[110] Davies, *The Beatles*, 321. Similar: Harrison, *I Me Mine*, 112; Tony King (quoted in Turner, *A Hard Day's Write*, 129).
[111] *Anthology* 243. See also *I Me Mine*, 112.

When George played it to the Beatles and George Martin, "nobody was overwhelmed," said engineer Geoff Emerick. "Personally, I thought it was just tedious. Of course, just hearing him run it down on acoustic guitar gave very little idea of the beautiful song that it was to turn into once all the overdubs were completed."[112] George Martin never did like the song, but worked carefully on the arrangement, using a string orchestra and Indian musicians from the "Asian Music Circle" of northern London playing exotic Indian instruments.[113] "We came along one night, he had about four hundred Indian fellows playing here and it was a great swinging evening, as they say," said John in 1967.[114]

The Indian influences on the Beatles from *Rubber Soul* (with the sitar on "Norwegian Wood") to *The White Album* (songs written in India) are remarkable. George had gone to India in September 1966, and had become more interested in Indian mysticism and music than in recording Beatle albums. Otherworldly religion began to pervade his lyrics. "We're all one," he said in 1967. ". . . The realisation of human love reciprocated, it's such a gas. . . . These vibrations that you get through Yoga, Cosmic chants and things like that, I mean it's such a buzz! It buzzes you out of everywhere. . . . It buzzes you right into the astral plane."[115]

• When I'm Sixty-Four — (McCartney-Lennon) (lead vocals: Paul) (recorded December 6 to 21, 1966)

Paul wrote this when he was about sixteen, around 1958, an instrumental piano piece in the music hall tradition — "rooty-tooty variety style," as he said in 1995.[116] He vaguely thought it might be used for a musical comedy someday.[117] The Beatles would play it at the Cavern when the

---

[112] *Here, There, Everywhere*, 179.
[113] Lewisohn, *Beatles Recording Sessions*, 103.
[114] "Interview with John Lennon & Paul McCartney." For John and Paul's reaction to the song, see further in that interview, also John in Lost Lennon Tapes, Sept. 16, 1991 ("One of George's best songs."), cf. Sheff, *The Playboy Interviews*, 196.
[115] Miles, "The Way Out Is In."
[116] Miles, *Many Years from Now*, 319.
[117] Gambaccini, "The Rolling Stone Interview," also Gambaccini, *Paul McCartney In His Own Words*, 17. This is his earliest comment on the song: "I wrote 'When I'm Sixty-Four'

amps blew out — Paul would bang it out on the piano, and, John reports, "This was just one of those that was quite a hit with us."[118]

In about 1966, Paul added words to it.[119] The following year, looking for material for *Sgt. Pepper*, he decided it would fit in. Its lyrics dealt with *Sgt. Pepper* themes of loneliness, and love possibly bridging that loneliness — or Paul may have added those themes as he and John prepared the song for recording. John remembers that "When I'm Sixty-Four" during the Cavern days was "half a song."[120] I suspect that Paul added the beautiful middle section as he worked up the song for *Sgt. Pepper*.

Though "When I'm Sixty-Four" had been Paul's for many years, it was subjected to the normal Lennon-McCartney songwriting, editing gauntlet. In 1967, John mentioned some phrases that he contributed to the song: "We just stuck in a few more words, like 'grandchildren on your knee,' and 'Vera Chuck and Dave.'"[121] And in 1971, he remembered that the song was written by "Paul." But, "I think I helped Paul with some of the words, like 'Vera, Chuck and Dave' and 'Doing the garden, digging the weeds.'"[122]

Paul pointed to Fred Astaire as the song's immediate influence. "Most of the songs I've written can be traced to some kind of influence — Elvis Presley, Carl Perkins, Chuck Berry to name a few. Even some of the Thirties-type tunes like 'When I'm Sixty-Four' or 'Honey Pie.' That's influenced by Fred Astaire and people like that," he said in 1980.[123] One of his

---

when I was about sixteen. I wrote the tune for that and I was vaguely thinking then it might come in handy in a musical comedy or something. I didn't know what kind of career I was going to take. So I wrote that on piano." See also Goodman, "Playboy Interview: Paul and Linda McCartney" (1984), 110; White, "Paul McCartney: Farewell," in White, *Rock Lives* (1988), 143; *Anthology* (2000), 22; McCartney, Autobiography, date unknown, on myspace; McCartney, in Badman, *Beatles Off the Record*, 285. There is reportedly a version of it on a 1960 Beatle rehearsal tape. Winn, *Way Beyond Compare*, 3.
[118] *Anthology*, 247.
[119] Goodman, "Playboy Interview: Paul and Linda McCartney" (1984), 110. McCartney, in Badman, *Beatles Off the Record*, 285.
[120] Lennon 1967 (*Anthology*, 247).
[121] *Anthology*, 247.
[122] Hennessey, "Who Wrote What."
[123] Garbarani, "Paul McCartney: Lifting the Veil" (1980. Du Noyer, *Conversations*, 213.

favorite songs was "Cheek to Cheek," written by Irving Berlin, and sung by Fred Astaire in the movie *Top Hat* (1935). Paul also pointed out that his home was filled with "music-hall music" when he was growing up.[124]

Despite the reliable evidence for John's contributions to the lyrics, both Paul and John often ascribed it to Paul alone. "I wrote 'When I'm Sixty-Four' when I was about sixteen," he said in 1973.[125] In 1980, John asserted, "Paul's completely."[126]

- **Lovely Rita — (McCartney-Lennon)
  (lead vocals: Paul) (recorded on February 23 and March 21, 1967)**

Paul got the title of this song "when someone told me that in America they call parking meter women meter maids. I thought that was great and it got to Rita Meter Maid and then Lovely Rita Meter Maid."[127]

Or he read about an American meter maid/traffic warden in the paper.[128] And with the character, came a story. "The song was imagining if somebody was there taking down my number and I suddenly fell for her, and the kind of person I'd be, to fall for a meter maid, would be a shy office clerk."[129] There was a "meter maid," Meta Davies, who claimed that the song was based on her after she gave Paul a ticket, but Paul discounts this as a coincidence.[130]

As he began to build characters and a story around this Americanism, he walked the streets near his father's house one night, working on the lyrics.[131] He had the music and most of the words, but at the last recording session for the song, there were still a few blank spots in the lyrics, so Paul,

---

[124] Paul in 1988 (White, *Rock Lives*, 143); see also in 2000 (*Anthology*, 22).
[125] Gambaccini, "The Rolling Stone Interview," also Gambaccini, *Paul McCartney In His Own Words*, 17. "It's pretty much my song," he said in 1995. Miles, *Many Years from Now*, 319.
[126] Sheff, *The Playboy Interviews*, 193.
[127] Aldridge, "Beatles Not All That Turned On," 144.
[128] *Anthology*, 247.
[129] Aldridge, "Beatles Not All That Turned On," 144.
[130] Miles, *Many Years from Now*, 320.
[131] Ibid., 319-20.

John, Mal and Neil retired to a corner of Studio 2 to complete them.[132] One photograph of the session shows Paul holding a lyric sheet with only the opening chorus and verse done; a couple more verses are written in Mal's handwriting.[133]

Paul claimed this song — "Yeah, that was mine," he said in 1984.[134] John agreed, in 1971, putting this in a list of songs written by Paul alone. And similarly, in 1980, John said, "That's Paul writing a pop song. *Q: Was there really a Rita, do you know?* Nah! He makes 'em up like a novelist."[135] But we know that there was some slight collaboration, finishing the lyrics at the studio.

- **Good Morning, Good Morning — (Lennon)**
  (lead vocals: John) (recorded February 8 to March 29, 1967)

This was another "found title," based on words from a television commercial. Hunter Davies wrote, in 1967,

> "Good Morning, Good Morning" was sparked off by listening to a cornflakes advertisement on TV. *[John:]* "I often sit at the piano, working at songs, with the telly on low in the background. If I'm a bit low and not getting much done, then the words from the telly come through. That's when I heard "Goodmorning, Goodmorning."[136]

Paul felt that some phrases in the song, such as "nothing to do," reflected John's life with Cynthia at the time, his boredom living in the suburbs.[137] But John, in 1968, said that "it was writing about my past . . . it was me at school, my whole bit."[138]

The rest of the Beatles certainly collaborated on the animal noises, which Paul described as "our first major use of sound effects, I think. We

---

[132] Winn, *That Magic Feeling*, 95.
[133] Ibid.
[134] "Paul and Linda McCartney Interview," *Playboy*, 110.
[135] Hennessey, "Who Wrote What," *Record Mirror*. Sheff, *The Playboy Interviews*, 206.
[136] Davies, *The Beatles*, 276. Similar: Sheff, *The Playboy Interviews*, 193.
[137] Miles, *Many Years from Now*, 320-21.
[138] Cott, "The Rolling Stone Interview."

had horses and chickens and dogs and all sorts running through it."[139] Calling this the first significant use of sound effects in the Beatles canon seems debatable, considering previous Beatle songs such as "Tomorrow Never Knows" and "Yellow Submarine." Nevertheless, Paul's statement shows that he thought the sound experimentation on this song was important, and he described the effects in detail in interviews.[140] Geoff Emerick made the point that John had thought carefully about the sequence of these sound effects: "John said to me during one of the breaks that he wanted to have the sound of animals escaping and that each successive animal should be capable of frightening or devouring its predecessor."[141]

So even on one of the lesser songs on *Sgt. Pepper*, there was complex aural experimentation going on.

John claimed this song, though it was not one of his favorites. "'Good Morning, Good Morning,' I was never proud of it," he said in 1968. "I just knocked it off to do a song."[142] He was a bit more sympathetic in 1971: "Me. A bit of gobbledygook one, but nice words."[143] But in 1980, he claimed the song, but looked at it more negatively, as a "throw-away piece of garbage."[144]

Paul, in 1984, agreed that it was a John song: "'Good Morning' — John's."[145] However, in 1995, he said, "This is largely John's song," and that "largely" opens up the possibility that there was some minor collaboration.[146]

○   Sgt. Pepper's reprise — (McCartney-Aspinall) (recorded on April 1, 1967)

The "Sgt. Pepper's reprise" unifies the album by closing the "show" just before the final song.

---

[139] "Paul and Linda McCartney Interview," *Playboy*, 110.
[140] Miles, *Many Years from Now*, 320-21.
[141] Quoted in Lewisohn, *The Beatles Recording Sessions*, 105.
[142] Cott, "The Rolling Stone Interview."
[143] Hennessey, "Who Wrote What," *Record Mirror*.
[144] Lost Lennon Tapes, May 2, 1988, cf. Sheff, *The Playboy Interviews*, 193.
[145] "Paul and Linda McCartney Interview," *Playboy*, 110.
[146] Miles, *Many Years from Now*, 320-21.

According to Neil Aspinall and George Martin, the idea of bringing back the first song as if we were at the end of a concert came from Neil. He remembers Paul and Mal coming to his apartment when Paul was working on "Sgt. Pepper's":

> At the end of every Beatles show, Paul used to say, "It's time to go. We're going to go to bed, and this is our last number." Then they'd play the last number and leave. . . . I said to Paul, "Why don't you have Sgt Pepper as the *compère* of the album? He comes on at the beginning of the show and introduces the band, and at the end he closes it." A bit later, Paul told John about it in the studio, and John came up to me and said, "Nobody likes a smart-arse, Neil."[147]

But, according to Martin, all the Beatles "thought this was a great idea," and thus we have "Sgt. Pepper's reprise."[148] Since Neil's statement is included in *Anthology*, presumably the Beatles agreed with it.

You could argue that Aspinall contributed to the words of this song, and the basic idea of the song, so I include him as a co-writer. Interestingly, for the band-within-the-band conceit of the album, the lyrics of the song are to a certain extent "found" words — Aspinall using Paul's words at the end of Beatle shows.

The applause and laughter were added from the EMI sound effects library.[149]

- **A Day in the Life — (Lennon-McCartney) (lead vocals: John; middle part, Paul) (recorded January 19 to February 10, 1967)**

According to John, he wrote the main song for "A Day in the Life" partially with "found" lyrics from the *Daily Mail*, a story dealing with the death of Tara Browne, heir of the Guinness fortune, who had been killed in a traffic accident on December 18, 1966. "I was writing the song with

---

[147] *Anthology*, 241.
[148] George Martin, *With a Little Help*, 147.
[149] Miles, *Many Years from Now*, 321-22.

the Daily Mail propped up in front of me on the piano," he said in 1967.[150] He started writing the song on January 17, 1967, when the *Daily Mail* reported the coroner's verdict on the Tara Browne case. John took some license with the story. Tara died in a straight traffic accident, but, John said, he "didn't copy the accident. Tara didn't blow his mind out. But it [the death of Browne] was in my mind when I was writing that verse."[151]

Paul strongly denied that the main character in the first verse was based on Tara Browne. "I don't think John had that in mind at all," Paul said in a very early interview.[152] And he emphasized, "The verse about the politician blowing his mind out in a car we wrote together."[153] In his view, there was actually a story of a man who was high on drugs, then stopped in the middle of an intersection, and didn't know that the lights had changed. He looked like a politician. Paul described the song as "black comedy," one of the Beatles' first "surreal" songs.[154] However, by 1995, Paul admitted, "as we were writing it, I was not attributing it to Tara in my head. In John's head it might have been."[155] In view of John's definite statements, I think we can accept that the story of the death of Browne certainly was in his mind.

More found lyrics came from the unlikely source of a news story on potholes in the roads of Lancashire: "There are 4000 holes in the road in Blackburn Lancashire, one twenty-sixth of a hole per person, according to a council survey. If Blackburn is typical then there are over two million holes in Britain's roads and 300,000 in London."[156] Later, as John worked

---

[150] Davies, *The Beatles*, 275. See also Connolly, *Ray Connolly Beatles Archive*, 109.

[151] Davies, *The Beatles*, 276. See also McCartney in 2000 (*Anthology*, 247).

[152] Aldridge, "Beatles Not All That Turned On," 144-45 (1967). See also Read, "McCartney on McCartney," (1989), episode 3. Miles, *Many Years from Now*, 323-24. However, in *Anthology*, 247, Paul seems to be speaking of Browne.

[153] Miles, *Many Years from Now*, 323-24.

[154] Aldridge, "Beatles Not All That Turned On," 144-45. Read, "McCartney on McCartney," (1989), episode 3.

[155] Miles, *Many Years from Now*, 324.

[156] This appeared in the *Daily Mail* on January 17, 1967, in the "Far and Near" column, "The holes in our roads." See Miles, *Many Years From Now*, 325. Sheff, *The Playboy Interviews*, 193-94. In *Anthology*, 247, this quote starts, "I had it [the Daily Mail] open at their

on the song, he knew the holes had some connection to the Albert Hall. As often, he turned to a Beatles insider for help. "For some reason I couldn't think of the verb. What did the holes do to the Albert Hall? It was Terry [Doran] who said 'fill' the Albert Hall. And that was it."[157] Doran was a friend of John who lived at Kenwood and helped run Apple for a time.

The fact that the song began from newspaper stories led to the first line of the song, "I read the news today oh boy."[158]

John brought the melody, the first verse, and the beginning of the second verse to Paul at Cavendish Avenue. John said, in 1968, "I'd written the first section and I let Paul hear it."[159] In the same year, he described how Paul was the first fan of the song. "I had the 'I read the news today' bit, and it turned Paul on. Now and then we really turn each other on with a bit of song, and he just said 'yeah' — bang bang, like that. It just sort of happened beautifully, and we arranged it and rehearsed it, which we don't often do, the afternoon before."[160] John had brought the newspaper to Paul's house, and they went up to the music room and began to fill in the second verse together.[161]

According to John, Paul added a lovely melodic fragment, "I'd love to turn you on," a nod to drugs and Timothy Leary, and the main song was almost complete.[162] Paul remembered the phrase as co-written.[163]

News in Brief, or Far and Near, whatever they called it." See also Davies, *The Beatles*, 275-76; Hennessey, "Who Wrote What," *Record Mirror*.
[157] Davies, *The Beatles*, 275.
[158] Sheff, *The Playboy Interviews*, 193-94.
[159] Davies, *The Beatles*, 277.
[160] Cott, "The Rolling Stone Interview."
[161] Miles, *Many Years from Now*, 323-24. Perhaps they polished the first verse too, as Paul remembers working on it.
[162] Hennessey, "Who Wrote What," *Record Mirror*. "I think Paul wrote, 'I'd love to turn you on.'" See also Sheff, *The Playboy Interviews*, 193-94.
[163] Read, "McCartney on McCartney," (1989), episode 3. "We kind of gave each other a look as it came up as we were writing it, was 'I'd love to turn you on.' It was kind of psychedelic period." Also, *The Paul McCartney World Tour*, (1989), 53. McCartney, Letter to John on John's Induction (1994). Miles, *Many Years from Now*, 323-24.

John felt the song was going so well that he didn't want to turn to writing a "middle-eight," and Paul suggested combining it with a song he'd written about an average day and a dream. John said, in 1968, "I needed a middle-eight for it . . . All the rest had come out smooth, flowing, no trouble . . . but instead Paul already had one there."[164] According to John, in 1967, "He [Paul] said what about this: 'Woke up, Fell out of bed, dragged a comb across my head.' This was a song he'd written on his own, with no idea of what I was working on. I said yeh, that's it."[165] And in 1970, John said that Paul "was a bit shy about it, cause I think he thought, 'Well, it's [already] a good song. . . . We were doing it in his room with the piano, and he's saying, 'Would you — should we do this?' I said, '*Yeah*, let's do that."[166]

The two songs seemed to fit together. Paul, in 1967, described his section as:

> It was just me remembering what it was like to run up the road to catch a bus to school, having a smoke and going into class. We decided: "The hell with this, we're going to write a turn-on song." It was reflection of my school days — I would have a Woodbine [a brand of cigarette] then, and somebody would speak, and I would go into a dream. This was the only one on the album written as a deliberate provocation.[167]

It was "a little party piece of mine," said Paul.[168] On the finished recording, Paul sings, "Somebody spoke and I went into a dream," and then there is a chanted, partially orchestral "dream" sequence that is presumably part of Paul's middle section.

---

[164] Cott, "The Rolling Stone Interview."

[165] Davies, *The Beatles*, 277.

[166] Wenner, *Lennon Remembers*, 115-16. See also McCabe and Schonfeld, *John Lennon: For the Record* (1971), 119: "And things like, 'A Day in the Life' was just my song and his song stuck together."

[167] Aldridge, "Beatles Not All That Turned On," 144-45.

[168] *Anthology*, 247.

At the studio, Paul evidently felt that somehow the two songs needed some separation, so he decided to record a sequence of percussion between them and fill it later.[169] George Martin, in 1971, said that he suggested they have a definite number of bars, twenty-four, and they would have Mal count them out, "One . . . two . . . three. . . ."[170] They asked Paul what they were going to do with it. "We'll worry about it later," he said.

Martin and the Beatles decided to have an orchestra play in the gap, and "freak out," starting quietly then making a crescendo to their highest register. This idea has been ascribed to John, Paul, and both of them. In 1967, John said, "Then we thought we needed some sort of connection bit, a growing noise to lead back into the first bit,"[171] which is an example of collaboration ascription. In 1971, George Martin said, "Paul said he wanted a symphony orchestra, and I said don't be silly, Paul, it's all right having 98 men, but you can do it with a smaller amount. He said, 'I want a symphony orchestra to freak out.'" Martin booked the smaller orchestra, then Paul and John (or Paul alone or John alone) came up with the idea to have a crescendo ending in a shriek.[172] According to Geoff Emerick, it was Paul who suggested that the musicians start with the lowest sounds on their instruments, then slowly rise to the highest part of their instruments. Then John suggested that they play louder and louder as they did this, till it became an "orgasm" of sound.[173]

Paul ascribes the huge crescendo to his immersion in avant-garde classical music:

---

[169] Martin said that this was Paul's idea. "It was also Paul's idea to leave 24 bars of the drum pattern." Pritchard and Lysaght, *The Beatles: an Oral History*, 237. Also, Badman, *Beatles Off the Record*, 287.
[170] Williams, "Produced by George Martin."
[171] Davies, *The Beatles*, 277.
[172] Williams, "Produced by George Martin."
[173] Emerick, *Here, There and Everywhere*, 152-53. George Martin agreed: "John said, 'I want it to be like a musical orgasm. I want it to start from absolutely nothing and increase in tremendous tension and build up to the most overpowering sound you've ever heard in your life." Badman, *Beatles Off the Record*, 287.

Because of all this Cage and Stockhausen stuff, what we did was I thought "OK I'd try this idea on John" and said let's take 15 bars, count 15 bars and we'll do one of these avant-garde ideas. We'll say to all the musicians, You've got to start at the lowest note on your instrument, which is like a physical limitation, and go to your highest note.[174]

As Paul remembers, he had to "sell" the idea to John.[175]

So there is no definitive answer to who originally came up with the idea of the orchestral "freak-out" crescendos. I tend to think the Paul had the idea for the orchestra rising in pitch, and John had the idea of increase in volume until the noise became absolutely overwhelming.

After the Beatles decided to put the gap with orchestra crescendo in the middle of the song, according to Emerick, Paul suggested that they use it again at the end of the song, and John agreed.[176]

After the second instrumental crescendo, there was a moment of silence, then a monumental crash of five pianos, then their continued echo, which ended the song.

Thus, this tragic story of someone committing suicide in a car, told with surreal additions, was combined with John's poignant elegiac melody. Then a contrasting middle section about a "day in the life," with experimental orchestral sections connecting the two songs, was added, leading to an overwhelming orchestral climax.

Paul in 1984 emphasized that "A Day in the Life" "was mainly John's, I think."[177] While John dominated the main part of the song, Paul's con-

---

[174] McCartney 1989 (in *The Paul McCartney World Tour*, 52-53). See also McCartney in 1984 ("Paul and Linda McCartney Interview," *Playboy*, 110); Lewisohn interview, 14 (1988), "I did a lot of work on the 'Day in the Life' crescendo because I was getting interested in *avant garde* things"; Read, "McCartney on McCartney" (1989), episode 3. Miles, *Many Years from Now*, 321-22. *Anthology*, 247. Lewisohn, *Beatles Recording Sessions*, 96; Du Noyer, *Conversations*, 70.

[175] *Anthology*, 247.

[176] Emerick, *Here, There and Everywhere*, 153.

[177] Goodman, "Paul and Linda McCartney Interview," *Playboy*, 110. Then he went on to mention collaboration: "But that was one of John's very good ones. I wrote . . . that was co-written." In the Beatles' Anthology video, Paul said, "It was mainly a John song. And

tribution to the finished recording was substantial. Aside from helping write the lyrics to the second and third verses, and providing the middle song, he worked on the song's unique avant-garde effects.[178] John in 1970 gave this as an example of a collaborative song: "Paul and I definitely were working together, especially on 'A Day in the Life.'"[179] It is one of the great Lennon-McCartney collaborations, and without it, *Sgt. Peppers* would not have been the masterpiece that it is.

---

he'd taken a lot of it from a newspaper. And then I had another bit, 'Woke up fell out of bed' . . . It was obviously a gorgeous song when he brought it. . . . I'd learn the chords off him and we'd develop it."

[178] MacDonald emphasizes McCartney's contribution to the performance — the "piano and (particularly) bass brim with invention, colouring the music and occasionally providing the main focus." *Revolution in the Head*, 184.

[179] Wenner, *Lennon Remembers*, 115. Also, Hennessey, "Lennon: the Greatest Natural Songwriter," 12.

11

"Perhaps they'll turn out to be different parts of the same song"

MAGICAL MYSTERY TOUR

Paul came up with the idea of the *Magical Mystery Tour* movie (and the title song) while the Beatles were flying back from L.A. on April 11, 1967.[1] In England they have "mystery tours" in which you sign up for a tour but don't know where you are going. Sometimes they are billed as "magical mystery tours," though they are never really magical. Why not have a "magical mystery tour" that is really magical, Paul thought? In 1974, he said,

> I did a few little sketches myself and everyone else thought up a couple of little things. John thought of a little thing and George thought of a scene and we just kind of built it up. Then we hired a coach and picked actors out of an actor directory and we just got them all along with the coach and we said, 'OK, act.' An off-the-cuff kind of thing.[2]

The surreal, plotless TV film, including six songs, was the Beatles' first major failure, though the musical releases connected with it did well.

The history of the *Magical Mystery Tour* album as a collection is complex. The American album, *Magical Mystery Tour*, included the songs from the *Magical Mystery Tour* movie and a collection of 1967 singles. It became the canonical album reproduced in modern CDs. But in Britain, this material was released only as singles, and then as a six-song double EP of songs from the movie. The first of the singles on the album, "Strawberry Fields

---

[1] Mal Evans and Neil Aspinall in 1967, see Evans and Aspinall, "Magical Mystery Tour," 8. Gambaccini, "The Rolling Stone Interview." Lost Lennon Tapes, Aug. 29, 1988.

[2] Gambaccini, "The Rolling Stone Interview."

Forever / Penny Lane," had been released much earlier, on February 17, 1967, before *Sgt. Pepper*.

"*Magical Mystery Tour* is one of my favourite albums, because it was so weird," said John in 1974.[3] It's one of those Beatle albums that has been overshadowed by *Sgt. Pepper*, *The Beatles* and *Abbey Road*, so you think of it as a lesser album. Then you remember that it includes masterpieces such as John's "Strawberry Fields," "All You Need is Love" and "I Am the Walrus," along with superb McCartney songs like "Hello Goodbye," "Penny Lane" and "Fool on the Hill." I'm also a fan of the quirky songs of the album, "Flying," "Blue Jay Way," "Your Mother Should Know."

------◦------

"All You Need is Love / Baby, You're a Rich Man" single, July 7, 1967

- All You Need is Love — (Lennon)
  (lead vocals: John) (recorded June 14 to 26, 1967)

In 1967, the BBC had the idea to broadcast a program to millions of people throughout the world, and asked the Beatles to contribute a song and a performance. Brian Epstein and the Beatles agreed, and Paul and John wrote songs in competition for the slot (as Paul in 1967 remembered, and George Martin remembered). Paul's song was "Hello Goodbye" while John's was "All You Need is Love."[4] Paul said, in 1967, "And we went to the session and we just decided to do his first. Anyway, by the time we'd done the backing track for his, we suddenly realized, that his — his was the one, you see, "All You Need Is Love," perfect. . . . So we've still got mine ready to do for the next one."[5]

However, there are alternate accounts. Geoff Emerick remembered that John specifically agreed to write a song. Brian Epstein explained the

---

[3] *Anthology*, 273.

[4] George Martin before 1999, in Pritchard and Lysaght, *The Beatles: an Oral History*, 251. For Martin on this song, see also *All You Need is Ears*, 199; *Anthology*, 257.

[5] Kenny Everett, Interview with Paul McCartney, June 26-30, 1967.

Our World deal to the Beatles, and said that a song was needed. "Paul didn't seem all that interested . . . With a distinct lack of enthusiasm, John finally said, 'Oh, okay. I'll do something for that.'" Then Paul reminded him two or three weeks before the program that he needed to come up with something. According to Emerick, John looked at Neil Aspinall, who said, "Couple of weeks' time, looks like." John moaned, "Oh God, is it that close? Well, then, I suppose I'd better write something."[6]

Strangely enough, John only made one short comment on this song in extant interviews. Asked in 1971 if "Give Peace a Chance" and "Power to the People" were propaganda songs, John replied, "Sure. So was 'All You Need is Love.'"[7]

In 1967, Paul ascribed "All You Need is Love" to John. Paul again described it as a John song in 1995, with the exception of a few minor additions by the other Beatles. "I threw in a few ideas, as did other members of the group, but it was largely ad libs like singing 'She Loves You' or 'Greensleeves' or silly little things at the end and we made those up on the spot."[8]

But in 1989, he tempered his attribution with "mainly": "it was quite a strange little song, mainly one of John's."[9] And in the 2000 *Anthology* interviews, he said, "It was John's song, mainly; one of those we had around at the time."[10]

Two insiders, in an early interview, described this as a co-written song. Mal Evans and Neil Aspinall, writing in 1967, described how the song was requested, then said: "That's the basis John and Paul worked on when they settled down to write the new song."[11] Probably Evans and Aspinall men-

---

[6] Emerick, *Here There Everywhere*, 203-4. Martin remembers himself cracking the whip, *All You Need is Ears*, 199.

[7] As cited in Turner, *A Hard Day's Write*, 136.

[8] Miles, *Many Years from Now*, 354.

[9] Read, "McCartney on McCartney," episode 3.

[10] *Anthology*, 257.

[11] Evans and Aspinall, "Mal and Neil Tell You How 'All You Need is Love' was Recorded."

tioned co-writing simply as a matter of custom. It's impossible to know for certain. 1967 is impressively early, and Evans and Aspinall were certainly insiders.

In view of Paul's 1967 memories, I ascribe the song fully to John, though the other Beatles helped with aspects of the recording.

Pieces of music by non-Beatles used in the recording were: the French national anthem "La Marseillaise"; "Two-Part Invention #8 in F" by Bach; "Greensleeves"; Glenn Miller's "In The Mood"; "She Loves You" (sung by John and Paul), "Chanson d'Amour" by Wayne Shanklin; and Jeremiah Clarke's "Prince of Denmark's March."

The broadcast took place on June 25, 1967. The Beatles sang to a pre-recorded backing track, surrounded by friends, relatives and various luminaries.

- **Baby, You're a Rich Man — (Lennon-McCartney) (lead vocals: John) (recorded on May 11, 1967)**

"Baby, You're a Rich Man" is another case where Paul and John stuck two independently written songs together. John had an incomplete song written from newspaper articles about American hippies, called "One of the Beautiful People."[12] Paul had an incomplete song called "Baby, You're a Rich Man." The two songwriters decided that this would fit as the middle section to John's song, so the two fragments were combined.

Both John and Paul agree about this songwriting scenario. "Both of us. In fact we just stuck two songs together for this one — same as 'A Day In The Life,'" said John in 1971.[13] Paul in 1995 remembered that the song "was co-written by John and me at Cavendish Avenue."[14]

I give Lennon first billing on this song because he wrote the "main" song, and Paul wrote the "chorus."

---

[12] Miles, *Many Years from Now*, 371.

[13] Hennessey, "Who Wrote What," *Record Mirror*. Sheff, *The Playboy Interviews*, 194.

[14] Miles, *Many Years from Now*, 371.

"Cat Call / Mercy Mercy Mercy" single — The Chris Barber Band, October 20, 1967

- Cat Call — (McCartney)
  (recorded on July 20, 1967)

Paul wrote this instrumental back in the early Beatles days. It was in the Beatles' live repertoire from 1958 to 1962, performed under the name "Catswalk."[15] It can be found on an early Beatle rehearsal tape.

In 1967, Paul became friendly with Chris Barber, a trombonist whose band was a leading jazz group in the U.K.[16] Barber asked Paul if he had any songs that would work for his band. Paul gave him "Cat Call," then helped produce the Chris Barber Band recording.[17]

In 1995, Paul said there was no collaboration with John on this song: "I wrote a few instrumentals: 'Cat Call' was one of those, then there was something called 'Cayenne Pepper,' but those tended to be me writing tunes by myself."[18] In about 1959, Paul listed it, "Catswalk," in a group of songs written collaboratively, but he may have been talking generally.[19] On the record, it is attributed to "Paul McCartney."

Later, in the Get Back sessions, the Beatles performed it again.[20]

- o Mercy Mercy Mercy (Joe Zawinul)

"Hello Goodbye / I am the Walrus" single, November 24, 1967

This is the last single from the *Magical Mystery Tour* period. John dominated the previous single, but Paul had the A-side on this one, though it

---

[15] Lewisohn, *Complete Beatles Chronicle*, Appendix, "What They Played"; Miles, *Many Years from Now*, 38; Sulpy and Schweighardt, *Get Back*, 246; Unterberger, *The Unreleased Beatles*, 348.

[16] Miles, *Many Years from Now*, 439. Engelhart, *Beatles Undercover*, 40.

[17] Chris Barber before 1987, quoted in Elson, *McCartney — Songwriter*, 170.

[18] Miles, *Many Years from Now*, 38.

[19] Letter to Mr. Low, in Davies, *The Beatles*, 63.

[20] Winn, *Way Beyond Compare*, 17; Unterberger, *The Unreleased Beatles*, 252.

was almost upstaged by John's "I am the Walrus," one of the strongest B-sides in the history of pop music.

- **Hello Goodbye — (McCartney)**
  (lead vocals: Paul) (recorded October 2 to November 2, 1967)

As we have seen, George Martin said that this was written in competition with "All You Need is Love" for performance on the My World TV show, and was dropped in preference to John's song.[21]

According to Alastair Taylor — Epstein's former personal assistant and later the general manager of Apple Corps — the song began at Cavendish Avenue, with Paul telling Taylor that anyone could write a song. They went to a harmonium, and Paul had Taylor play a note, any note, then Paul also played a note to create a rhythm. Next Paul told Taylor to shout out opposites as he (Paul) spoke words.[22] "'Black,' he started. 'White,' I replied. 'Yes.' 'No.' 'Good.' 'Bad.' 'Hello.' 'Goodbye.'" Paul came up with a tune as they echoed opposites to each other.[23]

Taylor was unsure whether this was the actual genesis of the song, or whether Paul had had the idea for it previously and was simply developing it with him.

This is an example of Paul working on the lyrics of a song with a non-musical friend. But probably Taylor's contribution can't be equated with songwriting.

Both Paul and John ascribe this to Paul. In 1988, Paul said, "The thing that lodges in my memory, in the writing aspect of 'Hello, Goodbye,' was the 'you say yes, I say no, you say hey, I say hello, you say black, I say white.' It almost wrote itself because it was to be 'Hello, Goodbye.'"[24] In 1995, he commented on the lyrics:

---

[21] Pritchard and Lysaght, *The Beatles: an Oral History*, 251.

[22] Taylor, *Yesterday: The Beatles Remembered*, 172-73.

[23] Forsyth, "The Alistair Taylor Interview."

[24] Interview in Lewisohn, *The Beatles Recording Sessions*, (1988), 16.

"Hello Goodbye" was one of my songs. There are Gemini-an influences here I think: the twins. It's such a deep theme in the universe, duality — man woman, black white, high low, right wrong, up down, hello goodbye — that it was a very easy song to write. It's just a song of duality, with me advocating the more positive. You say goodbye, I say hello. You say stop, I say go. I was advocating the more positive side of the duality, and I still do to this day.[25]

John ascribed it to Paul in 1971 and 1980.[26]

- **I Am the Walrus — (Lennon)**
  (lead vocals: John) (recorded on September 5, 1967)

This song began when John heard a two note police siren in the middle of the night at Kenwood, and was fascinated by its power as it faded in and out. In an undated interview he said that the siren "was so hypnotic, you know, *dee doo dee doo dee dooo* fading in and getting loud and then fading away again."[27]

Why not write a song with that two-note melody? he thought. This gave him the minimalist melody for the main part of the song, though it subsequently was expanded beyond the two notes. "You couldn't really sing the police siren," he said in 1968.[28]

The lyrics came slowly. First came "sitting pretty, like a policeman." He told Hunter Davies, in 1967, that this "would be a basis for a song, but there was no need to develop now. It could be dragged out next time he

---

[25] Miles, *Many Years from Now*, 370. For Paul's further comments on the philosophy of the song, Ray Coleman, Interview with Lennon and McCartney, *Disc and Music Echo* (Dec. 16, 1967), in Sandercombe, *The Beatles*, 224; Read, "McCartney on McCartney," (1989), episode 4.

[26] Hennessey, "Who Wrote What," *Record Mirror*; Sheff, *The Playboy Interviews*, 207-8.

[27] Pritchard and Lysaght, *The Beatles: an Oral History*, 257. Davies, *The Beatles*, 276-77.

[28] Cott, "The Rolling Stone Interview."

needed a song. 'I've written it down on a piece of paper somewhere. I'm always sure I'll forget it, so I write it down, but I wouldn't.'"[29]

However, in 1968, John stated that the first words of the song that came to him were "I am he as you are he as we are all together."[30] Then, one day, he wrote down a few more words, "just daft words, to put to another bit of rhythm. 'Sitting on a cornflake, waiting for a man to come.'" Davies thought he said 'van to come' and Lennon liked that better.[31]

As John said in 1980, "The first line written on one acid trip one weekend, the second line written on the next acid trip the next weekend, and subsequently filled in after I met Yoko."[32]

One part of the song — "sitting in an English country garden" — started out as an entirely different song, which he later connected to the main "I Am the Walrus" song. Hunter Davies wrote, in 1967,

> He also had another piece of tune in his head. This had started from the phrase "sitting in an English country garden." This is what John does for at least two hours every day, sitting on the step outside his window, looking at his garden. This time, thinking about himself doing it, he'd repeated the phrase over and over till he'd put a tune to it. "I don't know how it will all end up. Perhaps they'll turn out to be different parts of the same song — sitting in an English country garden, waiting for the van to come. I don't know."[33]

As to the surreal obscurity of the lyrics, John said, "'Walrus' is just saying a dream, the words don't mean a lot."[34]

---

[29] Davies, *The Beatles*, 276-77.

[30] Cott, "The Rolling Stone Interview."

[31] Davies, *The Beatles*, 276-77.

[32] Lost Lennon Tapes, March 28, 1988, cf. Sheff, *The Playboy Interviews*, 194-95.

[33] Davies, *The Beatles*, 276-77.

[34] Ray Coleman, Interview with Lennon and McCartney, *Disc and Music Echo*, Dec. 16, 1967, in Sandercombe, *The Beatles*, 224.

Pete Shotton described the genesis of another section of the song, which can be viewed as "found" poetry, of a sort. John had received a fan letter from a student at Quarry Bank High School, who described how the teachers were giving solemn interpretations of obscure Beatle lyrics. Then Lennon thought of the 'Dead Dog's Eye' song they'd sung as boys, and asked Shotton if he remembered it. "Yellow matter custard, green slop pie / All mixed together with a dead dog's eye / Slap it on a butty, ten foot thick / Then wash it all down with a cup of cold sick." "'That's it!' said John, 'Fantastic!' He found a pen and commenced scribbling . . ." Then he "threw in the most ludicrous images his imagination could conjure . . . He turned to me, smiling. 'Let the so-and-sos work *that* one out, Pete!'"[35]

The walrus of the title came from Lewis Carroll's "Walrus and the Carpenter," though John later regretted that he had used the rapacious walrus for the title.[36]

Both John and Paul ascribe this to John. "Me — I like that one," he said in 1971.[37] Paul in 1988 said that John "obviously wrote" it, and in 1995 affirmed, "That was John's baby, great one, a really good one."[38]

———————————◦———————————

Magical Mystery Tour, **U.S. album, November 27, 1967**

Magical Mystery Tour, **U.K. double EP, December 8, 1967 (Magical Mystery Tour; Your Mother Should Know; I Am the Walrus; The Fool on the Hill; Flying; Blue Jay Way)**

Magical Mystery Tour **TV movie, aired on BBC1 on December 26, 1967**

---

[35] Shotton and Schaffner, *The Beatles, Lennon and Me,* 217-18. Lost Lennon Tapes, March 28, 1988.

[36] Lennon in 1970, see *Anthology,* 273. Sheff, *The Playboy Interviews,* 194-95.

[37] Hennessey, "Who Wrote What," *Record Mirror.* Similar: John in Badman, *Beatles Off the Record,* 310. *Anthology,* 273.

[38] White, "Paul McCartney: Farewell," 50; Miles, *Many Years from Now,* 357.

The canonical U.S. *Magical Mystery Tour* album starts with the songs from the TV movie, then fills side two with all the extraordinary singles they'd been releasing in 1967.

- **Magical Mystery Tour — (McCartney-Lennon-Harrison-Starkey)**
  (lead vocals: Paul) (recorded April 25 to May 3, 1967)

As Paul thought of magical mystery tours, he remembered the barker recruiting participants. This gave him the first line of the song ("Roll Up, Roll Up, for the Magical Mystery Tour,"), and he added music. Mal Evans and Neil Aspinall wrote, in 1967, "Flying home to London (Tuesday April 11) Paul worked on the first words for a 'Magical Mystery Tour' song."[39]

Paul brought the words and music for that first line to the studio, played what he had for the other Beatles, and asked them for suggestions to finish the lyrics.[40] Davies writes:

> At the recording session, all they had was a title and a few bars of music. "Paul played the opening bars of 'Magical Mystery Tour' on the piano, showing the others how it would go." They started with one line: "Roll Up, Roll Up, for the Magical Mystery Tour." "Paul told Mal to write down the order of how they would do the song." "As they shouted out ideas, Mal wrote them all down. "Reservation," "Invitation," "Trip of a Lifetime,' 'Satisfaction guaranteed."' Paul came back later with the completed lyrics.[41]

Paul, in 1995, gave a vague ascription of this song to collaboration.

> "Magical Mystery Tour" was co-written by John and I, very much in our fairground period. One of our great inspirations was always the barker: "Roll up! Roll up!". . . If you look at all the Lennon / McCartney things, it's a thing we

---

[39] Evans and Aspinall, "Magical Mystery Tour," 8.
[40] Winn, *That Magic Feeling*, 103.
[41] Davies, *The Beatles*, 272-73.

do a lot. . . . John and I remembered mystery tours, and we always thought this was a fascinating idea.[42]

John ascribed the song mainly to Paul, though he agreed that he had worked on it. In 1971, he said, "Paul. I helped with some of the lyric." And, "Paul's song. Maybe I did part of it, but it was his concept," he remembered in 1980. In an undated interview, he stated that he "contributed to the Mystery Tour song."[43]

Thus it looks like the music and beginning of the song were written by Paul, and the lyrics were collaborative, with John, then all of the Beatles (and Beatle insiders?) contributing phrases and ideas.

- **Fool on the Hill — (McCartney) (lead vocals: Paul) (recorded September 25, 1967)**

In 1995, Paul remembered writing the music for "Fool": "I was sitting at the piano at my father's house in Liverpool hitting a D 6th chord, and I made up 'Fool On The Hill.' There were some good words in it, 'perfectly still,' I liked that, and the idea that everyone thinks he's stupid appealed to me, because they still do."[44]

Davies records that in mid-March 1967 (during the *Sgt. Pepper* sessions), Paul played it for John for the first time. The lyrics weren't yet complete.[45]

Both Paul and John ascribe this to Paul. In 1980, John praised its lyric and its sense of completeness.[46]

---

[42] Miles, *Many Years from Now*, 352. Barkers at carnivals had shouted "Roll up! Roll up!" from time immemorial, but Paul said there was also the double meaning of rolling a joint in it. For the history of fairgrounds, see The Dingles Fairground Heritage Center website.
[43] Badman, *Beatles Off the Record*, 310.
[44] Miles, *Many Years from Now*, 365-66. See also Hilburn, "From 'Yesterday' to Today" (1989). Turner, *A Hard Day's Write*, 143–144, suggests that a mystical experience Paul and Alistair Taylor had on Primrose Hill led to the song. However, Taylor does not link the experience to "Fool on the Hill." *Yesterday*, 167-68. In addition, Taylor dates the mystical experience to the time after Paul broke up with Jane Asher (mid-1968), but Paul started writing the song in 1967.
[45] Davies, *The Beatles*, 268.

Paul recorded a demo version on September 6, 1967, now available on *Anthology 2*.

- **Flying — (McCartney-Lennon-Harrison-Starkey) (recorded September 8, 1967)**

This song, originally called "Aerial Tour Instrumental," was the Beatles' first released instrumental since "Cry Like a Shadow" in the Hamburg-Tony Sheridan era. I've found one firsthand comment on the creation of this song. According to Paul, he asked the Beatles to make up an instrumental filler in the studio. He even called it a "non-song."

> In the studio one night I suggested to the guys that we make something up. I said, "We can keep it very very simple, we can make it a twelve-bar blues. We need a little bit of a theme and a little bit of a backing." I wrote the melody. The only thing to warrant it as a song is basically the melody, otherwise it's just a nice twelve-bar backing thing. It's played on the Mellotron, on a trombone setting. It's credited to all four, which is how you would credit a non-song.[47]

However, since Paul wrote the melody, and it was his idea, he is the dominant contributor.

The first take ended with a jazz instrumental, a recording on the Mellotron. This was replaced by a long ending of tape loops and special effects, created by the unlikely creative combination of John and Ringo, according to Lewisohn. This version of the song — 9:36 in length — was edited down to 2:14, as found on the final recording.[48]

---

[46] Sheff, *The Playboy Interviews*, 195-96, 208. See also Hennessey, "Who Wrote What," *Record Mirror*.

[47] Miles, *Many Years from Now*, 364.

[48] Lewisohn, *Beatles Recording Sessions*, 123, 127.

- **Blue Jay Way — (Harrison)**
  (lead vocals: George) (recorded September 6–7 and October 6, 1967)

Strangely enough, the lyrics to this song are autobiographical. After arriving at Los Angeles on August 1, 1967, George, with his wife and Neil Aspinall, arrived at a rented house on a street named Blue Jay Way in the Hollywood Hills. Derek Taylor, the Beatles' press officer, was going to meet them there, and though George was exhausted, he decided to stay awake till Derek arrived. But he was delayed, lost in the foggy back-streets of L.A. George said, in 1968,

> I waited and waited. I felt really nackered with the flight, but I didn't want to go to sleep until he came. There was a fog and it got later and later. To keep myself awake, just as a joke to fill in the time, I wrote a song about waiting for him in Blue Jay Way. There was a little Hammond organ in the corner of this rented house which I hadn't noticed. I messed around on this and the song came.[49]

From this prosaic situation came a rather outré, Indian-flavored song.

- **Your Mother Should Know — (McCartney)**
  (lead vocals: Paul) (recorded August 22, 23 and September 16, 29, 1967)

Paul wrote this at Cavendish Avenue, on a harmonium in his dining room, when his Aunty Jin (of "I've Just Seen a Face" and "Let 'Em In" fame) and Uncle Harry were visiting. Their presence inspired him to write a song against the generation gap — the opposite of the Who's "My Generation."

> I dreamed up "Your Mother Should Know" as a production number. . . . It's a very music-hall kind of thing . . . I've always hated generation gaps. . . . In "Your Mother Should

---

[49] Davies, *The Beatles*, 321-22. See also *I Me Mine*, 114; Somach et al., *Ticket to Ride*, 221 (Derek Taylor's account). Neil Aspinall in 1967 ("George's California Trip," 25).

Know" I was basically trying to say your mother might know more than you think she does. Give her credit.[50]

In 1971, John put this on a list of songs that Paul had written alone.[51]

o   I am the Walrus (Lennon)

See the "Hello Goodbye / I Am the Walrus" single, above.

SIDE TWO

o   Hello, Goodbye (McCartney)

See the "Hello Goodbye / I Am the Walrus" single, above.

o   Strawberry Fields Forever (Lennon-McCartney)

See the "Strawberry Fields Forever / Penny Lane" single, above.

o   Penny Lane (McCartney-Lennon)

See the "Strawberry Fields Forever / Penny Lane" single, above.

o   Baby, You're a Rich Man (Lennon-McCartney)

See the "All You Need is Love / Baby, You're a Rich Man" single, above.

o   All You Need Is Love (Lennon)

See the "All You Need is Love / Baby, You're a Rich Man" single, above.

"Christmas Time (Is Here Again)," from Christmas fan club disc, December 11, 1967

- Christmas Time (Is Here Again) — (Lennon-McCartney-Harrison-Starkey)
  (recorded on November 28, 1967)

Released only to members of the Beatles fan club on the annual Christmas record in 1967, this song was attributed to all the Beatles. It was

[50] Miles, *Many Years from Now*, 355.

[51] Hennessey, "Who Wrote What," *Record Mirror*. See also, Sheff, *The Playboy Interviews,* 208.

originally 6:17 seconds long, including spoken sections (only parts of which are on the Christmas record), but a three minute version was released as the B-side of the "Free as a Bird" CD single in 1995.[52]

Paul said, in 1989, that the Christmas records

> were ad-libbed. Hardly ever scripted. I mean, I think some of them are great. It developed each year, we thought, "Well, we can't do that, we've said hello. So this year, let's make up a Christmas song." [*sings*] "Oh, Christmas Time Is Here Again." 'Cause we knew that the fans would like anything that was just exclusive for them.[53]

It is not known whether any of the Beatles dominated in the composition of this song.

---

[52] Unterberger, *The Unreleased Beatles*, 185-86.
[53] Read, "McCartney on McCartney," episode 4.

12

"I was going humity-humity in my head and the songs were coming out"

THE BEATLES (THE WHITE ALBUM)

Most of the songs we have covered so far were written in England, in the homes of the Beatles, or during tours or vacations. Most of the White Album songs were written in the most exotic locale imaginable — Rishikesh, at the foot of the Himalayas, in northern India, from February to March 1968, as the Beatles attended a Transcendental Meditation training camp at the ashram of Maharishi Mahesh Yogi. Which is one more example of how much George's Indian leanings had influenced the whole group. A number of other celebrities were attending: actress Mia Farrow, her sister Prudence, Donovan, and Mike Love of the Beach Boys. All would impact the White Album, in different ways.

The White Album songs represent an important development in the Lennon-McCartney songwriting relationship: there is much more complete ownership of songs on this album than on previous albums — in other words, in previous albums often a song was a Paul song or a John song, but the other songwriter helped finish it. Only occasionally a song might be all Paul or all John. However, in *The Beatles*, most "Lennon-McCartney" songs were either all Lennon or all McCartney. In fact, John later regarded this as not even a Beatle album, but as the first album after the real Beatles breakup.[1] Both John and George Martin agree that *The Beatles* marked a point of much less collaboration among the Beatles, both in songwriting and recording. There were still a few collaborative songs — such as "Glass Onion" and "Birthday" — but they were in the minority.

---

[1] Wenner, *Lennon Remembers*, 24.

218

On the other hand, the album represents an upsurge in creativity, judging by the quantity of songs alone. While these songs were mostly written in the peace of the Transcendental Meditation sessions in India, they were often recorded in the midst of intra-Beatle conflict. Sometimes all the Beatles were not present during a particular song session, but when they were present bitter arguments often took place. In fact, engineer Geoff Emerick abruptly quit one day, depressed by the expletive-filled, non-stop back and forth. John had found a new partner, Yoko Ono, and he often introduced her into recording sessions, which was another source of tension, and it was often hard to communicate with him due to his use of drugs at the time.

John regarded the White Album as his return to productivity after a couple years of lying "fallow." The stay at the ashram gave the Beatles time to write without distractions.[2] "I was going humity-humity in my head and the songs were coming out. For creating it was great. It was just pouring out!"[3]

John also felt that the White Album was better than the previous two albums:

> Paul was always upset about the White Album. He never liked it because on that one I did my music, he did his, and George did his. And first, he didn't like George having so many tracks. He wanted it to be more a group thing, which really means more Paul. So he never liked that album, and I always preferred it to all the other albums, including *Pepper*, because I thought the music was better. The Pepper myth is bigger, but the music on the White Album is far superior, I think. *Q: That's your favorite, of all the Beatle albums?* Yeah, because I wrote a lot of good shit on that. I like all the stuff

---

[2] Sheff, *The Playboy Interviews*, 197, 199-200. Wenner, *Lennon Remembers*, 24.
[3] As cited in Goldman, *The Lives of John Lennon*, 350, paperback edition.

I did on that, and the other stuff as well. I like the whole album.[4]

Whether or not Paul disliked the album, as John contended, he contributed many memorable songs to it, from full-tilt rockers such as "Back in the U.S.S.R" and "Helter Skelter" to the haunting folk ballads "I Will," "Mother Nature's Sun" and "Blackbird."

George Martin felt it was an album in which the individual Beatles "tended to go off in their own directions," after the death of Brian Epstein on August 27, 1967. And he felt it varied widely in quality, due to quantity of songs supplied.[5] Some songs might have been left off the final recording, but it would not be easy to reach a consensus on which ones should have stayed and which should have been deep-sixed. The album has been recognized as a masterpiece,[6] including many songs by Lennon and McCartney at the top of their form, and also four top-drawer Harrison songs, including two really great songs, "While My Guitar Gently Weeps" and "Long Long Long."

After they came home from India, the Beatles met at George's home, Kinfauns, in Esher, a suburb of London, in late May 1968, and made rough demos of the new songs (called either the Kinfauns demos or the Esher demos).[7] Some of these demos were released on *Anthology 3*. Aside from the White Album songs, a number of songs from later Beatle albums and solo albums were written during this period, such as George's "Not Guilty," Paul's "Junk" and "Teddy Boy," Lennon's "Look at Me" and "Jealous Guy" (with different lyrics). In more ways than one, the White Album harked forward to the Beatles' solo careers.

---

[4] McCabe and Schonfeld, interview with John Lennon, Sept. 5, 1971.

[5] George Martin, Interview.

[6] See chapter 16, below, on polls, for the White Album's reputation and standing.

[7] Winn, *That Magic Feeling*, 169.

"Step Inside Love / I Couldn't Take My Eyes Off You" single — Cilla Black, March 8, 1968

- Step Inside Love — (McCartney)
  (recorded on February 28, 1968)

Cilla Black was starting a TV show in early 1968, produced by Michael Hurll, and she and Hurll approached Paul backstage one night and asked him to write a song for the show. "So I said yes," said Paul. "I did a little demo of it, with myself double-tracked, up at Cavendish, and that was it. I quite like the song, it's very cabaret, it suited her voice. It was just a welcoming song for Cilla."[8]

Cilla, herself, seems to portray Paul as hoping to write the theme song for the TV show: "Paul said he'd like to write a signature theme for my television series *Cilla* at the beginning of 1968."[9] Apparently, at first Paul wrote only the tune and first verse. "He wrote enough for the TV show itself," said Cilla. This was used for the first few weeks of the show, but before too long Cilla and Hurll asked for the complete song, and he gave her more lyrics.[10] Hurll remembered that

> Paul came over to the BBC Theatre in Shepherd's Bush and sat with me and Cilla and worked on a second verse. It started off with the line, 'You look tired, love', because Cilla was tired after a lot of rehearsing and most of what he wrote related to what was going on that day.[11]

Paul added a third verse, and Paul and Cilla recorded a demo of the finalized song on November 21, 1967.[12] When the complete song was rec-

---

[8] Miles, *Many Years From Now*, 181.

[9] Cilla Black before 1970 (Aldridge, *Beatles Illustrated Lyrics*, 154). Du Noyer, *Conversations*, 188-89.

[10] Cilla Black before 1970 (Aldridge, *Beatles Illustrated Lyrics*, 154).

[11] Turner, *A Hard Day's Write*, 215.

[12] Winn, *That Magic Feeling*, 136.

orded, Paul "came to all the band calls," said Black, "just to look after the backing."[13] The song reached number eight in Britain.

Both Paul and John agreed that this was a Paul song.[14] The Beatles did an informal version of it on September 16, 1968, during the White Album sessions, and this can be heard on *Anthology 3*.

   o   I Couldn't Take My Eyes Off You (Bobby Willis, Clive Westlake)

"Lady Madonna / The Inner Light" single, March 15, 1968

- Lady Madonna — (McCartney-Lennon)
  (lead vocals: Paul) (recorded on February 3 and 6, 1968)

One day at Cavendish, Paul sat down at the piano and tried to write "a bluesy boogie-woogie thing." He began playing an "an ascending boogie-woogie left hand," "an arpeggio thing," against a descending right hand. The song reminded him of Fats Domino, so he started singing in that style.[15]

The song may have also been influenced by "Bad Penny Blues," by the Humphrey Lyttleton band, a jazz recording produced by George Martin in 1956. In a 1968 interview, Ringo said, "Paul plays piano on it [Lady Madonna]. What he's doing on piano is a sort of 'Bad Penny Blues.' We said to George Martin, 'How did they do it on 'Bad Penny Blues'?"[16] In 1989, Paul admitted that this influence was possible, as "Bad Penny Blues" had been a favorite record of the early Beatles, but he then downplayed that possibility, instead pointing to Fats Domino as an influence.[17]

The words are Paul's ode to "all women": "How do they do it? — bless 'em — it's that one, you know. Baby at your breast, how do they get

---

[13] Cilla Black before 1970 (Aldridge, *Beatles Illustrated Lyrics*, 154).

[14] John: "Who Wrote What," *Record Mirror*; Sheff, *The Playboy Interviews*, 208.

[15] Miles, *Many Years from Now*, 449.

[16] Walsh, "Will the real Richard Starkey please stand up?"

[17] Read, "McCartney on McCartney," episode 4.

the time to feed them? Where do you get the money? How do you do this thing that women do?" he asked, in 1986.[18] A photo of a Malayo-Polynesian woman with three small children gave Paul the original inspiration for the song. He apparently thought of the Virgin Mary, then "working-class woman," then everywoman, an amalgamation of the Madonna and ordinary working-class women.[19]

John, in 1971, put this in a list of songs that Paul wrote alone.[20] Ringo also attributed it to Paul.[21] In 1980, John ascribed it to Paul, but said that he "maybe" helped with some of the lyrics.[22] Mal Evans and Neil Aspinall also seemed to reflect some collaboration, stating that Paul had "done most of the words and music for this item."[23]

- **The Inner Light — (Harrison-*Tao Te Ching*-Mascaró) (lead vocals: George) (recorded on January 12, February 6 and 8, 1968)**

On September 29, 1967, George and John appeared on the David Frost show to discuss Transcendental Meditation, and a Sanskrit translator from Cambridge University, Juan Mascaró, was included in a panel of experts. Later Mascaró wrote a letter to George, praising "Within You Without You," and sent him his book, *Lamps of Fire* (1958), suggesting that George write a song from the Chinese mystical text, *Tao Te Ching*, the words on page 66 of the book. George obliged, using those words to create the lyrics for this song.[24] In Legge's translation, the *Tao Te Ching* reads:

---

[18] Salewicz, "Tug of War," 67.

[19] "Paul McCartney Reveals." Miles, *Many Years from Now*, 449. According to Richie Havens, the song came from a picture of an African woman. Somach, *Ticket to Ride*, 261.

[20] Hennessey, "Who Wrote What," *Record Mirror*.

[21] Badman, *Beatles Off the Record*, 344.

[22] Sheff, *The Playboy Interviews*, 211.

[23] Evans and Aspinall, "New Single Sessions," 11.

[24] See Harrison, *I Me Mine*, 118; Harrison in Badman, *Beatles Off the Record*, 345; Everett II, 152; Dowlding, *Beatlesongs*, 202. Mascaro, *Lamps of Fire: the Spirit of Religions* (1958). *Tao Te Ching*, verse 48 (sometimes 47). For Paul's comments on the song, Aldridge, *Illustrated Lyrics*, 108; Badman, *Beatles Off the Record*, 345.

Without going outside his door,
one understands (all that takes place) under the sky;
without looking out from his window,
one sees the Tao of Heaven.
The farther that one goes out (from himself),
the less he knows.
Therefore the sages got their knowledge without travelling;
gave their (right) names to things without seeing them;
and accomplished their ends without any purpose of doing so.

After telling this story, George said, in 1980, "The song was written especially for Juan Mascaró because he sent me the book and is a sweet old man. It was nice, the words said everything. *Amen*."[25]

"Sour Milk Sea / The Eagle Laughs at You" single — Jackie Lomax, August 26, 1968 (U.S.), September 6, 1968 (U.K.)

- **Sour Milk Sea — (Harrison)**
  (recorded on June 24–26, 1968)

This was written in India, and Harrison recorded it in May 1968, as one of the Kinfauns demos.[26] George said that in Tantric cosmology, the central continent, Jambudvipa is surround by oceans, the "sour milk sea." "I used 'Sour Milk Sea' as the idea of — if you're in the shit, don't go around moaning about it: do something about it."[27] It was also a song about meditation.

The Beatles had founded Apple in January 1968, and began recruiting recording artists. They signed Jackie Lomax, an old friend they had known in Liverpool, in early 1968, and George Harrison ended up producing this

---

[25] *I Me Mine*, 118.

[26] Unterberger, *The Unreleased Beatles*, 349. Harrison, *I Me Mine*, 142.

[27] Harrison, *I Me Mine*, 142.

single, and Lomax's album, *Is This What You Want?* (released in March 1969), which included "Sour Milk Sea."[28] Geoff Emerick engineered the "Sour Milk Sea" session, and was impressed with Harrison's talents as a producer.[29] Ringo played drums, Paul bass, Eric Clapton guitar.

   ○   <u>The Eagle Laughs at You (Jackie Lomax)</u>

"Hey Jude / Revolution" single, August 30, 1968

- Hey Jude — (McCartney)
(lead vocals: Paul) (recorded July 31 to August 2, 1968)

This McCartney song reflects the intertwined stories of Paul, John, John's first wife, Cynthia, their son Julian, and John's second wife, Yoko. John had met Yoko on November 9, 1966, and gradually developed a serious relationship with her. John went to India with Cynthia from February to April, 1968, but wrote songs for Yoko when he was there. He and Cynthia separated in about May 1968, John moving out of Kenwood and starting to live with Yoko.

Paul wrote "Hey Jude" after this separation. He had always been good friends with Cynthia, and was very fond of Julian, so he drove out to Kenwood to visit them. "I happened to be driving out to see Cynthia Lennon," he said in 1973. "I think it was just after John and she had broken up, and I was quite mates with Julian. He's a nice kid, Julian." As he drove, he turned off the radio and began "just vaguely singing this song, and it was like 'Hey Jules.'"[30] "You know, Don't be too brought down by this

---

[28] For Lomax, see Engelhart, *Beatles Undercover*, 248-50.

[29] *Here, There and Everywhere*, 242. Everett II, 199.

[30] Gambaccini, "The Rolling Stone Interview," also Gambaccini, *Paul McCartney In His Own Words*, 24. Paul's earliest comment on the songwriting is similar: "It was going to be 'Hey Jules,' but it changed. I was driving down to Weybridge one day to see Cynthia and Julian and I just started singing 'Hey Jules, don't make it bad' and then I changed it to 'Hey Jude.'" Aldridge, *The Beatles Illustrated Lyrics*, 49. See also Cynthia Powell Lennon, who remembered, "During the divorce proceedings, I was truly surprised when, one afternoon, Paul arrived on his own. I was touched by his obvious concern for our wel-

divorce, lad. It'll be all right kind of style. And I'd basically written that on my own."[31]

He later finished the song at Cavendish, changing the title to "Hey Jude."[32]

When Paul first played the song for John, he "took it very personally," as John remembered in 1968. "'Ah, it's me,' I said, 'It's me.' He [Paul] says, 'No, it's me.' I said, 'Check. We're going through the same bit.' So we all are."[33]

Paul said that John contributed to the lyrics by keeping him from changing the line, "The movement you need is on your shoulder." When he played the song for John and Yoko, he said in 2007, "I turned round to John and said: 'I'll fix that if you want.' And he said: 'You won't, you know, that's a fucking great line, that's the best line in it.'" So it stayed.[34]

Paul's girlfriend at the time, Francie Schwartz, claimed that the song was about Paul and her. "'Hey Jude' was 'our song', written and rewritten while I lived with Paul. I know it, he knows it, and now, you do," she said.[35]

The ending melody, repeated at length, was not a song fragment added on but an integral part of the song. Paul said, "The end refrain . . .

---

fare. . . . On the journey down he composed 'Hey Jude' in the car. He said it was for Julian. I will never forget Paul's gesture of care and concern in coming to see us." *The Beatles for the Record*, 64.

[31] Read, "McCartney on McCartney," episode 4 (1989). See also, *Anthology*, 297.

[32] Miles, *Many Years From Now*, 465.

[33] Cott, "The Rolling Stone Interview" (1968). Also Hennessey, "Who Wrote What," *Record Mirror.* Transcript by Sauter, "One John Lennon"; see also Sheff, *The Playboy Interviews*, 196.

[34] Doherty, "Pete Doherty meets Paul McCartney." See also Gambaccini, "The Rolling Stone Interview," and Gambaccini, *Paul McCartney In His Own Words*, 23. Miles, *Many Years From Now*, 465. *Anthology*, 297.

[35] Fontenot, "Francie Schwartz: The About.com Interview," (1999), p. 4. She said she heard Paul "rewriting Jude on the piano for several WEEKS." John also thought the song was about Paul and Francie, Lost Lennon Tapes, Sept. 16, 1991, cf. Sheff, *The Playboy Interviews*, 196. Paul and Jane Asher had broken up in summer 1968.

wasn't intended to go on that long at the end but I was having such fun ad-libbing over the end when we put down the original track that I went on for a long time. So then we built it with the orchestra."[36]

Both Paul and John ascribed this to Paul. He said, in 1989, "That was basically my song."[37] In 1980, John praised its lyrics and said he did not contribute to it.[38] As often in the Beatle songs, we apparently have arrived at great clarity. But then — according to Mal Evans, in 1968, this song was collaborative:

> "Hey Jude" is a more recent number [than 'Revolution,' written in India], based on one of Paul's ideas, but worked on with much joint effort from both John and Paul before it reached the recording studios. . . . On Friday, July 26, John and Paul spent most of the day at Paul's house putting the final touches to their latest composition, "Hey Jude."[39]

Evans's statements are impressively contemporaneous. But John and Paul's statements are more firsthand, so I accept them. I think it is probable that John and Yoko came to Paul's house and Paul simply performed the song for them, or played a demo, and asked for comments, and Evans assumed they had been collaborating.

---

[36] Miles, *Many Years From Now*, 466.

[37] Read, "McCartney on McCartney," episode 4.

[38] Sheff, *The Playboy Interviews*, 151. See also Lost Lennon Tapes, Sept. 16, 1991, cf. Sheff, *The Playboy Interviews*, 196, in which he described the song as one of Paul's "masterpieces." Asked if he contributed to it, he replied, "I don't think I had anything to do with it." Hennessey, "Who Wrote What," *Record Mirror*: "Paul. That's his best song." See also George Harrison in *Anthology*, 297, and George Martin in Badman, *Beatles Off the Record*, 381.

[39] Evans, "The Eighteenth Single," 6, 8.

Chapter 12

- **Revolution — (Lennon)**
  (lead vocal: John) (fast version, recorded on July 9-13, 1968)

This is the second, hard rock recording of this song. "Revolution 1," on the White Album, is the slower, original recording.

John wrote "Revolution" in India,[40] and hoped to make it a single, to give the Beatles a political voice, and put them on record as opposing the Vietnam War. "When George and Paul and all of them were on holiday, I made 'Revolution,' which is on the LP, and 'Revolution No. 9,'" he said in 1970.[41]

However, Paul and George didn't think the slow version of this song would work as a single.[42] So John decided to do a faster, hard rock version, which became the B-side of the "Hey Jude" single. This story, Paul and John objecting to "Revolution" as a slow song, is odd, as "Hey Jude," the A-side, is a slowish rock ballad. One could understand political objections better.

John claimed this song: "Completely me," he said in 1980.[43] Paul, in 1995, stated, "It was a great song, basically John's. . . . I don't think he was sure which way he felt about it at the time, but it was an overtly political song about revolution."[44] I conclude that this is a full Lennon song.

———————◦○◦———————

---

[40] Frederick James, "Revolution Report" (1968), 6-8; Mal Evans, "The Eighteenth Single" (1968), 6. It is one of the Kinfauns demos.

[41] Lennon, Rolling Stone Interview, Dec. 1970, BBC, part 4; Wenner, *Lennon Remembers*, 110. This is an odd statement, as both "Revolution 1" and "Revolution" were recorded with the full group, and "Revolution No. 9" was recorded with George and Ringo.

[42] Sheff, *The Playboy Interviews*, 196-97. George never did warm up to "Revolution," *Anthology*, 298.

[43] Sheff, *The Playboy Interviews*, 196-97. Also: Hennessey, "Who Wrote What," *Record Mirror*. "Me. I should never have put that in about Chairman Mao."

[44] Miles, *Many Years from Now*, 484-85.

"Thingumybob / Yellow Submarine" single —
Black Dyke Mills Band, September 6, 1968

- Thingumybob — (McCartney)
  (recorded on June 30, 1968)

In this song, a brass band instrumental, Paul returned to his northern heritage. In 2000, he said, "I was also asked to write the theme tune for a London Weekend Television series that Stanley Holloway was going to be in, called Thingumybob. I've always loved brass bands, so I wrote and produced a song for the Black Dyke Mills Band."[45] In northern England, mills and factories would each have a band, and these would compete. The Black Dyke Mills Band had won that year.[46] Bands are "a roots thing for me," Paul said, "my dad's type of music."[47]

They recorded the song up north, in Saltaire, near Bradford. They did "Yellow Submarine" in a big hall, but, Paul said, "For the A side, I wanted a really different sound so we went out and played it on the street. It was lovely, with very dead trumpety sounding cornets."[48]

- o Yellow Submarine

See *Revolver* album, above.

Wonderwall Music album — George Harrison, November 1, 1968

In 1968 Joe Massot asked George Harrison to do the music for his movie *Wonderwall*, about a man peeping through a wall at a model living next door, and becoming obsessed with her. "I don't know how to do mu-

---

[45] *Anthology*, 289. See also Derek Taylor, Press Release, "Thingumybob," in *Scraping the Barrel: An Apple Singles Collection Catalogue*.
[46] Peter Asher, as quoted in Unterberger, *The Unreleased Beatles*, 349. Engelhart, *Beatles Undercover*, 58.
[47] Miles, *Many Years from Now*, 24, see also 458. McCartney 1968, see [no author], "Paul Joins Band" and Pearson, "Paul's Shout Up at Shipley."
[48] *Anthology*, 289.

sic for films," George protested, and Massot replied that he would use whatever music George gave him. George agreed, and decided he would do the score as a "mini-anthology of Indian music" to popularize Indian music.[49]

The album was recorded in London in December 1967, with English performers, and in Bombay, India, in January 1968, with Indian performers. The London songs were performed by Eric Clapton and Ringo Starr, under pseudonyms, and session musicians, the Remo Four, a Liverpool group. The London songs are by George, but the Indian songs are traditional Indian pieces. He did not play on any of them.

Wonderwall premiered at Cannes on May 17, 1968.

- **Microbes**

  Recorded in India.

- **Red Lady Too**

  Recorded in England.

- **Tabla and Pakavaj**

  Recorded in India.

- **In the Park**

  Recorded in India.

- **Drilling a Home**

  Recorded in England.

- **Guru Vandana**

  Recorded in India.

- **Greasy Legs**

  Recorded in India.

---

[49] George Harrison (liner notes for *Wonderwall* CD). See also White, "George Harrison Reconsidered" (1987), 56.

- **Ski-ing**

  Recorded in England.

- **Gat Kirwani**

  Recorded in India.

- **Dream Scene**

  Recorded in England.

SIDE TWO

- **Party Seacombe**

  Recorded in England.

- **Love Scene**

  Recorded in India.

- **Crying**

  Recorded in India.

- **Cowboy Music**

  Recorded in England.

- **Fantasy Sequins**

  Recorded in India.

- **On the Bed**

  Recorded in India.

- **Glass Box**

  Recorded in England.

- **Wonderwall to Be Here**

  Recorded in England.

- **Singing Om**

  Recorded in India.

Unfinished Music No.1: Two Virgins **album — John Lennon and Yoko Ono, November 11, 1968 (US) November 29, 1968 (UK)**
(recorded on May 19, 1968)

This is experimental music, with no real composed songs. It continues the tape loop style of "Revolution 9." John said,

> Well, after Yoko and I met, I didn't realize I was in love with her. I was still thinking it was an artistic collaboration, as it were — producer and artist, right? . . . My ex-wife was away . . . and Yoko came to visit me. . . . we went upstairs and made tapes. I had this room full of different tapes where I would write and make strange loops and things like that for the Beatles' stuff. So we made a tape all night. She was doing her funny voices and I was pushing all different buttons on my tape recorder and getting sound effects.[50]

Paul said, in 1994, in his letter to John, "After that I set up a couple of Brennell recording machines we used to have and you stayed up all night and recorded *Two Virgins*."[51]

———————————◦◦◦———————————

The Beatles **(*White Album*), November 22, 1968**

- **Back in the U.S.S.R. — (McCartney)**
  (lead vocals: Paul) (recorded August 22–23, 1968)

Paul wrote this in India as a parody of Chuck Berry's "Back in the U.S.A." In 1968, he said that the track, "just sort of came. Chuck Berry once did a song called 'Back In The U.S.A.,' which is very American, very Chuck Berry. Very sort of, uhh . . . you know, you're serving in the army

---

[50] John Borack, *John Lennon: Music, Memories, and Memorabilia*, 110, citing Sheff's interview with John.

[51] Letter to John on John's Induction.

— And when I get back home I'm gonna kiss the ground."[52] He also said that the song was "a kind of Beach Boys parody. . . . I just liked the idea of Georgia girls and talking about places like the Ukraine as if they were California, you know? It was also hands across the water, which I'm still conscious of."[53]

Adding to these two influences was Jerry Lee Lewis: "I remember trying to sing it in my Jerry Lee Lewis voice, to get my mind set on a particular feeling. We added Beach Boy style harmonies."[54] So this song is actually a complex combination of early rock influences.

According to Mike Love, he (Love) suggested that Paul talk about girls all over Russia:

> I was sitting at the breakfast table and McCartney came down with his acoustic guitar and he was playing "Back in the USSR," and I told him that what you ought to do is talk about the girls all around Russia, the Ukraine and Georgia. He was plenty creative not to need any lyrical help from me but I gave him the idea for that little section.[55]

So this song that is in part a Beach Boys pastiche was actually influenced by a Beach Boy.

In 1971 John wondered if he helped a bit on this, but doubted it: "Paul. Maybe I helped a bit, but I don't think so."[56] And in 1980, he said, "Paul completely."[57]

[52] McCartney, Interview, Radio Luxembourg, Nov. 21, 1968. Miles, *Many Years from Now*, 422-23.

[53] Goodman, "Paul and Linda McCartney Interview," *Playboy* (1984), 110.

[54] Miles, *Many Years from Now*, 422-23. Du Noyer, *Conversations*, 32.

[55] As quoted in Miles, *Many Years from Now*, 422.

[56] Hennessey, "Who Wrote What," *Record Mirror*.

[57] Sheff, *The Playboy Interviews*, 198.

Chapter 12

- **Dear Prudence — (Lennon)**
  (lead vocals: John) (recorded August 28–30, 1968)

John wrote this at Rishikesh when Prudence Farrow, Mia Farrow's sister, would not come out of her hut for three weeks, and he and George were deputized to try to get her to come out.[58] So John wrote this song, "Dear Prudence, won't you come out and play." As Paul remembers, "We walked up to her chalet, a little delegation, and John sang it outside her door with his guitar. And she looked out, she improved after that."[59]

Prudence herself remembered the incident differently. "At the end of the meditation course in India, just as we were leaving," she said, "he mentioned that they had written a song about me, but I didn't hear it until it came out on the album. I was flattered by it."[60]

Donovan felt that this song was influenced by his folk "finger-style guitar method." John "wrote 'Dear Prudence' soon after learning the new style,"[61] he said.

All the best relevant sources view this as a John song.[62]

- **Glass Onion — (Lennon-McCartney)**
  (lead vocals: John) (recorded on September 11, 1968)

As he began this song, John had the idea of writing a "joke tune" which contained "all kinds of answers to the universe."[63] Then he brought

---

[58] Ibid., 208.

[59] Miles, *Many Years from Now*, 417. See also Read, "McCartney on McCartney," episode 4; *Anthology*, 284.

[60] Badman, *Off the Record*, 390. Naturally, Farrow's perspective is much more sympathetic to herself than is John's, see Farrow, *What Falls Away*, 139-40; Turner, *A Hard Day's Write*, 151-52. Patti Boyd Harrison also remembered the Beatles singing the song to Prudence, *Wonderful Tonight*, 117. Farrow, *What Falls Away*, 139-40, quotes Prudence as saying that John played the song to her, but was surprised when it appeared on an album.

[61] Donovan, *Uncut* interview (2005). See also Donovan, quoted in Unterberger, *The Unreleased Beatles*, 197.

[62] Lennon in Hennessey, "Who Wrote What," *Record Mirror* (1971); Mal Evans, "Thirty New Beatles Grooves," (1968), 12. Mia Farrow, *What Falls Away*, 139-40, remembered John and Paul writing this, but this can be discounted as secondhand.

it to a collaboration session with Paul, and they worked on it together. It referred back to enigmatic lines from earlier Beatles songs. Since many people had written to John, asking who the walrus was, John decided he would give the answer: the walrus would be Paul. Which caused John and Paul a "great giggle."[64] John remembered doing this partly as an act of generosity, because he felt guilty that he was starting a major relationship with Yoko and leaving Paul as a creative partner:

> At that time [I was] still in my love cloud with Yoko, I thought, well, you know, I'll just say something nice to Paul, that it's all right and 'You did a good job over these few years holding us together.' He was trying to organize the group and that; *and* do the music *and* be an individual artist and all that.[65]

Lennon claimed this song in 1971 and 1980.[66] But Paul had definite memories of collaborating on it. "John wrote the tune 'Glass Onion,' I mean he wrote it mainly, but I helped him on it," he said before 1979.[67] And in 1995, he asserted: "We still worked together, even on a song like 'Glass Onion' where many people think there wouldn't be any collaboration."[68]

I regard this as a song started by John, finished with collaboration.

---

[63] Paul, in Cowan, *Behind the Beatles Songs*, 21.

[64] Ibid.

[65] Lennon, Rolling Stone Interview, Dec. 1970, BBC, part 4; cf. Wenner, *Lennon Remembers*, 87. See also Sheff, *The Playboy Interviews*, 208-9.

[66] Hennessey, "Who Wrote What," *Record Mirror*; Sheff, *The Playboy Interviews*, 208-9. See also Mal Evans, "Thirty New Beatles Grooves," (1968), 12, "Mostly John's idea this one."

[67] As quoted in Cowan, *Behind the Beatles Songs*, 21.

[68] Miles, *Many Years from Now*, 537.

- **Ob-La-Di, Ob-La-Da — (McCartney-Scott)
(lead vocals: Paul) (recorded on July 3, 1968)**

A friend of Paul whom he knew in the clubs, Jimmy Scott, a Nigerian conga player, used to say, "'Ob-la-di, ob-la-da, life goes on."[69] Paul liked the phrase, and used it as the basis for the lyrics of this song. He developed it in India, achieving the chorus. "And it was very very pleasant; walking along in the dust slightly downhill through a path in the jungle from the meditation camp with my guitar and singing 'Ob-La-Di Ob-La-Da,' which I was writing, accompanying the process on the way."[70] Paul Saltzman remembered Paul and John repeating the chorus over and over again as they worked on the song.[71]

Then the verses started to come. Paul remembered singing "Desmond has a barrow in the marketplace" as he walked down a jungle path to see a movie in a nearby village.[72]

Both Paul and John remember this as a Paul song. In 1968, Paul, asked if he'd written the song alone, answered, "I think it was mainly me. Mainly me. (*jokingly*) John's a bit more Nigerian influenced." (*laughter*)"[73] Paul later sent Scott a check "because even though I had written the whole song and he didn't help me, it was his expression. It's a very *me* song, inasmuch as it's a fantasy about a couple of people who don't really exist."[74]

In 1971, John attributed the song directly to Paul.[75] But nine years later, he left open the possibility that he had contributed to the lyrics, saying

---

[69] Goodman, "Paul and Linda McCartney Interview," *Playboy*, (1984), 110. Miles, *Many Years from Now*, 419.

[70] Miles, *Many Years from Now*, 419.

[71] Saltzman, Excerpt on "Ob-La-Di Ob-La-Da."

[72] *Anthology*, 284.

[73] McCartney, Interview, Radio Luxembourg, Nov. 21, 1968.

[74] Miles, *Many Years from Now*, 419. See also Mal Evans, "The Eighteenth Single," (1968), 6; "Mal's Diary," (1968), 11.

[75] Hennessey, "Who Wrote What," *Record Mirror*.

"I might've given him couple of lyrics, but it's his song, his lyric."[76] In view of John's lack of certainty, I attribute this entirely to Paul.

John influenced the performance of the song in a major way. Evidently, Paul was playing it slower, and was requiring the Beatles to do the song over and over again in the studio. Finally, John, one day, lost patience, left, then hours later burst into the studio and yelled, 'I AM FUCKING STONED!!' 'I am more stoned than you have ever been. In fact, I am more stoned than you will ever be!' 'And this,' Lennon added with a snarl, 'is how the fucking song should go.' He lurched to the piano and played the opening chords for "Ob-la-di" at a breakneck speed. Paul accepted the new tempo and the piano introduction.[77]

Jimmy Scott's contribution to the song is significant — providing the title and the mantra of the chorus. This is not to deny that the essential magic of the music and lyrics are from McCartney, and Jimmy Scott's phrase never would have amounted to a song without Paul's eye for a good phrase and his musical talent. On the other hand, Paul's talent saw the phrase as charming and profound, in its way. It was "found poetry" — but does a found phrase, if it comes from another human being, amount to collaboration? Jimmy Scott thought it did, and Paul agreed with him enough to send him a check at one point.

- ## Wild Honey Pie — (McCartney)
  ### (lead vocals: Paul) (recorded August 20, 1968)

Paul was in an experimental mood after doing John's "Yer Blues," and he asked, "'Can I just make something up?' and was given permission. He made up this song in the studio, having fun with double-tracking, adding layers of harmony to it.

> It was very home-made; it wasn't a big production at all. I just made up this short piece and I multitracked a harmony

---

[76] Sheff, *The Playboy Interviews*, 208.
[77] Geoff Emerick, *Here There Everywhere*, 246-47. George Martin tells the story in a much more restrained fashion in Pritchard and Lysaght, *The Beatles: an Oral History*, 263. For the recording, see also Shotton and Schaffner, *The Beatles, Lennon and Me*, 348.

to that, and a harmony to that, and a harmony to that, and built it up sculpturally with a lot of vibrato on the strings, really pulling the strings madly. Hence "Wild Honey Pie," which was a reference to the other song I had written called "Honey Pie." It was a little experimental piece.[78]

This fragment (53 seconds long) nearly didn't make the cut for the final album, but Pattie Harrison liked it, so it survived.[79]

Turner reports that this came from a "spontaneous singalong in Rishikesh,"[80] which seems to conflict with Paul's explanation above, where it is something made up in the studio. The recording session records give support to Paul's story.[81]

- **The Continuing Story of Bungalow Bill — (Lennon) (lead vocals: John) (recorded on October 8, 1968)**

This song is based on an actual person at the ashram in India, a fellow "who . . . took a short break to go away and shoot a few poor tigers, and then came back to commune with God," as John said in 1980. He took the character Jungle Jim, changed the name to Buffalo Bill, then deformed that to Bungalow Bill. "It's a sort of teen-age social-comment song, it was a bit of a joke. Yoko's on that one, actually, I believe, singing along," John said.[82]

In 1995, Paul remembered John singing it at Rishikesh: "This is another of his great songs and it's one of my favorites to this day because it stands for a lot of what I stand for now. 'Did you have to shoot that tiger' is its message."[83]

---

[78] Miles, *Many Years from Now*, 497.

[79] Aldridge, *Beatles Illustrated Lyrics*, 218.

[80] *A Hard Day's Write*, 154.

[81] Lewisohn, *The Beatles Recording Sessions*, 150.

[82] Lost Lennon Tapes, Nov. 14, 1988, cf. Sheff, *The Playboy Interviews*, 209. Farrow, *What Falls Away*, 139.

[83] Miles, *Many Years from Now*, 421. Hennessey, "Who Wrote What," *Record Mirror*.

- **While My Guitar Gently Weeps — (Harrison)**
  (lead vocals: George) (recorded on September 5-6, 1968)

George wrote this song at his mother's house in Warrington,[84] using bibliomancy — the tried and true divinatory method of opening a book and accepting the first phrases you read as a revelation. He said, in 1980, "I picked up a book at random — opened it — saw 'Gently weeps' — than laid the book down again and started the song."[85] It is another example of "found poetry" in Beatle lyrics.

George said that because John and Paul were so prolific, he never felt secure bringing his own songs in and pushing to get them recorded. One night the Beatles were doing takes of "While My Guitar Gently Weeps" at the studio and George was disappointed at the lack of commitment and inspiration in these performances.

So the next day he brought in Eric Clapton to overdub the lead guitar part. Eric was nervous, thinking the Beatles might object, George remembered. "And I was saying, "Fuck 'em, that's my song."[86] Clapton's introduction into the studio caused everyone to "act better." Paul went to the piano and played an intro that George liked. Everyone took the song more seriously because of Clapton's presence.[87] So the stars aligned to produce a great performance of a great song.

- **Happiness is a Warm Gun — (Lennon-Taylor)**
  (lead vocals: John) (recorded on September 24-25, 1968)

For this cut, John simply combined three separately-composed songs. It was a natural solution to his problem of not finishing songs! "Oh yeah, I like that, one of my best," he said in 1970. "I just like all the different things that are happening in it. That was like 'God.' I put together three

---

[84] *Anthology*, 306.

[85] Harrison, *I Me Mine*, 120, see also Yorke, Interview with George Harrison.

[86] Glazer, "Growing Up at 33 1/3."

[87] *Anthology*, 306. Paul's memories of the session are substantially similar, ibid.

sections of different songs. But it was meant to be like — . . . it seemed to run through all the different kinds of rock music."[88]

In *Anthology*, John summarized each verse with a handwritten word: first verse, "Dirty old man." Second, "the junkie." Third, "the gunman."[89] Musically, the three sections are each defined by a different style of rock.

The first and third sections were based on found poetry. In fact, the first part came from random phrases shouted out by John's friends Derek Taylor, Neil Aspinall and Pete Shotton while everyone was relaxing in a rented house. John had told them that he needed to finish a song, then said, "Neil, take some notes, we'll get some stuff down. Think of phrases."[90] The first line came when John wanted to know how you described a girl who was really smart, and Derek remembered his father's phrase: "She's not a girl who misses much." After that the song continued in entirely surreal fashion, though each phrase has an explanation. According to Taylor, he supplied many of the lines.[91]

The second song was about Yoko ("Mother Superior") and heroin. John publicly denied that it was about the drug,[92] but his handwritten summary of this section, and the song's first line, "I need a fix cause I'm going down," are hard to ignore.

The third song came from the cover of an American gun magazine, which had the picture of a smoking gun that had just been shot. In an undated interview, John said, "I thought, 'Wow! Incredible,' you know, the fact that happiness was a warm gun that had just shot something or somebody and that's why I wrote that song."[93]

---

[88] Wenner, *Lennon Remembers*, 114. See also Badman, *Off the Record*, 392.

[89] *Anthology*, 307.

[90] Taylor in Somach et al., *Ticket to Ride*, 221.

[91] Derek Taylor, as quoted in Turner, *A Hard Day's Write*, 157.

[92] Lennon 1971 (*Anthology*, 306).

[93] Badman, *Off the Record*, 392. See also George Martin in Williams, "Produced by George Martin" (1971). Mal Evans in 1968 ("Thirty New Beatles Grooves," 12). Chris Thomas, in Pritchard and Lysaght, *The Beatles: An Oral History*, 266.

Both Paul and John ascribed this song to John. In 1971, John said, "They were advertising guns and I thought it was so crazy that I made a song out of it."[94] And in 1980, he affirmed, "Me completely."[95] Paul, in 1968, said, "And it was so sick, you know, the idea of 'Come and buy your killing weapons,' and 'Come and get it.' But it's just such a great line, 'Happiness Is A Warm Gun' that John sort of took that and used that as a chorus. And the rest of the words . . . I think they're great words, you know. It's a poem."[96] And in 1995, Paul explained,

> It's very similar to "Bungalow Bill" in that it's a piss-take of all the people who really do think happiness is a warm gun. There's a great vocal on it, good lyrics, and it's a very interesting song because it changes tempo a lot, it's quite a complex piece. It's very Lennon. . . . I was thinking the other day how poignant it was that John, who was shot in such tragic circumstances, should have written this song.[97]

While it seems clear that Paul was not involved in writing it, Derek Taylor apparently contributed substantially to it.

SIDE TWO

- **Martha My Dear — (McCartney)**
  (lead vocals: Paul) (recorded on October 4, 1968)

This song started as a piano exercise, an instrumental, in which Paul made the conscious effort to come up with something slightly above his "level of competence" as piano player.[98] When he tried to find some words

[94] Lennon (*Anthology*, 306). Hennessey, "Who Wrote What," *Record Mirror*. Badman, *Off the Record*, 392.
[95] Sheff, *The Playboy Interviews*, 199. Hennessey, "Who Wrote What," *Record Mirror* (1971): "Me. That's another one I like. They all said it was about drugs, but it was more about rock and roll than drugs. It's sort of a history of rock and roll."
[96] McCartney, Interview, Radio Luxembourg, Nov. 21, 1968.
[97] Miles, *Many Years from Now*, 497.
[98] Ibid., 497-98.

that fit the music, "Martha my dear, though I spend my days in conversation" suddenly came into his head. Martha was Paul's sheepdog, so, he said, "It's me singing to my dog." (*laughs*)[99] It turned into a "fantasy song," with fictional characters. The song was written in a way that was typical for Paul: he had a tune, and an accompaniment, then some words "came into [his] head."

Both Paul and John attributed it to Paul.[100]

"Martha My Dear" was recorded by Paul, without any of the other Beatles, on October 4, 1968. According to Alistair Taylor, it was written during the Magical Mystery Tour period.[101]

- **I'm So Tired — (Lennon)**
  (lead vocals: John) (recorded on October 8, 1968)

John wrote this, one of his autobiographical songs,[102] one night during a bout of insomnia after meditating all day with the Maharishi. And in an undated interview, he remembered, "The funny thing about the Maharishi camp was that, although it was very beautiful and I was meditating about eight hours a day, I was writing the most miserable songs on earth, like 'I'm So Tired' and 'Yer Blues.'"[103]

Both John and Paul ascribed it to John. In 1970 and 1980, John said he'd written it in India.[104] Jenny Boyd, Patti Harrison's sister, remembered John being unable to sleep, in India, and singing "those sad songs he wrote during those evenings, like 'I'm So Tired.'"[105]

Paul said, in 1995,

---

[99] McCartney, interview, Radio Luxembourg, Nov. 21, 1968.

[100] Hennessey, "Who Wrote What," *Record Mirror.* See also Sheff, *The Playboy Interviews*, 209.

[101] Taylor, *Yesterday*, 151. See also Winn, *That Magic Feeling*, 216.

[102] Wenner, *Lennon Remembers*, 12.

[103] Badman, *Beatles Off the Record*, 342.

[104] Wenner, *Lennon Remembers*, 12; Sheff, *The Playboy Interviews*, 209. See also Hennessey, "Who Wrote What," *Record Mirror* (1971).

[105] Badman, *Beatles Off the Record*, 341.

"So Tired" is very much John's comment to the world, and it has that very special line, "And curse Sir Walter Raleigh, he was such a stupid git." That's a classic line and it's so John that there's no doubt that he wrote it. I think it's 100 per cent John. Being tired was one of his themes.[106]

- ## Blackbird — (McCartney) (lead vocals: Paul) (recorded on June 11, 1968)

Strangely enough, this song started out as a piece by Bach. "The original inspiration was from a well-known piece by Bach," Paul said in 1995, "which I never know the title of, which George and I had learned to play at an early age."[107] Paul played it at his "Chaos and Creation at Abbey Road" concert, and it is the Bourrée in E minor, from Lute suite no. 1 BWV 996 (though, as Paul notes, he didn't play it correctly).[108] While at his farmhouse in Scotland, in spring 1968,[109] not long after returning from India, Paul began thinking of the Bach tune: "Bach was always one of our favourite composers ... I developed the melody on guitar based on the Bach piece and took it somewhere else, took it to another level."[110]

Having composed the music, he then added the lyrics. Just as John's "Revolution" had been a response to recent anti-war protests, this was a response to the civil rights movement in the United States.

I had in my mind a black woman, rather than a bird. Those were the days of the civil-rights movement, which all of us cared passionately about, so this was really a song from me to a black woman, experiencing these problems in the

---

[106] Miles, *Many Years from Now*, 421.

[107] Ibid., 485-86.

[108] Hilton, *Chaos and Creation at Abbey Road*. This may have been a Bach piece played by Chet Atkins, "Bourée," see Lewisohn, *Tune In*, 150.

[109] Chris Douridas, Interview with Paul McCartney, May 25, 2002; Everett II, 190. Paul had bought High Park Farm in Campbeltown near the Mull of Kintyre, Scotland on June 16, 1966.

[110] Miles, *Many Years from Now*, 485-86. Du Noyer, *Conversations*, 209.

states: "Let me encourage you to keep trying, to keep your faith, there is hope." As is often the case with my things, a veiling took place so, rather than say "Black woman living in Little Rock" and be very specific, she became a bird, became symbolic, so you could apply it to your particular problem. This is one of my themes: take a sad song and make it better, let this song help you.[111]

Paul claimed this song,[112] and John generally agreed.[113] However, in 1980, he said that he contributed a line to it.[114] I lean toward his earlier testimony.

• Piggies — (Harrison-Lennon-Harrison) (lead vocals: George) (recorded on September 19, 1968)

George Harrison wrote this, for the most part, and put most of the lyrics in a notebook. Years later, he resurrected it, and brought the unfinished song to John, who contributed "a couple of lines about forks and knives and eating bacon."[115] But there was still one gap, one line missing from the song's middle eight. So he turned to, of all people, his mother, Louise French Harrison, who provided the perfect line, "What they need's a damn good whacking!"[116]

---

[111] Ibid., 485-86. In a studio session for Mary Hopkins, about November 22, 1968, Paul told Donovan that he wrote this for blacks, after he "read something in the paper about riots and that." You Tube, "Paul McCartney Donovan -1968,1969," at 3:55.

[112] Miles, *Many Years from Now*, 485. See Paul's Nov. 21, 1968 Interview, Radio Luxembourg; *"Q: "Blackbird' I think is quite a beautiful song."* "Thank you, Tony."

[113] Hennessey, "Who Wrote What," *Record Mirror* (1971). See also George Martin in Pritchard and Lysaght, *The Beatles: An Oral History*, 264.

[114] Sheff, *The Playboy Interviews*, 209.

[115] Ibid., 210.

[116] Badman, *Off the Record*, 394. *I Me Mine* 126.

- ### Rocky Raccoon — (McCartney-Lennon-Donovan) (lead vocals: Paul) (recorded on August 15, 1968)

This song was written when Paul, John and Donovan were "sitting on a roof" at the Maharishi's ashram, playing together. "I started playing the chords of 'Rocky Raccoon,' you know, just messing around," Paul said in 1968. "We just started making up the words, you know, the three of us — and started just to write them down." The title was originally Rocky Sassoon, but Paul changed it to Raccoon "because it sounded more like a cowboy." Paul disavowed any actual knowledge of "the Appalachian mountains or cowboys and Indians or anything. But I just made it up, you know."[117]

Though John and Donovan helped, Paul stated, in 1995: "'Rocky Raccoon' is quirky, very me. I like talking-blues so I started off like that, then I did my tongue-in-cheek parody of a western and threw in some amusing lines . . . it's me writing a play."[118]

In 2008, Paul described it as a "pastiche" of the "George Formby sensibility" mixed with a spoof of folk music. (George Formby was a British singer and actor known for his comic songs.) "Rocky Raccoon was a freewheeling thing, the fun of mixing a folky ramble with Albert In The Lion's Den with its 'orse's 'ead 'andle,' ha ha.'"[119] (Comedian Stanley Holloway was well known for his rendition of the comic poem "The Lion and Albert," by Marriott Edgar.)

John, in 1971, couldn't remember this song very well: "Paul — I might have helped with some of the words. I'm not sure."[120] By 1980, he ascribed it completely to Paul.[121]

---

[117] Interview, Radio Luxembourg.

[118] Miles, *Many Years from Now*, 423. See also McCartney before 2003 (Quantick, *Revolution*, 114).

[119] Mat Smith, "Paul McCartney Speaks." According to author David Quantick, this was a parody of Robert W. Service's melodramatic poem, "The Shooting of Dan McGrew," which also has a Dan and a Lil. Quantick, *Revolution*, 114.

[120] Hennessey, "Who Wrote What," *Record Mirror*.

[121] Sheff, *The Playboy Interviews*, 199.

- **Don't Pass Me By — (Starkey)**
  (lead vocals: Ringo) (recorded on June 5, 1968)

Ringo, in 2000, remembered writing this at his home, on the piano. He was banging away at the piano, playing the three chords he knew, and the melody came, and some words.[122] According to some reports, Starr was working on this as far back as 1963, even before he joined the Beatles.[123] When he played it for the other Beatles, they reportedly went into hysterics, "and said it was a rewrite of a Jerry Lee Lewis B-side."[124]

However, just to show that song authorship with the Beatles is never straightforward, in June 1964, when John said the song was not finished, both Ringo and Paul asserted that it was finished, and Ringo said, "We finished it." (Not "*I* finished it.")

> **George:** But, as far as Ringo and I are concerned, we'll leave the songwriting to ... **Ringo:** Excuse me! Paul's gonna sing the one I've written! **Paul:** No, I can't re — I can't quite remember it. **Ringo:** Well, I'll get — just for a plug, Paul. **Paul:** But even so, we just — Ringo has written one called "Don't pass me by, don't make me cry, don't make me blue." A beautiful melody. Sincere, folks. . . . No, but you really — this is Ringo's first venture into songwriting. . . . **John:** Unluckily, there's never quite enough time to fit Ringo's songs on. Because he never finishes it! **Ringo:** It's finished! **Paul:** It's finished. **Ringo:** We finished it. **John:** After 18 years . . .[125]

---

[122] Kenny Everett, Interview with the Beatles, June 5, 1968.

[123] Everett, *Beatles as Musicians* I, 173, 206. Lewisohn, *Tune In*, 691. Ringo mentioned it in April 1964, Winn, *Way Beyond Compare*, 176.

[124] Lewisohn, *Tune In*, 691.

[125] The Beatles, Interview, Dunedin, June 26, 1964, Bob Rogers, New City Hotel. Winn, *Way Beyond Compare*, 210. See also Starr interview, unknown date, Badman, *Beatles Off the Record*, 370: "I have already recorded my song for the new LP."

Clearly, Paul knew something about the song being finished that John didn't. But he explicitly says that Ringo wrote it.

In a July 1964 Top Gear interview with the Beatles, Ringo when asked how his songwriting was going, and said, "Oh, yes, I've written a good one and nobody seems to want to record it." And once again, Paul sang the beginning of it.[126]

It's odd that Paul sang it (twice), and not Ringo. Possibly the drummer had brought it to Paul for help with arranging it.

When an interviewer brought up the Top Gear interview in 1992, Ringo said, "They [the Beatles] didn't help me at all writing it."

> *Q: You're listed as the author of "Don't Pass Me By."* I am the author of "Don't Pass Me By." *Q: But there's a tape of a BBC interview [Top Gear, July 14, 1964] where you and Paul noted that the two of you were working on your song "Don't Pass Me By."*[127] You sure that wasn't George. *Q: No, I'm pretty sure it was Paul.* Ok. Well, I don't remember Paul working on it. Paul would have said that as the band was working on it; he wasn't working on it as the writer.[128]

John said, in a 1968 interview, that the Beatles had just recorded "Ringo's first song that we're working on this very moment. *Q: He composed it himself?* He composed it himself in a fit of lethargy. *Q: And what do you think about it?* I think it's the most wonderful thing I've ever heard since Nilsson's 'River Deep Mountain Dew.'"[129]

In a 1964 interview, Ringo said that "his songwriting technique is to hum a tune to himself and let the others work out the chords on guitar."[130]

I accept that this is a pure Ringo song.

----

[126] Interview with the Beatles on the Top Gear program, July 14, 1964.

[127] This is not true, by my transcription of the Top Gear interview.

[128] Wiener, "Interview with Ringo Starr."

[129] Kenny Everett, Interview with the Beatles, June 5, 1968.

[130] Beatles, on *Ready Steady Go!* Nov. 23, 1964, see Winn, *Way Beyond Compare*, 286.

- **Why Don't We Do It in the Road — (McCartney)
(lead vocals: Paul) (recorded on October 9–10, 1968)**

In Rishikesh, Paul was on the ashram roof, meditating, one day, when he saw two monkeys copulating briefly. This led him to pose the question in this song, asking whether civilized rules are necessary. "And I thought, bloody hell, that puts it all into a cocked hat, that's how simple the act of procreation is, the bloody monkey just hopping on and hopping off.... And it's that simple. We have horrendous problems with it."[131]

Both Paul and John ascribed this to Paul. In 1968, after mentioning "I Will" and this song, Paul said, "Just completely different things — completely different feelings and . . . But it's me singing both of them. It's the same fella. Uhh, and I've wrote both of them, you know."[132]

But paradoxically, Paul described it as written in the Lennon style. "It was a very John sort of song anyway. That's why he liked it, I suppose. It was very John, the idea of it, not me. I wrote it as a ricochet off John."[133] John would sometimes sing it, and was offended when Paul recorded it without him (an example of how the Beatles were drifting apart during this album).[134] He later said, "Paul — one of his best."[135]

- **I Will — (McCartney)
(lead vocals: Paul) (recorded on September 16, 1968)**

As Paul tells the story, he had had the melody to this for a long time. "It's still one of my favorite melodies that I've written. You just occasionally get lucky with a melody and it becomes rather complete," he said in 1995.[136] He played it with Donovan and "maybe" a few others at Rishikesh, and he and Donovan began to think of lyrics for the song, but

---

[131] Miles, *Many Years from Now*, 499.

[132] Interview, Radio Luxembourg. For John, Sheff, *The Playboy Interviews,* 199.

[133] Davies, *The Beatles* (1981), 369.

[134] Ibid. Sheff, *The Playboy Interviews,* 199.

[135] Hennessey, "Who Wrote What," *Record Mirror.*

[136] Miles, *Many Years from Now*, 420.

they weren't quite satisfactory, for Paul. Finally, he wrote a new set of lyrics.[137]

Paul and John agreed, repeatedly, that this was written by Paul, and that John did not contribute to it. As we have seen, Paul said in 1968 that he wrote both this and "Why Don't We Do It."[138] John, in 1971, put it on a list of songs Paul wrote alone.[139]

John almost collaborated on the song. During the Get Back sessions, one day, when John was absent, Paul talked with Michael Lindsay-Hogg about songwriting with John and Yoko. Paul defended her somewhat, and explained that once he and John were trying to work on the last verse of "I Will," unsuccessfully, and Yoko tried to stay out of it. Finally, Paul did the last verse himself.[140]

This incident shows why and how Paul and John were collaborating less now. Their "Beatles family" was being replaced by Linda and Yoko.

- ## Julia — (Lennon-Ono-Donovan-Gibran) (lead vocals: John) (recorded on October 13, 1968)

John wrote this to his mother, Julia Stanley Lennon, after "opening up" about his feelings relating to her during Transcendental Meditation sessions. He also had Yoko in mind as he wrote it.[141]

While Paul did not contribute to "Julia," three other people did. First, John said in 1971 that Yoko "helped me with this one," so she both partially inspired the song and helped write it.[142] In the same year, John said, 'She had written other things, even 'Julia' back in the Beatles days."[143]

---

[137] Ibid.

[138] Interview, Radio Luxembourg. See also *Anthology*, 284.

[139] Hennessey, "Who Wrote What," *Record Mirror*. Similar: John in 1980, in Sheff, *The Playboy Interviews*, 209; Mal Evans in 1968, "Thirty New Beatles Grooves," 12.

[140] Paul, on January 13, 1969, available on YouTube. Cf. Sulpy, *Get Back*, 182.

[141] Donovan, as cited in Turner, *Hard Day's Write*, 163. Sheff, *The Playboy Interviews*, 199-200.

[142] Hennessey, "Who Wrote What," *Record Mirror*.

[143] Smith, "Lennon: Doing The Rounds For Publicity."

Then, Donovan said that he helped John with the words "a bit," after John asked him for help.[144] He also taught John the "finger-picking" method that is used on the song.[145]

Finally, some of the lyrics, including the opening lines, are from Kahlil Gibran's book of poetry, *Sand and Foam* (1926).[146]

Both John and Paul ascribed this gentle, lyrical song to John. "That was mine," said John in 1980.[147] And Paul, in 1995, said, "That was John's song about his mum, folk finger-picking style, and a very good song."[148]

SIDE THREE:

- **Birthday — (McCartney-Lennon)
  (lead vocals: Paul and John) (recorded on September 18, 1968)**

On the night of September 18, 1968, the Beatles wanted to see the movie *The Girl Can't Help It* on TV — it had a number of their early rock heroes performing, such as Little Richard, Gene Vincent and Fats Domino. In addition, a number of the Beatles' friends were present at the studio and the atmosphere was like a party. So instead of working on a detailed song or overdubs, Paul suggested that they just make up a song in the studio — a "useful song," like a birthday song. This would fit with the party atmosphere of the recording session.[149]

They recorded a very simple harmonic backing, and went to Paul's house to watch the movie. "Then we went back to the studio again and

---

[144] Donovan in 2005 (*Uncut* interview). See also Donovan, as cited in Turner, *Hard Day's Write*, 163. Leitch, *The Autobiography of Donovan*, 210. Donovan in 2005 (Leitch, "Poet John," 135).

[145] Donovan, in Unterberger, *The Unreleased Beatles*, 179, and in Turner, *Hard Day's Write*, 163.

[146] Everett II, 170.

[147] Sheff, *The Playboy Interviews*, 199-200.

[148] Miles, *Many Years from Now*, 422. See also, p. 48; Donovan in 1995 (as cited in Miles, *Many Years*, 421-22).

[149] Press Release, in Harry, *The Paul McCartney Encyclopedia*, "Birthday (single)." See also a 1990 interview, Baker, "Paul McCartney," 11.

made up some words to go with it all," Paul said in an early interview. "So this song was just made up in an evening. Umm, you know. We hadn't ever thought of it before then. And it's one of my favorites because of that."[150] Elsewhere, he remembered: "So we came up with this really simple lyric, put a riff in the middle, a little instrumental break and we got the crowd of guests there to sing along to the chorus."[151]

Paul described this song as a joint composition, improvised in the studio: "that is 50-50 John and me, made up on the spot," he said in 1995.[152] John, in 1971, seemed to agree: "Both of us. We wrote it in the studio."[153] However, both Paul and John remembered that writing the song was Paul's idea. "I think Paul wanted to write a song like 'Happy, Birthday Baby,' the old Fifties hit," John said.[154] So I accept that the song was Paul's idea, developed in collaboration.

However, if we turn to early insiders, such as Chris Thomas (the acting producer) and Mal Evans, Paul's contribution was more pronounced than 50-50. (And while insiders were generally not first-hand witnesses for a song's composition, for this song, they were, because the song was created in the studio.) According to Thomas, Paul came in early because the Beatles were scheduling the session on both sides of the movie:

> Paul was the first one in, and he was playing the "Birthday" riff. Eventually the others arrived, by which time Paul had literally written the song, right there in the studio. We had the backing track down by about 8:30, popped around to watch the film as arranged and then came back and actually finished the whole song. It was all done in a day.[155]

---

[150] Interview, Radio Luxembourg (1968).
[151] Press Release, in Harry, *The Paul McCartney Encyclopedia*, "Birthday (single)."
[152] Miles, *Many Years from Now*, 496.
[153] Hennessey, "Who Wrote What," *Record Mirror*.
[154] Sheff, *The Playboy Interviews*, 200. For Paul, Press Release, in Harry, *The Paul McCartney Encyclopedia*, "Birthday (single)," quoted above.
[155] In Lewisohn, *The Beatles Recording Sessions*, 156.

Evans, in a nearly contemporaneous article, remembered the song as a collaboration of all four Beatles, but dominated by Paul. "This was written in the recording studio with all four fellows working on it as a joint effort even if Paul seemed to contribute the most ideas."[156]

I conclude that this song was collaborative, but a collaboration dominated by Paul.

- **Yer Blues — (Lennon)**
  (lead vocals: John) (recorded on August 13, 1968)

Like "I'm So Tired," this was written in India, and reflects John's feelings during the Transcendental Meditation camp, the duality between peaceful, happy meditation during the day and insomnia and misery at night. In this song, he bordered on suicidal: "I was right in Maharishi's camp writing 'I want to die.'"[157] John put this in the tradition of autobiographical or self-revealing songs that culminated in *Plastic Ono Band*.[158]

- **Mother Nature's Son — (McCartney-Lennon)**
  (lead vocals: Paul) (recorded on August 9, 1968)

According to John, this song was inspired by a lecture on nature by the Maharishi, as was John's "Jealous Guy," originally titled "I'm Just a Child of Nature."[159] Miles, perhaps reflecting Paul, perhaps reflecting this interview by John, agreed.[160]

Though the Maharishi lecture might have given Paul the original idea for the song, he remembered writing it at his dad's house in Liverpool, and that he had a song sung by Nat King Cole, "Nature Boy," in mind when he wrote it.[161] "'Mother Nature's Son' was inspired by that song. I'd always

---

[156] Mal Evans 1968 ("Thirty New Beatles Grooves," 12).

[157] Lennon, Rolling Stone Interview, Dec. 1970, BBC, part 1, cf. Connolly, *Ray Connolly Beatles Archive*, 108. Wenner, *Lennon Remembers*, 12. Sheff, *The Playboy Interviews*, 209; Badman, *Beatles Off the Record*, 342. Hennessey, "Who Wrote What."

[158] Badman, *Beatles Off the Record*, 395. Paul on the song: Miles, *Many Years from Now*, 497.

[159] Sheff, *The Playboy Interviews*, 209. Miles, *Many Years from Now*, 423.

[160] Miles, *Many Years from Now*, 423.

[161] Ibid., 490. "Nature Boy" was written by eden ahbez (born George Alexander Aberle).

loved nature, and when Linda and I got together we discovered we had this deep love of nature in common."[162]

John ascribed this song fully to Paul.[163] Paul generally claimed it,[164] but in 1995, he said, "There has been a little help from John with some of the verses."[165] Mal Evans, in 1969, referred to it as collaborative. "John and Paul wrote this while they were in India."[166] Evans was in India with the group, but was possibly simply speaking generally — he doesn't even reflect that Paul was dominant.

Though this is definitely a McCartney song, John evidently contributed to the lyrics in a minor way.

- **Everybody's Got Something to Hide Except for Me and My Monkey — (Lennon)**
  (lead vocals: John) (recorded June 27 and July 1, 1968)

John said that this song expressed the love and closeness that he and Yoko shared in the early days of their relationship: "It was about me and Yoko. Everybody seemed to be paranoid except for us two, who were in the glow of love. Everything is clear and open when you're in love."[167]

According to George, the opening phrase, "Come on is such a joy," came from the Maharishi.[168] This, and the fact that the song was performed as one of the Esher demos in May 1968, suggest that it was written in India.

Paul observed that "monkey" was a jazz-musician idiom for heroin,[169] so this might reflect hard drug use, but this is not certain.

---

[162] Miles, *Many Years from Now*, 490.

[163] Hennessey, "Who Wrote What," *Record Mirror*. Sheff, *The Playboy Interviews*, 209.

[164] See Paul in 1968 (Interview, Radio Luxembourg). The song "says 'Born a poor young country boy' and I was born in Woolton hospital actually — so it's a dirty lie."

[165] Miles, *Many Years from Now*, 490.

[166] "Your Album Queries," 10.

[167] Sheff, *The Playboy Interviews*, 200-1.

[168] Harrison, quoted in Everett II, 180.

[169] Miles, *Many Years From Now*, 486.

John and Paul both ascribed "Everybody's Got Something to Hide" to John. In 1971, John said, "Me," and in 1980, he remembered, "That was just a sort of a nice line that I made into a song."[170] Paul felt that this song "very much reflected the early days of John and Yoko's life together at Montagu Square."[171] This chronology is not quite correct, as John and Yoko moved into 34 Montagu Square in late July, long after the song was written, but Paul's main point is valid.

- **Sexy Sadie — (Lennon)**
  (lead vocals: John) (recorded July 19, 24, August 13, 21, 1968)

The incident behind this song is still shrouded in controversy. After Paul left India in late March 1868, with John and George continuing to stay in Rishikesh, John's friend, the unstable "Magic" Alex Mardas, accused the Maharishi of making a pass at one of the women there (Mia Farrow, according to John).

John fully accepted the story, and was outraged. John and George confronted the religious leader and told him they were leaving.[172] Just before they left India, when their bags were packed, John wrote "Sexy Sadie" about the meditation guru, but at the time with lyrics explicitly about Maharishi: "Maharishi, what have you done, you've made a fool of everyone."[173]

Back in London, John told Paul the story and sang the song. Paul later came to believe that the story about Maharishi was untrue, that Alex Mar-

---

[170] Hennessey, "Who Wrote What," *Record Mirror*. Sheff, *The Playboy Interviews*, 200-1.

[171] Miles/McCartney, *Many Years from Now*, 486.

[172] Wenner, *Lennon Remembers*, 27. Here John said that the Maharishi tried to rape Mia Farrow or seduce her, which seems unlikely. Mia Farrow, in her autobiography, does mention that the Maharishi put his arms around her unexpectedly at one point, and that she misinterpreted it initially. Prudence told her that an embrace was customary after meditation. Nevertheless, Farrow immediately left the ashram. Farrow, *What Falls Away*, 141.

[173] Sheff, *The Playboy Interviews*, 201. See also Lennon 1970 (Wenner, *Lennon Remembers*, 27-28); Hennessey, "Who Wrote What," *Record Mirror* (1971).

das had fabricated it to lessen the Maharishi's influence on the Beatles.[174] George also denied that anything had happened: "Now, historically, there's the story that something went on that shouldn't have done — but nothing did."[175] Eventually, George persuaded John to take out any explicit reference to the Maharishi, and suggested the title "Sexy Sadie" instead.[176]

Both Paul and John ascribed this to John,[177] but the title came from George. Paul's piano is also notable, adding a tuneful introduction and a contrapuntal overlay. It would be possible to ascribe this song to "Lennon-Harrison-McCartney."

- **Helter Skelter — (McCartney)**
  (lead vocals: Paul) (recorded on September 9, 1968)

According to interviews with Paul in the eighties and nineties, the idea for this song came when he read an interview with Peter Townshend of the Who, in which Townshend said the Who's next single, "I Can See for Mile and Miles," was "the loudest, most raucous rock 'n' roll, the dirtiest thing they'd ever done." That made Paul think: 'Right. Got to do it.' And I totally got off on that one little sentence in the paper, and I said, "We've got to do the loudest, most raucous . . ."[178] "So I sat down and wrote 'Helter Skelter' to be the most raucous vocal, the loudest drums, et cetera et cetera."[179]

---

[174] Miles, *Many Years from Now*, 422. Mardas later denied that he had concocted the story, and once again affirmed that Maharishi had made advances toward a woman. Incidentally, he said that he was not at the ashram when Mia Farrow was. Kozinn, "Meditation on the Man Who Saved the Beatles."

[175] *Anthology*, 286.

[176] George and John in *Anthology*, 286. Miles, *Many Years from Now*, 422.

[177] Hennessey, "Who Wrote What," *Record Mirror.*(1971): John said, of the song, "Me. That was about the Maharishi." In 1995, Paul asserted: "John wrote 'Sexy Sadie.'" Miles, *Many Years from Now*, 422.

[178] Garbarani, "Paul McCartney: Lifting the Veil" (1980), 98. Miles, *Many Years from Now*, 488.

[179] Miles, *Many Years from Now*, 488. "I was always trying to write something different, trying to not write in character, and I read this and I was inspired, Oh, wow! Yeah!" See

In a much earlier interview, in 1968, Paul seems to describe a different sequence of events. He read a review of an unidentified record in which the reviewer said that "this group really goes wild, there's echo on everything, they're screaming their heads off." Paul was annoyed that the group had beat the Beatles to it. Then he heard the actual record and was disappointed. "It was quite straight, and it was very sort of sophisticated." "So I thought, 'Oh well, we'll do one like that, then.'" But instead of sitting down and writing the song, Paul thought of a song he already had that would lend itself to such a performance. "And I had this song called 'Helter Skelter' which is just a ridiculous song. So we did it like that, 'cause I like noise."[180]

The helter skelter is a ride in which a slide spirals down around a tower.[181] Paul used the symbol of a slide to represent the rise and fall of empires — "and this was the fall, the demise, the going down."[182]

Whatever the details of the songwriting, both Paul and John ascribed "Helter Skelter" to Paul. Paul, in 2000, said, "So I said to the guys, 'I think we should do a song like that; something really wild.' And I wrote 'Helter Skelter.'"[183] In 1971 John put it on a list of songs written by Paul alone, and nine years later, said, "That's Paul *completely*."[184]

The recording session for this song has become legendary. "'Helter Skelter' was a track we did in total madness and hysterics in the studio," said Ringo. He also stated that Paul virtually wrote the song in the studio, though Paul's interviews suggest he'd worked on the song before the recording.[185]

---

also Garbarini and Baird, "Has Success Spoiled Paul McCartney?" 61; Read, "McCartney on McCartney," episode 4; *Anthology*, 311.

[180] McCartney, Interview, Radio Luxembourg, Nov. 21, 1968.

[181] Radice, "A Welter Of Helter Skelters."

[182] Miles, *Many Years from Now*, 488.

[183] *Anthology*, 311.

[184] Hennessey, "Who Wrote What," *Record Mirror*; Sheff, *The Playboy Interviews*, 210.

[185] *Anthology*, 311.

- **Long, Long, Long — (Harrison)**
  (lead vocals: George) (recorded on October 7, 1968)

This great song by George was allegorical, addressed to God. He used the chords from Dylan's "Sad Eyed Lady of the Lowlands" to write the music.[186]

The eerie percussive coda at the end was a wine bottle that would rattle when Paul, who performed Hammond organ on the song, played a certain note. Ringo added a snare drum roll.[187]

SIDE FOUR:

○ <u>Revolution 1 — (Lennon)</u>
(recorded on May 30-31, and June 4, 21, 1968)

See "Hey Jude / Revolution" single, above. This is the original, slower, doo-wop version.

- **Honey Pie — (McCartney)**
  (lead vocals: Paul) (recorded on October 1, 2, 4, 1968)

Paul said that both he and John loved the music hall tradition. Paul listened to the Billy Cotton Band Show as he grew up, and Fred Astaire was a favorite.[188] "My dad's always played fruity old songs like that, you know. And I liked 'em. I like the melody of old songs, and the lyrics actually as well."[189] So for this song, he pretended he was living in 1925,[190] and wrote a "fantasy song" in that style, about a woman in Hollywood named Honey Pie. He emphasized that it was not a parody, but "a nod to the vaudeville tradition that I was raised on."[191]

Both Paul and John ascribed this to Paul.[192]

---

[186] *I Me Mine*, 132.

[187] Lewisohn, *The Beatles Recording Sessions*, 159; Harrison, *I Me Mine*, 132.

[188] Miles, *Many Years from Now*, 497. See "When I'm Sixty-Four," in *Sgt. Pepper's*, above.

[189] McCartney, Interview, Radio Luxembourg. See also Garbarani, "Paul McCartney: Lifting the Veil," (1980), 46.

[190] McCartney, Interview, Radio Luxembourg, Nov. 21, 1968.

[191] Miles, *Many Years from Now*, 497.

[192] Ibid. Hennessey, "Who Wrote What," *Record Mirror*.

While Paul would make these obvious nods to this music from a different generation, the impact of this kind of carefully crafted melodic writing on his rock music has not been sufficiently recognized or understood.

- **Savoy Truffle — (Harrison-Taylor)**
  (lead vocals: George) (recorded on October 3, 1968)

George wrote this to tease Eric Clapton, who had a weakness for candy. When he saw a box of candy, he "had to eat them all," said George. As a result Clapton was undergoing major dental work at the time.[193] The lyrics are partially found poetry, as George took a number of candy names from a box of chocolates. He remembered that Clapton "was over at my house, and I had a box of 'Good News' chocolates on the table and wrote the song from the names inside the lid."[194]

Derek Taylor helped with the lyrics. "I got stuck with the two bridges for a while," said George, "and Derek Taylor wrote some of the words in the middle — 'You know that what you eat you are.'"[195]

- **Cry Baby Cry — (Lennon)**
  (lead vocals: John) (recorded on July 15, 16 and 18, 1968)

John got the idea for this song from an advertisement back in *Sgt. Pepper* days. In 1967 he told Hunter Davies, "I've got another one here, a few words, I think I got them from an advert: 'Cry baby cry, make your mother buy.' I've been playing it over on the piano. I've let it go now. It'll come back if I really want it."[196]

The lyrics are also partly based on the nursery rhyme, "Sing A Song Of Sixpence":

> The king was in his counting house counting out his money,
> The queen was in the parlour eating bread and honey

---

[193] Harrison in Glazer, "Growing Up at 33 1/3" (1977).

[194] Harrison, *I Me Mine*, 128.

[195] Ibid. Taylor also remembered this, Somach et al., *Ticket to Ride*, 221. He had a friend, Barry Feinstein, who had just done a film called *You Are What You Eat*.

[196] Davies, *The Beatles*, 277.

The maid was in the garden hanging out the clothes,
When down came a blackbird and pecked off her nose!

John worked on this song in India.[197] There is a home tape of it, Lennon on guitar and piano, which Winn dates to December 1967 or January 1968.[198] It was also one of the Esher demos, in May 1968.

Generally, both John and Paul ascribed this to John. Miles/Paul gave it as an example of a song that Paul first heard in the studio, because John was spending so much time with Yoko.[199] Mal Evans agreed, in 1968: "This is John's number all the way with strong, heavy and very Lennon vocals."[200]

However, just to prevent an easy solution to a Lennon-McCartney song, John, in 1980, denied writing it: "Not me. A piece of rubbish."[201] He must have simply been confused, as the evidence for his authorship is conclusive.

- **Can You Take Me Back Where I Came From — (McCartney)**
  (lead vocals: Paul) (recorded on December 16, 1968)

This is an ad-lib by Paul, recorded during the "I Will" sessions, Take 19. It was originally two minutes and 21 seconds in length, and a 28-second segment was cut out of this for the White Album.[202] Not listed on the record, it serves as an intro to Revolution 9, or the outro to "Cry Baby Cry." A haunting bit of McCartney between two classic John cuts.

I know of no comments on the song by Paul, John or any insider.

---

[197] *Many Years from Now*, 487.

[198] Winn, *That Magic Feeling*, 150.

[199] Hennessey, "Who Wrote What," *Record Mirror*. Miles, *Many Years from Now*, 487.

[200] "Thirty New Beatles Grooves," 7.

[201] Sheff, *The Playboy Interviews*, 209.

[202] Lewisohn, *The Beatles Recording Sessions*, 155.

- **Revolution 9 — (Lennon-Ono-Harrison-Starkey) (recorded May 30 to June 21, 1968)**

As has been mentioned (see the "Hey Jude / Revolution" single, above), this experimental montage of sounds developed from an extended jam after "Revolution 1." John said, in 1980, that the slow version of the song continued on and on, and he added sounds to the extended fade out.[203]

John was the main creator of this piece. Geoff Emerick remembered, "On this night John sat with me behind the console, like a kid with a new toy. He was the composer and he knew what he wanted, so he manned the faders instead of me."[204]

Tape loops were an important component of the composition. John said, in 1970: "All the thing was made with loops. I had about thirty loops going, I fed them onto one basic track. . . . It was an engineer's tape, and I was just using all the bits like to make a montage."[205] George Martin described the cut as "an extension of 'Tomorrow Never Knows'" in its use of tape loops.[206]

Another influence was "classical" experimental music. John described this cut in 1971 as "just abstract, musique concrete, kind of loops and that, people screaming. I thought I was painting in sound a picture of revolution."[207] The phrase "musique concrète" points to the electronic music of Karlheinz Stockhausen and Edgard Varèse.

Yoko's impact on this cut was considerable, as she was present for the recording and even chose particular loops.[208] So Yoko contributed directly

---

[203] Sheff, *The Playboy Interviews*, 198.

[204] *Here, There and Everywhere*, 241-42. "I spent more time on 'Revolution 9' than I did on half the other songs I ever wrote," he said ten years later. Sheff, *The Playboy Interviews*, 198.

[205] Lennon, Rolling Stone Interview, Dec. 1970, BBC, part 4; cf. Wenner, *Lennon Remembered*, 111. Sheff, *The Playboy Interviews*, 198.

[206] Williams, "Produced by George Martin." See also Chris Thomas before 1999 (Pritchard and Lysaght, *The Beatles: An Oral History*, 266).

[207] Blackburn and Ali, "Lennon and Ono interview."

[208] Sheff, *The Playboy Interviews*, 198.

to the piece, and also inspired it. John and Yoko alone did the final editing, which took four hours.[209]

George Harrison, George Martin and Ringo also helped John on this piece. (Paul was in New York when it was recorded.) Once John wrote to *Melody Maker* to assert he was the main creator of "Revolution 9," not George Martin; however, he said that he recorded it "with <u>Yoko</u> plus the help of Ringo, George and Martin."[210]

George Harrison remembered that he and Ringo went into the EMI tape library and pulled tapes for John to use in his collage, and John would "cut them together."

> The whole thing, 'Number nine, number nine,' is because I pulled the box number nine. It was some kind of educational program. John sat there and decided which bits to cross-fade together, but, if Ringo and I hadn't gone there in the first place, he wouldn't have had anything.[211]

Lennon's friend Pete Shotton claimed that he helped substantially with this cut. "'Revolution 9,' of course, was the impressionistic sound-effects montage that John and I had conceived during our LSD trip hours before he revealed himself to me as Jesus Christ. John subsequently completed it with a little help from Yoko . . . '*This* is the music of the future,' John would tell everybody who'd listen. 'You can forget all the rest of the shit we've done — this is *it!*'"[212] Shotton said that he and John started Revolution 9 at John's home, using "John's network of Brunell tape recorders."[213] Shotton was not there when Lennon was working on the piece in

---

[209] Letter to George Martin/Richard Williams, Sept. 1971, in Davies, *The John Lennon Letters*, 213.

[210] Ibid.

[211] Badman, *Beatles Off the Record*, 397. See also Yorke, Interview with George Harrison (1969).

[212] Shotton & Schaffner, *The Beatles, Lennon and Me*, 338.

[213] Ibid., 321-24.

the studio, however. George Harrison *was* an important presence.[214] Perhaps Shotton helped with some of the tape loops before John brought them to the studio.

According to Miles/McCartney, the other three Beatles and George Martin all tried to convince John to leave this off the White Album.[215] In 1969, John said "Working on my own with Yoko, I can go as far out as I like. Take Revolution No. 9. I thought I imposed that on the Beatles."[216] This was one time when John's instincts were right; one can't imagine the White Album without this extended avant-garde moment near the end.

- **Good Night — (Lennon)**
  (lead vocals: Ringo) (recorded on June 28, 1968)

John wrote "Good Night" as a lullaby for his son Julian,[217] and it is a classic example of John writing against type, with its lush orchestral accompaniment. It offers a striking contrast to "Revolution 9," and serves as a moving ending for the White Album.

John either wrote it for Ringo to sing, or decided to give it to him, so he recorded a demo for the drummer.[218]

George Martin did the orchestral arrangement. John remembered, in 1969, "So I just said to George Martin 'Arrange it just like Hollywood.' Yeah, corny."[219] Martin thus is probably responsible for counter-melodies in the orchestra.

John, Ringo and Paul ascribed this to John.[220] In 1969, he said, "When I wrote it, it was just like a child's lullaby. I just picked it out on guitar."[221]

---

[214] Lewisohn, *The Beatles Recording Sessions*, 135-39.

[215] *Many Years from Now*, 487.

[216] B. P. Fallon, Interview with John Lennon, *Melody Maker*, Apr. 12, 1969 (Sandercombe, *The Beatles*, 262).

[217] Sheff, *The Playboy Interviews*, 209; Miles, *Many Years from Now*, 487.

[218] Emerick, *Here There Everywhere*, 245.

[219] Fallon, "Will the Real John Lennon" (1969). Also quoted in Schaffner, *The Beatles Forever*, 115. See also Paul, Interview, Radio Luxembourg.

[220] Hennessey, "Who Wrote What," *Record Mirror*.

[221] Fallon, "Will the Real John Lennon."

In 1968, Paul said, "It's his tune, uhh, which is surprising for John — 'cause he doesn't normally write this kind of tune."[222] Twenty years later, Paul said that John had a well-earned reputation as a rocker. "But he wrote songs like 'Good Night,' for Ringo, which is the most sentimental ballad you'll ever hear."[223] "It was John who wrote it for me," Ringo said in an early interview.[224]

But as nearly always in the Beatle songs, after this clarity, ambiguity intrudes. In the same 1968 interview cited above, Paul said, "John wrote it, mainly." There is a slight opening for collaboration. Mal Evans, probably not a firsthand witness, though an insider, twice in 1968 stated that John and Paul wrote it. "Ringo has recorded two titles — the one he wrote himself and another which John and Paul did for him."[225] And again, he said, "John and Paul wrote this sad, wistful song for Ringo to sing."[226] Evans may have been simply giving the "Lennon-McCartney" party line, or he may have witnessed collaboration sessions that were later forgotten by the principals. I lean toward the former theory, and accept this as a song by John alone.

Paul cites this as evidence for John's love of old standards. "One of his favourite songs was 'Girl of My Dreams'. And he loved 'Little White Lies'. . . . That side of John he'd never dare show, except in very rare moments."[227]

---

[222] McCartney, Interview, Radio Luxembourg, Nov. 21, 1968.

[223] Lewisohn interview, 12 (1988). See also Coleman, *McCartney: Yesterday . . . and Today* (1995), 98.

[224] Beatles, *Illustrated Lyrics*, 40. See also Ringo in *Anthology*, 306.

[225] "The Eighteenth Single," 8.

[226] "Thirty New Beatles Grooves," 7.

[227] Coleman, *McCartney: Yesterday . . . and Today* (1995), 98; Du Noyer, *Conversations*, 27. "Girl of My Dreams," by Sonny Clapp, was first recorded by Blue Steele and His Orchestra with Vocal Chorus in 1927. "Little White Lies," by Walter Donaldson, was first recorded by Fred Waring's Pennsylvanians in 1930.

13

"I wanted to do something bigger, a kind of operatic moment"

THE GET BACK SESSIONS AND *ABBEY ROAD*

As the formal Beatles breakup approached, full collaboration between Paul and John became less frequent, and most Lennon-McCartney songs were pure John or pure Paul.[1] However, in a few songs from the Get Back sessions — such as the title song, which was developed in live performance in the studio — there was some significant collaboration. In "I've Got a Feeling" Paul and John put separate songs together, just as they had sometimes done in the *Sgt. Pepper* era.

In *Abbey Road*, the last album the Beatles recorded, even those minor moments of limited collaboration were few and far between. Only "Come Together," seems collaborative, though John clearly dominated the song. There is no substantial songwriting collaboration between Paul and John on any of the other songs. As the two main Beatle songwriters reached their collaborative nadir, the album achieved a triumphant culmination of the Beatles' musical career — a paradox that has rarely been recognized.

The Get Back Sessions

After the elaborate instrumentations and orchestrations of *Revolver*, *Sgt. Pepper's*, *Magical Mystery Tour*, and the White Album, the Beatles had the idea to do a back-to-basics album, with just them, the band, playing live, without overdubs. In addition, they owed United Artists another movie, and so it was agreed that they would tape the sessions on film, and end the

---

[1] For an recent treatment of the breakup, see Mikal Gilmore, "Why the Beatles Broke Up."

movie with a live show. These sessions became known as the Get Back sessions.[2]

So the Beatles began rehearsing at Twickenham Film Studios, with the cameras rolling, on January 2, 1969. Michael Lindsay-Hogg, who had directed some short Beatle films previously, acted as film director. Since the Beatles often brought songs to the studio unfinished, the film footage documents various Beatle songs in primitive form, and shows the group working on them together. In addition, the Beatles played many covers during these sessions, often in fragmentary form, some of their early songs, and a number of songs that later appeared on their solo albums after the breakup. One of their early songs, "One After 909," ended up on the *Let It Be* album. Some of the covers ended up in the movie.

George Martin was still formally the music producer, but the format of the album (rehearsals, then "live" performance) did not lend itself to his normal role in the studio. In Martin's absence, Glyn Johns, the engineer, often functioned as producer.

After the rehearsals, the Beatles began recording at the new recording studio at Apple headquarters on January 22. Finally, on January 30, they gave an impromptu performance on the top of the Apple building in central London, which later became the climax of the movie *Let It Be*. They recorded again in the studio on January 31, and continued to add overdubs to the Get Back songs in the following months.

Glyn Johns made four possible album lineups, more or less within the boundaries of the original idea of the album, and all were rejected by the Beatles, or some majority of the Beatles (Paul later said he liked them). The release of the album for this movie, and the movie itself, both titled *Let It*

---

[2] The Get Back sessions have been widely bootlegged, and Doug Sulpy and Ray Schweighardt describe them in detail in their excellent book, *Get Back: The Unauthorized Chronicle of the Beatles' "Let It Be" Disaster* (1999). (Though I would not call any album that included such masterpieces as "Get Back," "Long and Winding Road," "Let It Be," and "Across the Universe" — not to mention solid contributions of the caliber of "Two of Us," "I've Got a Feeling," "Don't Let Me Down" and "I Dig a Pony" — a disaster.) A more compressed summary can be found in Unterberger, *The Unreleased Beatles*.

Be, were delayed until after the Beatles' real final album, *Abbey Road*. (And then, the album *Let It Be* was radically re-produced by Phil Spector.) Although many of the songs seemed to have a valedictory tone, from "Let It Be" to "Long and Winding Road," they were generally written much earlier than the *Abbey Road* songs (though a few of the *Abbey Road* songs were played in the Get Back sessions). To understand the Beatles' progression as songwriters, we must always remember that the *Let It Be* songs were written during and soon after the White Album sessions.

The Get Back sessions sometimes continued the miserable, combative tone of the White Album studio experience. John's continued drug use and his focus on Yoko made it difficult to communicate with him. George Harrison called the Get Back sessions "the low of all time." Lennon agreed: he said that the Get Back sessions were "hell . . . the most miserable sessions on earth."[3] George Martin said, "*Let It Be* was such an unhappy record (even though there are some great songs on it) that I really believed that was the end of The Beatles, and I assumed that I would never work with them again. I thought, What a shame to end like this."[4]

Paul had a more mixed view:

> We were being constantly filmed or taped. We suddenly realized there were these tensions and being under the glare of the camera, there was no way you could keep it out. I think Michael Lindsay-Hogg realized this and he sort of said "This is the film; it's cinema vérité, let's shoot what happens." It was painful for us and I think it did contribute to the break-up. At the same time we had some great times.[5]

On January 10, Harrison, bitterly resentful of Lennon and McCartney, announced he was leaving the band, and walked out of the rehearsal studi-

---

[3] As quoted in Lewisohn, *Complete Beatles Chronicle*, 310.
[4] *Anthology*, 337.
[5] Beatles-unlimited.com website.

os and off the movie set.[6] He only returned, after setting definite conditions, on the 14th. However, while he was gone, he attended a Ray Charles concert, and met an old friend, keyboardist Billy Preston, whom the Beatles had known earlier when Preston had toured with Little Richard. Billy joined the Get Back sessions and became, for a while, a welcome Fifth Beatle.

Despite the occasional misery of these sessions, as the group was slowly, agonizingly breaking up, John and Paul had written some great songs for this album, and the cameras captured some magnificent performances. If the Beatles were sometimes bored, bitter, resentful, petulant and angry, their musical instincts clicked in when they were performing to create recordings with magical live chemistry. In fact, some insiders, such as Glyn Johns, remembered the sessions as essentially funny and positive. Johns said:

> John Lennon only had to walk into a room, and I'd just crack up. Their whole mood was wonderful. There was all this nonsense going on at the time about the problems surrounding the group . . . in fact, there they were, just doing it, having a wonderful time and being incredibly funny. I didn't stop laughing for six weeks.[7]

In addition, we might underline the difference between songwriting and recording sessions in the Beatles' history (not to mention personal and legal conflicts). An author looking for obvious dramatic personal stories, from a storytelling point of view, would highlight the conflicts during these sessions. However, for a historian of the Beatles' creativity (as evidenced by their songwriting), the recording is less important than songwriting (though the recording sessions are easier to document and dramatize).

---

[6] Sulpy and Schweighardt, *Get Back*, 169. The authors emphasize George's conflicts with John as the cause of his departure, but undoubtedly, George resented Paul also. See also Winn, *That Magic Feeling*, 246, 267; Irvin, "Get It Better."; Doggett, *You Never Give Me Your Money*, 60.
[7] Quoted in *The Record Producers*, as cited in Doggett, *Abbey Road*, 78; Matteo, *Let It Be*, 54.

Songwriting was sometimes finished at the studio, but the main structure of songs was usually done by the writer alone, at home, without the cameras running. (For example, Paul wrote "Long and Winding Road" during the White Album sessions, at his farm in Scotland.) This kind of creativity is more elusive, and arguably more important, than the recording sessions. ("Get Back," developed in the studio, is the exception.)

Yellow Submarine album, January 17, 1969

The animated movie *Yellow Submarine* was released in November 1968. There were four new Beatle songs on the soundtrack album, including two by George. These aren't top drawer Beatle songs, by any stretch of the imagination, but they're nevertheless good fun — especially John's "Hey Bulldog."

o   Yellow Submarine

See *Revolver* album, above.

- **Only a Northern Song — (Harrison)**
  (lead vocals: George) (recorded February 13–14, April 20, 1967)

This song, which represents the Beatles' growing business sophistication, was written by George for *Sgt. Pepper*.[8] George referred to it as a "joke."[9] He said that when he signed the contract with Dick James, he didn't realize he was giving up ownership of his own songs. "It was just a blatant theft. By the time I realized what had happened, when they were going public and making all this money out of this catalog, I wrote 'Only A Northern Song' as what we call a 'piss-take,' just to have a joke about it."[10]

---

[8] Emerick, *Here, There, Everywhere*, 165-66.

[9] *I Me Mine*, 100.

[10] White, "Billboard Interview" (1999). See also George in Badman, *Beatles Off the Record*, 415. In 1989, Paul said, "They forced us to do one [song] specially [for the movie]," said Paul, "which was 'It's Only a Northern Song,' which George did with a very big tongue in his cheek, because Northern Songs was the name of the publishing company." *The Paul*

Though it was recorded during the *Sgt. Pepper* sessions, George Martin did not think it measured up to the other *Sgt. Pepper* songs. "I suggested he [George Harrison] come up with something a bit better," Martin said.[11] So the recording was shelved, then resurrected two years later for *Yellow Submarine*.

The following is a good example of how completely non-factual anecdotes pop up even around the lesser Beatle songs. Al Brodax, producer and screenwriter for *Yellow Submarine*, said:

> At two o'clock in the morning, in EMI's studio, with the London Symphony Orchestra patiently waiting to go home, we were still one song short for the film. George told me to sit tight while he knocked out another tune. After an hour or two, he returned to the studio with the final song, "Here, Al," he said, "it's only a northern song."[12]

Not only was this song not written for *Yellow Submarine*, it had been recorded two years earlier, in February and April 1967!

- **All Together Now — (McCartney-Lennon) (lead vocals: Paul) (recorded on May 12, 1967)**

This is another of Paul's songs written for children. He took the title from a music hall catchphrase. "When they were singing a song, to encourage the audience to join in they'd say 'All together now!'" said Paul in 1995. "So I just took it and read another meaning into it, of we are all together now. So I used the dual meaning." His evaluation of the song is entirely realistic: "A bit of a throwaway."[13]

Both Paul and John ascribed this to Paul as the main writer.[14] In 1980, he described it with one word: "Paul." But then, not to leave a song attrib-

---

McCartney World Tour, 55. This doesn't seem to jibe with the recording history of the song. Possibly Paul confused this song with "Hey Bulldog."

[11] *With a Little Help from My Friends* (1994), 124.

[12] Badman, *Beatles Off the Record*, 415. Also, McCabe, *Apple to the Core*, 106.

[13] Miles, *Many Years from Now*, 481.

[14] Ibid. Hennessey, "Who Wrote What," *Record Mirror*.

ution without ambiguity, he continued, "I put a few lines in it somewhere, probably."[15]

It was recorded in May 1967, during the *Magical Mystery Tour* era of the Beatles.

• Hey Bulldog — (Lennon-McCartney) (lead vocals: John) (recorded on February 11, 1968)

In February 1968, just before the Beatles left for India, Paul told John that they needed to do a "real song in the studio" for *Yellow Submarine*, and could "John whip one off?" John had "a few words" for this song at home, so he brought them to the studio.[16] At some point John recorded a home demo of the chorus called "She Can Talk to Me." At the studio, Paul helped finish the song.[17] Reportedly, it was originally titled "Hey Bull-frog," but after Paul started barking at the end, they kept the barking in and John re-titled the song 'Hey Bulldog.'[18] Paul also misread "Some kind of solitude is measured out in news" as "Some kind of solitude is measured out in you," and John decided to keep the mistake.

In 1980, John described the song as something he'd "knocked off" when the movie people requested another song.[19] Paul agreed that it was mainly a John song, but remembered some collaboration on it: "I helped him finish it off in the studio."[20]

---

[15] Sheff, *The Playboy Interviews*, 211. Further comments on the song: Blackburn and Ali, "Lennon and Ono interview." George Harrison in White, "Billboard Interview."

[16] Miles, *Beatles in their Own Words*, 102.

[17] Miles, *Many Years from Now*, 481.

[18] Dowlding, *Beatlesongs*, 213. Cowan, *Behind the Beatles Songs*, 24. For the ad-lib barking at the end, see Lewisohn, *Beatles Recording Sessions*, 134.

[19] Lost Lennon Tapes, Oct. 21, 1991, cf. Sheff, *The Playboy Interviews*, 213. See also Miles, *Beatles in their Own Words*, 102, quoted above. George Harrison and Mal and Neil also referred to it as John's song. Harrison in 1999 (White, "The Billboard Interview"). Evans and Aspinall, "New Single Sessions," 11.

[20] Miles, *Many Years from Now*, 481.

- **It's All Too Much — (Harrison)**
(lead vocals: George) (recorded on May 25–26 and June 2, 1967)

This is George's psychedelic song — as he said, "written in a childlike manner from realizations that appeared during and after some LSD experiences and which were later confirmed in meditation."[21] As he remembered that era, you'd "trip out . . . and then you'd just be back having your evening cup of tea!"[22]

It was recorded in May and June 1967, and so was another *Magical Mystery Tour* vintage song.

  o   All You Need Is Love

See the "All You Need Is Love" single, above, and the *Magical Mystery Tour* album.

SIDE TWO

Side two of the album was orchestral music by George Martin.[23]

Goodbye album — Cream, February 15, 1969

- **Badge — (Clapton-Harrison-Starkey)**

This is another example of how haphazard and collective songwriting could be in the Beatles circle that included Eric Clapton. Clapton started this song, then a collaboration session with George Harrison ensued. According to George, he helped with both the music and the words: "Eric had some of the melody and I helped him finish the tune and then wrote the words."[24]

Eric took the title, "Badge" from an upside down misreading of "Bridge," a word which George had written on the lyric sheet.

---

[21] *I Me Mine*, 106.

[22] White, "Billboard Interview."

[23] For his comments on this, see Hieronimus, "Interview with George Martin."

[24] *I Me Mine*, 148.

An inebriated Ringo also wandered in to make a contribution.[25] George said, "we were up to the lines: 'I told you not to drive around in the dark / I told you' — and Ringo said: '… about the swans that live in the park.' It's a bit silly, but that's what happened, folks."[26]

―――――◗◦◖―――――

"Goodbye / Sparrow" single — Mary Hopkin, March 28, 1969

- Goodbye — (McCartney) (recorded March 1, 1969)

  Mary Hopkin had won a vocal competition, and when Paul heard her, he was impressed. He signed her to Apple, produced her first single, "Those Were the Days," a phenomenal international hit, then her first album, *Post Card.*[27]

  In February 1969,[28] Paul reportedly dashed off "Goodbye," one of the best of the songs the Beatles gave away, in great haste, because a follow-up to "Those Were the Days" was needed. Miles wrote, "Over in Cavendish Avenue Paul quickly wrote one called 'Goodbye.'"[29] Mary later said, "He said he wrote 'Goodbye' in about ten minutes. I'm not sure how true that is! It probably is."[30] He made a demo for Mary, still extant.

  - Sparrow (Benny Gallagher, Graham Lyle)

―――――◗◦◖―――――

"Get Back / Don't Let Me Down" single, April 11, 1969

This single was the only release from the Get Back sessions for more than a year.

---

[25] Glazer, "Growing Up at 33 1/3" (1977).

[26] *I Me Mine*, 148. Similar: White, "George Harrison Reconsidered" (1987), 57.

[27] Engelhardt, *Beatles Undercover*, 199-201.

[28] *New Muscial Express*, March 15, 1969, as quoted in Winn, *That Magic Feeling*, 264.

[29] Miles, *Many Years From Now*, 457.

[30] Mary Hopkins in 1995 (*Goldmine* interview, April 14, 1995, vol. 21 no. 8, Issue 384, as cited in Unterberger, *Unreleased Beatles*, 350). See also Mary Hopkin in 1984 (Giuliano, *The Lost Beatles Interviews*, 249).

- **Get Back — (McCartney-Lennon)**
  (lead vocals: Paul) (recorded on January 27, 1969)

This song's genesis is captured on tape, remarkably enough. On January 7, Paul plays a "galloping bass riff," then vocalizes a melody over it, while George plays a few "discordant" comments on guitar. Paul repeats it, and on the third trial it "comes together" and we have the verse tune of "Get Back." Two days later, the chorus has been added, and a few mentions of Arizona and California. (Paul had recently visited Arizona.) On the same day, Jo Jo appears in the lyrics. On the thirteenth, Paul and John are working on the lyrics as they rehearse. Loretta is now a character. The third verse is political, dealing with the issue of too many Pakistanis living in small flats.

When the Beatles rehearsed the song again on the 23rd, the political lyrics had been dropped, but the lyrics and music were nowhere near finished. Nevertheless, the song became more polished with repeated rehearsals. The performance used for this single, and the album, was recorded on January 27th.[31]

Paul sometimes claimed this song: "I originally wrote it as a political song," he said sometime before 1979.[32] However, at other times, he emphasized that it was the product of group improvisation. In 1969, he said, "We were sitting in the studio and we made it up out of thin air . . . we started to write words there and then . . . when we finished it, we recorded it at Apple Studios and made it into a song to roller-coast by."[33] Twenty years later, he explained, "We were jamming, and then we were just making up words. . . . [About too many Pakistanis living in small flats. Then they realized] It's gonna be seen as racist or something . . . So we dumped that, and we got these other lyrics.[34] 'Jo Jo was a man.' It's all silly stuff really,

[31] Sulpy and Schweighardt, *Get Back*, 84, 153, 188-90, 222-24, 282. Unterberger, *Unreleased Beatles*, 240, 243, 245, 250-51. Everett II, 221-22. Doggett, *Abbey Road*, 97-98.

[32] Cowan, *Behind the Beatles Songs*, 17.

[33] Quote in a press advertisement for the single, see Doggett, *Abbey Road*, 47.

[34] The original Pakistani lyrics, Paul said, were anti-racist, not racist. "If there was any group that was not racist it was the Beatles." Miles, *Many Years from Now*, 535.

but — it was a jam that just developed through that."[35] And before 1999, he mentioned "'Get Back,' which we were making up on the set of *Let It Be*."[36]

Miles/McCartney described this as a Paul song in genesis developed during jams and rehearsals, which I believe is correct. "It was basically Paul's song, composed in the studios at Twickenham for the now abandoned television show. Paul had a rough idea for the words and music and began jamming it out. John joined him and together they worked on some lyrics."[37]

John also ascribed this to Paul. In 1971 he put it on a list of songs written by Paul alone, and nine years later he said "'Get Back' is Paul."[38] However, I believe John made a substantial contribution to the lyrics.

- **Don't Let Me Down — (Lennon-McCartney) (lead vocals: John) (recorded on January 28, 1969)**

"That's me, singing about Yoko," John said in 1980.[39] Paul felt it reflected John's feelings of vulnerability and paranoia as a heroin user during the period.[40] "It was saying to Yoko, '. . . I'm really letting my vulnerability be seen, so you must not let me down.' I think it was a genuine cry for help."[41]

Both John and Paul ascribed this song to John.[42] Paul doubted that he worked on the song: "I sang harmony on it, which makes me wonder if I helped with a couple of the words, but I don't think so. It was John's song."[43] However, the Get Back tapes show he contributed to the song.

---

[35] Read, "McCartney on McCartney," episode 4.

[36] Morse, *Classic Rock Stories*, 68, cf. Badman, *The Dream is Over*, 14.

[37] Miles, *Many Years from Now*, 535.

[38] Hennessey, "Who Wrote What," *Record Mirror*. Sheff, *The Playboy Interviews*, 211.

[39] Lost Lennon Tapes, Oct. 21, 1991, cf. Sheff, *The Playboy Interviews*, 214.

[40] Miles, *Many Years from Now*, 535-36. He had begun writing it by late 1968. Everett II, 222.

[41] Miles, *Many Years from Now*, 535-36.

[42] Ibid. Hennessey, "Who Wrote What," *Record Mirror*.

[43] Miles, *Many Years from Now*, 535-36.

Sulpy and Schweighardt write, "John . . . wants to retain Paul's lyrics [for the middle section] because he doesn't see much merit in his own lines either." After a rehearsal, they write that "Paul and George have been doing most of the songwriting on what is essentially John's number."[44]

Unfinished Music No.2: Life with the Lions album — John Lennon and Yoko Ono, May 9, 1969

Yoko had a miscarriage in November 1968, and on March 2, 1969, John and Yoko gave a live improvisatory performance at Cambridge. These events are reflected in this second experimental John and Yoko album.[45]

Electronic Sound album — George Harrison, May 9, 1969

On the cover, we read "Electronic Sound. Produced by George Harrison." Another example of the Beatles' interest in experimental music, this includes two long pieces performed on Moog synthesizer. Harrison himself said, "Whatever came out when I fiddled with the knobs went on tape."[46]

- "Under the Mersey Wall" (Harrison)

This is eighteen minutes long.

- "No Time or Space" (Harrison)

This is twenty-five minutes long. Bernie Krause, who demonstrated the Moog to George, later claimed that this was essentially a recording of

---

[44] *Get Back*, 63, 67. One critic writes, "After John plays all the potential sections of the song, Paul steps in and essentially shapes the song. He advises John to jettison one of the sections of the song. They end with the first full performance of the song, essentially structured as we know it today." *Get Back to Let It Be Dissected*, at Jan. 2, 1969, Roll 8-A.

[45] Everett II, 238. See also Drummond, Interview with John Lennon and Yoko Ono, May 8, 1969; Badman, *Off the Record*, 446-47.

[46] Everett II, 242. White, "George Harrison Reconsidered" (1987), 56.

his demonstration.[47] Harrison bought a Moog and the Beatles used it extensively on *Abbey Road*, on such songs as "Because" and "Here Comes the Sun."

"The Ballad of John and Yoko / Old Brown Shoe" single, May 30, 1969

- The Ballad of John and Yoko — (Lennon-McCartney) (lead vocals: John) (recorded on April 14, 1969)

John wrote most of this song on his honeymoon with Yoko, and the lyrics tell, in "old-time ballad" fashion (that is, it's a storytelling song), about their marriage on March 20, 1969, on the Rock of Gibraltar, and their subsequent honeymoon in Amsterdam and Vienna, which included their first bed-in for peace.

When John returned to England, he was anxious to record this song. He came to Paul and said, as Paul remembers, "'I've got this song about our wedding and it's called 'The Ballad Of John And Yoko, Christ They're Gonna Crucify Me,' and I said 'Jesus Christ, you're kidding aren't you? Someone really is going to get upset about it.' He said, 'Yeah, but let's do it.'"[48]

John was having trouble with the last verse, so he and Paul sat down and worked it out, then on April 14, went to the studio. George and Ringo were out of town, but John wanted to record it as quickly as possible, so Paul agreed to play drums and bass. "So we did it," Paul said, "and stood back to see if the other guys would hate us for it. Which I'm not sure about. They probably never forgave us. John was on heat, so to speak. He needed to record it so we just ran in and did it."[49] They recorded the song in nine hours, John doing lead vocal, guitars and percussion, while Paul did drums, bass, piano and backing vocals.

---

[47] Pinch and Trocco, *Analog Days*, 123-24.
[48] Lewisohn interview (1988), 14.
[49] Ibid.

So we have one more late example of a real Lennon-McCartney collaboration.

Both John and Paul agreed that this was mainly a Lennon song. John said, in 1969, "It's something I wrote, and it's like an old-time ballad. It's the story of us going along getting married, going to Paris, going to Amsterdam, all that. It's 'Johnny B. Paperback Writer.'"[50] In 1980, he explained, "I wrote that in Paris on our honeymoon. It's a piece of journalism. It's a folk song."[51] However, there was some slight collaboration with Paul.[52]

- **Old Brown Shoe (Harrison)**
  (lead vocals: George) (recorded on April 16 and 18, 1969)

George began writing the chords for this song on piano, and then began lyrics from the idea of opposites in nature. Thus somewhat in the tradition of "Hello Goodbye."[53]

It was performed during the Get Back sessions, on January 27-29.[54] George made a demo of it on February 25, which can be heard on *Anthology 3*.

"Give Peace A Chance / Remember Love" single — Plastic Ono Band, July 4, 1969

- **Give Peace A Chance — (Lennon-Ono)**
  (recorded June 1, 1969)

In 1970, John said, "In me secret heart, I wanted to write something that would take over 'We Shall Overcome,' you know."[55] And in the fol-

---

[50] Alan Smith, "Beatles Music Straightforward On Next Album."

[51] Sheff, *The Playboy Interviews*, 210. John actually started it on March 20, in Paris. Lennon interview, Fred Peabody, June 2, 1969, as summarized in Winn, *That Magic Feeling*, 299.

[52] Miles, *Many Years from Now*, 537.

[53] *I Me Mine* 134.

[54] Unterberger, *The Unreleased Beatles*, 257-61.

[55] Lennon, Rolling Stone Interview, Dec. 1970, BBC, part 4; cf. Wenner, *Lennon Remembers*, 93. See also Everett II, 239.

lowing year, "I was also pleased when the movement in America took up 'Give peace a chance' because I had written it with that in mind really. . . . I felt an obligation even then to write a song that people would sing in the pub or on a demonstration."[56]

According to Derek Taylor, John wrote it for the Beatles,[57] but, as it was a Lennon-Ono composition, it ended up being performed and released by the Plastic Ono Band, which included John, Yoko, and whoever was performing with them at the time. It was recorded at a bed-in at the Hotel Le Reine Elizabeth in Montreal, Canada, on June 1, 1969, with many "guest artists," including Tommy Smothers on guitar, and as back-up vocalists, Timothy Leary, Derek Taylor, singer Petula Clark, members of the hotel staff, and visitors from the local Radha Krishna Temple.[58] "By now, it was nearing midnight, and John decided that he wanted to record his newly-written song 'Give Peace a Chance,'" wrote one journalist.[59]

It is a Lennon-Ono song, and Paul made no contribution to it. When it was first released, however, it was credited to "Lennon-McCartney." John says he gave Paul this credit at first because he felt bad that he (John) was leaving the Beatles. "I was guilty enough to give McCartney credit as co-writer on my first independent single instead of giving it to Yoko, who had actually written it with me,"[60] he admitted. In re-issues, it has been credited to Lennon alone.

This is arguably the first post-Beatle solo record.

o   Remember Love (Yoko Ono)

---

[56] Blackburn and Ali, interview.

[57] Derek Taylor, "Congratulations on a hit, everybody!" (1969).

[58] Ibid. Greenfield, *Timothy Leary: A Biography*, 358.

[59] Renard and Shnurmacher, "Eight Days in Montreal with John and Yoko," 24. Lost Lennon Tapes, Feb. 22, 1988. See also The Plastic Ono Band Unfinished Discography website; Winn, *That Magic Feeling*, 297.

[60] *Anthology* 148.

"Penina / Wings Of Revenge" single — Carlos Mendes, July 18, 1969

- Penina — (McCartney)

While Paul and his new girlfriend, Linda Eastman, were on vacation in Portimão, Portugal in December 1968, one night he turned up "pissed out of [his] skull,"[61] at the hotel La Penina, and played drums with the band, Jota Herre.

> And they said, "Give us a song," so I said, "Yeah ... I've been to Alberferra, I had a great time there," you know. It was called "La Penina," which was the name of the hotel, and I ended up in La Penina and they were all digging and singing along. ...

Jota Herre asked if they could record the song, and Paul agreed. "So, William Hickey said that I had given away this 20,000 pound song. But then, Derek Taylor said, "It's not that he gave away a song, he gave away more of a riff for them to build around."[62]

Jota Herre did record the song, but they were preceded by Carlos Mendes.

The song is attributed to Paul alone. It is probably the least of all the songs the Beatles gave away, not surprising considering it isn't really a song that was written; he just started singing it in public while playing drums in a state of inebriation one night.

- o Wings Of Revenge (João Magalhães Pereira, Nuno Nazareth Fernandes)

―――――――――◦◦――――――――

Abbey Road album, September 26, 1969

After the misery and chaos of the Get Back sessions, and with the Get Back tapes making no progress toward release, the Beatles decided to make

---

[61] Badman, *The Dream is Over*, 23-24.

[62] Ibid. See also Unterberger, *Unreleased Beatles*, 353, citing a 1994 *Club Sandwich*.

another album the old way, a studio album with George Martin as full producer. Martin, who had thought he would never work with the Beatles again, was stunned when Paul rang him up and told him that the Beatles wanted him to produce the album. "John included?" he asked incredulously. "Yes, honestly," said Paul.[63]

So, as their last hurrah, the Beatles returned to Abbey Road, to make a real Beatles album. Everyone was upbeat because they knew it would be their last album.

Abbey Road ended up divided into two parts: side one was "normal" songs, two by John, two by Paul, one by Ringo, and one by George. But for side two, Paul had the idea of creating an extended rock suite; this allowed them to use a number of song fragments. "I wanted to do something bigger, a kind of operatic moment," Paul said.[64]

John didn't like the idea, at first. But he ended up accepting it, and contributed some of his own songs to the second side suite. George Martin said,

> John objected very much to what we did on the second side of Abbey Road, which was almost entirely Paul and I working together, with contributions from the others. . . . But even on the second side, John helped. He would come and put his little bit in, and have an idea for sewing a bit of music into the tapestry.[65]

---

[63] George Martin, in *Anthology*, 337. See also Martin, "George Martin Interview" and Tobler and Grundy, "George Martin."

[64] Lewisohn, McCartney interview, 14. In 2000, Paul is cautious: "I think it was my idea to put all the spare bits together, but I'm a bit wary of claiming these things. I'm happy for it to be everyone's idea." *Anthology*, 33.

[65] *Anthology*, 338. John later had little good to say about this album. "I liked the 'A' side, I never liked that sort of whatever, pop opera on the other side . . . [*Abbey Road*] had no life in it." Lennon, Rolling Stone Interview, Dec. 1970, BBC, part 4; Miles, *Beatles in their Own Words*, 102. And in 1980 he described it as an album of fragments that had no unified center. Sheff, *The Playboy Interviews*, 212. More positive views by John are in *Anthology*, 337.

In fact, John has quite a substantial presence on side two, four songs, including his great song "Because."

Somehow, the suite worked (for most listeners), and side two of *Abbey Road* became a fitting culmination for the entire Beatles era.

- **Come Together — (Lennon-McCartney-Harrison-Leary-Berry)**
  (lead vocals: John) (recorded July 21–30, 1969)

The labyrinthine story of the songwriting for this particular song begins when Timothy Leary, the psychedelic guru, decided to run for governor of California in 1969. Leary, it should be remembered, had become a hero to John Lennon, and helped inspire *Revolver*'s climax, "Tomorrow Never Knows."

Leary attended John and Yoko's bed-in in Montreal in June 1969, on John's invitation, and asked the Beatle to write him a campaign song, based on the slogan, "Come together, join the party." John reportedly improvised a song on the spot, with the lyrics, "Come together right now, don't come tomorrow, don't come alone. Come together, right now, over me." John made a demo of the song, and it was reportedly played on the radio and used in Leary's campaign appearances.[66] "Leary was saying, 'Write me a song' for his campaign. And his campaign slogan was 'Come Together.' But obviously 'Come Together' is not a good campaign song," John said in 1969.[67]

Leary was arrested for narcotics possession, his political career ended, and John began thinking of using the lyrics for a Beatles record.[68] Soon

---

[66] Leary, *Flashbacks*, 281. Greenfield, *Timothy Leary: A Biography*, 358. Conners, *White Hand Society* (seen in Google books, no page number). Friedman, *Tripping*, 155. A primitive rendition of this campaign song can be found in "outtakes from Lennon's second bed-in event in Canada." Wikipedians, *The Beatles*, 553. Winn describes a song he titles "Get It Together" that "may or may not be John's attempt at writing a campaign song for Timothy Leary." This was recorded from May 26 to June 2, 1969. Winn, *That Magic Feeling*, 299.

[67] Miles, "My Blue Period" (interview conducted on Sept. 23-24, 1969). See also Sheff, *The Playboy Interviews*, 210-11. Connolly, *Ray Connolly Beatles Archive*, 107.

[68] For Leary's perspective, see Turner, *Hard Day's Write*, 188.

after his car crash on July 1, 1969, he began to rework the improvised campaign jingle into a real song.[69]

He turned to Chuck Berry's "You Can't Catch Me" as a model, musically and lyrically. He was, he said, "writing obscurely around an old Chuck Berry thing."[70]

> I was writing in the office just sort of — I can't say this 'cause we're gonna get sued, because it's silly. But I was writing this, um, like, 'You Can't Catch Me,' you know, the same rhythm and using the old words, I often do it, you know. If I'm trying to write one like 'Long Tall Sally,' or I'm just singing, . . . 'gonna tell unk Mary' and just make up, change, parodize the words. I was doing that and then when I got — I stopped and then said, just came out, 'Come together,' 'cause 'come together' was rolling around in my head.[71]

"I left the line in 'Here comes old flat-top,'" he said in 1980.[72] It was a quirky choice, but it shows he wasn't trying to mask his debt to Berry. "And I think it's a compliment to Chuck Berry."[73]

According to Paul, John played the song for him, at a very up-tempo speed, and Paul pointed out that it was very similar to the Chuck Berry song, and they should try to find distance somehow. Paul suggested that they slow it down. As he put it, "John came in with an up-tempo song that sounded exactly like Chuck Berry's 'You Can't Catch Me,' even down to the 'flat-top' lyric. I said, 'Let's slow it down with a swampy bass-and-drums vibe.' I came up with a bass line and it all flowed from there. Great record."[74]

---

[69] Yorke, Interview with George Harrison, September, 1969.

[70] Sheff, *The Playboy Interviews*, 210-11.

[71] Lost Lennon Tapes, March 14, 1988.

[72] Sheff, *The Playboy Interviews*, 210-11.

[73] Lost Lennon Tapes, March 14, 1988.

[74] *Anthology*, 339. See also Miles, *Many Years from Now*, 553.

John remembered the slowing down as a collective idea. In 1969, he said, "We said, 'Let's slow it down. Let's do this to it, let's do that to it,' and it ends up however it comes out."[75] "With 'Come Together' I just said to them, 'I've got no arrangement for you, but you know how I want it. Give me something funky.'"[76]

And in fact, he said, "The thing was created in the studio."[77] Geoff Emerick, back on the controls at Abbey Road, remembered, however, "It was Paul who suggested that it be done at a slower tempo, with a 'swampy' kind of sound, and Lennon went along with it uncomplainingly."[78] Emerick also said that Paul added a piano lick, which John learned and then played on the record.[79] George Harrison said that he "wrote some of the lyrics" of the song.[80]

All this came together, and the song became an impressive opening cut for *Abbey Road.*

Not surprisingly, Morris Levy, the owner of Berry's "You Can't Catch Me," sued the Beatles in 1973 (compare "Here come ol' flattop, he come groovin' up slowly" to Berry's "Here come a flattop, he was movin' up with me"), and in a settlement, John agreed to record three other songs by the same publisher. He recorded "You Can't Catch Me" and one of the other two required songs on his 1975 album of oldies, *Rock 'n' Roll.* Since the third song was not released, this opened him up to be sued again!

This is mainly a John song. "That's my song," he said in late 1969.[81] And, it was "one of my favorite Lennon tracks," he said in 1980.[82] Paul

[75] *Anthology* 339.
[76] Miles, "My Blue Period" (1969).
[77] Sheff, *The Playboy Interviews,* 210-11.
[78] *Here, There and Everywhere*, 284-85.
[79] Paul, in the 1984 *Playboy* interview, remembers playing the lick, but he may be remembering playing it the first time, not the performance on record.
[80] Smith, *Off the Record*, 261. See also Winn, *That Magic Feeling*, 323.
[81] Williams, "John & Yoko (part 1)." Similar: Hennessey, "Who Wrote What," *Record Mirror.* Aldridge, *Beatles Illustrated Lyrics*, 196. Miles, *Beatles in their Own Words*, 102. Badman, *Beatles Off the Record*, 468.
[82] Sheff, *The Playboy Interviews,* 210-11.

agreed, in 1969: "Well, I like 'Come Together.' That's a great one, which is John's one, yeah."[83] In the same year, George Harrison referred to it as "One of John's songs."[84] But its title comes from Timothy Leary; the first line from Chuck Berry. George Harrison says that he contributed to the lyrics. Paul convincingly describes reshaping the originally quite fast music into a slow, "smoky," "swampy" song.

I accept this as mainly a John song, built on Leary and Chuck Berry, with contributions from Paul and George.

- **Something (Harrison-Taylor)**
  (lead vocals: George) (recorded April 16 to August 15, 1969)

One day, during the White Album sessions, when Paul was busy doing overdubs, George went into a room with a piano, and wrote the main part of this song, though with incomplete lyrics, and perhaps lacking the chorus. He played it for Chris Thomas, often the functional producer for the *White Album* sessions, on October 19, 1968.[85] Since it was unfinished, it had to wait to find a home two albums later.

In 1969, George said that it was "maybe" "probably" written for his wife, Pattie: "**David:** *What inspired 'Something' for example?* **George:** Maybe Pattie, probably. **David:** *Really?* **George:** I wrote it at the time when we were making the last double album."[86] And Pattie said that George "told me, in a matter-of-fact way, that he had written it for me."[87] Later, he strongly denied that it was about Pattie. "*Now, you wrote that about Pattie, is*

---

[83] Wigg interview.

[84] Yorke, Interview with George Harrison, September, 1969. George said that John wrote this soon after his car crash on July 1, 1969. See also Winn, *That Magic Feeling*, 323.

[85] Lewisohn, *The Beatles Recording Sessions*, 156; Chris Thomas in Pritchard and Lysaght, *The Beatles: An Oral History*, 265; Harrison, *I Me Mine*, 152. For the White album vintage, see also Harrison before 1979 (transcript from Sold on Song website; abridged version in Cowan, *Behind the Beatles Songs*, 43). Yorke, Interview with George Harrison, 1969.

[86] Interview with David Wigg, Apple Offices, London, October 8, 1969.

[87] Boyd, *Wonderful Tonight*, 117.

that right? Well no, I didn't. . . . everybody presumed I wrote it about Pattie, but actually, when I wrote it, I was thinking of Ray Charles."[88]

It was evidently influenced, in its first line, by a James Taylor song named "Something In The Way She Moves," which would appear on Taylor's first album in December 1968. George had heard the song because Taylor was an Apple artist. The two songs are not otherwise similar, musically or lyrically. He admitted the influence in 1969,

> "Something" is a song of mine I wrote towards the end of . . . the White Album. . . . But I never finished it off. I could never think of words for it. And, um, also because there was a James Taylor song called 'Something In The Way She Moves,' which is the first line of that.[89]

George recorded a demo of this on February 25, 1969; it is available on *Anthology 3*.

- **Maxwell's Silver Hammer — (McCartney) (lead vocals: Paul) (recorded July 9–11 and August 6, 1969)**

Paul wrote this during the White Album sessions, and it was almost recorded for that album.[90] It was another of Paul's "fantasy songs" with fictitious characters.[91] Its gleefully macabre humor makes it a McCartney song "against type," in one sense, but Paul's humor could always lean toward the surreal. In 1995 Paul gave a surprisingly serious explanation of the song's philosophy: "'Maxwell's Silver Hammer' is my analogy for when

---

[88] Harrison 1996 (Cashmere, "George Harrison Gets 'Undercover'"). See also an interview in Badman, *Beatles Off the Record*, 469: "It wasn't about Patti. Everybody says it was, but it wasn't. It was just a song. It wasn't about anyone specific."

[89] Yorke, Interview with George Harrison. Comments from John and Paul: Lennon 1969 (Badman, *Beatles Off the Record*, 469). McCartney 1969 (Wigg interview). McCartney 2000 (*Anthology*, 96).

[90] Lewisohn, *Beatles Recording Sessions*, 179.

[91] *Anthology*, 339.

something goes wrong out of the blue, as it so often does, as I was beginning to find out at that time in my life."[92]

According to Linda, the song's story reflects the influence of avant-garde dramatist Alfred Jarry.[93] Paul used Jarry's word "Pataphysical" (the next step beyond metaphysical) in the lyrics.

This was performed during the Get Back sessions, on January 3, 7, 8 and 10.[94] The movie *Let It Be* shows some rehearsals of the song.

Paul, John and George all ascribed "Maxwell" to Paul. John called it "a typical McCartney sing-a-long."[95]

In Beatle lore, this song is remembered primarily as the focus for attacks by the other Beatles, and the time it took to record it. John said, in 1980, "That's Paul's. I hate it. 'Cause all I remember is the track — he made us do it one hundred million times."[96] (Strangely enough, given this quote, John did not perform on the song.[97]) Ringo turned the three days into "It went on for fucking weeks."[98] Actually, it took two days to record, and part of another; the third day was divided between "Maxwell" and two other songs.[99] Winn thinks John may be referring to the Get Back sessions, but this seems unlikely, as the song was only rehearsed for a few days in

---

[92] Miles, *Many Years from Now*, 554. Cf. earlier, Aldridge, *Beatles Illustrated Lyrics*, 246.

[93] Linda McCartney, *Linda McCartney's Sixties*, 153.

[94] Sulpy and Schweighardt, *Get Back*, 50, 95-100, 123, 171.

[95] Miles, "My Blue Period," (1969); Badman, *Beatles Off the Record*, 469, cf. *Anthology*, 339. See also Sheff, *The Playboy Interviews*, 211, quoted below. Yorke, Interview with George Harrison. See also Glazer, "Growing Up at 33 1/3."

[96] Lost Lennon Tapes, Oct. 21, 1991, cf. Sheff, *The Playboy Interviews*, 211.

[97] Badman, *Beatles Off the Record*, 469; also in *Anthology*, 339, but slightly different.

[98] Scaggs, "Ringo Starr" (2008), 22.

[99] Lewisohn, *Beatles Recording Sessions*, 179. Paul's replies to these criticisms: *Anthology*, 340; Salewicz, "Tug of War" (1986). John also despised the song itself, saying in late 1969: "The Beatles can go on appealing so a wide audience as long as they make albums like *Abbey Road*, which have nice little folk songs like 'Maxwell's Silver Hammer' for the grannies to dig." Williams, "John & Yoko (part 1)."

those sessions, many other songs were rehearsed on the same days, and it did not end up on the *Let It Be* album.[100]

- **Oh! Darling — (McCartney)**
  (lead vocals: Paul) (recorded April 20 to August 11, 1969)

  The Beatles began to play this song during the Get Back rehearsals.[101] Like many Beatles songs, it was modeled on black rhythm and blues performance.[102]

  Paul has never commented on writing this song, but he sings the lead, and has made proprietary comments on performing the song. In an early interview, he said that when he was recording the vocals, he came to the studio early every day to sing it by himself, as he wanted his voice to sound strained, "as though I'd been performing it on stage all week."[103] As there wasn't a lot of melody or "chordal magnificence" in the song, he felt he had to turn in a really good performance to bring it to life.[104]

  One person who frankly thought that Paul had failed in this objective was John, who said that Paul "didn't sing it too well. . . . He wrote it, so what the hell, he's going to sing it. If he'd had any sense, he should have let me sing it. [*Laughing*]"[105]

  "'Oh! Darling' was a great one of Paul's," he said in 1980.[106]

- **Octopus's Garden — (Starkey-Harrison)**
  (lead vocals: Ringo) (recorded April 26 to July 18, 1969)

  On August 22, 1968, during the White Album sessions, Ringo had a moment of despair, and decided to leave the Beatles. After announcing his

---

[100] Winn, *That Magic Feeling*, 305.

[101] Sulpy and Schweighardt, *Get Back*, 51-52, 96, 99, 126, 143, 203, 282.

[102] Pritchard and Lysaght, *The Beatles: An Oral History*, 289.

[103] Aldridge, *The Beatles Illustrated Lyrics*, 253. See also Miles, *Many Years from Now*, 555.

[104] Pritchard and Lysaght, *The Beatles: An Oral History*, 289.

[105] Sheff, *The Playboy Interviews*, 212. George, in 1969, also ascribed it to Paul, Ritchie Yorke, Interview with George Harrison.

[106] Sheff, *The Playboy Interviews*, 212. See also Hennessey, "Who Wrote What," *Record Mirror.*

decision to John and Paul, he left for Sardinia with his family. While he was there, a sea captain began telling him stories of octopi.[107] "He told me all about octopuses," Ringo said in 1981, "how they go round the sea bed and pick up stones and shiny objects and build gardens. I thought, 'How fabulous!' 'cause at the time I just wanted to be under the sea, too. I wanted to get out of it for a while."[108] (Ringo returned to the group about a week later.)

Though this song is credited to Ringo alone, and it started out as his idea, the Get Back tapes and the *Let It Be* movie show that George helped Ringo develop the song during the Get Back sessions.[109] On January 26, the chorus is non-existent, and George shows Ringo some piano chords that would work for it. Sulpy and Schweighardt write, "even these few minutes of rehearsal show George making a significant contribution to the song."[110] George and Ringo worked on the song through the day, with George Martin occasionally pointing out sections missing.

George referred to it as a Ringo song in 1969, but said, in 1988, "I've helped Ringo finish songs."[111] John, in an undated interview, said it was "the only song that he [Ringo] wrote on the album . . . It's a 'Ring-a-Long' 'Sing-A-Long.'"[112]

---

[107] Sulpy and Schweighardt, *Get Back*, 56; 273, at 26.15. See also Newborn, "Ringo in the Afternoon" (1981), 61.

[108] Newborn, "Ringo in the Afternoon"(1981), 61. See also *Anthology*, 312.

[109] George Harrison described it as a pure Ringo song, probably out of politeness. Yorke, Interview with George Harrison (1969).

[110] Sulpy and Schweighardt, *Get Back*, 271.

[111] Yorke, Interview with George Harrison (1969); Harrison in 1988 (Smith, *Off the Record*, 261).

[112] Badman, *Beatles Off the Record*, 470. John also comments briefly on the song in *Anthology*, 339.

- **I Want You, She's So Heavy — (Lennon)
(lead vocals: John) (recorded February 22 to August 11, 1969)**

The Beatles first played this toward the end of the Get Back sessions, on January 29, 1969.[113] It was a love song from John to Yoko,[114] and its minimalist lyrics were the product of Yoko's aesthetics.[115]

Paul has never commented on this song, but John's authorship is not in doubt.[116]

SIDE TWO

- **Here Comes the Sun (Harrison)
(lead vocals: George) (recorded July 7 to August 19, 1969)**

George started writing this one day when he decided to skip depressing business meetings at Apple and spend an afternoon at Eric Clapton's house, "Hurtwood" in Ewhurst. In a 1969 interview, he said, after describing the meetings with lawyers and bankers,

> And it was really awful, 'cause it's not the sort of thing we enjoy. And one day I didn't come in to the office. I just sort of, it was like sagging off school. ***David:*** *(laughs)* **George:** And I went to a friend's house in the country. And it was just sunny and it was all just the release of that tension that had been building up on me. And it was just a really nice sunny day. And I picked up the guitar, which was the first time I'd played the guitar for a couple of

[113] Sulpy and Schweighardt, *Get Back*, 293-94.

[114] Sheff, *The Playboy Interviews,* 211.

[115] Miles, "My Blue Period" (1969).

[116] Hennessey, "Who Wrote What," *Record Mirror.* Wenner, *Lennon Remembers*, 83. Aldridge, *Beatles Illustrated Lyrics*, 236. Yorke, Interview with George Harrison. Ringo, interview with David Jensen, September 26, 1969, as summarized in Winn, *That Magic Feeling*, 326.

weeks because I'd been so busy. And the first thing that came out was that song. It just came.[117]

After thus getting the beginning of it, he finished it later, when he and Pattie were on holiday in Sardinia, from June 1 to 23, 1969.[118]

Once again, George pointed to a Byrds influence on this song. "The riff going through it is the same as, uh — y'know, all those 'Bells Of Rhymney' sort of Byrd-type things," he said in 1969.[119]

- **Because — (Lennon-Ono)**
  (lead vocals: John, with Paul and George singing harmony)
  (recorded August 1 to 5, 1969)

This is another Beatle song that came directly from a classical source. Yoko, a classical trained musician, was playing Beethoven's Moonlight Sonata on the piano one day, and John said, "Play that backwards."[120] She played the chord progression backwards, and a song developed. "Well, it wasn't quite the reverse," said Ono, "I mean, it wasn't exact or anything — that was the inspiration."[121]

John brought the song to the recording studio, then worked on it with George Martin and the Beatles. Geoff Emerick remembered that at first John was singing it and "gently picking individual notes" on guitar "rather than playing chords." So John and the Beatles and George Martin worked

---

[117] Interview: Apple Offices, London, October 8, 1969. Similar statements: Yorke, Interview with George Harrison (1969); BBC interview, as quoted in Doggett, *Abbey Road*, 107 (1969); *I Me Mine*, 144.

[118] Interview: Apple Offices, London, October 8, 1969.

[119] Yorke, Interview with George Harrison.

[120] Smith, "Beatles Music Straightforward." Lennon, Interview with Tony Macarthur, late September, 1969: "Yoko plays classical piano, and she was playing one day. I dunno, it was Beethoven or something. I said, give me those chords backwards. And I wrote 'Because' on top of it." **[Yoko:]** Moonlight Sonata. **John:** Moonlight Sonata backwards. [laughter.]" Similar: Connolly, *Ray Connolly Beatles Archive*, 108. Aldridge, *The Beatles Illustrated Lyrics*, 257. Hennessey, "Who Wrote What." Sheff, *The Playboy Interviews*, 201.

[121] From a bootleg, *The Beatles In Their Own Words*, CD3 27.0, as cited in Beathoven, a website. Cf. Pritchard and Lysaght, *The Beatles: An Oral History*, 290.

on the chords to the song. John said, "I just asked George Martin, or whoever was round, "What's the alternative to thirds and fifths?" they're the only ones I know, and he plays them on a piano, and we'd say, "Oh, we'll have that one."[122]

At some point, John and the Beatles decided to do the song in three part harmony, a return to the style of early Beatle songs such as "Yes It Is" or "This Boy." John, Paul and George worked these harmony parts out, then started recording them, doing take after take. Finally, John rebelled, "at one point snapping, 'Jesus Christ, give me a break already . . . I wish I hadn't written the bloody thing!'"[123]

The song's authorship is not controversial. "I've just written a song called "Because," John told Alan Smith in 1969.[124] Paul said he had nothing to do with "Because," but thought that Yoko was probably a co-writer.[125] George, in an early interview, said, "'Because' is one of the most beautiful tunes. And I think it's three-part harmony, John, Paul and George all sing it together. John wrote this tune."[126] George Martin commented: "'Because' was a strange song for John to write. He got the idea from the arpeggios in Beethoven's Moonlight Sonata but the choral work was really classical Beatles."[127]

However, in the 1969 interview with Alan Smith, after describing the genesis of the song in the Moonlight Sonata, John said, "and we [John and Yoko] had a tune. We'll probably write a lot more in the future." Here he seems to reflect collaboration with Ono.[128]

---

[122] Lennon, Interview with Tony Macarthur, late September, 1969. See also Winn, *That Magic Feeling*, 326; Badman, *Beatles Off the Record*, 471.

[123] Emerick, *Here, There and Everywhere*, 292-93.

[124] Alan Smith, "Beatles Music Straightforward On Next Album."

[125] Wigg interview (1969). Miles, *Many Years from Now*, 555.

[126] Yorke, Interview with George Harrison (1969).

[127] George Martin, *In My Life* album, cover notes. See also Pritchard and Lysaght, *The Beatles: An Oral History*, 290.

[128] Alan Smith, "Beatles Music Straightforward On Next Album."

In light of this early statement, I accept Yoko as a collaborator on "Because," though John was far and away the dominant writer. One could also make a case for George Martin as a minor collaborator, as he contributed to working out the harmony, by Lennon's own account.

- **You Never Give Me Your Money — (McCartney) (lead vocals: Paul) (recorded May 6 to August 6, 1969)**

This song is another document reflecting McCartney's pain as the Beatles were breaking up. "I wrote this when we were going through all our financial difficulties at Apple," he said in an early interview.[129] It has the patented Beatle organization of song fragments thrown together. The main song is apparently addressed to Allen Klein.

> That was me directly lambasting Allen Klein's attitude toward us: no money, just funny paper, all promises and it never works out. It's basically a song about no faith in the person, that found its way into the medley in *Abbey Road*. John saw the humour in it.[130]

It's curiously gentle, lyrical music to accompany such a theme.

Another song fragment dealt with Paul and Linda on one of their "going nowhere" trips — expeditions in which they would jump into a car and drive for hours without a definite goal, simply enjoying the scenery, getting away from everything.[131]

Paul wrote this song while the Beatles (and Linda) were in New York, in May 1968. He and Linda would marry on March 12, 1969.

Both Paul and John ascribed this to Paul.[132] George selected it as one of his favorites on Abbey Road. "You know, Paul always writes nice melodies. In fact, I don't know where he finds them half the time."[133]

---

[129] Aldridge, *Beatles Illustrated Lyrics*, 196. Miles, *Many Years from Now*, 556.

[130] Miles, *Many Years from Now*, 556. Also, Snow, "We're a damn good little band."

[131] Miles, *Many Years from Now*, 556. See also "Two of Us" in *Let It Be*, below.

[132] *Anthology*, 337. For John, Hennessey, "Who Wrote What," *Record Mirror* (1971); Sheff, *The Playboy Interviews*, 212.

[133] Interview: Apple Offices, London, October 8, 1969. See also *Anthology*, 337.

- ## Sun King — (Lennon-McCartney) (lead vocals: John) (recorded on July 24 and 25, 1969)

According to Miles/McCartney, John dreamed this song, though I haven't been able to find John himself saying this.[134] Paul also thought John had been influenced by Nancy Mitford's biography of Louis XIV, *The Sun King* (1966). John described it as "just half a song that I had which I never finished, which was one way of getting rid of it without every finishing it, you know."[135]

Paul helped with the "Spanish" lyrics, as John explained:

> [On "Sun King"] when we came to sing it, to make them different, so it wasn't just the same riff, we just started joking, you know, saying "*cuandopara mucho.*" So we just made it up. Paul knew a few Spanish words from school, so we just strung any Spanish words that sounded vaguely like something. And of course we got "*chickaferdi*" in — that's a Liverpool expression; just like it doesn't mean anything, just like "ha ha ha."[136]

This is a John song. "My contribution [to the medley] is 'Polythene Pam,' and 'Sun King' and 'Mean Mr Mustard,'" he said in 1969. "So we just juggled them about until it made vague sense."[137] However, Paul helped with the Spanish.

---

[134] Miles, *Many Years from Now*, 556; Turner, *Hard Day's Write*, 194.

[135] Lennon, Interview with Tony Macarthur, late September, 1969.

[136] Ibid.

[137] Lennon, Interview with Tony Macarthur, late September, 1969. Hennessey, "Who Wrote What," *Record Mirror*. Sheff, *The Playboy Interviews*, 214.

- **Mean Mr. Mustard — (Lennon)**
  (lead vocals: John) (recorded for *Abbey Road* from July 24 to 29, 1969)

John wrote this song in India, and it became "another half a song which I never finished."[138] As was the case with many Beatle songs, its lyrics were based on a newspaper story.[139] John wrote it after reading an account of a man who kept his money in his rectum. "I'd read somewhere in the newspaper about this mean guy who, something about he hid five-pound notes, not up his nose but somewhere else. It had nothing to do with cocaine or snorting," he said in 1980.[140] John changed the name of Mr. Mustard's sister to Pam in order to lead into "Polythene Pam."[141]

Both John and Paul ascribed this to John, though John had no great fondness for it. "That's me, writing a piece of garbage," he said in 1980.[142] Paul in 1995, said, "'Mean Mr Mustard' was very John. I liked that. A nice quirky song."[143]

It was performed as one of the Esher demos in May 1968, which is on *Anthology 3*. The Beatles also played it during the Get Back sessions.[144]

- **Polythene Pam — (Lennon)**
  (lead vocals: John) (recorded July 25 to 30, 1969)

The Beatles knew Royston Ellis, a beat poet, in Liverpool — John called him "England's answer to Allen Ginsberg." In August 1963, they ran into him after a show in Guernsey, in the Channel Islands, and Ellis introduced John to his girlfriend, Stephanie, who dressed in polythene.

---

[138] Lennon, Interview with Tony MacArthur, late September, 1969. See also *Anthology*, 337. Yorke, Interview with George Harrison. Miles, "My Blue Period" (September 1969).

[139] Lennon, Interview with Tony MacArthur, late September, 1969.

[140] Lost Lennon Tapes, March 14, 1988, cf. Sheff, *The Playboy Interviews,* 212.

[141] Lennon, Interview with Tony MacArthur, late September, 1969. *Anthology*, 337.

[142] Lost Lennon Tapes, March 14, 1988, cf. Sheff, *The Playboy Interviews,* 212. See also Connolly, *Ray Connolly Beatles Archive*, 109. Hennessey, "Who Wrote What," *Record Mirror*. Miles, "My Blue Period" (September 1969). *Anthology*, 337.

[143] Miles, *Many Years from Now*, 421.

[144] Sulpy and Schweighardt, *Get Back*, 121-23, 201.

"She didn't wear jack boots and kilts, I just sort of elaborated. . . . Perverted sex in a polythene bag. . . . I was just looking for something to write about."[145]

Paul remembered, in 2000: "He came back with all these tales about a girl who dressed in polythene: 'Shit! There was this chick and it was great . . .' and we thought, 'Oh, wow!' Eventually he wrote the song."[146] This memory of Ellis and "Polythene Pam" was so vivid to John, that when he was in India, some five years later, he wrote the song there.[147]

Both Paul and John ascribed this to John. In an early interview, John said, "I wrote this one in India, and when I recorded it I used a thick Liverpool accent because it was supposed to be about a mythical Liverpool scrubber [groupie] dressed up in her jackboots and kilt."[148]

Like "Mean Mr. Mustard" this became one of the Esher demos (recorded in May 1968), now available on *Anthology 3*, then was performed during the Get Back sessions.[149]

- **She Came in Through the Bathroom Window — (McCartney)**
  (lead vocals: Paul) (recorded July 25 to 30, 1969)

John said that Paul came up with the title of the song in May 1968, when the pair were in New York, doing publicity for Apple. "We were just

---

[145] Lost Lennon Tapes, March 14, 1988, cf. Sheff, *The Playboy Interviews,* 212-13. Ellis's memories were substantially the same. Ghosh, "The Beatles In 1960 Liverpool: Royston Ellis Remembers." Turner has another theory: The Beatles had a friend, Pat Dawson, "Polythene Pat," who ate polythene. *Hard Day's Write*, 196-97. Long-time Beatle associate Tony Bramwell, in Badman, *The Beatles Off the Record*, 473, felt that the song dealt with a specific homeless lady who kept her possessions in plastic bags. Both these theories seem weak in the face of John's explicit mention of Royston Ellis and his polythene-wearing girlfriend.

[146] *Anthology*, 337. Also, Miles, *Many Years from Now*, 556.

[147] Aldridge, *Beatles Illustrated Lyrics*, 232. Connolly, *Ray Connolly Beatles Archive*, 107.

[148] Ibid. See also John's comments in Lennon, Interview with Tony MacArthur, late September, 1969; *Anthology*, 337 (full quote at "Sun King"). Hennessey, "Who Wrote What," *Record Mirror*. Miles, *Beatles in their Own Words*, 75. Badman, *The Beatles Off the Record*, 472.

[149] Sulpy and Schweighardt, *Get Back*, 240. Unterberger, *The Unreleased Beatles*, 251.

in the flat we were staying in and he just came out with that line, y'know, 'She Came in Through the Bathroom Window.' So, he'd had it for years, so he eventually finished it."[150]

According to Paul, he got the words for the third verse ("And so I quit the police department") from something he saw during a cab ride in New York. The cabbie's name, Eugene Quits, was underneath his photo, and beneath it was written, "New York Police Dept." This verse had no logical coherence with the rest of the lyrics, but "This was the great thing about the randomness of it all," Paul said.[151] Or one could easily call this avant-garde aesthetic of randomness flawed.

John, in 1980, tentatively suggested that it might have been Linda who came in through the bathroom window.[152] Paul, two years later, disagreed: "No she wasn't." He explained that it might have been a subconscious meaning but he didn't knowingly write the song with her in mind. "A lot of the time when I do songs like that, it's just because the words sound good."[153]

Two non-Beatles have offered theories for the song's title. The "Apple Scruffs" who would hang around Paul's house once broke in while he was gone, using the bathroom window to gain entrance, and stole some photos and clothes.[154] One of the Scruffs, Carol Bedford, said Paul told her, "I've written a song about the girls who broke in."[155] John, however, explicitly said that the song was not about the Apple Scruffs.[156]

Mike Pinder of the Moody Blues said that he told Paul of a groupie who climbed through a bathroom window into the band's house. Paul

---

[150] Lennon, Interview with Tony MacArthur, late September, 1969.

[151] Miles, *Many Years from Now*, 521.

[152] Sheff, *The Playboy Interviews*, 212.

[153] Bonici, "Paul McCartney Wings It Alone."

[154] Turner, *Hard Day's Write*, 198.

[155] Carol Bedford, *Waiting for the Beatles* (1985), as cited in Turner, *Hard Day's Write*, 198.

[156] Badman, *The Beatles Off the Record*, 473.

took up a guitar and sang, "She came in through a bathroom window."[157] This does not have the support of any statement by Paul or John.

Paul, John and George ascribed this to Paul. In 1982, Paul said, "I wrote it."[158] The song was played frequently during the Get Back sessions. A slower version appears on *Anthology 3*.

- ### Golden Slumbers — (McCartney-Dekker) (lead vocals: Paul) (recorded July 2 to August 15, 1969)

Paul started writing this when he was visiting his father's home, Rembrandt, in Cheshire, near Liverpool. He sat down at the piano and found a music book of his half-sister, Ruth, which had "Cradle Song" in it, a song with lyrics by Elizabethan dramatist and poet Thomas Dekker (1572–1632), a poem that was first published in 1603. In his earliest account of the song, Paul said,

> So I was just flicking through it and I came to Golden Slumbers, . . . I can't read music so I didn't know the tune, and I can't remember the old tune, you know. . . . So I started just playing MY tune to it. And then I liked the words so I just kept that, you know. And then it fitted with another bit of song I had which is the verse in between it. So I just made that into a song.[159]

Here is the original Dekker poem:

> Golden slumbers kiss your eyes,
> Smiles awake you when you rise ;
> Sleep, pretty wantons, do not cry,
> And I will sing a lullaby,

---

[157] *The Classic Artists Series: the Moody Blues*, a DVD documentary, as cited in Wikimedia, *The Beatles*, 1284.

[158] Bonici, "Paul McCartney Wings It Alone." Sheff, *The Playboy Interviews*, 212. Hennessey, "Who Wrote What," *Record Mirror*. Yorke, Interview with George Harrison.

[159] David Wigg interview, September 19, 1969. See also Aldridge, *The Beatles Illustrated Lyrics*, 246; Miles, *Many Years from Now*, 537.

Rock them, rock them, lullaby.

Care is heavy, therefore sleep you,

You are care, and care must keep you ;

Sleep, pretty wantons, do not cry,

And I will sing a lullaby,

Rock them, rock them, lullaby.

Paul, John and George ascribed this to Paul (with help from Dekker).[160] It was played during the Get Back sessions.[161]

- **Carry That Weight — (McCartney)
(lead vocals: Paul) (recorded July 2 to August 15, 1969)**

Paul said he wrote this song at a time of great stress. "I'm generally quite upbeat but at certain times things get to me so much that I just can't be upbeat anymore and that was one of those times. We were taking so much acid and doing so much drugs and all this Klein shit and [things were] getting crazier and crazier and crazier."[162] The music, strangely enough, is joyful.

Paul has never specifically talked about writing this song, though he has discussed the lyrics frequently. John ascribed it to Paul. In 1969, when asked if the song was co-written, he said, "No, that's Paul's line." And ten years later, "That's Paul again."[163]

"Golden Slumbers" and "Carry that Weight" were recorded as a single song. Paul played them that way during the Get Back sessions.[164]

- **The End — (McCartney)
(lead vocals: Paul) (recorded July 23 to August 18, 1969)**

The Beatles were looking for an end to *Abbey Road*, and Paul remembered how Shakespeare would end a scene with a couple of memorable tag

---

[160] Sheff, *The Playboy Interviews*, 213. Hennessey, "Who Wrote What," *Record Mirror*. Yorke, Interview with George Harrison.

[161] Sulpy and Schweighardt, *Get Back*, 80, 141.

[162] Miles, *Many Years from Now*, 557-58.

[163] Hennessey, "Who Wrote What," *Record Mirror*. Sheff, *The Playboy Interviews*, 213.

[164] Sulpy and Schweighardt, *Get Back*, 56-57, 77, 80, 84, 141-42.

lines. Paul wanted the album to end "with a little meaningful couplet, so I followed the Bard and wrote a couplet."[165] And the thought just came into his mind: "And in the end the love you take is equal to the love you make."

Each of the Beatles took an instrumental solo as they recorded the song,[166] and *Abbey Road*, and the Beatles era was over.

Until "Her Majesty," of course.

Both Paul and John ascribed this to Paul.[167]

• Her Majesty — (McCartney) (lead vocals: Paul) (recorded July 2, 1969)

Paul wrote this little ditty in Scotland. "I just wrote it as a joke, you know."[168] He described the political philosophy of the song as "basically monarchist . . . It's almost like a love song to the Queen."[169]

In the *Abbey Road* lineup, "Her Majesty" originally followed "Mean Mr. Mustard," but Paul decided it didn't work, and told the engineer, John Kurlander, to throw it away. Kurlander cut it out of the master tape, but attached it to the end of the reel, separated by a stretch of leader, which was a common practice. When the album was transferred to acetate, "Her Majesty" suddenly started playing at the very end, by accident. Paul liked that effect, and kept the song as a coda to the album.[170]

Both Paul and John ascribed this to Paul.[171] He performed it during the Get Back sessions.[172]

---

[165] Miles, *Many Years from Now*, 558.

[166] *Anthology*, 337. Badman, *The Beatles Off the Record*, 474.

[167] Hennessey, "Who Wrote What," *Record Mirror*. Sheff, *The Playboy Interviews*, 213.

[168] Wigg interview.

[169] Miles, *Many Years from Now*, 558. See also Badman, *The Beatles Off the Record*, 474.

[170] Miles/McCartney, *Many Years from Now*, 558; Kurlander, in Dowlding, *Beatlesongs*, 294.

[171] For John, see Hennessey, "Who Wrote What," *Record Mirror*.

[172] Sulpy and Schweighardt, *Get Back*, 141, 244.

14

"Writing the song was my way of exorcizing the ghosts"

LET IT BE

The original idea of the Get Back sessions was to watch the Beatles developing an album, filming them as they rehearsed, ending in a live performance. In addition, the Beatles would retreat from their orchestrated, elaborately overdubbed studio recordings and create a recording of the band alone. John somewhat undiplomatically told George Martin, "I don't want any of your production rubbish on this one. I don't want any overdubbing of voices. I don't want any editing. Everything has got to be performed live like it used to be. It's got to be real, man, it's got to be honest."[1] However, as the Get Back sessions progressed, the Beatles gradually began to depart from this ideal.

Ironically, John led the way in bringing in Phil Spector (who had recently produced John's Plastic Ono Band single, "Instant Karma!") to "reproduce" the album, and Spector added many overdubs, and even full orchestrations in some places. Here we have John going against type again; while we often associate him with hard rock, he is the Beatle most responsible for the lush strings, harps and choral voices added by Spector on *Let It Be*. Apparently Paul (and certainly George Martin) had no idea that Spector was "re-producing" the album in this way. (Paul knew Spector was working on the album, but did not realize that he was adding many overdubs with orchestral instruments.) Paul, always extremely concerned about the details of recording and arranging his own songs, was understandably

---

[1] Quoted in Torrance, "Don't Let It Be." See also Tobler and Grundy, "George Martin." George Harrison, on the bonus fly-on-the wall disk *Let It Be . . . Naked*, also emphasized the necessity for no overdubs on this album.

upset to hear that some of his songs had received this Spector treatment. George Martin said,

> I knew that John was going in the studios, doing some work on *Let It Be*, but I understood that as they were making a film of it, they were doing some film tracks. When the record finally came out, I got a hell of a shock. ***Melody Maker:*** *You didn't know anything about it?* **George M.:** Nothing. Neither did Paul, and Paul wrote to me to say that he was pretty appalled, if you'll forgive the pun. All the lush un-Beatle-like orchestrations with harps and choirs in the background.[2]

As a result, John was sensitive about how he and George had brought Spector in, and perhaps overemphasized the low quality of the Glyn Johns compilations and of the Get Back sessions in general. "He [Spector] was given the *shittiest* load of badly recorded shit that — and with a lousy feeling to it — ever. And he made *something* out of it," he said in 1970. "It wasn't fantastic, but it was — when I heard it, I didn't puke."[3]

Paul, on the other hand, had liked the bare Glyn Johns mixes. "We then mixed it once with Glyn Johns, who'd done a very straightforward mix, very plain, but I loved it because it was just the Beatles. It was us. It had a lot of character," he said.[4] He thought that Allen Klein pulled in Phil Spector, when he didn't think the Get Back tapes were good enough. Paul, of course, hadn't signed with Klein. In 1989, Paul said that Spector's contribution was not a total disaster: "For what he was pulled in to do I

---

[2] Williams, "Produced by George Martin." This is slightly unfair; Martin had given a Beatle song like John's "Goodnight" a lush orchestration, though at John's request. See also George Martin (interview in *Melody Maker*, quoted in Doggett, *Abbey Road*, 78); George Martin in Pritchard & Lysaght, *The Beatles: An Oral History*, 307.

[3] Lennon, Rolling Stone Interview, Dec. 1970, BBC, part 4, cf. Wenner, *Lennon Remembers*, 120. See also 118-21.

[4] Read, "McCartney on McCartney," episode 4. Salewicz, "Tug of War," 60.

thought he did a good job. And you can't blame him, he was hired in and he thought we all agreed and knew what was happening."[5]

In any event, the Spector version of *Let It Be* was released and became part of the Beatles canon. However, in November 2003, the surviving Beatles released a de-Spectorized version of the album, *Let It Be . . . Naked*. Time will tell if this supplants the 1970 *Let It Be*, or if the two versions of the album are eventually regarded as equally valid.

Wedding Album — John Lennon and Yoko Ono, October 20 (U.S.), November 7 (U.K.), 1969

John and Yoko's third experimental album commemorated their marriage on March 20, 1969. John explained,

> It was like us sharing our wedding with whoever wanted to share it with us. We didn't expect a hit record out of it. People make a wedding album, show it to relatives when they come round. Well, our relatives are what you call fans, or people that follow us outside. So, that was our way of letting them join in on the wedding.[6]

It included no real songs, except for an early version of Yoko's "John John Let's Hope for Peace" and John doing an acoustic performance of "Goodnight."

Side one ("John and Yoko") recorded John and Yoko calling to each other over the sound of heartbeats; it was recorded on April 22 and 27, 1969. John said, "It's in stereo and our heartbeats are bumping along there, like African drums and we howl over the top. I sing 'Yoko' and she sings 'John', continuously through one side of it. It's like an extended, very extreme, . . . It really makes your hair stand on end."[7]

---

[5] Read, "McCartney on McCartney," episode 4.

[6] As quoted in The Plastic Ono Band Unfinished Discography website. See also Williams, "John & Yoko (part 2)."

[7] As quoted in The Plastic Ono Band Unfinished Discography website.

Side two ("Amsterdam") was recorded in a hotel in Amsterdam from March 25 to 31, 1969, including moments from John and Yoko's "bed-in" honeymoon, mixed with random sounds.

———————◦———————

"Cold Turkey / Don't Worry Kyoko (Mummy's Only Looking for a Hand in the Snow)" single — Plastic Ono Band, October 24, 1969

- Cold Turkey — (Lennon)
  (recorded September 25 to 28, 1969)

As has been mentioned, John and Yoko became addicted to heroin during the White Album sessions. Finally, they realized they needed to stop taking the drug, so subjected themselves to complete withdrawal — "cold turkey." This song describes that experience; it is directly in John's confessional mode of songwriting. In 1970, he said that it wasn't a song, but a diary.[8] "I wrote this about coming off drugs and the pain involved," he stated in an early interview.[9]

John offered this to the Beatles as a single, but they were not enthusiastic, either put off by the drug lyrics or the minimalist music. John said, in late 1969, "When I wrote it, I went to the other three Beatles and said, 'Hey, lads, I think I've written a new single.' But they all said, 'Ummm . . . arrr . . . wellll,' because it was going to be my project, and so I thought, 'Bugger you, I'll put it out myself.'"[10]

So John released it as a solo record, with the Plastic Ono Band, which now included John, Yoko, Eric Clapton, Klaus Voorman from Hamburg days on bass, and Ringo on drums. It's typical of this time period, which was a bridge between the Beatles and the solo Beatles eras. "Cold Turkey" might have been a Beatles single, but ended up being the second Plastic

---

[8] Wenner, *Lennon Remembers*, 15.
[9] Aldridge, *Beatles Illustrated Lyrics*, 210.
[10] Williams, "John & Yoko (part 1)".

Ono Band single, though the band included two Beatles. It was the first Lennon song credited to Lennon, not Lennon-McCartney.

The Plastic Ono Band premiered "Cold Turkey" at the Toronto Rock & Roll Revival Festival on September 13, 1969, and so it was included on *Live Peace in Toronto, 1969.*

   o   <u>"Don't Worry Kyoko (Mummy's Only Looking for a Hand in the Snow) (Yoko Ono)</u>

"Come and Get It / Rock Of All Ages" single — Badfinger, December 5, 1969

- **Come and Get It — (McCartney) (recorded by Badfinger on August 2, 1969)**

The idea of this song came to Paul late at night, when he was in bed at Cavendish Avenue. He left Linda in bed, went downstairs, "and just whispered it into my tape recorder. I played it very quietly so as not to wake her."[11]

The next day, July 24, 1969, he came in early to a recording session at Abbey Road and did a demo of the song, playing all the instruments himself. "Because I lived locally, I could get in half an hour before a Beatles session at Abbey Road — knowing it would be empty and all the stuff would be set up — and I'd use Ringo's equipment to put a drum track down, put some piano down quickly, put some bass down, do the vocal and double track it."[12] He recorded the demo in about twenty minutes and was satisfied with it. (This has been released on *Anthology 3*.)

Paul ended up giving the song to Badfinger, a group that had signed with Apple.[13] Originally known as The Iveys, they hailed from Wales (except for one Liverpudlian), and were talented songwriters in their own right. They went on to a career that was at times very successful, though

---

[11] Miles, *Many Years from Now*, 550. Thomson, "Paul McCartney," (2005).
[12] *Anthology*, 289.
[13] Bill Collins, manager of Badfinger, in Aldridge, *Beatles Illustrated Lyrics*, 227.

business and tragic personal problems eventually caused the group to split up.

Paul produced the recording session, on August 2; Badfinger followed the demo closely,[14] and the single became a solid success. This song, with two other Badfinger songs, appeared in the comedy *The Magic Christian* (released December 1969).

"Come and Get It" was correctly credited to Paul alone.

- **Rock Of All Ages (Evans, Ham, Gibbins, McCartney) (recorded on September 18, 1969)**

While this song is credited to members of Badfinger, Tom Evans, Pete Ham, and Mike Gibbins, Paul helped develop it. Evans said:

> So we started making up a song similar to "Long Tall Sally" in G. We just did the backing track. When it came time to do the vocal I was just floundering over it. He [Paul] started to sing with me and we both kind of made it up. There's a great take of me and him singing it together. I said, "You've got to use that on the record, please use that on the record." He said, "No, you go down and do it properly."[15]

No One's Gonna Change Our World album — various artists, December 12, 1969

- **Across the Universe — (Lennon) (lead vocals: John) (recorded February 4, 8, 1968)**

This great song, written back in 1967 during the *Sgt. Pepper* era, finally sees the light of day. For a full treatment, see the *Let It Be* album, below.

---

[14] For the session, Lewisohn interview, *Beatles Recording Sessions*, (1988), 11; *Anthology* 289; Matovina, *Without You*, 63; Tom Evans of Badfinger, in Badman, *Beatles Off the Record*, 480.
[15] Matovina, *Without You*, 62.

Live Peace in Toronto 1969 album — Plastic Ono Band, December 12, 1969

The Plastic Ono Band lineup that had recorded "Cold Turkey" performed on September 13, 1969 at the Toronto Rock and Roll Revival festival (but now with Alan White playing drums, instead of Ringo), and this live album of the performance was released.[16] It is arguably the first post-Beatles solo album.

o Blue Suede Shoes (Carl Perkins)

Carl Perkins released this rock 'n' roll standard in 1956, and it was widely covered, including a version by Elvis, also in 1956. The Beatles had performed it as part of a medley during the Get Back sessions, and this can be found on *Anthology 3*.

o Money (That's What I Want) (Janie Bradford, Berry Gordy)

See above, *With the Beatles*.

o Dizzy Miss Lizzy (Larry Williams)

See above, *Help!*.

o Yer Blues

See above, *White Album*.

o Cold Turkey

See above, "Cold Turkey" single.

o Give Peace a Chance

See above, "Give Peace a Chance" single.

---

[16] For this performance, see Mal Evans, "John and Yoko's Toronto Concert."; Winn, *That Magic Feeling*, 321.

Let It Be

SIDE TWO

- o <u>Don't Worry Kyoko (Mummy's Only Looking for Her Hand in the Snow) (Yoko Ono)</u>
- o <u>John, John (Let's Hope for Peace) (Yoko Ono)</u>

———————————◦●◦———————————

There is no absolute dividing line between the Beatles era and the solo Beatles era. However, one possible point of demarcation is January 4, 1970, which is the last day when the Beatles (minus John, who was on vacation in Denmark) got together at Abbey Road to re-record and add overdubs to "Let It Be" from the Get Back sessions. (The day before, they had re-recorded George's "I Me Mine.")

In this book I will use January 4, 1970 as the end of the Beatles era, for practical purposes, though, as we have seen, the Beatles' solo careers had already begun. John had released Plastic Ono Band recordings before this, and Paul had started recording *McCartney* in December 1969. *Let It Be* had yet to be released, but it had been substantially recorded long before *Abbey Road*.

In another sense, the Beatles era continued, as songs written and rehearsed during the Beatles heyday continued to appear on the Beatles' solo albums, and later in important collections such as the three *Anthology* albums and *Let It Be . . . Naked*. So I will continue to look at the solo songs that had direct roots in the Beatles era, and new releases of recordings from that time period.

Of course, in another sense, the Beatles era continued in new songs written by the Beatles after the breakup. A careful examination of the Beatle solo albums shows close connections, in quality, subject matter, and aesthetics, between them and the Beatles' earlier work. I don't see a sudden disastrous drop-off in content or quality, though there were obvious stylistic changes at times. For me, the dream continued, if we view the dream as the high songwriting skills of the Beatles. Certainly, there have been high and low points, great, good, and bad songs, during the solo Beatles' career, but we tend to forget that there were great, good and bad songs during the

Beatles' career. John could write "Strawberry Fields," "I'm Only Sleeping," as well as "Run for Your Life." Paul could write "Hey Jude, "Here There Everywhere," as well as "All Together Now." George could write "Something" and "Here Comes the Sun" on one album, and "For You Blue" and "I Me Mine" on the next.

From this point on, I will consider songs that were written before January 4, 1970, but were released after that date.

───────●○●───────

This Girl's In Love With You album — Aretha Franklin, February 21, 1970

○ Let It Be — (McCartney) (recorded December 1969)

Possibly the first release of "Let It Be."[17] See below, "Let it Be / You Know My Name Look Up My Number" single, and the *Let It Be* album.

───────●○●───────

"Ain't That Cute / Vaya Con Dios" single — Doris Troy, February 13, 1970

• Ain't That Cute (Harrison-Troy)

George wrote this with soul singer Doris Troy, best known for the song, "Just One Look." She had come to England to live, and George signed her to Apple and helped with her album, *Doris Troy*.[18] He said,

> We did her single, "Ain't That Cute," which we wrote in the studio, actually. This is a good exercise because ... I wouldn't consider going in there and just making it up on the spot, which is what we did with "Ain't That Cute." We didn't have a song, so we made it up, and I just pinched the chords from (Leon Russell's) "Delta Lady" and away I

---

[17] See Engelhardt, *Beatles Undercover*, 175. The Franklin album may have been delayed.

[18] Unterberger, *The Unreleased Beatles*, 354.

went. We wrote that, and it's very nice, with Pete Frampton playing guitar.[19]

The album, *Doris Troy*, was recorded during the Beatles era, mid-1969 to end of the year.

○   <u>Vaya Con Dios (Larry Russell, Inez James, Buddy Pepper)</u>

———————

"Let It Be / You Know My Name Look Up My Number" single, March 6, 1970

- **Let It Be — (McCartney)**
  (lead vocals: Paul) (recorded January 31, April 30, 1969, January 4, 1970, March 26, 1970)

"Let It Be," written during the White Album sessions,[20] was another song that came from a dream. Paul experienced dark, paranoid times in the late sixties, caused by drugs, the breakup of his working relationship with John (in part due to John's relationship with Yoko), and the looming bitter breakup of the Beatles and the accompanying business and legal problems.

Paul had always been close to his mother, Mary Patricia Mohin McCartney, who had died in 1956, when Paul was fourteen. More than a decade later, as the Beatles were approaching their breakup, as emotionally painful and catastrophic as a divorce, Paul had a dream and "saw my mum, who'd been dead ten years or so." They talked, and to Paul, he and she seemed "to both be physically together again. It was so wonderful for me." She might not have said "let it be," but she was very reassuring. Things would work out. "It was such a sweet dream I woke up thinking, Oh, it was really great to visit with her again. I felt very blessed to have that dream. So that got me writing the song "Let It Be." I literally started off "Mother Mary," which was her name."[21]

---

[19] George Harrison, quoted in liner notes from *Doris Troy*. Possibly from a 1970 interview, see Winn, *That Magic Feeling*, 376.

[20] Everett II, 198.

[21] Miles, *Many Years from Now*, 538.

Paul wrote the song as therapy: "Writing the song was my way of exorcizing the ghosts."[22]

Both Paul and John ascribed this song to Paul.[23] In 1980, John said, "That's Paul. . . . Nothing to do with the Beatles, no, it could've been Wings, right? . . . I don't know what he's thinking when he writes 'Let It Be.'"[24] This comment parallels John's contention that the real Beatle breakup happened before the White album.

Mal Evans has a severely revisionist account of this song's writing, in which Paul saw *him* in a dream, and changed the lyrics to "mother Mary."[25] This must be rejected in favor of Paul's strong, consistent testimony through the years.

The Beatles started performing "Let It Be" during the Get Back sessions, on January 3, 1969. The master recording was made on January 31. George Harrison added overdub solos on April 30, 1969 (used for the single release) and January 4, 1970 (used for the album release). The single version of the song was produced by George Martin, with Paul's help, and included orchestrations and overdubs, also added on January 4.[26] This single version can be found on *Past Masters 2*.

Later, on March 26, 1970, Phil Spector added more orchestration and used only George's January 4, 1970 solo. This version appeared on the album.

For the first release of "Let it Be," see above, Aretha Franklin's *This Girl's In Love With You* album.

---

[22] As quoted in Turner, *Hard Day's Write*, 180. Similar: Salewicz, "Tug of War," (1986), 68; Read, "McCartney on McCartney," episode 4 (1989); McCartney interview, transcribed from "Sold on Song" website.

[23] For Paul, Interview in Smith, *Off the Record*, 201. Coleman: *McCartney: Yesterday . . . and Today*, 38-39. Snow, "Paul McCartney." For John, Hennessey, "Who Wrote What," *Record Mirror*.

[24] Sheff, *The Playboy Interviews*, 211.

[25] Badman, *The Beatles Off the Record*, 490.

[26] See the relevant dates in Lewisohn, *The Beatles Recording Sessions*, Sulpy and Schweighardt, *Get Back*.

- **You Know My Name (Look Up My Number) — (Lennon-McCartney-Harrison-Starkey)**
  (lead vocals: John and Paul) (recorded from May 17, 1967 to April 30, 1969)

During the *Sgt. Pepper* era, John was at Paul's house one day, and saw a phone book on the piano. Prominently displayed was the phrase, "You know the name, look up the number." John took that sentence home and began to write a song around it, changing the words slightly. It was intended to be a rhythm and blues, Four Tops kind of tune, but it never developed into a finished song.[27] In fact, John apparently added no lyrics to the one phrase, instead repeating it over and over.

Paul remembered John coming to the studio with a new song, and Paul asked him, "'What's the words?'" And John said, "You know my name look up my number." Paul asked: "What's the rest of it?" "No, no other words, those are the words. And I wanna do it like a mantra!"[28] Paul described it as "originally . . . a fifteen-minute chant" brought in by John "when he was in space-cadet mode."[29]

So during the *Sgt. Pepper* period, the Beatles began to rehearse and record this song. They never turned it into an actual rhythm and blues song. Instead, it became, "a comedy record," in the Goon Show spirit, and, John explained, "We made a joke of it."[30]

First, they recorded the backing. "and we did these mad backings," said John.[31] The first recording, mostly backing, took place on May 17, 1967. Paul called this song "probably my favorite Beatles track" because of all the memories connected with it, such as Mal Evans shoveling gravel (as a "rhythmic device") and Brian Jones of the Rolling Stones playing sax

---

[27] Sheff, *The Playboy Interviews*, 214.

[28] McCartney 1988 (Lewisohn interview, 15).

[29] As quoted in Winn, *That Magic Feeling*, 282.

[30] Sheff, *The Playboy Interviews*, 214.

[31] Smith, "Beatles Music Straightforward On Next Album."

(which he did not know how to play).[32] Paul remembered it as a song that they kept trying over and over and never quite getting it right, but "we had these endless, crazy fun sessions."

A master edit of the backing was done on June 9, 1967, but vocals and many special effects were not added till two years later, on April 30, 1969. Engineer Nick Webb remembered Paul and John singing together around one microphone.[33] Paul remembered, "And eventually we pulled it all together and I sang [*sings in a jazzy style*] "You know my name . . ." and we just did a skit, Mal and his gravel. . . . And it was just so hilarious to put that record together."

John considered releasing this as a Plastic Ono Band record, and cut it from six to four minutes,[34] but the song finally appeared as a Beatles song, a B-side, a remarkable contrast to the A-side, "Let it Be."

John often claimed this.[35] In 1969, he said, "There was another song I wrote around 'Pepper' time that's still in the can, called 'You Know My Name Look Up The Number.' . . . But I never finished it, and I must."[36] However, in 1980, he said, "That was a piece of unfinished music that I turned into a comedy record with Paul."[37] Based on this statement, and Paul's substantial contributions, such as the parodic lounge singing, he deserves secondary credit. John definitely was the main writer, though.

McCartney album — Paul McCartney, April 17, 1970

This album is part of the "Beatles to solo album" transitional period. Some of the songs were written during the middle Beatles period (in India), and were performed during the Get Back sessions. Two are even of

---

[32] McCartney 1988 (Lewisohn interview, 15). Miles, *Many Years from Now*, 438. Lewisohn, *The Beatles Recording Sessions*, 116.

[33] Lewisohn, *The Beatles Recording Sessions*, 175.

[34] Ibid., 194.

[35] For example, in 1971, Hennessey, "Who Wrote What," *Record Mirror*.

[36] Smith, "Beatles Music Straightforward On Next Album."

[37] Sheff, *The Playboy Interviews*, 214.

pre-Beatles vintage. Other songs were written (or improvised) in late 1969 or early 1970.

The first songs were recorded at Cavendish, on Paul's newly-installed four-track recorder, from December 1969 to January 1970. On February 12th, 1970, Paul recorded two songs ("Kreen-Akrore" and "Suicide") at Morgan Studios, in Willesden Green, London, and added overdubs to his home tapes. Then he recorded three songs at Abbey Road, "Every Night," and "Maybe I'm Amazed" on February 22, 1970, and "Man We Was Lonely" on February 25.[38]

Three of these songs (such as "Man We Was Lonely," "Ooh You" and "Kreen-Akrore") were written/improvised after my January 4, 1970 cutoff date, but I will look at all the cuts on the album, as the exact recording or songwriting dates are not known for all of them.

These songs are all accepted as written by Paul, as they were released on a McCartney solo album.

• The Lovely Linda

This was a song from Paul's and Linda's early time together, so it was possibly written in 1968. (They met on May 15, 1967, but started a serious relationship about a year later.) It was written in Scotland.[39]

While Paul at first thought he would "finish" this song, it remains as a fragment.[40] As such, this, and other songs on this album, continued the aesthetics of the song fragment as found in the White Album ("Can You Take Me Back," "Wild Honey Pie") and *Abbey Road*.

• That Would Be Something

This was written in Scotland in 1969.[41]

---

[38] "The McCartney Recording Sessions," website.

[39] Ibid. White, "Paul McCartney On His Not-So-Silly Love Songs" (2001).

[40] Ibid. "I was always going to finish it, and I had another bit that went into a Spanish song, almost mariachi, but it just appeared as a fragment and was quite nice for that reason."

[41] "The McCartney Recording Sessions."

- **Valentine Day**

This instrumental was improvised and recorded at home. Paul explained:

> Made up as I went along — acoustic guitar first, then drums (maybe drums were first). Anyway — electric guitar and bass were added and the track is all instrumental. . . . This one and Momma Miss America were ad-libbed with more concern for testing the machine than anything else.[42]

- **Every Night**

Paul had the first two lines of this song for a few years before this album. He played an unfinished version of it during the Get Back sessions, on January 22 and 24, 1969.[43] In June 1969, while on holiday in Benitses, Greece, he developed it further. The finished product reflects his depression at the breakup of the Beatles and his newfound love for Linda.

- **Hot as Sun/Glasses**

"Hot as Sun" was a very early song — Paul said he wrote it in 1958, 1959 or "maybe earlier."[44] It was "one of those songs that you play now and then," he said.[45] He performed "Hot as Sun" during the Get Back sessions,[46] recorded this version at home, then added the middle at Morgan Studio.

Sulpy and Schweighardt suggest that it had a Polynesian inspiration, and was part of a musical movement that looked to exotic music during the 1950s.[47]

---

[42] Ibid.

[43] Sulpy and Schweighardt, *Get Back*, 210, 245.

[44] McCartney 1970 (self-interview insert for *McCartney*, as reprinted in DiLello, *Longest Cocktail Party*, 248).

[45] Ibid.

[46] Sulpy and Schweighardt, *Get Back*, 245-46; Unterberger, *Unreleased Beatles*, 253.

[47] Sulpy and Schweighardt, *Get Back*, 245-46.

Paul said, of "Glasses," "Wine glasses played at random and over-dubbed on top of each other."

• Suicide

An eight-second fragment of "Suicide," not listed on the album credits, follows "Glasses." Paul explained, "the end [of "Glasses"] is a section of a song called Suicide — not yet completed."

This song was written when Paul was a teenager, and a version was recorded during the Get Back sessions.[48] The mature Paul, in 1995, had no fondness for the song. "It was murder! Horrible song! But you had to go through all those styles to discover your own. I only had one verse, so I cobbled together another."[49]

Paul sent the song to Frank Sinatra in 1974, but the singer rejected it.

> Apparently he thought it was an almighty piss-take . . . I think he couldn't grasp it was tongue in check. It was only supposed to be a play on the word 'suicide,' not the actual physical suicide. . . . Looking back on it I'm quite relieved he did [reject it], actually, it wasn't a good song, it was just a teenage thought.[50]

Paul performed it on TV in 1999, but the complete song was not officially released until it appeared as a bonus track on the remastered special edition of *McCartney* in 2011.[51]

---

[48] Lewisohn, *Tune In*, 91-92; Sulpy and Schweighardt, *Get Back*, 275. By Lewisohn's chronology this, not "I Lost My Little Girl," might be the first song Paul every wrote. *Tune In*, 811n16. Du Noyer, *Conversations*, 194.

[49] Miles, *Many Years from Now*, 183.

[50] Ibid. See also McCartney in 2003, quoted in Barnes, "Sinatra Rejected My Song, Says Sir Paul."

[51] Miles, *Many Years*, 182-83; Unterberger, *Unreleased Beatles*, 256; Benitez, *The Words and Music of Paul McCartney*, 22.

- **Junk**

Paul wrote this song, originally entitled "Jubilee," in India,[52] and played it as one of the Esher demos in May 1968. This performance can be heard on *Anthology 3*. He completed it gradually in London during the White Album recordings,[53] and played it during the Get Back sessions.[54] He remembered, "'Junk' was intended for *Abbey Road*, but something happened."[55]

  o <u>Man We Was Lonely</u>

This was written fairly late, and is definitely of post-January 4 songwriting vintage. Paul said, "The chorus ('Man We Was Lonely') was written in bed at home shortly before we finished recording the album. The middle ('I used to ride...') was done one lunchtime in a great hurry as we were due to record the song that afternoon. Linda sings harmony on this song which is our first duet together."[56]

SIDE TWO

  o <u>Oo You</u>

Paul said, in 1970, "This, like 'Man We Was Lonely,' was given lyrics one day after lunch just before we left for Morgan Studios, where it was finished that afternoon."

- **Momma Miss America**

According to Paul, this was "An instrumental recorded completely at home. Made up as I went along — first a sequence of chords, then a mel-

---

[52] Information included in *McCartney* (1970), as reprinted in DiLello, *Longest Cocktail Party*, 253.

[53] Ibid. See also Unterberger, *TheUnreleased Beatles*, 198.

[54] Sulpy and Schweighardt, *Get Back*, 155; Unterberger, *Unreleased Beatles*, 244.

[55] Self-interview insert for *McCartney* (1970), as reprinted in DiLello, *Longest Cocktail Party*, 248-49.

[56] Self-interview insert for *McCartney* (1970), as reprinted in DiLello, *Longest Cocktail Party*, 248-49.

ody on top. Piano, drums, acoustic guitar, electric guitar. Originally it was two pieces but they ran into each other by accident and became one."

- **Teddy Boy**

Paul wrote this in India,[57] and it was repeatedly rehearsed during the Get Back sessions.[58] Glyn Johns included it in some of the *Get Back* lineups. A version edited from two Get Back performances appeared on *Anthology 3*. Paul explained, "On the new *Anthology* we do 'Teddy Boy' which was considered as a Beatles song but we never got around to it."[59]

  o <u>Singalong Junk</u>

- **Maybe I'm Amazed**

This was written in 1969, as a tribute to Linda. Paul said, in 1970, "Written in London, at the piano, with the second verse added slightly later, as if you cared." Later, asked if the song was written for *McCartney*, Paul replied, "Yeah, that was very much a song of the period."[60]

  o <u>Kreen-Akrore</u>

This experimental track sounds odd, but the explanation, by Paul, is even odder.

On February 11, 1970, the BBC aired *The Tribe That Hides from Man*, by Adrian Cowell, a documentary about the Kreen-Akrore Indians, living in the Brazilian rainforest.[61] Paul and Linda watched it, and decided to create an experimental percussion track based on how the Kreen-Akrore Indians hunted. Paul did drumming, then later added piano, guitar, organ, voices, the sounds of running, animal noises, an arrow sound, "then animals stampeding across a guitar case." The McCartneys even built a fire in the

---

[57] McCartney 1970 (self-interview insert for *McCartney* (1970), as reprinted in DiLello, *Longest Cocktail Party*, 254). "Another song started in India and completed in Scotland and London, gradually."

[58] Sulpy and Schweighardt, *Get Back*, index.

[59] McCartney ca 1996 (Gobnotch, "Recording Sessions Update - Part 12").

[60] White, "Paul McCartney: Farewell" (1988), 47.

[61] Internet Movie Database gives February 17, 1970 as the date of release.

studio, though they ended up not using this sound. But they did include the "sound of the twigs breaking."

Since none of this was explained in the liner notes to *McCartney*, virtually all listeners simply listened with incomprehension to the last song on this remarkable album, as I did many years ago.

———————◦◦◦———————

Let It Be album, May 8, 1970

• Two of Us — (McCartney)
  (lead vocals: Paul) (recorded January 24 to 31, 1969)

This was written during one of Paul's and Linda's wandering trips through the countryside. They would put Martha in the back seat and drive out of London. "Let's get lost," Linda would say, and they would stop looking at signs and drive at random. They'd try to find beautiful, isolated places to stop, then just do nothing.

Well, not entirely nothing. Paul had his guitar with him, and he began writing "Two of Us" on one of these trips. "Hence the line in the song, 'Two of us going nowhere,'" said Linda. "Paul wrote that on one of those days out."[62]

Linda took a picture of him — with a day's growth of stubble, sitting in the driver's seat with open door, playing his guitar. Paul said "Two of Us" was a favorite song of his because it reminded him of those days, "getting together with Linda, and the wonderfully free attitude we were able to have, I had my guitar with me and I wrote it out on the road, and then maybe finished some of the verses at home later, but that picture is of me writing it."[63]

The authorship of the song is straightforward enough, it seems. John, in 1971 ascribed it to Paul.[64] But then in the 1980 *Playboy* interviews, Len-

---

[62] Quoted in Badman, *The Beatles: The Dream is Over*, 13.

[63] Miles, *Many Years from Now*, 471. Du Noyer, *Conversations*, 203-4.

[64] Hennessey, "Who Wrote What," *Record Mirror*.

non is reported as saying, about this song, "Mine."[65] And Ringo remembered John bringing the song to the sessions. "When John brought it in, he called it 'On Our Way Home.' And when we'd finished with it in the studio it became 'Two Of Us.'"[66]

However, Beatle historian Donald Sauter checked the original tapes of the *Playboy* interview, and concluded that the word "Mine" is actually not present in the interview. Sheff asked about 'Don't Let Me Down,' to which Lennon responded, "That's me, singing about Yoko...." Then Sheff asked about "Two of Us," but Lennon, disregarding "Two of Us," continued talking about "Don't Let Me Down": "... *which Rod Stewart took note for note and turned* into (singing) "Maggie don't go-o-o", *some girl's name, "Maggie don't go-o-o"*. That's one the publishers never noticed."[67] This is consistent with Lennon's 1971 ascription of "Two of Us" directly to Paul. Sauter also notes that in the Get Back sessions, Paul teaches the song to the other Beatles, and takes the lead in rehearsing it.[68]

This leaves Ringo as the odd man out on this song! He was undoubtedly simply confused, if the interview was transcribed correctly.

Paul brought the song to the session thinking of it as a rock song with electric guitars. This kind of performance is captured in the *Let It Be* movie. But Glyn Johns suggested acoustic guitars, and this inspired suggestion was eventually adopted.[69]

- **Dig a Pony — (Lennon)**
  (lead vocals: John) (recorded January 22 to 30, 1969)

Lennon brought this as a song fragment at the beginning of the Twickenham sessions, and improvised the lyrics. Beatles historian Peter Doggett writes:

---

[65] Sheff, *The Playboy Interviews*, 214.

[66] Ringo, in Yellow Submarine radio series, as cited in Sauter, "One John Lennon."

[67] Transcript from Sauter, "One John Lennon."

[68] See also Sulpy and Schweighardt, *Get Back*, 22.

[69] Ibid., 39.

The song's lyrics were, as Lennon conceded, 'interchangeable,' and when serious rehearsals resumed at Apple on 22 January, he admitted that he was inspired less by the meaning of the words than by their sounds: 'Lots of d's and b's.' When Harrison queried the order of the verses, Lennon admitted, 'I just make it up as I go along,' and he continued to do so even as the final version of the song was being taped on the Apple rooftop a week later.[70]

John had no high opinion of the song: "Another piece of garbage," he said in 1980.[71]

The chorus is from a separate song about Yoko called 'All I Want Is You.'[72]

John claimed this. "Yeah, I was just having fun with words. It was literally a nonsense song," he said in 1972.[73] Paul agreed. Miles/McCartney wrote, "Paul had no input on 'Dig a Pony,' which was entirely John's."[74]

o <u>Across the Universe — (Lennon)</u>
  <u>(lead vocals: John) (recorded February 4, 8, 1968, October 2,</u>
  <u>1969, April 1, 1970)</u>

The writing of this song dates to 1967, when one night John's wife Cynthia was talking on and on in bed. But after she went to sleep, he kept hearing the words repeating over and over, "flowing out like an endless stream." He went downstairs and created a "cosmic song" rather than an irritated song. "Such an extraordinary meter and I can never repeat it! It's not a matter of craftsmanship; it wrote itself. It *drove* me out of bed," he

---

[70] Doggett, *Abbey Road*, 83.

[71] Lost Lennon Tapes, Oct. 21, 1991, cf. Sheff, *The Playboy Interviews*, 214.

[72] Turner, *Hard Day's Write*, 176.

[73] From the film, *Imagine*. See also Connolly, *Ray Connolly Beatles Archive*, 106.

[74] Miles, *Many Years from Now*, 537.

said in an interview.[75] He wrote out the lyrics first, then added the music later.[76]

John used a Sanskrit mantra in this song: *"Jai guru deva om,* "hail to the divine guru," with the mystic syllable *om* added.

The Beatles recorded this on February 4 and 8, 1968 (at about the same time as "Hey Bulldog" and "Lady Madonna"), before they flew to India.[77] So this song, which we associate with the last-released Beatle album, *Let It Be*, was actually recorded before most of the songs on the White Album were even written. There is a composing tape in which John sings part of this, which Winn dates to December 1967 or January 1968.[78]

John disliked the Beatles recording, which he felt was out of tune because the other Beatles weren't really involved or helpful. This is where he accused the Beatles, especially Paul, of "subconsciously" sabotaging his songs.[79] I read this critique of Paul as a byproduct of his ambiguous role as co-writer, and un-official arranger and producer for the Beatles. When he produced actively, in his typical driven, detail-oriented way, John and George often resented his bossiness and his relentless quest for perfection (which resulted in many takes); when he held back, they resented his not getting involved in their songs.

The version found on the charity anthology album is the February 1968 studio version, with wildlife effects (birds chirping, children playing in a sandbox) added in the remix — this is also on the CD *Past Masters, Volume Two.* The Beatles played "Across the Universe" in the Get Back sessions, but the version that appears on the supposedly "live" *Let It Be* album is once again the February 1968 studio version, without the wildlife effects, but with Phil Spector's orchestral additions! (The version on the *Let It Be . . . Naked* is also the 1968 studio version, without the Spector ad-

---

[75] Sheff, *The Playboy Interviews,* 201-3.

[76] Lost Lennon Tapes, Apr. 18, 1988, cf. Sheff, *The Playboy Interviews,* 201-3.

[77] Lewisohn, *Beatles Recording Sessions,* 133-34. Overdubs were added in subsequent sessions.

[78] Winn, *That Magic Feeling,* 150.

[79] Lost Lennon Tapes, Apr. 18, 1988, cf. Sheff, *The Playboy Interviews,* 201-3.

ditions.) An alternate take, with pronounced Indian sitar and tambura, can be found on *Anthology 2*.

Both John and Paul ascribed this to John. "It's one of the best lyrics I've written," he said in 1970, and the following year, he referred to it as, "One of my best songs."[80] Paul, in 1995, agreed that "Across The Universe" was "one of John's great songs."[81]

For the first release of this song, see *No One's Gonna Change Our World*, charity album, above.

- **I Me Mine — (Harrison-McCartney)**
  (lead vocals: George)(recorded on January 3, 1970)

George wrote this song quickly during the Get Back rehearsals, and one day came to Twickenham and played it for Ringo. This was filmed, and turned out to be an engaging moment, so was used in the film. However, this was not a proper recording, and the song would be needed for the soundtrack album, so the Beatles (minus John) re-recorded it from the ground up on January 3, 1970. George called it "a very strange song which I wrote the night before it was in the film," in about five minutes.[82] It was "about the ego problem." At the time, he said, he "hated everything about my ego — it was a flash of everything false and impermanent which I disliked."[83]

When John complained that the song was too short, "McCartney mended that problem by leading the group into an improvised, up-tempo middle section."[84]

---

[80] Lennon, Rolling Stone Interview, Dec. 1970, BBC, part 4, cf. Wenner, *Lennon Remembers*, 99, see also 85. Connolly, *Ray Connolly Beatles Archive*, 109. Hennessey, "Who Wrote What," *Record Mirror*. Similar: Miles, *Beatles in Their Own Words*, 105.

[81] Miles, *Many Years from Now*, 421. See also Brown, "McCartney: Life after Death" (1974), 63.

[82] George Harrison, Interview with Johnny Moran, March 11, 1970.

[83] *I Me Mine*, 158.

[84] Doggett, *Abbey Road*, 86-87; see also Sulpy and Schweighardt, *Get Back*, 133.

- **Dig It — (Lennon-McCartney-Harrison-Starkey)
(lead vocals: John) (recorded January 24 to 29, 1969)**

All four Beatles are credited with this song, but John claimed it.[85] "I made this up on the spot. Sounds like it? Yes doesn't it," he said in an early interview.[86] However, according to Miles/McCartney, "Dig It" "was a studio improvisation led by John,"[87] but all the Beatles contributed lines.

  o <u>Let It Be — (McCartney)</u>

See "Let It Be / You Know My Name Look Up My Number" single, above.

  o <u>Maggie Mae (COVER) (traditional)
(lead vocals: John) (recorded on January 24, 1969)</u>

"Maggie Mae" was a well-known Liverpool folk song.

SIDE TWO

- **I've Got a Feeling — (McCartney-Lennon)
(lead vocals: Paul and John) (recorded January 30, 1969)**

As the "Get Back sessions approached, Paul had an exuberant rock song, "I've Got a Feeling," ready. John came to Cavendish one day with a song called "Everybody Had a Hard Year," and they decided the two songs would fit well together. So this is a song such as "A Day in the Life" or "Baby I'm a Rich Man," in which separately composed songs were combined and created a seemingly cohesive whole. In fact, both songs expressed general optimism (except for the first line of John's song, oddly enough).[88] Paul taught the song to George and Ringo on January 2, the first day of the Get Back sessions.

Paul and John agreed that Paul wrote the main song (which he sings), and John wrote the counter-melody, which he sings. "Paul," said John in

---

[85] For example, Hennessey, "Who Wrote What," *Record Mirror*.

[86] Aldridge, *Beatles Illustrated Lyrics*, 208..

[87] Miles, *Many Years from Now*, 536.

[88] Miles, *Many Years from Now*, 537. Similar: Paul in 2003 (Sennett, "At last, they let it be").

1980. "And there's part of me on it."[89] In 1971, he put it on a list of songs he and Paul had collaborated on.[90] Miles/McCartney, in 1995, agreed: "Just as Paul had an inclusion in the middle of "A Day in the Life," so John had one in the middle of Paul's "I've Got a Feeling.""[91] Paul gave it as an example of how his collaboration with John had continued even into the late Beatles time period, though the song was probably written during or just after the White Album's release. John had written his part by December 1968, when it shows up on a demo. The songs were joined together by January 2, 1969.[92]

- **One After 909 — (Lennon-McCartney)**
  (lead vocals: John) (recorded on January 30, 1969)

During the Get Back sessions, the Beatles played this, one of the really early Beatle songs, out of good-humored nostalgia. John says he started writing the song when he was seventeen or eighteen, which would have been 1957 or 1958. After this start, he worked on it with Paul at the McCartney home at Forthlin Road. Paul stated, "It's a great favourite of mine because it has great memories for me of John and I trying to write a bluesy freight-train song. There were a lot of those songs at the time, like 'Midnight Special,' 'Freight Train,' 'Rock Island Line,' so this was the 'One After 909.'"[93]

The song can be found on a summer 1960 Beatle rehearsal tape, and again on a 1962 Cavern Club recording.[94] They also played it in Hamburg.[95] A great early version was recorded in the studio on March 5, 1963 — this never made it onto a Beatle record, but can be found on *Anthology 1*. The

---

[89] Lennon 1980, Sauter, "One John Lennon"; cf. Sheff, *The Playboy Interviews*, 215.

[90] Hennessey, "Who Wrote What," *Record Mirror*.

[91] Miles, *Many Years from Now*, 537. Similar: Paul in 2003 (Sennett, "At last, they let it be").

[92] Winn, *That Magic Feeling*, 231.

[93] Miles, *Many Years from Now*, 536. Paul also put it in a list of early collaborative songs, an improvement on "Just Fun," "In Spite of All the Danger," "Like Dreamers Do," and leading up to "Love Me Do." Ibid., 36.

[94] Winn, *Way Beyond Compare*, 4, 17.

[95] Lewisohn, *Tune In*, 440.

song was not performed or released till it was sung as an "oldie" during the Get Back sessions. Apparently, in the early Beatle period Paul and John were dissatisfied with this song; either they regarded it as unfinished, or felt the lyrics were lacking.[96]

John claimed it starting in 1970, saying "it's one I wrote when [I was] seventeen or eighteen in Liverpool separately from Paul."[97] And in 1980, he remembered: "That was something I wrote when I was about seventeen."[98]

But in an early interview, in 1969, John talked about the song as something he and Paul hadn't finished. "**Paul:** Our kid [Mike McCartney] has been saying, 'You should do that [the song One after 909],' for years. But, I said, 'Well, you know, Mike, you don't understand about these things, you know.... **John:** It's like, we always thought it wasn't finished. We couldn't be bothered finishing it."[99]

Paul remembered collaboration. In a very early booking letter that he wrote in 1960 he listed "One After 909" among the songs he and John had written.[100] In 1969, he said:

> It's from one of the first songs we ever wrote. *Glyn Johns: "John wrote it when he was about 15, didn't he?* **Paul:** Yeah, we used to sag off every school day, go back to my house and the two of us would write: "Love Me Do," "Too Bad About Sorrows." ["Just Fun"] .... But we hated the words to "909."[101]

[96] Lennon and McCartney 1969 (Fly on the Wall bonus disc on *Let It Be ... Naked*). McCartney in Cott and Dalton, *The Beatles Get Back*, p. 85.

[97] Lennon, Rolling Stone Interview, Dec. 1970, BBC, part 2. Cf. Wenner, *Lennon Remembers*, 26. Hennessey, "Who Wrote What." Hennessey, "Lennon: the Greatest Natural Songwriter," 12. *Ray Connolly Beatles Archive*, 106. Aldridge, *Beatles Illustrated Lyrics*, 192.

[98] Lost Lennon Tapes, Sept. 23, 1991, cf. Sheff, *The Playboy Interviews*, 213.

[99] Lennon and McCartney 1969 (Fly on the Wall bonus disc on *Let It Be ... Naked*).

[100] McCartney to "Mr. Low," about 1959, see Davies, *The Beatles*, 63.

[101] McCartney in Cott and Dalton, *The Beatles Get Back*, p. 85. See also Miles, *Many Years from Now*, 536, quoted above. Paul also put it in a list of early collaborative songs, an im-

Probably John started it, then he and Paul worked on it in collaborative sessions.

- ## The Long and Winding Road — (McCartney)
  ## (lead vocals: Paul) (recorded January 26 and 31, 1969, April
  ## 1, 1970)

Paul wrote this in Scotland, during the White Album sessions, from May to October, 1968. He sat down at the piano and started playing and came up with the song.[102] He once played it, with the lyrics not yet finished, for Alistair Taylor after a White Album recording session.[103]

It is a nexus for a number of influences. One was "the dissension and troubled atmosphere within the band at the time."[104] Paul said that writing sad songs such as this one often serves as therapy. "It's a good vehicle, it saves having to go to a psychiatrist."[105] Counterbalancing the negative feelings from the looming Beatle breakup was the "calm beauty of Scotland."[106] One theory is that the "long and winding road" is the road that led to his farm in Scotland, BH42.[107]

On a musical level, Paul was channeling Ray Charles, which led to the song's "slightly jazzy" chord structure.[108]

Paul and John both ascribed this to Paul. In 1988, he affirmed, "John never had any input on 'The Long and Winding Road.'"[109] In 1980, John had agreed: "Paul again." John felt that "the shock of Yoko" caused Paul

---

provement on "Just Fun," "In Spite of All the Danger," "Like Dreamers Do," and leading up to "Love Me Do." Ibid., 36.

[102] In Merritt, "Truth behind ballad that split Beatles."

[103] Taylor is quoted in Matteo, *Let It Be*, 43-44.

[104] Miles/McCartney, *Many Years from Now*, 539.

[105] Miles, *Many Years from Now*, 539.

[106] In Merritt, "Truth behind ballad that split Beatles,"

[107] Matteo, *Let It Be*, 43.

[108] Miles, *Many Years from Now*, 539.

[109] White, "Paul McCartney: Farewell," 48. See also: See Merritt, "Truth behind ballad that split Beatles." Coleman, *McCartney: Yesterday . . . and Today*, 38; Interview in Smith, *Off the Record*, 201.

to have a little "creative spurt" just before the breakup, which produced this song.[110]

As has been mentioned, this song later became the main victim of Phil Spector's orchestrations on the *Let It Be* album, to the dismay of Paul and George Martin. Paul said, in 2000:

> So now we were getting a 're-producer' instead of just a producer, and he added on all sorts of stuff — singing ladies on 'The Long and Winding Road' — backing that I perhaps wouldn't have put on. I mean, I don't think it made it the worst record ever, but the fact that now people were putting stuff on our records that certainly one of us didn't know about was wrong.[111]

"Plain" versions of this can be found on *Anthology 3* (the January 26 version) and *Let It Be . . . Naked* (the January 31 version). I do prefer the plain versions, but have developed a fondness for Spector's over-the-top orchestrated version over the years, which historically has been the most influential version. So we have three canonical versions of this great song — not to mention numerous recordings and live performances by Paul after the breakup.

- **For You Blue — (Harrison)**
  (lead vocals: George) (recorded on January 25, 1969)

Harrison's second song on *Let It Be* is slight. His songs on *Let It Be* are dwarfed by his great songs on the *White Album* and *Abbey Road*. This is a 12-bar song, in the blues tradition, but instead of the blues, it's "happy-go-lucky."[112]

---

[110] Lost Lennon Tapes, Oct. 21, 1991, cf. Sheff, *The Playboy Interviews*, 214. Also Hennessey, "Who Wrote What," *Record Mirror*.

[111] *Anthology*, 350.

[112] *I Me Mine*, 156. See also Harrison, interview with Johnny Moran, March 30, 1970; Mal Evans in 1969 ("The Beatles Get Back," 27). As George's spoken reference to Mississippi blues guitarist Elmore James shows, it's modeled on that style. Womack, *Long and Winding Roads*, 260.

o   Get Back — (McCartney-Lennon)

See "Get Back / Don't Let Me Down" single, above.

———————◦◦———————

Let It Be, movie, May 13, 1970

The *Let It Be* movie included some songs not on the *Let It Be* album.

- **Paul's Piano Piece — (McCartney)**

This song opens the film. Per Sulpy and Schweighardt, this is based on Barber's "Adagio for Strings," but to me and some classical music friends, it does not sound like that piece at all.[113]

o   Maxwell's Silver Hammer — (McCartney)

To state the obvious, the performances of this, "Oh Darling," and "Octopus's Garden," predated the *Abbey Road* versions.

o   Oh Darling — (McCartney)

See *Abbey Road*, above.

- **Jazz Piano Song — (McCartney-Starkey)**

A primitive blues improvisation.

- **Suzy Parker — (Lennon-McCartney-Harrison-Starkey)**

John seems to lead this improvised song, performed on January 9, 1969.[114] Some give it the title "Suzy's Parlour."

o   Bésame Mucho (COVER) (Consuelo Velázquez, Sunny Skylar)

This performance is one of the charming highlights of the *Let It Be* film. The Beatles performed the bizarre Coasters song at the Decca audition, January 1, 1962, and at the EMI audition, on June 6 of the same year. The EMI version can be heard on *Anthology 1*.

Paul said, in 1989, "You see we had a very sort of strange repertoire because of Hamburg and 'cause all these little B sides we'd looked up. We

---

[113] Sulpy and Schweighardt, *Get Back*, 26.
[114] Ibid., 148.

tried things like 'Besame Mucho.' 'Du dudududu. Cha chacha, oy! Besame. Besame mucho.' Weird song to do."[115] Paul, typically, commented on the music and harmony of the song: "It's a minor [key] song and it changes to major, and where it changes to major is such a big moment musically. That major change attracted me so much."[116]

o   Octopus's Garden — (Starkey-Harrison)

See *Abbey Road*, above.

o   You Really Got a Hold on Me (COVER) (Smokey Robin-son)

John's version of this is one of the high points of the movie. The Beatles first released it on *With the Beatles*, above.

Medley:

o   Rip It Up (COVER) (Robert Blackwell, John Marascalco)

This was performed by Bill Haley and his Comets and Little Richard in 1956.

o   Shake Rattle and Roll (COVER) (Jesse Stone, under his working name Charles E. Calhoun)

Written in 1954, this was recorded by Big Joe Turner and Bill Haley and his Comets the same year. It became a rock standard.

Medley:

o   Kansas City (COVER) (Jerry Leiber, Mike Stoller)

See *Beatles For Sale*, above.

o   Miss Ann (COVER) (Richard Penniman, Enotris Johnson)

A Little Richard song, released as the B-side of his 1956 single "Jenny, Jenny."

---

[115] Read, "McCartney on McCartney," episode 1.
[116] Miles, *Many Years from Now*, 81

  ○ <u>Lawdy Miss Clawdy (COVER) (Lloyd Price)</u>

A 1952 hit single by Lloyd Price, this song was successfully covered by Elvis four years later.

- **Just Fun — (collaboration)**

Paul sings the first verse of this in the *Let It Be* movie, and reportedly performed the whole song on acoustic guitar during a soundcheck in Zurich in 2004.[117] In 1969, he said,

> Yeah, we used to sag off every school day, go back to my house and the two of us would write: "Love Me Do," "Too Bad About Sorrows." There's a lot from then. We have about a hundred that we never recorded because they're all very unsophisticated songs. (singing in a very dumb voice) "They said our love was just fun/ The day that our friendship begun,/ There's no blue moon that I can see/ There's no blue moon in history" and we just thought "great, too much."[118]

Twenty years later, Paul remembered: "One of the earliest [collaborations with John] I can remember, I can't remember if it was exactly the earliest, was a song called 'Just Fun.'" But the song had one bad line they never could fix: "'There's no blue moon that I can see, There's never been in history.' Terrible."[119]

---

[117] "Early Beatle Songs" website. Sulpy and Schweighardt, *Get Back*, 119.

[118] McCartney 1969 (*Let It Be* movie; Cott and Dalton, *The Beatles Get Back*, p. 85).

[119] Read, "McCartney on McCartney," episode 1. See also Miles, *Many Years from Now*, 36.

15

"Both inspired from the same lecture of Maharishi"

BEATLE SONGS AFTER THE BREAKUP

As was mentioned in the previous chapter, I'm using January 4, 1970 as the somewhat arbitrary dividing line between the Beatles era and the solo Beatles era. From the standpoint of songwriting, I regard songs written before that date as part of the Beatles canon; songs written after as part of the solo Beatles era. This chapter deals with songs written *before* January 4, 1970, though they may appear on later solo albums. If we are concerned mainly about songwriting, such songs are fully Beatle songs, Beatle music. Many of the songs in George's *All Things Must Pass*, for example, were written during the Beatles era. His "Not Guilty," a key song for understanding George's place in the Beatles, was recorded as one of the Kinfauns demos after India, but did not appear until the 1979 album *George Harrison*.

Paul's "Cosmically Conscious," written during the India residence, could have been included on the White Album, but did not appear until his 1993 album *Off the Ground*.

Of course, some songs are hybrid: John's "Jealous Guy," from his 1971 album *Imagine*, uses music written during the India period, but its present lyrics were written post January 4, 1970.

―――――――∋●∈―――――――

Doris Troy album — Doris Troy, September 11, 1970

This Apple album with four George collaborations was recorded from mid-1969 to the end of the year.[1]

---

[1] Liner notes from *Doris Troy*.

- ○ <u>Ain't That Cute — (Harrison-Troy)</u>

See "Ain't That Cute" single, February 13, 1970.

- **Give Me Back My Dynamite — (Harrison-Troy)**
- **Gonna Get My Baby Back — (Harrison-Starkey-Troy-Stills)**

Ringo and Stephen Stills from Crosby, Stills and Nash helped write and perform this song, and "You Give Me Joy Joy."

- **You Give Me Joy Joy — (Harrison-Starkey-Troy-Stills)**
  - ○ <u>Jacob's Ladder (traditional, arranged Harrison-Troy)</u>

Encouraging Words album — Billy Preston, September 11, 1970

This Apple album appeared the same day as the Doris Troy album. George Harrison co-produced it, and an all-star cast of musicians (George Harrison, Eric Clapton, Keith Richards, Ginger Baker) helped record it. This is the first appearance of two solo Harrison classics, and the only appearance of an obscure Harrison collaboration.[2]

- ○ <u>My Sweet Lord — (Harrison)</u>

See at Harrison's *All Things Must Pass* album, below. The Preston version was recorded with the Edwin Hawkins Singers, the group that George says inspired the song.

- **Sing One for the Lord — (Harrison-Preston)**

This song was co-written by George and Billy during the Get Back sessions. It was recorded and mixed by February 12, 1969. Billy said: "The names change. His [George's] is Krishna; mine is Christ. The spiritual promotion — praising God, chanting, spreading it, turning people onto it — these are the things we have in common."[3]

---

[2] Liner notes from Billy Preston, *Encouraging Words*.
[3] As quoted in the liner notes from *Encouraging Words*.

o   <u>All Things Must Pass — (Harrison et al.)</u>

See at George's *All Things Must Pass*, below.

———————————◦◦———————————

All Things Must Pass album — George Harrison, November 27, 1970

This album includes many superb songs written during the Beatles era, some of which were rather inexplicably rejected by the other Beatles and denied a place on a Beatle album.

• I'd Have You Anytime — (Harrison-Dylan)

George and Bob Dylan wrote this song in November 1968 in Dylan's front room in upstate New York when the Beatle was visiting the Band and Dylan. George asked him how he wrote words so easily, and Dylan replied, "How do *you* get all them chords?" George played two major seventh chords, which turned into the main melody. He sang the opening lyric, "Let me in here / I know I've been here." Then Bob "wrote the middle": "All I have is yours / all you see is mine / I'm glad to hold you in my arms / I'd have you anytime."[4]

• My Sweet Lord — (Harrison-Preston-Clapton-Delaney-Bonney-traditional Hindu prayer)

George wrote this in December 1969, in Copenhagen, Denmark, when he was touring with Billy Preston, Eric Clapton, and Delaney & Bonnie.[5] He left a press conference and, thinking of the Edwin Hawkins Singers' version of "Oh Happy Day,"[6] began to play chords on his guitar,

---

[4] White, "George Harrison Reconsidered" (1987), 62. See also Harrison, *I Me Mine*, 164; Unterberger, *The Unreleased Beatles*, 218.

[5] Self, "The 'My Sweet Lord'/'He's So Fine' Plagiarism Suit." See also Leng, *The Music of George Harrison*, 45. For background, Winn, *That Magic Feeling*, 344.

[6] Harrison, *I Me Mine*, 176.

adding the words "Hallelujah" and "Hare Krishna." "Later," he said, "members of the band joined in and lyrics were developed."[7]

In England, as George was working with Preston on his *Encouraging Words* album, Preston suggested they record the song that had begun in Denmark. Beatles historian Joseph Self writes, "The unfinished 'My Sweet Lord' was brought up, and was worked into a finished version. Part of this completed song included a second section that differed significantly from the first section."[8] A Hindu prayer, "Hare Krishna / Hare Krishna / Krishna Krishna / Hare Hare / Hare Rama / Hare Rama," was included.

So this song began as George's idea, was developed in a jam session with Billy Preston, Eric Clapton, Delaney & Bonnie, and later was finished in collaboration with Preston, for Preston's album.

There was a plagiarism suit regarding this song and Ronnie Mack's "He's So Fine," a hit for the Chiffons in 1962.[9] The suit was successful, though George was convicted of unconscious plagiarism only, and he had to pay Allen Klein, who had purchased "He's So Fine," $587,000.

George said, on the two songs:

> I wasn't consciously aware of the similarity between "He's So Fine" and "My Sweet Lord" when I wrote the song as it was more improvised and not so fixed, although when my version of the song came out and started to get a lot of airplay people started talking about it and it was then I thought 'Why didn't I realise?'. It would have been very easy to change a note here or there, and not affect the feeling of the record.[10]

---

[7] Self, "The 'My Sweet Lord'/'He's So Fine' Plagiarism Suit," citing George's court testimony.

[8] Ibid.

[9] Ibid.

[10] Harrison, *I Me Mine*, 176. For the comments of two Beatles on the suit, Lennon, in Sheff, The *Playboy Interviews*, 162; Starr, in Badman, *The Beatles Diary, Vol. 2, After the Break-Up*, at Oct. 2, 1976.

- ## All Things Must Pass — (Harrison-*Tao Te Ching*-Leary)

George wrote this song during his visit to the Band and Bob Dylan in Woodstock in November 1968, and he cited the Band's "The Weight," with its religious overtones, as his immediate model.[11] It is a curious mixture of religious, oriental and psychedelic drug mysticism, as it was modeled after a "psychedelic prayer" by Timothy Leary, which was in turn based on the *Tao Te Ching*.[12] "I remembered one of these prayers and it gave me the idea for this thing," said George.[13] The chapter of the *Tao Te Ching*, titled "All Things Pass" by Leary, begins, "All things pass / A sunrise does not last all morning / All things pass / A cloudburst does not last all day."[14]

This was performed frequently during the Get Back sessions, first on January 2, 1969, and finally on January 29, and must have been seriously considered as an album cut for *Let It Be*.[15] It would have been a much stronger Harrison song than "I Me Mine" or "For You Blues." George recorded it alone as a demo on February 25, 1969, and this version is on *Anthology 3*.

- ## Isn't It a Pity — (Harrison)

This song, which we associate with George's solo career, was apparently written in 1966! George performed it during the Get Back sessions, on January 25, 1969, at which time he mentioned that John had rejected it three years earlier.[16]

---

[11] White, "George Harrison Reconsidered" (1987), 60, 62. Harrison, *I Me Mine*, 184.
[12] See Timothy Leary's *Psychedelic Prayers After the Tao Te Ching* (1966).
[13] As quoted in Turner, *Hard Day's Write*, 216.
[14] Ibid.
[15] See Sulpy and Schweighardt, *Get Back*, index.
[16] Ibid., 182, 269.

- **Behind That Locked Door — (Harrison)**

George wrote this song about Bob Dylan when Dylan was performing at the Isle of Wight in August 1969. George said, "It was a good excuse to do a country tune with pedal steel guitar."[17]

- **Let It Down — (Harrison)**

This was performed during the Get Back sessions.[18] George taught John the chords to the song on January 2, 1969.

- **Hear Me Lord — (Harrison)**

Written just before January 6, 1969, this was performed during the Get Back sessions.[19]

- **Wah Wah — (Harrison)**

This was written on January 10, 1969, the day George left the Get Back sessions, after he'd had an argument with Paul.[20] In 1977, George said:

> That was the song, when I left from the "Let It Be" movie, there's a scene where Paul and I are having an argument, and we're trying to cover it up. Then the next scene I'm not there and Yoko's just screaming, doing her screeching number. Well, that's where I'd left, and I went home to write "Wah-Wah." It had given me a wah-wah, like I had such a headache with that whole argument. It was such a headache.[21]

———————◦◦———————

---

[17] Harrison, *I Me Mine*, 206.

[18] Sulpy and Schweighardt, *Get Back*, 7-8, 270, 293, 296.

[19] Winn, *That Magic Feeling*, 244. Sulpy and Schweighardt, *Get Back*, 55-56, 73-75.

[20] Sulpy and Schweighardt, *Get Back*, 169-70.

[21] Glazer, "Growing Up at 33 1/3" (1977). Similar: White, "George Harrison Reconsidered" (1987), 55.

Plastic Ono Band album — John Lennon and Plastic Ono Band, December 11, 1970

The songs for this album were mostly written in spring and summer 1970, and reflected John's intense involvement with Dr. Arthur Janov's Primal Scream therapy. However, one song, "Look at Me," was written during the Beatles era.

- Look at Me — (Lennon)

This was written when the White Album was being recorded (May to October, 1968), "but I just never got it, got it done," said John in 1970.[22]

"Another Day / Oh Woman, Oh Why" single — Paul McCartney, February 19, 1971

- Another Day — (P. McCartney-L. McCartney)

This song was performed during the Get Back sessions, on January 9 and 25, 1969.[23] It became the A-side of Paul's first solo single. He listed Linda as co-writer. Some have sneered at the idea of Linda as co-writer of songs in Paul's solo career, but it was a traditional modus operandi for the Beatles to turn toward friends and family for feedback, and to get phrases to finish songs (as we have seen, George Harrison's mother helped him finish "Piggies"). John and Paul often enlisted friends to help in brainstorming/collaboration sessions, and when they were married, their wives would be natural sounding boards.

---

[22] Lennon, Rolling Stone Interview, Dec. 1970, BBC, part 1; see also Wenner, *Lennon Remembers*, 2.

[23] Sulpy and Schweighardt, *Get Back*, 140, 260.

Ram album — Paul McCartney, May 17, 1971

- **Back Seat of My Car — (P. McCartney-L. McCartney)**

This song, the dramatic conclusion of the *Ram* album, was performed during the Get Back sessions, on January 14, 1969.[24] Paul described it as "a good old driving song" and "the ultimate teenage song."[25]

Imagine album — John Lennon, September 9, 1971

Five of the ten songs on this album were started during the Beatles period.

- **Jealous Guy — (Lennon)**

One day, when the Beatles were in India, the Maharishi lectured on nature. Paul and John both wrote songs in India influenced by the lecture, according to John — this one, originally titled "I'm Just a Child of Nature" or "On the Road to Marrakesh," and Paul's "Mother Nature's Son."[26]

"Child of Nature" was performed as one of the Esher demos in May 1968 (when the lyric says "on the way to Rishikesh") and during the Get Back sessions in January 1969 (when the lyric says, "on the way to Marrakesh" (in Morocco)).[27]

At some point John changed the lyrics completely, and "Jealous Guy," on *Imagine*, was the result.[28]

- **Give Me Some Truth — (Lennon-McCartney)**

Started in India, this was performed during the Get Back sessions. According to John, "The middle eight was written with Paul." [29]

---

[24] Ibid., 194.

[25] White, "Paul McCartney On His Not-So-Silly Love Songs."

[26] Sheff, *The Playboy Interviews*, 209. See on "Mother Nature's Son" in the White Album, above.

[27] Sulpy and Schweighardt, *Get Back*, 9, 236; also see *Let It Be . . . Naked*, below.

[28] Unterberger, *The Unreleased Beatles*, 197.

[29] Davies, *John Lennon Letters*, 220. Sulpy and Schweighardt, *Get Back*, 41-42, 102, 104. Peter Doggett felt that Paul wrote the complete middle section. *Art and Music*, 151.

- ## Oh My Love — (Lennon-Ono)

John made a demo of this in late 1968. John said the song was 80% Yoko Ono's lyric "and 50% her tune."[30]

- ## How Do You Sleep — (Lennon-Ono-Klein)

The lyrics for this controversial song, a direct attack on Paul, were post-Beatles, written in response to perceived attacks on Lennon in Paul's *Ram*. However, the music dates back to the Beatles period. In notes to *Imagine* that were never used, John wrote, "I know you'll all be wondering about this one! it's been around since late '69 in a similar form to this — but not quite (i.e. more abstract)."[31] Allen Klein contributed to the lyrics, as did Yoko.[32]

- ## Oh Yoko! — (Lennon)

In a May 3, 1969 interview with the *New Musical Express*, John described a new song: "It's one I've written myself, and it's about Yoko, but I'll just change the word 'Yoko' to 'John,' and she can sing it about me."[33] It was recorded in the Montreal bed-in, from May 26 to June 2, 1969.[34]

---

[30] Unterberger, *The Unreleased Beatles*, 221, 253. Winn, *That Magic Feeling*, 230. Sauter, "One John Lennon."

[31] Davies, *The John Lennon Letters*, 221.

[32] Ibid: "I must thank Mark Allen Klein publicly for the 'line' 'just another day', a real poet." Klein also affirmed this. Felix Denis of *Oz* magazine, present when the song was being recorded, said that "Yoko wrote many of the lyrics. I watched her writing them and then watched her race into the studio to show John, and they'd burst out laughing." Blaney, *Lennon and McCartney*, 55.

[33] Alan Smith, "Beatles Music Straightforward."

[34] Winn, *That Magic Feeling*, 299.

Chapter 15

Live in Japan: *Spring Tour 1973* album — Donovan, 1973

- Hurdy Gurdy Man — (Donovan-Harrison)
  recorded March 25 or 26, 1973

According to Donovan, George wrote a verse of this song while they were in India.[35] The verse was not included on the single or album version because of time constraints, but Donovan often sang it during live performances.

Another Rishikesh vintage song.

"My Love"/ "The Mess" single — Paul McCartney, March 23, 1973

- My Love — (McCartney)

Paul said that "My Love," the big ballad from *Red Rose Speedway*, "was my definitive one for Linda, written in the early days of our relationship, and that came easily."[36] Dating exactly when this song was written might be difficult, as Paul met Linda on May 15, 1967, before the release of *Sgt. Pepper*. But they started getting more serious in fall 1968, during the White Album recordings. So this was probably written in the same era as "Two of Us" or "Maybe I'm Amazed," one of the many songs to Linda that Paul wrote during this period.

Thirty Three & 1/3 album — George Harrison, November 19, 1976

- Woman Don't You Cry for Me — (Harrison-Delaney)

George said that he wrote this "around 1968," in Gothenburg, Sweden, when he was touring with Eric Clapton, and Delaney & Bonnie, but the group actually played there on December 14, 1969, so that is the prob-

---

[35] *The Autobiography of Donovan*, 210.
[36] White, "Paul McCartney On His Not-So-Silly Love Songs."

able date of songwriting. Delaney & Bonnie's record, *Coming Home*, had just come out and they must have been listening to it. Delaney handed George a bottle-neck slide guitar, and asked him to play a line that David Mason had played on the record. George tried the new instrument, "and that was how 'Woman Don't You Cry for Me' came about," George said.[37] He thought the title came from Delaney.

———————◦●◦———————

Live! at the Star-Club in Hamburg, Germany; 1962 album — The Beatles, April, 1977

This is a low quality mono tape of the Beatles recorded December 18 to 31, 1962, at the Star Club in Hamburg. It has historical significance, and includes two early performances of Lennon-McCartney songs, "I Saw Her Standing There" and "Ask Me Why," and many covers. Though the Beatles tried to block its appearance, it was legally released in Germany in April, 1977; in the U.K. the following month; and in the U.S. in June 1977. George Harrison said, "The Star-Club recording was the crummiest recording ever made in our name!"[38] However Beatles historian Richie Unterberger regards it as "an invaluable document of the group . . . a diploma of sorts for a five-year apprenticeship."[39]

Many of these covers can be found in vastly better quality in *Live at the BBC* (1994), *Anthology 1* (1995), *Anthology 2* (1996), and *On Air – Live at the BBC Volume 2* (2013). Only unique songs are listed below.

- Your Feet's Too Big (COVER) (Ada Benson, Fred Fisher) (Lead vocals: Paul)

This was composed in 1936, and Fats Waller had a hit with it three years later.

---

[37] Harrison, *I Me Mine*, 172. See also White, "George Harrison Reconsidered" (1987), 57.

[38] Harrison court testimony, May 6, 1998, as quoted in Unterberger, *The Unreleased Beatles*, 41.

[39] Unterberger, *The Unreleased Beatles*, 42.

    o   <u>Reminiscing (COVER) (credited to King Curtis (pseud. for Curtis Ousley); reportedly written by Buddy Holly) (Lead vocals: George)</u>

The title song for Buddy Holly's second posthumous album, released in 1963. King Curtis was a well-known saxophonist who did sessions with Holly; Holly reportedly wrote this song, but gave Curtis songwriting credit. It was recorded in 1958.

    o   <u>Nothin' Shakin' (But the Leaves on the Trees) (COVER) (Eddie Fontaine, Cirino Colacrai, Diane Lampert, John Gluck) (Lead vocals: George)</u>

This was released as a single by Eddie Fontaine in 1958.

    o   <u>Little Queenie (COVER) (Chuck Berry) (Lead vocals: Paul)</u>

This was a single in 1959; it has since become a rock standard. Though John sang many Chuck Berry songs, Paul sings this one.

    o   <u>Falling in Love Again (Can't Help It) (COVER) (Frederick Hollander, Sammy Lerner) (Lead vocals: Paul)</u>

This was originally performed by Marlene Dietrich in the movie *The Blue Angel* (1930), and it became a standard. Sammy Lerner wrote the English lyrics.

    o   <u>Be-Bop-A-Lula (COVER) (Gene Vincent, Bill Davis) (Lead vocals: Fred Fascher, Star-Club waiter)</u>

This song, a hit for Gene Vincent in 1956, was a key song for the early Beatles. John performed it the night he met Paul, on July 6, 1957,[40] and much later, he recorded it on his 1975 album of oldies, *Rock 'n' Roll*. Paul chose it as one of his Desert Island Disks in 1982 and performed it on *Unplugged: The Official Bootleg* (1991).

---

[40] Cott, "John Lennon: The Last Interview."

- o <u>Red Sails in the Sunset (COVER) (Jimmy Kennedy, Hugh Williams (pseud. for Wilhelm Grosz))</u>
  <u>(Lead vocals: Paul)</u>

This was recorded by Al Bowly, Guy Lombardo and Bing Crosby in 1935, and became a standard. The Beatles may have heard Nat King Cole's 1951 version. The Beatles version has turned the ballad into a rock song.

- o <u>Shimmy Like Kate (aka I Wish I Could Shimmy Like My Sister Kate or Sister Kate) (COVER) (Armand Piron, Fred Smith, Cliff Goldsmith)</u>
  <u>(Lead vocals: Paul)</u>

This song was published in 1919, but the Beatles version is based on the 1960 rhythm and blues version by the American group The Olympics.

- o <u>I Remember You (COVER) (Johnny Mercer, Victor Schertzinger)</u>
  <u>(Lead vocals: Paul)</u>

This song was sung by Dorothy Lamour in the film *The Fleet's In* (1942), and it became a standard. The Beatles would have known it from a 1962 yodeling version by English singer Frank Ifield that was a huge hit in England.

- o <u>Where Have You Been All My Life? (COVER) (Barry Mann, Cynthia Weil)</u>
  <u>(Lead vocals: John)</u>

This was the flip side of Arthur Alexander's 1962 "Soldier of Love" single. Gene Vincent also recorded it.

- o <u>Sheila (COVER) (Tommy Roe)</u>
  <u>(Lead vocals: George)</u>

Roe first recorded this Buddy Holly-like song in 1960, but it became a hit for him two years later.

George Harrison album — George Harrison, February 23, 1979

- Not Guilty — (Harrison)

George wrote this in early 1968, just after returning from India, and it was one of the Kinfauns demos in May 1968.[41] It expresses his resentment against Paul and John:

> It was me getting pissed off at Lennon and McCartney for the grief I was catching during the making of the *White Album*.[42] I said I wasn't guilty of getting in the way of their careers. I said I wasn't guilty of leading them astray in our all going to Rishikesh to see the Maharishi. I was sticking up for myself and the song came off strong enough to be saved and utilized.[43]

The Beatles did a remarkable 102 takes of this in August of 1968, so they must have seriously considered putting it on the White Album. However, as it turned out, it did not make the cut.[44] One of these takes appears on Beatles *Anthology 3*.

Gone Troppo album — George Harrison, November 5, 1982

- Circles — (Harrison)

This was another of the Kinfauns demos from May 1968.[45] The lyrics for this version for full band were substantially changed.

---

[41] Brown, "A Conversation with George Harrison" (1979).

[42] Since it was a Kinfauns demo, it was actually written before the White Album sessions.

[43] White, "George Harrison Reconsidered," 55. See also Shapiro, *Behind Sad Eyes*, 85.

[44] See Lewisohn, *The Beatles Recording Sessions*, 147. Mal Evans in 1968 ("Thirty New Beatles Grooves," 7).

[45] Unterberger, *Unreleased Beatles*, 198.

Unplugged (The Official Bootleg) album — Paul McCartney, May 20, 1991

- I Lost My Little Girl — (McCartney-Lennon)

Paul said that "I Lost My Little Girl," was the first song he ever wrote; he came up with it when he was about fourteen, which would have been about June 1956.[46] His friend Ian James remembered him singing it at Forthlin Road.[47] When Paul met John, they began working on it in songwriting sessions at the McCartney home. In a very early interview, he reflects this collaboration:

> Then we started composing songs. John had a song he had written and I had one — it was, 'I Lost My Little Girl' — and I'd sing him one and he'd sing me one and we would work on them on holidays and even sometimes when we were supposed to be in school. We'd just belt away — my father would be out working and he wouldn't know it.[48]

John probably didn't have much impact on the song. He never commented on it, but he sang lead on it once during the Get Back sessions, so he definitely remembered it.[49]

The song was primitive, with its three chords, but Paul typically analyzes an idiosyncrasy in the music. "I think the sort of interesting thing about it now is I've got the chords going down and the melody going up,

---

[46] Read, "McCartney on McCartney," episode 1, quoted below. Lewisohn, *Tune In*, 818n47, holds that Paul wrote two piano songs, primitive versions of "Suicide" and "When I'm Sixty-Four," before this, his first guitar song. See also Wyndham, "Paul McCartney As Songwriter"; Gambaccini, "The Rolling Stone Interview" (1973); Miles, *Many Years from Now*, (1995), 21, 34; *Anthology* (2000), 20. Interview, date unknown, in Badman, *The Beatles Off the Record*, 13; Paul, Autobiography, on myspace.

[47] Lewisohn, *Tune In*, 153.

[48] Sann, "The Beatles: The Intimate Portrait."

[49] Unterberger, *The Unreleased Beatles*, 254.

it's a little obvious musical trick, but there's a little jiggery-pokery starting on the first song."[50]

━━━━━━━━◦◦━━━━━━━━

Off the Ground album — Paul McCartney, February 2, 1993

- **Cosmically Conscious — (McCartney)**

In India, the Maharishi used to repeat, "Be Cosmically Conscious, peace and joy." So Paul wrote a song with those lyrics and nothing else — basically a fragment, or a "snippet," as he described it.[51]

He included it, at 1:50 minutes, as an unlisted track on his ninth solo album, *Off the Ground*. A longer version of the song, at 4:39 minutes, was included as a bonus track on the U.S. CD single, "Off the Ground," released April 19, 1993.

━━━━━━━━◦◦━━━━━━━━

Live at the BBC album — The Beatles, November 30, 1994

This album, recorded from January 22, 1963 to May 26, 1965, represents a marvelous document of the early Beatles live, and presents many songs they performed live that never made it onto the albums. One of the highlights is the McCartney-Lennon song, "I'll Be On My Way," the only recorded performance by the Beatles. Other solid pleasures are a number of Chuck Berry songs sung by John, "Hippy Hippy Shake" sung by Paul, "A Shot of Rhythm and Blues," Arthur Alexander's "Soldier of Love," and the earliest recording of "Long Tall Sally." I will consider only the unique songs here.

   o I Got a Woman (COVER) (Ray Charles, Renald Richard) (lead vocals: John)

This was a 1954 Ray Charles single, though the Beatles may have heard the song on a 1956 U.K. Elvis album, *Rock 'n' Roll*.

---

[50] Read, "McCartney on McCartney," episode 1.

[51] Giuliano, *Glass Onion*, 122.

- o <u>Too Much Monkey Business (COVER) (Chuck Berry)</u>
  <u>(lead vocals: John)</u>

This Chuck Berry single was released in 1956.

- o <u>Keep Your Hands Off My Baby (COVER) (Gerry Goffin,</u>
  <u>Carole King)</u>
  <u>(lead vocals: John)</u>

Little Eva had a number 12 hit with this in 1962.

- o <u>I'll Be On My Way (McCartney-Lennon)</u>
  <u>(lead vocals: Paul, John)</u>

See "Do You Want to Know a Secret / I'll Be On My Way" single —
Billy J. Kramer with The Dakotas, above. This Buddy Holly-flavored rendition is the only version by the Beatles that has been released. It was
taped on April 4, 1963 and broadcast on the radio show *Side by Side* on
June 24, 1963.[52]

- o <u>Young Blood (COVER) (Jerry Leiber, Mike Stoller, Doc</u>
  <u>Pomus)</u>
  <u>(lead vocals: George)</u>

The Coasters released this, as the B-side for the famous "Searchin',"
in 1957.

- o <u>A Shot of Rhythm and Blues (COVER) (Terry Thompson)</u>
  <u>(lead vocals: John)</u>

This was the B-side of Arthur Alexander's single, "You Better Move
On," released in 1961. In 1988, Paul singled this song out, saying that records were the "currency" of music in the early Beatles era. "That's where
we got our repertoire from, the b-sides, the 'Shot Of Rhythm And Blues,'
the lesser known stuff that we helped bring to the fore, the R&B stuff."[53]
The Beatles also performed it during the Get Back sessions.

---

[52] Lewisohn, *Complete Beatles Chronicles*, 105.
[53] Lewisohn, *Beatles Recording Sessions*, 6.

○ <u>Sure to Fall (in Love with You) (COVER) (Carl Perkins, Bill Cantrell, Quinton Claunch)</u>
<u>(lead vocals: Paul)</u>

Carl Perkins's version of this song was released in 1957. The Beatles had performed it at the Decca audition.

○ <u>Some Other Guy (COVER) (Jerry Leiber, Mike Stoller, Richard Barrett)</u>
<u>(lead vocals: John, Paul)</u>

Richard Barrett's version of this appeared as a single in 1962. It became something of a rock touchstone for the Beatles. They played it on August 22, 1962 when a local TV station was filming at the Cavern, about a week after Ringo replaced Pete Best in the group. Paul explained the importance of the song for the Beatles: "Some Other Guy" is a great song . . . It really got us started because that's one of the earliest bits of film of The Beatles. . . . It was also a bit of a muso song."[54] John, in 1968, said,

> I mean, we got a bit pretentious. . . . Really, I just like rock'n'roll. I mean, these [pointing to a pile of Fifties records] are the records I dug then, I dig them now and I'm still trying to reproduce "Some Other Guy" sometimes or "Be Bop A Lula."[55]

○ <u>That's All Right (Mama) (COVER) (Arthur Crudup)</u>
<u>(lead vocals: Paul)</u>

This was Elvis's first single, released in 1954; Crudup had released a version in 1946.

---

[54] *Paul McCartney's Rock 'n Roll Roots*, BBC Radio 2, Dec. 25, 1999, as cited in Pedler, *The Songwriting Secrets of the Beatles*, 232.
[55] Cott, "The Rolling Stone Interview with John Lennon."

- o <u>Carol (COVER) (Chuck Berry)</u>
  <u>(lead vocals: John)</u>

This Chuck Berry single appeared in 1958. It was one of the early rock songs that John learned on his guitar.[56]

- o <u>Soldier of Love (Lay Down Your Arms) (COVER) (Buzz</u>
  <u>Cason, Tony Moon)</u>
  <u>(lead vocals: John)</u>

"Soldier of Love," one of the great Beatles covers, had appeared in 1962 as the B-side of Arthur Alexander's single "Where Have You Been."

<u>Clarabella (COVER) (Frank Pingatore)</u>
<u>(lead vocals: Paul)</u>

The Jodimars (former members of Bill Haley and the Comets) released this as a single in 1956.

- o <u>I'm Gonna Sit Right Down and Cry (over You) (COVER)</u>
  <u>(Joe Thomas, Howard Biggs)</u>
  <u>(lead vocals: John, Paul)</u>

Written in 1953, this appeared on Elvis's first album three years later.

- o <u>Crying, Waiting, Hoping (COVER) (Buddy Holly)</u>
  <u>(lead vocals: George)</u>

This song was released in 1959 as the B-side to Holly's "Peggy Sue Got Married." The Beatles also performed it in the Decca audition.

- o <u>To Know Her Is to Love Her (COVER) (Phil Spector)</u>
  <u>(lead vocals: John, Paul, George)</u>

This song, recorded by Spector's first band, The Teddy Bears, in 1958, supplied the Beatles a model for their close-harmony vocal songs. Paul, in 1995, said:

> We used to do a close-harmony version of the Teddy
> Bears' "To Know Her Is To Love Her," which was good
> for the versatility in the band. We weren't all rock n' roll,

---

[56] Lennon, in *Anthology*, 11.

we could change the pace, which was always nice after you'd played for three hours. So this ["This Boy"] was our attempt to write one of those.[57]

The Beatles also performed it for the Decca audition.

○ The Honeymoon Song (COVER) (Mikis Theodorakis, William Sansom)
(lead vocals: Paul)

This was the theme song for the 1959 movie, *Honeymoon*. In 1988, Paul reminisced:

> "The Honeymoon Song" was Marino Marini, an Italian, and his backing group. They used to appear on telly and the greatest thing about them was they had a volume pedal! "The Honeymoon Song" wasn't a big hit but I liked it, thought it was a nice tune. I was the force behind that, the others thought it was a real soppy idea, which I can see now![58]

○ Johnny B. Goode (COVER) (Chuck Berry)
(lead vocals: John)

This rock standard was released as a single by Berry in 1958. It was one of the early rock songs that John learned on his guitar.[59]

○ Memphis, Tennessee (COVER) (Chuck Berry)
(lead vocals: John)

This was the B side of "Back in the U.S.A." in 1959, but it became a hit on its own in 1963. According to historian Kevin Howlett, Paul remembered learning this song in John's bedroom "when the two lads decided it had 'the greatest riff ever'."[60]

---

[57] Miles, *Many Years From Now*, 155.

[58] Lewisohn interview, *Beatles Recording Sessions*, 9.

[59] Lennon, in *Anthology*, 11.

[60] Howlett, Liner notes for *On Air — Live at the BBC Volume 2*, 35.

- Lucille (COVER) (Albert Collins, Richard Penniman (Little Richard))
(lead vocals: Paul)

Little Richard released this single in 1957.

- Sweet Little Sixteen (COVER) (Chuck Berry)
(lead vocals: John)

This was a Chuck Berry single in 1958. The Beatles sang it during the Get Back sessions, and Paul chose it as one of his Desert Island Disks in 1982.

- Lonesome Tears in My Eyes (COVER) (Johnny Burnette, Dorsey Burnette, Paul Burlison, Al Mortimer)
(lead vocals: John)

This was released by Johnny Burnette and his Rock 'n' Roll Trio in 1957.

- Nothin' Shakin' (COVER) (Eddie Fontaine, Cirino Colacrai, Diane Lampert, John Gluck, Jr.)
(lead vocals: George)

This was an Eddie Fontaine single in 1958. The full title is "Nothin' Shakin' (But the Leaves on the Trees)."

- The Hippy Hippy Shake (COVER) (Chan Romero)
(lead vocals: Paul)

American rocker Chan Romero released this song in the U.S. and Australia in 1959. Though it was covered by Little Tony in the U.K. in the same year, Paul heard the Romero recording, according to Bob Wooler, DJ at the Cavern. Wooler couldn't tell if the falsetto vocals were by a man or a woman. "I played it at a lunchtime session at the Cavern, and Paul McCartney asked me about it. He always fancied himself as a high-voiced singer. I lent him the record and the Beatles started doing it."[61] The song became a Beatles staple.

---

[61] Leigh, "Cavern King," Interview with Bob Wooler (1998).

Paul reminisced: "We had too much material anyway. We couldn't record it all when we did get a deal, so other groups took songs from our act and made hits out of them — like The Swinging Blue Jeans with 'The Hippy Hippy Shake,' which was one of my big numbers."[62]

The Beatles performed this during the Get Back sessions.

- o <u>Glad All Over (COVER) (Aaron Schroeder, Sid Tepper, Roy Bennett)</u>
  <u>(lead vocals: George)</u>

This song, performed by Carl Perkins, appeared in the movie *Jamboree* in 1957, then was released as a single the following year.

- o <u>I Just Don't Understand (COVER) (Marijohn Wilkin, Kent Westberry)</u>
  <u>(lead vocals: John)</u>

This was released by Ann-Margret (Olsson) in 1961.

- o <u>So How Come (No One Loves Me) (COVER) (Felice and Boudleaux Bryant)</u>
  <u>(lead vocals: George, John)</u>

This appeared on the Everly Brothers' fourth album, *A Date With The Everly Brothers*, in 1960.

- o <u>I Forgot to Remember to Forget (COVER) (Stan Kesler, Charlie Feathers)</u>
  <u>(lead vocals: George)</u>

This was one of Elvis's Sun singles, released in 1955.

- o <u>I Got to Find My Baby (COVER) (Chuck Berry)</u>
  <u>(lead vocals: John)</u>

Chuck Berry released this as a single in 1960. Some believe that it was written by Peter Clayton in 1941.

---

[62] *Anthology*, 68.

○ <u>Ooh! My Soul (COVER) (Richard Penniman)</u>
   <u>(lead vocals: Paul)</u>

This appeared as the B-side of Little Richard's "True, Fine Mama" single in 1958.

○ <u>Don't Ever Change (COVER) (Gerry Goffin, Carole King)</u>
   <u>(lead vocals: Paul, George)</u>

Written in 1961, this was a hit for the Crickets in the U.K. the following year.

Anthology 1 album — The Beatles, November 20, 1995

Between November 1995 and October of the following year, the Beatles released what amounted to the Beatle fan's ultimate dream — three two-CD "official" bootlegs, *Anthology 1*, *Anthology 2*, and *Anthology 3*. They offered songs written and performed by the Beatles that had never been released, including alternate takes, demos and covers. While some of this material had been available on bootlegs, some hadn't. And the recordings on the Anthology CDs were understandably often of much higher quality than the bootlegs.

Some of the early material, such as the Decca audition tape, has been mentioned above in chronological order of recording.

I will discuss only the unique songs here.

○ <u>Free as a Bird — (Lennon-McCartney-Harrison-Starkey)</u>

As a part of the Anthology series, the living Beatles agreed to "complete" two demos by John, adding instrumentation, background vocals, and sections of the songs that were missing. Per Everett, this song was written by Lennon "around 1977, reportedly as an exhilarated reaction to [Lennon] obtaining his hard-won U.S. 'green card'."[63] The Beatles re-recorded it in February and March, 1994.

---

[63] Everett II, 287.

Paul said: "I fell in love with 'Free As A Bird.' I thought I would have loved to work with John on that. I liked the melody, it's got strong chords and it really appealed to me. Ringo was very up for it, George was very up for it, I was very up for it."[64] The Beatles especially liked the fact that they could fill in a middle eight. Paul said: "That was really like working on a record with John, as Lennon/McCartney/Harrison, because we all chipped in a bit on this one. George and I were vying for best lyric."[65] According to George, they also changed some chords.[66]

o <u>That'll Be the Day (COVER) (Jerry Allison, Buddy Holly, Norman Petty)</u>
<u>(lead vocals: John)</u>

"That'll Be the Day" and "In Spite of All the Danger" were two sides of the demo that the Quarrymen (John, Paul and George, with Colin Hanton on drums, and John 'Duff' Lowe on piano) recorded on July 12, 1958. Thus this is the earliest high quality recording of the proto-Beatles.

"That'll Be the Day," a Buddy Holly single released in May 1957, was one of the earliest rock songs that John learned to play.[67] "John did 'That'll Be the Day' which was one of our stage numbers, and George played the opening guitar notes and I harmonised with John singing lead," explained Paul in 1995.[68]

• **In Spite of All the Danger — (McCartney)**
(lead vocals: John)

This is one of Paul's two or three earliest songs.[69] He wrote it when he was about fourteen, around 1956. It was very influenced by Elvis — "It's

---

[64] Gobnotch, "Recording Sessions Update - Part 1."

[65] Ibid.

[66] Ibid.

[67] *Anthology*, 11.

[68] Lewisohn, "The Paul McCartney Interview," 6-7.

[69] *Anthology*, 23. Lewisohn, "The Paul McCartney Interview," 6-7.

me doing Elvis," he explained.[70] When it came time to record two songs onto an actual disk at a semi-professional studio in Liverpool, this was one of the songs chosen.[71] John 'Duff' Lowe, the pianist for the recording, remembered that in the rehearsal for the recording at Forthlin Road, Paul "was quite specific about how he wanted it played and what he wanted the piano to do. There was no question of improvising. We were told what we had to play."[72] Paul as driven producer and arranger was already well in evidence.

John sang lead on this song for this demo. He once said, "I sang both sides [of this single]. I was such a bully in those days I didn't even let Paul sing his own song."[73] This is a point worth emphasizing — Paul and John did not always sing lead on their own songs. Sometimes John sang lead on Paul songs so he (Paul) could sing harmony, and this is probably what happened here.

When the disk received a sticker, a handwritten note on it attributed the song to "McCartney-Harrison." Paul later explained, "It says on the label that it was me and George but I think it was written by me and George played the guitar solo! We were mates and nobody was into copyrights and publishing . . . and because George did the solo we figured that he 'wrote' the solo."[74]

There are no statements from George Harrison on the song, but John attributed it to Paul: "The first thing we ever recorded was 'That'll Be The Day,' a Buddy Holly song, and one of Paul's called 'In Spite Of All The Danger.'"[75]

---

[70] Lewisohn, "The Paul McCartney Interview," 6-7. For young Paul, Elvis was the "ultimate groove," Du Noyer, *Conversations*, 30.

[71] Lewisohn, *Tune In* (extended), 444-46.

[72] Quoted in Turner, *A Hard Day's Write*, 208-9.

[73] Interview by Paul Drew, US Radio, April 1975, as cited in Lewisohn, *Tune In*, 178. Paul, however, had fuzzy (incorrect) memories that he sang the lead, see Lewisohn, "The Paul McCartney Interview," 6-7.

[74] Ibid.

[75] Lennon, 1974, in *Anthology*, 14.

McCartney played this song throughout his 2005 world tour.

    o   <u>Hallelujah, I Love Her So (COVER) (Ray Charles)</u>
        <u>(Lead Vocal: Paul)</u>

A performance from the spring-summer 1960 rehearsals at the McCartney home. This had been a 1956 Ray Charles single, but the Beatles followed the Eddie Cochran version from 1958.

- **You'll Be Mine — (McCartney-Lennon) (Lead Vocal: Paul)**

This is from the spring-summer 1960 rehearsals at the McCartney home. A parody of the Inkspots, according to Lewisohn, it was sung by Paul, with a nonsensical spoken word interlude by John.[76] I have not as yet found any commentary on this song by any of the Beatles, so my attribution is based on the main singer. This is arguably the earliest Lennon-McCartney song recording, but the track has historical interest only.

- **Cayenne — (McCartney)**

One more performance from the spring-summer 1960 rehearsals at the McCartney home. Paul claims authorship of this instrumental. This version lasts 1:14 minutes, while the original ran to two and a half minutes. "I wrote a few instrumentals," Paul said in 1995. "'Cat Call' was one of those, then there was something called 'Cayenne Pepper,' but those tended to be me writing tunes by myself."[77] Paul realistically stated that this has mainly historical interest: "It's not brilliant. But when you listen to it you can hear a lot of stuff I'm going to write. So, it's interesting from that point of view."[78]

---

[76] Lewisohn, Liner notes on *Anthology I*, p. 8.

[77] Miles, *Many Years from Now*, 38.

[78] As quoted in Turner, *Hard Day's Write*, 210.

o   <u>Searchin' (COVER) (Jerry Leiber, Mike Stoller)</u>
    <u>(lead vocals: Paul)</u>

From the Decca Audition, January 1, 1962. This was a single for the Coasters in 1957. It was a touchstone song for the Beatles, and Paul chose it as one of his Desert Island Disks in 1982. He said, in 1995,

> Another thing we went across town for was the record 'Searchin' by The Coasters. Nobody had it. The drummer in the Quarry Men, Colin Hanton, knew some guy that had it, but we had to get on the bus, do two changes of bus routes. Didn't matter. Half an hour away. There was such a passion about that song 'Searchin.'[79]

After they learned it, it became "a big Cavern number, that one."[80]

o   <u>Three Cool Cats (COVER) (Jerry Leiber, Mike Stoller)</u>
    <u>(lead vocals: George)</u>

From the Decca Audition, January 1, 1962. Another Coasters song — this was the B-side of their 1959 single, "Charlie Brown."

o   <u>The Sheik of Araby (COVER) (Harry B. Smith, Francis</u>
    <u>Wheeler, Ted Snyder)</u>
    <u>(lead vocals: George)</u>

Another from the Decca Audition. This Tin Pan Alley song was written in 1921, in honor of Rudolf Valentino's role in *The Sheik*, and became a jazz standard in the twenties. George said, in 2000,

> In those days a lot of the rock 'n' roll songs were actually old tunes from the Forties, Fifties or whenever, which people had rocked up. That was the thing to do if you didn't have a tune: just rock up an oldie. Joe Brown had recorded a rock n' roll version of 'The Sheik Of Araby.' He was really popular on the Saturday TV show *Six-Five Special*

---

[79] Miles, *Many Years From Now*, 30.

[80] Read, "McCartney on McCartney," episode 1. See also *Anthology* 22.

and *Oh Boy!*. I had the Joe Brown records, so I sang 'Sheik Of Araby.'"[81]

o <u>Like Dreamers Do — (McCartney)</u>
<u>(lead vocals: Paul)</u>

From the Decca Audition, January 1, 1962. It was first released by the Applejacks in 1964, see above. This is the only Beatles version.

o <u>Hello Little Girl — (Lennon-McCartney)</u>
<u>(lead vocals: John)</u>

Also from the Decca Audition. It was first released by the Fourmost in 1963, see above. This is the only Beatles version.

o <u>Bésame Mucho (COVER) (Consuelo Velázquez, Sunny Sky-</u>
<u>lar)</u>
<u>(lead vocals: Paul)</u>

From the EMI audition, recorded on June 6, 1962. See the *Let It Be* movie for another version. It was also played at the Decca Audition.

o <u>How Do You Do It? (COVER) (Mitch Murray)</u>
<u>(lead vocals: John)</u>

The Beatles recorded this, reluctantly, on September 4, 1962, at George Martin's urging. But they disliked the song, so Martin gave it to Gerry and the Pacemakers, who made it a hit.[82]

o <u>Lend Me Your Comb (COVER) (Kay Twomey, Fred Wise</u>
<u>and Ben Weisman)</u>
<u>(lead vocals: John and Paul)</u>

The Beatles live at the BBC Maida Vale Studios, July 16, 1963. This had been the B-side of Carl Perkins's 1958 single, "Glad All Over."

---

[81] *Anthology*, 67.

[82] See Lewisohn, "The Paul McCartney Interview," 7; Read, "McCartney on McCartney," episode 2. Williams, "Produced by George Martin" (1971). More in Badman, *Beatles Off the Record*, 44-45.

- ○ <u>Moonlight Bay (COVER) (Percy Wenrich, Edward Madden)</u>
  <u>(lead vocals: John)</u>

Performed on The Morecambe and Wise Show, December 2, 1963, broadcast on April 18, 1964. This song had been published in 1912.

- ○ <u>Shout! (COVER) (Rudolph Isley, Ronald Isley, O'Kelly Is-</u>
  <u>ley, Jr.)</u>
  <u>(lead vocals: John, Paul, George, Ringo)</u>

Live for the ITV show, "Around The Beatles," recorded April 19, 1964. This was recorded by the Isley Brothers in 1959, and became a rock standard.

- • **You Know What to Do — (Harrison)**
  (lead vocals: George) (recorded on June 3, 1964)

This demo was recorded with Jimmy Nicol on drums, as Ringo was sick. Then it was apparently forgotten. Paul said, in 1995,

> There was a song of George's that the engineer Allan Rouse discovered. EMI didn't know they had it. . . . I do believe there will be a bunch of people interested in hearing the George Harrison song from thirty years ago that no one to this day had heard. It's not the greatest thing that George ever wrote, but it's an undiscovered nugget.[83]

After it was rediscovered, George reportedly said that he had no memories of it at all.

- ○ <u>Leave My Kitten Alone (Take 5) (COVER) (Little Willie</u>
  <u>John, James McDougal and Titus Turner)</u>
  <u>(Lead Vocal: John) (recorded August 14, 1964)</u>

Little Willie John released this in 1959, and Johnny Preston did a version of it the following year. The Beatles recorded it for the *Beatles for Sale* album, but it was not used. Paul said, in 1988, "That was a Johnny Preston song that we'd rehearsed in Liverpool along with all our Cavern stuff and it

---

[83] Gobnotch, "Recording Sessions Update - Part 8."

was just in our repertoire. It wasn't a big one that we used to do, we'd pull it out of the hat occasionally, and we also recorded it."[84]

───────◦○◦───────

"Free as a Bird / "Christmas Time (Is Here Again)" single — The Beatles, Dec. 4, 1995

    ○   "Free as a Bird — (Lennon-McCartney-Harrison-Starkey)

See *Anthology 1*.

    ○   "Christmas Time (Is Here Again)"

See Christmas record, at December 11, 1967. This is its first general release.

───────◦○◦───────

Anthology 2 album — The Beatles, March 18, 1996

    ○   Real Love — (Lennon)

This was written in 1979-80, then was re-recorded with the other Beatles in February 1995.[85] Paul said, in 1996,

> I don't quite like it as much as 'Free As A Bird' because I think 'Free As A Bird' is more powerful. But it's catchier. There was one real nice moment when we were doing 'Real Love' and I was trying to learn the piano bit, and Ringo sat down on the drums, jamming along. It was like none of us had ever been away.[86]

Paul, as we have seen, preferred doing the more collaborative "Free as a Bird," and "Real Love" was more like "being side men to John — but that was very joyful and good fun and I think we did a good job."[87]

---

[84] Lewisohn, "The Paul McCartney Interview," 11.
[85] Everett II, 289.
[86] Gobnotch, "Recording Sessions Update — Part 5."
[87] Press Release for "Real Love."

- **If You've Got Trouble (Take 1) — (Lennon)
  (lead vocals: Ringo) (recorded on February 18, 1965)**

  This was recorded during the *Help!* sessions, and apparently became another lost Beatle song, until much later it was rediscovered in the vaults.[88] John claimed it in 1965. Journalist Ray Coleman observed, "They are just completing a song which features Ringo singing. 'I wrote it,' says John. 'It's the funniest thing I've ever done — listen to the words.'"[89]

  o <u>That Means a Lot (Take 1) — (McCartney-Lennon)
  (lead vocals: Paul) (recorded February 20, March 30, 1965)</u>

  P. J. Proby released this in 1965, see above.

- **12-Bar Original (Edited Take 2) — (Lennon, McCartney, Harrison, Starkey)
  (recorded November 4, 1965)**

  A rare Beatles instrumental, recorded during the *Rubber Soul* sessions.

Anthology 3 album — The Beatles, 28 October 1996

  o <u>Junk — (McCartney)</u>

  A demo recorded at Kinfauns in May 1968. See the *McCartney* album, above.

  o <u>Not Guilty (Take 102) — (Harrison)</u>

  Another Kinfauns demo. See George's album, *George Harrison*, above.

- **What's the New Mary Jane (Take 4) — (Lennon-Mardas)
  (Lead vocal: John) (Recorded August 14, 1968)**

  In 1969, John described this song as "a mad thing I wrote half with our electronics genius, Alex. . . . It was real madness."[90] "Alex" was Yanni

---

[88] *Anthology*, 172.
[89] Coleman, "Here We Go Again."
[90] Smith, "Beatles Music Straightforward On Next Album." In a January 1, 1976 interview with Elliott Mintz, Lennon called it "a crazy song that I wrote," Lost Lennon Tapes, Apr. 18, 1988.

(John) Alexis Mardas, "Magic Alex," a close associate of John in 1967 and 1968.[91]

This song was one of the Esher demos, from May 1968. In an undated, unsourced interview, John is quoted as saying, "That was me, Yoko, and George sitting on the floor at EMI fooling around. Pretty good, huh?"[92] It was on the short list for inclusion on the White Album, but was rejected at the last moment. Mal Evans, in 1968, said this was "a recording you WON'T hear on the new LP… Very strange this one. John thought it up and John sings it."[93]

Lennon wanted to release it as a single, but the other Beatles vetoed the idea.[94] This is the song's first release.

- o Step Inside Love — (McCartney) / Los Paranoias — (McCartney-Lennon-Harrison-Starkey) (Lead vocals: Paul) (recorded September 16, 1968)

Cilla Black recorded "Step Inside Love" in 1968, see above. This Beatles performance led to a studio jam, "Los Paranoias," credited to Lennon-McCartney-Harrison-Starkey. It's a fragment, but Paul sings it and it is connected with a Paul composition. According to Turner, "Los Paranoias" is "an extended studio joke initiated by Paul."[95]

- o Teddy Boy — (McCartney)

See the *McCartney* album, above.

- o Medley: Rip It Up (COVER) (Robert Blackwell, John Marascalco) / Shake, Rattle and Roll (COVER) (Jesse Stone, under his working name Charles E. Calhoun) / Blue Suede Shoes (COVER) (Carl Perkins)

See the *Let It Be* movie, above.

---

[91] See "Sexy Sadie" in the White Album, above.

[92] Wikipedia, "What's the New Mary Jane." Winn, *That Magic Feeling*, 200.

[93] Evans, "Thirty New Beatles Grooves," 11.

[94] Emerick, *Here, There and Everywhere*, 312.

[95] Turner, *Hard Day's Write*, 216. See also Lewisohn, *The Beatles Recording Sessions*, 155.

- o <u>All Things Must Pass (Demo) — (Harrison)</u>

See Harrison's album, *All Things Must Pass*, above.

- o <u>Mailman, Bring Me No More Blues (COVER) (Ruth Roberts, Bill Katz, Stanley Clayton)</u>
  <u>(Lead vocals: John)</u>

From the Get Back sessions. This was the B-side of the 1957 "Words of Love" single by Buddy Holly. It was in the early Beatles repertoire.

- o <u>Come and Get It (Demo) — (McCartney)</u>

This demo, performed entirely by Paul, was recorded on July 24, 1969. See "Come and Get It / Rock Of All Ages" single, Badfinger, above.

The Beatles Anthology DVD — The Beatles, April 1, 2003.

McCartney, George Harrison and Ringo Starr reminisced and sang some old songs for the Anthology documentary in June 1994. This session was not released until the DVD version of the series appeared.

- o <u>Baby What You Want Me to Do (COVER) (Jimmy Reed)</u>

This was recorded by blues musician Jimmy Reed in 1959.

- o <u>Raunchy (instrumental) (COVER) (Bill Justis, Sid Manker)</u>

This was a hit for Bill Justis and his band in 1957. It was one of the first instrumentals with pronounced lead guitar that became popular in early rock. George's mastery of this song reportedly got him into the Beatles.

- **Thinking of Linking — (McCartney-Lennon)**

Paul got the germ of this song in the movies, when a character said, "We're thinking of linking." Paul thought, "That should be a song. Thinking of linking, people are gonna get married, gotta write that!' . . . Pretty corny stuff."[96] So Paul said in 1988. However, in 1968, an interviewer, the-

---

[96] Lewisohn, "The Paul McCartney Interview," 12 (1988).

oretically reflecting statements by Paul and John, wrote that the title came from "the television commercial for the Link Furniture Company."[97]

However the title came into being, the song was worked on in songwriting sessions with Paul and John — in about 1959, Paul put it in a list of songs he and John had written.[98] It was performed during the Get Back sessions,[99] purely out of nostalgia, because, as Paul said, "'Thinking of Linking' was terrible!"

The words were fairly primitive, but the music is actually quite likable, very Buddy Holly, better than many other early Beatle songs.

○ <u>Blue Moon of Kentucky (COVER) (Bill Monroe)</u>

This was a hit single for Bill Monroe and the Bluegrass Boys in 1947, as a somewhat slow waltz. It became the B-side of Elvis's first single, "That's All Right," in 1954, in a faster, more rock version, and was just as popular as the A-side.

Let It Be . . . Naked album — The Beatles, November 17, 2003

And yet another attempt to get the Get Back sessions right as an album! This strips all the Spector overdubs from the songs, and is a significant contrast to the original *Let It Be* for that reason. The song order is also completely different. A Lennon song, "Don't Let Me Down," formerly the B-side to the "Get Back" single, is added, while "Maggie Mae" and "Dig It" are jettisoned.

Purists have objected to many aspects of this album. For example, "Across the Universe" is a studio recording, made long before the Get Back sessions. For our purposes, we can note that the main album includes no new Beatles songs. However, a whole extra disk, the Fly on the Wall disk, includes conversations and excerpts from songs. It is only twenty-two

[97] Lydon, "Lennon and McCartney: Songwriters."
[98] Letter to Mr. Low, in Davies, *The Beatles*, 63.
[99] Unterberger, *The Unreleased Beatles*, 260.

minutes long, a collection of fragments that is more tantalizing than satis-fying. It does include snippets of some early Lennon-McCartney songs that have historical interest.

Notable songs on the Fly on the Wall disk are as follows:

- **Because I Know You Love Me So — 1:32 (Lennon-McCartney)**

After the Beatles played "One After 909" on January 3, 1969, John remembered and played this old Lennon-McCartney tune.[100]

- **Taking a Trip to Carolina — 0:19 (Starkey)**

Ringo performed this fragment on January 3, 1969.[101]

- **John's Piano Piece — 0:18 (Lennon)**
  - Child of Nature — 0:24 (Lennon)

See "Jealous Guy" in Lennon's *Imagine*, above.

  - All Things Must Pass — 0:21 (Harrison)

See Harrison's *All Things Must Pass*, above.

- **John's Jam — 0.19 (Lennon)**
- **Paul's Bass Jam — 0.14 (McCartney)**
  - Paul's Piano Piece — 1:01 (McCartney)

See *Let It Be*, the movie, above.

- **Fancy My Chances With You (or I Fancy Me Chances) — 0:27 (Lennon-McCartney)**

This song had been part of the Beatles' live repertoire in 1962.[102] They played it in the Get Back sessions on January 24, 1969.

---

[100] Sulpy and Schweighardt, *Get Back*, 37.

[101] Ibid., 30.

[102] Lewisohn, *The Beatles Chronicle*, appendix, "What They Played."

McCartney album, Deluxe Edition — Paul McCartney, June 13, 2011

- ○ <u>Suicide — (McCartney)</u>

See *McCartney*, above. This bonus track on disk 2 of the *McCartney* re-master, deluxe edition, is the first complete recording of this song on disk. A 1974 version from the unreleased TV documentary, *One Hand Clapping*, is on the bonus film DVD.

On Air — Live at the BBC Volume 2 album — The Beatles, November 11, 2013

Only unique songs are discussed below.

- ○ <u>I'm Talking About You (COVER) (Chuck Berry)</u>
  <u>(lead vocals: John)</u>

Chuck Berry released this as a single in 1961.

- ○ <u>Beautiful Dreamer (COVER) (Stephen Foster, Gerry</u>
  <u>Goffin, Jack Keller)</u>
  <u>(lead vocals: Paul)</u>

This classic song was written by Foster in 1862, thus is probably the oldest cover song the Beatles ever recorded. They followed a speeded up version by Tony Orlando that had been released in the U.K. exactly a hundred years later. It included new lyrics by Goffin and Keller.

The Beatles Bootleg Recordings 1963 album — The Beatles, December 17, 2013

This was released through the iTunes Store. It includes 15 studio recordings and 44 live BBC recordings, reportedly released for copyright reasons.

- ○ <u>"Bad to Me" (Demo) — (Lennon-McCartney)</u>

This was released as a single by Billy J. Kramer with The Dakotas in July 1963, see above.

o "I'm in Love" (Demo) — (Lennon-McCartney)

This was released as a single by the Fourmost in November 1963, see above.

16

Who Wrote the Lennon-McCartney Songs?

Sweeping Away the Myths

There are multiple levels of misapprehensions about the standard "Lennon-McCartney" songwriting attribution that appeared on most of the Beatle songs. In order to understand John, Paul and the Beatles, we must clear those away.

"Lennon-McCartney": The Beatles as Magical Synergy

First, many have accepted the "Lennon-McCartney" attribution as literally true, which actually is not an unreasonable assumption. "Lennon-McCartney" suggests that all those songs were the result of systematic 50-50 collaboration (as in songwriting partnerships such as George and Ira Gershwin, Elton John and Bernie Taupin, and Burt Bacharach and Hal David, in which one person wrote music and the other words). To the best of our knowledge, once, but only once, did John and Paul come close to that, John writing most or all of the lyrics to a song and Paul writing the music — "In My Life."[1]

This idea, that all Lennon-McCartney songs represented full collaboration, is contradicted by all the best evidence, as is well known to anyone with more than a passing interest in the Beatles. Both Paul and John wrote lyrics and music. Some of their songs were "full" collaborations, "written eye-to-eye," but many were entirely written by either John or Paul alone. Many, probably the majority until the White Album era, were "supportive," "finishing," collaborations: they were substantially started by either Paul or John, then were finished with some collaboration. In other words, John might have written the music and first verse of a song, then Paul came in and they had a songwriting session to finish it up. Paul might have

---

[1] As Paul tells the story. See discussion above.

worked with him on the second or third verse and "middle eight" — often a substantial middle section.[2] While this is not a full collaboration — the main song is John's — it still includes some significant collaborative work, and the attribution Lennon-McCartney is valid (as long as we understand that it was not 50-50).

In the same way, sometimes Paul would start a song, then bring it to John to finish it off. Though, again, this is not a full collaboration, there was joint work on the song, so a joint attribution again would be appropriate (though "McCartney-Lennon" would have been correct, rather than "Lennon-McCartney").

Sometimes Paul and John would combine songs that had been written independently (as with "A Day in the Life," "Baby I'm a Rich Man," or "I've Got a Feeling"). However, this would not be full collaboration, as the writer of the "main" song would dominate — thus "A Day in the Life" is correctly attributed to "Lennon-McCartney," though Paul made a major contribution to the song.

Sometimes Paul or John would write a song, and the other would merely act as an "editor," changing a word or two in the lyrics. Sometimes the "editor" would add just a bit to the other's song, a phrase in the lyrics or a counter-melody.

However, many of the Lennon-McCartney songs were actually written by either Paul or John entirely separately, and "Lennon" or "McCartney" would have been the correct attribution.

Of the 203 "Lennon-McCartney" songs written from the "Love Me Do" single to *Let It Be*, only about twelve seem to have been literal, nearly-equal collaborations.[3] On all the rest of the songs, one or the other of the

[2] For the "middle eight" in Beatle songs, see chapter two at "Love Me Do."
[3] There is no scientific way of isolating all full collaborative songs. The following list represents my best judgment, based on the evidence I've seen. Very equal collaborations are "Misery," "There's a Place," "I'll Get You," "Little Child," "I Want to Hold Your Hand," and "Baby's In Black." I also put "In My Life" in this category. In other songs, there was extensive collaboration, from the ground up, though either Paul or John may have dominated the collaboration session slightly: "From Me To You," "Thank You Girl," "She

two writers either wrote the song entirely alone or substantially dominated the writing. "Full" collaborations were more common in the early Beatles period. However, "supportive" collaborations, in which one of the Beatles helped finish a song the other had begun, extended from the early Beatles period to *Abbey Road*.

This only reaffirms what Beatle insiders have been saying through the years. John said, "All our best work — apart from the early days, like 'I Want to Hold Your Hand,' we wrote together, and things like that — *we wrote apart, always*."[4] Tony Barrow, the Beatles' early publicist, correctly wrote,

> Only a mere handful of songs were written in total and equal collaboration with each writer doing half the job. As a rule, most of the number was the solo work of John or Paul, the one thinking up the idea in the first place and creating most of the music as well as the words, whilst the other added useful trimmings towards the end of the whole operation. Very occasionally, the two lads really did sit down together and work out a new piece of material.[5]

George Martin has also said about the same thing:

> ***Rolling Stone:*** *It's sad that the end of their touring meant the end of their collaborative songwriting.* **Martin:** Well, they never really wrote songs together . . . John and Paul never sat down and

---

Loves You," "This Boy," and "The Word." See Compton, "Lennon-McCartney Song Database."

[4] My emphasis. Lennon, Rolling Stone Interview, Dec. 1970, BBC, part 2, cf. Wenner, *Lennon Remembers*, 26.

[5] Barrow, "Lennon and McCartney Songbook," 17. See also Barrow, "The Songs John Wrote," 17: "John confessed quite readily in private that he and Paul did all their best work alone. He could count on a single handful of fingers those few major songwriting successes which had been true Lennon-McCartney collaborations from start to finish." Barrow, "Lennon and McCartney Songbook," 21: "Of all these [all Lennon-McCartney songs], only a couple of dozen were written by both composers in true collaboration."

said, 'Let's write a song.' John would write the germ of something and say, 'I'm having trouble with the middle eight, what do you think?' Paul would say, 'Try this.' But it was fairly soon after we started recording that they started really going their own ways in songwriting, and just helping out occasionally with the odd lyric.[6]

Thus the idea that John and Paul were equal collaborators on all their songs (or even on a majority of their songs) can be definitively rejected. Sometimes they wrote songs entirely separately; sometimes one was the main writer for a song, and the other provided "finishing" collaboration; sometimes they simply polished each other's songs in a minor way. But except for the thirteen or so songs written with nearly equal collaboration, either Paul or John dominated on any specific song, or wrote the song separately.

Those who accept this fundamental misapprehension of Lennon-McCartney creativity — which I call the "magical synergy" theory of Beatles creativity — will misunderstand both the Beatles and the Beatles after the breakup. Paul and John often wrote separately on many widely admired and popular Beatles songs, with no collaboration at all, and so this "magical synergy" (on an all-or-nothing level) was never present. Instead of Lennon or McCartney dependent on collaboration, then, actually we had two superior writers, generally writing alone, and sometimes helping to put finishing touches on each other's songs. We might define the process of composition of many of the Beatle songs as writing (almost always alone; the music and the beginnings of lyrics are usually done here); then editing/finishing (often on lyrics, though there were musical contributions as

---

[6] In Hodenfield, "George Martin Recalls" (1976), 87. Cf. "George Martin on the Beatle Days," 14.

well).[7] Thus on many songs, there was no collaboration at all on the music of the song; there was only minor collaborative work on lyrics.

We should not underestimate either side of the song's creation: writing (alone), and editing; though the writing is obviously most important, the editing was also there. Thus John could say, "We both had our fingers in each other's pies."[8] In other words, there was separate ownership of songs, but the other Beatle served a final editing function — no more mysterious than an editor working through a manuscript with a novelist before publication. McCartney can say, "For ten years together he [John] took my songs apart, he was paranoiac about my songs. We had great screaming sessions about them."[9] The songs are Paul's; but he and John would fight about the editing/finishing process (which, in the case of Paul's songs, probably centered primarily on lyrics).

The Other Pole: "We Never Wrote Together"

A second level of misapprehension concerning the "Lennon-McCartney" attribution is to overemphasize how much John and Paul wrote alone. When the Beatles began to break up, John said that he was so tired of the "Lennon-McCartney" label and the Beatle image (and the misapprehension that he and Paul had written all their songs in "full" collaboration) that he claimed that he and Paul had written just about all their songs separately.

He agreed that there was "full" collaboration in the early Beatles period: "We wrote a lot of stuff together, one-on-one, eyeball to eyeball . . . In those days we really used to absolutely write like that-both playing into each other's noses. We spent hours and hours and hours."[10] But by the

---

[7] Cf. McCartney, in Aldridge, "Beatles Not All That Turned On" (1967). The song starts out as an individual writing the song, then "playing it to the others." Then there is the editing stage, "letting them think of bits"; then recording.

[8] Wenner, *Lennon Remembers*, 83. Cf. ibid., p. 115, where John describes how he and Paul would help each other when they got "stuck."

[9] In Davies, *The Beatles*, 371.

[10] Sheff, *The Playboy Interviews*, 149-50.

time of the White Album, he stated in May 1970, he and Paul were mostly going their own way:

> **Rolling Stone:** When did the Beatles break up? **Lennon:**
> The Beatles' white album. Listen — all you experts listen,
> none of you can hear. Every track is an individual track —
> there isn't any Beatle music on it . . . it was John and the
> band, Paul and the band, George and the band, like that.[11]

However, John later admitted that he had previously overemphasized separate authorship of songs because he was tired of the idea of Lennon-McCartney co-authorship. However, he says, the truth was that he and Paul wrote "a *lot* of stuff together, one-on-one."[12]

McCartney also correctly counters this second misapprehension:

> John and I gradually started to write stuff together. Which
> didn't mean that we wrote everything together. We'd kind
> of write 80% together and the other 20% for me were
> things like 'Yesterday' and for John things like 'Strawberry
> Fields' that he'd write mainly on his own.[13]

In other words, Paul was saying that 80% of the Beatle songs were written with "full" or "finishing"/"supportive" collaboration (with "finishing" collaboration including, substantial help in finishing songs, or lyric and musical edits). Only 20% of the songs were written entirely apart. Paul, in individual discussions of songs, agreed that in the "supportive" collaborations one writer dominated, often writing the music and the beginnings of the lyric before bringing it to the other writer. However, in discussing individual songs in interviews since the breakup, he has often served as a

---

[11] In Wenner, "One Guy Standing There," 6.

[12] Sheff, *The Playboy Interviews,* 149-50. See Introduction, above.

[13] Gambaccini, *Paul McCartney In His Own Words,* 17. Another statement by Paul is similar: "There's probably only about, say, twenty [Lennon-McCartney songs] that are really our own. On the rest there's quite a lot of collaboration. I suppose you do get a little niggled, you wish people knew that was mine. But hell, how much credit do you want in a lifetime?" (Quoted in Gambaccini, "A Conversation," 45.)

corrective to John's post-breakup emphasis on "full" individual authorship of many specific songs. Even if one writer dominated on a specific song, Paul affirmed, he often remembered some collaboration, helping to finish a song, an important addition or lyrics or music. I believe he has been fairly even-handed in these interview attributions. Sometimes he stated that he contributed to a song that was mainly John's, but at other times he has emphasized the importance of John's contributions to songs that were mainly his own.

I believe John's generalization on songwriting in the White Album, while not precisely accurate, reflects a general truth. "Full" collaboration between the Beatles was infrequent on that record, and even "finishing" collaboration was less common than in previous albums.

And, as can be seen from the catalogue, John is correct in stating that most of the "full" collaboration (writing songs together from the ground up) happened in the early Beatles period. Of the twelve songs with significant collaboration listed above, all were written before 1966, and nine of the twelve were written in 1963. Two were written in 1964, and one in 1965. Full collaboration became more and more infrequent as the Beatles continued their career, and even "supportive" collaboration gradually decreased.

Thus, after we reject the two main misapprehensions about the Lennon-McCartney authorship — (1) that they were always "full" collaborators, with no individual authorship or even domination of songs and (2) that after the early Beatles albums, Paul and John wrote all or the great majority of their songs separately — we can arrive at what I believe is the correct view: a minority of the "Lennon-McCartney" songs (say, about twelve of them) were written in "full" or "nearly full" collaboration. Another minority of the "Lennon-McCartney" songs (say about 20 percent of them) were written wholly apart. The great majority of the "Lennon-McCartney" songs were written with supportive or finishing collaboration. One writer dominated, often writing the substantial framework of the song, and the other writer helped finish it, often making limited edits.

Thus, many of the Beatles' great songs are the result of independence, rather than "magical synergy." And the songs that would logically represent such magical synergy, their full-bore collaborations, are found mostly in the Beatles' early albums and singles.

The Beatles: Performance and Songwriting

Another popular misconception about the Beatles is that they were great because they had great chemistry as a performing and recording band. While the Beatles *were* great musicians, and *did* have great live chemistry, this was not their essential greatness. The Beatles were never solo virtuosos as, for example, Jimmy Hendrix or Eric Clapton were. Their performances would never have been as electric without their songwriting, their original material. Their career would have been entirely different if they had been a cover band only. Some might reasonably argue that their greatness was a combination of their original material and their performances. However, if their performances had dominated, it's probable that they wouldn't have stopped live performance beginning in the *Revolver-Sgt. Pepper* era. Thus emphasis on the Beatles as instrumentalists and vocalists, and on the recording of their songs, does not get at the heart of their creativity. Their performances interpreted and supported the remarkable songwriting. (On the other hand, you can't make an absolute demarcation of songwriting from performance and recording in the studio. Often songs were finished in the studio. Often musical counter-melodies were thought of and added in the studio. Avant-garde music, an important part of the Beatles' music from *Revolver* on, was often developed in the studio. In classical music, scoring a piece is part of composition, though the final part that chiefly "interprets" music that has already been composed.) The Beatles' recording and their performances as musicians were obviously important, but songwriting was at the heart of their creativity and artistic accomplishment.[14]

---

[14] See Introduction.

Some critics regard the Beatles as essentially performers, and essentially a performance rock group. Such a view is a fundamental misunderstanding of Paul, John and George as songwriters. In the beginning of their career, George Martin wanted them to sing "How Do You Do It," a song written by someone else, for their first single; instead they convinced him to let them sing one of their own songs. The number of songs that John and Paul wrote for other groups in their early days of success shows how seriously they took their songwriting identity. They were fundamentally different from performers like Elvis, who interpreted the songs other people wrote, and often sang songs selected by his handlers.

Lyrics and Music

Clearing aside popular myths of the Beatles, and realistically understanding how the songs of the Beatles were written, allows us to look at the individual songwriting gifts and tendencies of McCartney and Lennon. While it is valid to look at the union of music and lyric in song, it is also necessary to judge them separately. This will allow us to look at complex triumphs and failures in the various Beatle songs — there are mediocre, hackneyed words in some early Beatle songs and original, enthralling music. Later, there were some Beatles songs with brilliant, original lyrics and repetitive, limited melodies. Understanding how each Beatle song was written allows us to assess the individual accomplishments of McCartney and Lennon, in music or in word.

Some critics and fans will focus on lyrics; others on music. But taking a song apart and understanding who wrote which parts of it is necessary to judge the accomplishments of the two chief Beatle songwriters.

Friends, Mothers and Roadies: "Communal" Songwriting in the Beatles Circle

Viewing lyrics and music separately gives insight into one of the most striking aspects of the Beatles' songwriting: its communal nature. Not only did the Beatles collaborate on each others' songs, but many Beatles insiders, from Mal Evans to Derek Taylor to Donovan, added to them. Mal

Evans contributed to "Sgt. Pepper's"; Donovan to "Yellow Submarine" and "Julia." Jan Vaughan, the wife of Paul's boyhood friend Ivan, came up with the French words to "Michelle" at Paul's request. Derek Taylor added phrases to Harrison and Lennon songs, such as "Savoy Truffle" and "Happiness is a Warm Gun." George Harrison's mother added the classic line, "What they need's a damn good whacking" to "Piggies."

Some might interpret this as one of the most remarkable and controversial insights that this book offers. In one sense, I think this phenomenon is important, and has been under-emphasized. This inner circle deserves some credit for what they contributed to the Beatle legacy. (Hiding the contributions of this inner circle is one more false assumption that the straitjacket label "Lennon-McCartney" has promoted.)

Nevertheless, in another way, this phenomenon gives valuable insight into Paul and John as songwriters, how they wrote songs. First of all, this kind of communal collaboration was rarely a musical contribution. It took place after the music and the beginnings of the lyric were in place. John or Paul would need to write another verse, or fill in a line, in the lyrics. So they'd sit down with whoever was available and brainstorm.

They would never do this with the music. Paul would never sit down with Mal Evans and work out the melody to, for instance, "Eleanor Rigby." On the other hand, one can imagine Paul sitting down with Evans or other friends and filling in the lyrics to a missing verse on the song. Or he could take a funny phrase from his friend Jimmy Scott and use it as the title for a song, as in "Ob-la-di, Ob-la-da."

Thus, finalizing lyrics with Beatle insiders was a verbal contribution, rarely (to the best of my knowledge) a musical collaboration. Finishing up lyrics, adding a phrase or two to a song, especially after the main lyrics were in place, was very supportive collaboration.

For example, Paul collaborated with Jan Vaughan to produce the French lines to "Michelle." But she has never written other songs. She was not a musician. The same point can be made about Mal Evans and Derek Taylor. Though they deserve credit for their contributions to lyrics in a few songs, they did not help with the music of the Beatles.

Another example of this is "Eleanor Rigby," widely accepted (correctly) as mainly a Paul song. Nevertheless, according to John, Paul brought the song to the studio with the lyrics unfinished, and turned to the people who just happened to be there to help him complete them. "We were sitting around with Mal Evans and Neil Aspinall, so [Paul] said to us, 'Hey, you guys, finish up the lyrics.'" John says that he, offended, then took Paul aside and the two of them put the actual finishing touches to the song's words. However, George Martin disagrees: "Neil and Mal and I were coming up with suggestions" for the missing lyrics, he said. It is possible that Ringo, George Martin, Neil Aspinall, Mal Evans, and Pete Shotton contributed to the lyrics of the song. This is a stark contrast to the control Paul exercised in the smallest details of the *music* to his songs.

And it is certain that the music in "Eleanor Rigby" is completely by Paul. He was also responsible for the basic story of the song and the first verse. He collaborated with John and possibly other Beatles and Beatle insiders on the rest of the lyrics.

The Beatles' Progress: Collaboration and Artistic Development

If we accept that the great majority of the Beatle songs were written or substantially started by John or Paul separately, we suddenly have a view of the Beatles' creativity that is radically different from generally accepted perceptions. We can at least substantially reject the over-simplified "magical synergy" theory of their songwriting creativity, replacing it with a perspective based on "individual creativity, sometimes followed by finishing collaboration."

While the Lennon-McCartney collaboration was important, the individual songwriting aesthetics of Paul and John in the Beatles is more important. First, the songs that were full collaborations were characteristic of the early Beatle period. Even from 1963 to 1966, most of the songs were mainly by Paul or John. Paul once said that the "Lennon-McCartney" label was created to soften the competition between the two writers as they competed for the A-side of singles.[15] But competition would have tended to isolate the two writers. Strong collaboration and strong competition are mutually exclusive. Interestingly, Martin ascribes the tension between Lennon and McCartney to the fact that they composed separately. "They did love each other very much ... But the tension was there mostly because they never really collaborated. They were never Rodgers and Hart. They were always songwriters who helped each other out with little bits and pieces."[16]

And as the Beatles progressed, full collaboration decreased. Proponents of the magical synergy theory would have to argue that the songs should have decreased in quality as Paul and John wrote more and more separately, with only occasional supportive collaboration. However, critical consensus polls put *Sgt. Pepper*, *Revolver*, the White Album, *Abbey Road* and *Rubber Soul* at the peak of the Beatles' accomplishment. For example, in a Rolling Stone top 500 albums poll in 2003, *Sgt. Pepper* was ranked number 1, *Revolver* was 3, *Rubber Soul* was 5, the White Album was 10, and *Abbey Road* was 14. Much further down the list, at 39, was an early album, *Please Please Me*.

A *Rolling Stone* readers poll in 2002 is fairly similar: *Revolver* was 1, *Sgt. Pepper* was 3, the White Album was 5, *Abbey Road* was 6, and *Rubber Soul* was 23.[17]

Such polls have no authority, but they do provide a temporary snapshot of collective critical taste. Judging by this rough consensus, the early

---

[15] As quoted in Barrow, "Why Paul and John started writing songs," 21.

[16] As quoted in Coleman, *Lennon*, 269.

[17] The Beatles had a startling four of the top six places, a remarkable witness to the Beatles' enormous impact. Just so we are not dependent on *Rolling Stone* alone, we could mention a few other polls. A 1974 poll from *NME* (*New Musical Express*) had *Sgt. Pepper's* at 1, *Revolver* at 4, *Abbey Road* at 8, and *Rubber Soul* at 15. A 1987 poll from *OOR* magazine, in Netherlands, had the *White Album* at 5, *Revolver* at 10, *Sgt. Pepper's* at 13, *Rubber Soul* at 14, and *Abbey Road* at 116. Two early albums were far down in the poll: *A Hard Day's Night* at 200, and *Please Please Me* at 265. In a 2006 *Q* magazine readers poll, we have the following results: *Revolver* at 4, *Abbey Road* at 14, the *White Album* at 17, *Sgt. Pepper's* at 19, and *Rubber Soul* at 29. All critical and readers polls that I have seen support my main point here.

Beatles albums, when there was more full collaboration, cannot measure up to the later Beatles albums, when full collaboration had dwindled, and individual songwriting, often with full individual authorship of songs, had largely replaced it. The conclusion is inescapable: As Paul and John gained in creative maturity, they wrote more and more apart.

Rock and Ballad, Music and Lyric: McCartney and Lennon as Individual Songwriters

When we have achieved informed, balanced views of which songs were fully or mainly written by either Paul or John, we can reach clearer conclusions concerning their individual creativity, their individual styles and aesthetic interests. As was discussed in the introduction, after the Beatles breakup, the feud between Paul and John made the Beatles and their songwriting a partisan phenomenon. In interviews, John and Paul took jabs at each other, and John in particular often attacked Paul's songs. He characterized himself as writing music that was part of the counter-culture, while Paul was writing music that appealed to the masses, the bourgeoisie. John wrote hard-edged rock, while Paul wrote sentimental ballads. John's songs were serious, while Paul's were light. John referred to some songs by Paul as "granny music," appealing to a former generation. John's songs often expressed pessimism in a serious way, while Paul's were shallowly optimistic. For example, John, in 1980, said that Paul "provided a lightness . . . where I would always go for the sadness and the 9th and the discords."[18]

John sometimes made these points, then added tempering statements later. But often his supporters simply took the main points and turned them into dogma. So these critiques require careful examination, and we will examine them one by one.

There is a widespread assumption that John wrote hard-edged rock, while Paul wrote ballads. For example, *Rolling Stone* writes that John was the Beatles' "most committed rock & roller."[19] This is certainly a half-

---

[18] Lost Lennon Tapes, Sept. 16, 1991, cf. Sheff, *The Playboy Interviews*, 148.
[19] "John Lennon: Biography."

truth. John did write some hard-edged rock songs, while Paul wrote a number of ballads. But they both also wrote an enormous range of many kinds of music.

To take Paul first. He wrote ballads such as "Yesterday," "She's Leaving Home" and "The Long and Winding Road," but he also wrote many driving, rave-up rock songs. Aside from the scorching "Helter Skelter," maybe the apotheosis of Paul's hard rock writing, he (mainly) wrote and sang, "I Saw Her Standing There," "Hold Me Tight," "Can't Buy Me Love," "She's a Woman," "I'm Down," "Back in the U.S.S.R," "Oh! Darling" and "Why Don't We Do It In the Road." He took the lead vocals on Little Richard screamers such as "Long Tall Sally," and "Kansas City/Hey Hey Hey," then wrote songs like "I'm Down" in this same style. On a less frantic level, but still magnificent, original rock songs, are such offerings as Paul's "Things We Said Today," "You Won't See Me," "Lady Madonna," "What You're Doing," "Got To Get You Into My Life," "Hello Goodbye" and "Lovely Rita." "Hey Jude" starts as a rock ballad, but ends up in an improvisatory rock frenzy.

In addition, Paul wrote gentler songs somewhere between ballads and rock songs, such as "I'll Follow the Sun." In fact, from the days of the early Beatles, he did not think that the group should be confined to writing and performing only rock; he wanted the Beatles to reflect the breadth of popular music. He felt that the group would stand apart from lesser groups because of this. But he has always loved to play and sing full-bore rock.

His use of strings in his ballads was often remarkably restrained, classical in flavor (as in "She's Leaving Home," "Yesterday," and "Eleanor Rigby"). George Martin deserves credit for influencing this element of Paul's style. It finally fell to Phil Spector, brought in by Lennon, ironically enough, to provide a really over-the-top orchestration for a McCartney song, on "Long and Winding Road" with its strings, angel choirs and harps.

In the same way, while John wrote great rockers such as "Everybody's Got Something to Hide Except for Me and My Money," and "She's So Heavy," and sang over-the-top covers such as "Twist and Shout," "Dizzy

Miss Lizzie," and "Money," he also wrote ballads remarkable for their tenderness and melodic power, such as "If I Fell," "Good Night," "Across the Universe," "Because," and "Julia." (Martin provided a "Hollywood" orchestral accompaniment for "Good Night" at John's request.)

The generalization that John's songs often expressed pessimism, while Paul's were optimistic, is again a half-truth, as some of Paul's songs certainly were optimistic. However, many of Paul's songs do not express simplistic optimism, and many of his most characteristic songs are tragic. He wrote a number of songs about relationships failing, such as "You Won't See Me" or "For No One." His most famous ballad, "Yesterday," is completely tragic. Some of his songs are sophisticated mixtures of light and shadow — examples are "Things We Said Today," "Let It Be," "Long and Winding Road," "Blackbird," and "Hey Jude." Often he wrote songs as therapy, to counter moods of darkness and hopelessness, as in "Let It Be" ("When I find myself in times of trouble") or "Long and Winding Road."

One of the important recurring themes in his songs is loneliness, as in "Eleanor Rigby." This important side of McCartney's artistic vision, capturing a haunting sense of emotional separation and isolation, which continued into his solo period, is not light optimism.

When John stated that he was part of the counter-culture, while Paul was writing light pop music for the mainstream, it almost amounted to an excommunication. While there is an element of this idea that is fairly subjective, and so hard to "prove" or "disprove," one can point to a number of factual details that do not fit this broad picture. For example, Paul was very much part of the late sixties counter culture, as psychedelic elements in his songs show. With John, he was influenced by Dylan to write lyrics that departed from Tin Pan Alley themes and were often enigmatic (as in "Paperback Writer," "Baby You Can Drive My Car" or "Fool on the Hill"). More importantly, for our purposes, he was very much into experimental music that was not top-forty teeny-bopper, or Mantovani Strings, fodder. Living in London, frequenting the Indica bookstore, he became interested in the experimental music of people like Stockhausen and Cage. He was the first of the Beatles to use backward tape loops that appeared on such songs as "Tomorrow Never Knows." He was instrumental in working out the avant-garde orchestral effects in "Day in the Life."

Sgt. Pepper, often the most highly regarded Beatle album (and rock album) in critical polls, is one of the central manifestos of the counter-culture, and McCartney was the dominant songwriter for this album. (He thought of the title song conceit for the album, an artificial group, and was the dominant writer for "Sgt. Pepper's," "With a Little Help," "Getting Better," "Fixing a Hole," "She's Leaving Home," "When I'm 64," "Lovely Rita," and "Sgt. Pepper's reprise." John was the dominant writer for "Lucy in the Sky with Diamonds," "Being for the Benefit of Mr. Kite," "Good Morning Good Morning," and "A Day in the Life." (However, songs that leaned toward collaborations were "With a Little Help," "Lucy in the Sky" and "A Day in the Life.")

Lennon complained of the *number* of songs McCartney was writing during the *St. Pepper, Magical Mystery Tour* era.[20] Lennon regarded Paul as the dominant writer for those albums, and saw himself as regaining his creativity during the White Album period.

When John accused Paul of writing "granny music," this is a critique that has some basis in fact. John scathingly mocked Paul's songs that were based on a former era, the music hall song, such as "Honey Pie," "Maxwell's Silver Hammer," "Your Mother Should Know," and "When I'm 64." However, as has been discussed above, Paul always consciously sought a breadth of style in the Beatles, to set them apart from lesser, one-dimensional groups. He liked, and likes, many types of music. When you talk about the challenge of creating a rock album that is listenable, that does not repeat the same song over and over, this is an intelligent point of view. Second, Paul has explained that he disagrees with the concept of generation gaps, and in his Beatle songs he sometimes consciously reached out to older people. He was strongly influenced, not just by Elvis and

---

[20] Wenner, *Lennon Remembers*, 26; Sheff, *Playboy Interviews*, 195. This shows both individual ownership of songs, behind the scenes, and Paul's prolific songwriting at the time.

Buddy Holly, Dylan and Brian Wilson, but by the jazz and pop standards of his parents' generation.

Purely from a personal, aesthetic point of view, you may not like the McCartney ballads or music hall songs; but he has a thoughtful rationale for them.

While I have responded to John's critique of Paul's music, and to overly schematic views based on them, it is important to also look at the impressive variety in the songs mainly written by John. His songs could range in tone from high seriousness to comic songs of lunatic whimsy and fantasy, such as "Hey Bulldog" or "Mean Mr. Mustard." He too could reach out to another generation (in "Julia" and "Goodnight"). "Happiness Is a Warm Gun" offers a brilliant historical overview of early rock styles. John's mother taught him old standards, much as Paul had learned standards from his father.[21] John could write exuberant rock, experimental oddities, and tender, quiet songs. In his final interview, he said, "That was the thing about the Beatles — they never stuck to one style. . . . We loved *all* music. . . . if you look down those Beatle tracks, I'm right there with all the sentimental [things,] — just the same as Paul or anyone else. I love that music just as much."[22]

Beyond Collaboration: Two Styles

Having removed the most obvious fallacies about the McCartney-Lennon songwriting, then, we may attempt an evaluation of their individual styles. McCartney writes strong unpredictable melodies; his harmonies are inventive (by the standards of twentieth-century popular music); he developed, during the *Revolver* and *Sgt. Pepper* albums, a technique of synthetically creative pastiche that allowed him to range over the whole gamut of popular music in this century. He has mastered both rhythmic rock, softer ballads, folk, and the music hall comic song. A perfectionist as an arranger/producer, he is continually exploring new textures of instrumentation while recording his music. His songs can be lighthearted, comic,

---

[21] Baird, *John Lennon, My Brother*, 38; Sheff, *The Playboy Interviews*, 175.
[22] Sholin and Kaye, "John Lennon's last interview."

even grotesque, but his artistic vision also contains a persistent thread of tragedy, loss, loneliness and darkness that balances his more upbeat songs (or provides depth to his otherwise positive-leaning songs). His lyrics are often unremarkable, seeming afterthoughts, but expressing his most basic concerns — loneliness and loss in human existence, the need for love, the warmth of family, comic celebration, comic sadness. He is more focused on music, harmonies and melody than on lyrics, as is obvious from many of his comments on writing his songs in the Beatles era.

Lennon, on the other hand, came to put his primary focus on lyrics. His style is (sometimes) defined by extended word play, often comic — "Strawberry Fields," "I Am the Walrus," "Glass Onion," "Come Together." Some of his characteristic songs can be dreamy in tone — "Strawberry Fields," "I'm Only Sleeping," "Across the Universe," "Imagine." Other Lennon songs can be political and topical, as in "Revolution." Though his music is generally first-rate, his melodies can be minimalist, serving as background for the lyrics, as in such songs as "Come Together," "I Am the Walrus," and "Tomorrow Never Knows." His lyrics, even in his early Beatle days, could be intensely autobiographical and personal — "Help," "Nowhere Man," "In My Life," "Norwegian Wood." On the other hand, they could be fantastic and fictional in the tradition of Lewis Carroll.

Paul was always more interested in music, and Lennon ended up more interested in lyrics (partly as a result of Bob Dylan's influence). They certainly crossed over and performed superbly outside of the field of their particular interest at times — Lennon sometimes wrote great, inspired music, and Paul occasionally wrote superior lyrics that have had a powerful impact on his audience over the years. But their main focus was always clear.

These two focuses come though clearly in their interviews: for instance, Paul tended to write music first, then add the lyrics (as in the case of "Yesterday"); when he wrote words first, he called it working "upside down."[23] Lennon described Paul as a lazy lyricist: "I always had an easier

---

[23] Goodman, "Paul and Linda McCartney," 104.

time with lyrics, although Paul is quite a capable lyricist who doesn't think he's a capable lyricist, therefore he doesn't go for it. Rather than face the problem he would avoid it."[24] Thus we have Paul writing music naturally, leaving the lyrics aside till later. Lennon's creative inclinations were exactly opposite. He said: "Paul has a special gift when it comes to making up tunes. I find myself using tunes which already exist and fitting my words to them . . . With me I have a theme which gets me started on the poetry side of the thing. Then I have to put the tune to it, but that's the part of the job I enjoy least. Words come easier."[25] Thus Lennon is avoiding the music. "It's the playing around with words I enjoy most," he said.[26] "I can't leave the lyrics alone; I have to make them make sense apart from the song," he explained in 1980.[27] He almost seems to yearn for words without music: "See, the ones I like are the ones that stand as words without melody, that don't have to have any melody. It's a poem, you know, you could read 'em."[28] George Martin, though he knew both Paul and John could write both good music and lyrics, was aware of their natural creative leanings: "Paul's melodies and his harmonic structures appealed to me more than John's because John's melodies and his music were tailor-made to fit his words rather than the other way around. The lyrics would lead and develop John's songs."[29]

Strangely enough, John and Paul did not collaborate much in what would have been a natural way: Lennon writing words, Paul writing music. Only in "In My Life" — if McCartney's account of how the song was written is correct — do we have a case of (mostly or all) Lennon lyrics combined with pure McCartney music. But the two writers' artistic visions probably became much too divergent early for this kind of thing to happen

---

[24] Lost Lennon Tapes, Sept. 16, 1991, cf. Sheff, *The Playboy Interviews*, 150.

[25] Quoted in Barrow, "Songs John Wrote," 15.

[26] Ibid., 14.

[27] Lost Lennon Tapes, Sept. 16, 1991, cf. Sheff, *Playboy Interviews*, 151.

[28] Lennon, Rolling Stone Interview, Dec. 1970, BBC, part 4, cf. Wenner, *Lennon Remembers*, 100.

[29] As quoted in Coleman, *Lennon*, 278.

regularly. However, they certainly influenced each other in their particular areas of expertise. John has said: "In the early days I wrote less material than Paul because he was more competent on guitar than I. He taught me quite a lot of guitar really."[30] Paul once (according to Lennon) "encouraged Lennon to introduce a larger variety of notes and chords into his compositions."[31] On the other hand, George Martin once said of McCartney that, "All the time he's trying to do better, especially trying to equal John's talent for words."[32] Lennon's style of free-associative word-play has influenced McCartney's lyric style to this day.

Thus it would be natural for Lennon to edit McCartney's words, or add lines when his lyrics were incomplete. And it would be equally natural for Lennon to write a poem, leave it lying around, and have McCartney pick it up and write music for it. "I can't leave lyrics alone," said John. His contributions to the lyrics of McCartney songs have been abundantly documented. One wonders how much McCartney contributed to the music of John's songs — suggesting a chord here, a melodic pattern there. There are hints of this in the interviews. On selected John songs, Paul remembered some collaboration (e.g., "Do You Want to Know a Secret," "A Hard Day's Night," "Help," "In My Life," "Glass Onion"[33]), and his natural contribution in a collaborative situation would be musical. He stated

---

[30] Aldridge, *The Beatles Illustrated Lyrics*, 235.

[31] In Okun, *Compleat Beatles* I, 114. Cf. Barrow, "Songs John Wrote," 17: "He [John] was anxious to keep up with Paul, which was not easy because the McCartney output was usually greater than his. For every new song Lennon finished, McCartney tended to complete a couple, even if one was ditched and never made it into a recording session."

[32] Davies, *The Beatles*, 280.

[33] We can consider cases where, in one interview, John claims a song as entirely his, while in other interviews he mentions Paul's involvement — e.g., "Norwegian Wood," "Day Tripper," "In My Life." This may be largely due to poor memory, but it may also reflect difference in artistic vision; to John, perhaps, the words were the song, and the music was simply not as important.

that sometimes John would be "stuck for a melody; I'd produce a melody for him."[34]

Paul also became the dominant music arranger of the Beatles. Those who have worked closely with the group have pointed this out; for example, one of the early Beatles engineers, Norman Smith said:

> [in the early recording sessions, it was] nearly always Paul who was the MD, the musical director, as early as this. Obviously John would have quite a lot to say, but overall it was always Paul who was the guv'nor. Which is fair, because he was the natural musician, and even at this stage, the natural producer ... With *Rubber Soul*, the clash between John and Paul was becoming obvious ...
>
> George was having to put up with an awful lot from Paul ... Paul was absolutely finicky ... Mind you, there is no doubt at all that Paul was the main musical force. He was also that in terms of production as well. A lot of the time George Martin didn't really have to do the things he did because Paul McCartney was around and could have done them equally well.[35]

Paul's role as informal music producer caused tension within the Beatles, yet the group was also dependent on him. He relates an anecdote of George and Ringo telling him to lay off when he was dominating a recording session; then, when he did lay off, and a session was flagging, telling him, "Come on ... Produce!"[36] As we have seen, in the case of "Across the Universe," Lennon went so far as to accuse McCartney of sabotaging

---

[34] deCurtis, "Beatlemania strikes again," 36. Paul said that he often contributed to middle eights for songs John had started — "those middle eights, John never had his middle eights." Miles, *Many Years From Now*, 270-71. See chapter two, at "Love Me Do" for middle eights.

[35] In Salewicz, *McCartney: the Definitive Biography*, 147; 177-78.

[36] Quoted in Chris Salewicz, "Tug of War," 62.

his songs, by not working on them enough.[37] George Martin responded that Paul's songs got more finishing touches because "Paul was more interested. John's irritation was a little unfair. John's songs got a great deal of attention . . . They worked out the way I wanted them . . . Paul would sit down and ask what I planned to do with his songs, every note virtually . . . Lots of the arrangements to his songs were very much his ideas which I would have to implement. John would be more vague in what he wanted."[38] McCartney recently responded to his reputation as domineering: "I'm pretty ruthless, ambitious, all that stuff . . . If we've gotta make a record, I'll actually sit down and write songs. This could be interpreted as being overpowering and forceful . . . It just seemed to me when we had a session booked it was a cool idea to turn up."[39] McCartney's productivity caused John's resentment. In addition, Paul's driven, detail-oriented, production understandably annoyed his band-mates; on the other hand, this kind of attention to detail arguably was essential for the high achievement of the Beatle albums.

Beatles biographer Philip Norman has said, "John Lennon was the Beatles."[40] Many rock critics explicitly or implicitly agree. This view is largely based on Lennon's brilliant lyrics, his politics and his persona, as well as his music. However, if you take the music of the Beatles seriously, and see it as a central aesthetic accomplishment of the group, then you cannot hold Norman's reductionist view, even in modified form. You can certainly see both Lennon and McCartney as central to the Beatles' achievement (and marvel that two such gifted songwriters ended up in the

---

[37] Sheff, *Playboy Interviews*, 201; cf. Wenner, *Lennon Remembers*, 22-26.

[38] Coleman, *Lennon*, 273, 275.

[39] Salewicz, "Tug of War," 60.

[40] King, "'Shout!': An Interview with Author Philip Norman"; Doggett, *You Never Give Me Your Money*, 275. I do not disagree with praise for Lennon's songwriting; but the idea that one person in the Lennon-McCartney duo had all the brilliance does not adequately reflect the complexity of the Beatles' story and music. This is a kind of aesthetic dualism, an unnecessary binary formulation in which the two main Beatle songwriters are seen as a pair in which one has to be all great and the other the complete opposite, and could not both be authentically extraordinary.

same group), but serious critics will reject the "Lennon was a genius and McCartney was nothing" position. McCartney was arguably the central musician in the Beatles (considering the characteristic interests of Paul and John) and music was a central accomplishment of the group.

Lennon and McCartney: Singles and Albums

If we examine the songwriting balance of Lennon and McCartney on specific records, the results show a constant ebb and flow between the two songwriters. To start with the singles, the first Beatles single ("Love Me Do / P.S. I Love You") was dominated by Paul, both sides; the second single ("Please Please Me / Ask Me Why") was dominated by John, both sides. So some singles were dominated by one writer. On the other hand, many singles were split—"Strawberry Fields Forever / Penny Lane" had a John song on side A, a Paul song on side B; "Hello Goodbye / I Am the Walrus" had Paul on side A, John on Side B. The A Side of a Beatles single was, of course, especially sought after; sometimes, when John had an A side, it was understood that Paul would have the next A side. For instance, after John's "Day Tripper" in December 1965, the next single was Paul's "Paperback Writer" in May 1966.

On albums, John, in interviews, said that he dominated in song-production during the early albums, but lay "fallow" in the *Sgt. Pepper / Magical Mystery Tour* era.[41] Then he was productive again in the White Album. My research has basically supported those perspectives. However, we should also factor in great songs by McCartney during the early albums (such as "I Saw Her Standing There," "All My Loving" and "Things We Said Today"), and great songs by Lennon when he was supposedly lying fallow. John's magisterial "Strawberry Fields Forever" initiated the *Sgt. Pepper* era, and "Lucy in the Sky with Diamonds" and "A Day in the Life" were key songs on the album.

In addition, one must remember that while one writer, Paul or John, might dominate or begin a song, the other might make a significant contri-

---

[41] Sheff, *The Playboy Interviews*, 197.

bution to it. So Paul wrote the middle section to John's "A Day in the Life" and worked on the avant-garde sections in it. On the same album, John helped with the lyrics of Paul's "She's Leaving Home" and "With a Little Help From My Friends." When there was well-documented collaboration on a song, we should take that into consideration. Sometimes we have the ebb and flow between Paul and John *within* a song.

Songwriting and the Elusive Beatles Breakup

A careful examination of the authorship of the Lennon-McCartney songs gives us an essential foundation for understanding and evaluating the Beatles' music. This examination will also give us a view of the group's breakup that differs significantly from simplistic views of the event that are based on the clichéd interpretations of Lennon and McCartney creativity.

After the breakup of the Beatles, when the group and their music became a partisan phenomenon, rock critics tended to side with John. They viewed the Beatle songs as collaborative, with the best of the Beatles being written or influenced by John. As they had a tendency to focus on lyrics rather than music, John seemed to emerge as the genius of the group. Paul, without the collaborative link with John, was seen as lacking the key component of the Beatles' artistic intelligence and creativity.

Not surprisingly, the critical consensus of rock critics has been that John's solo albums have been artistic successes, while Paul's albums have been shallow. Jon Landau, in a *Rolling Stone* review of McCartney's *Ram* (1971) wrote:

> If it was Paul who used to polish up Lennon's bluntness and forced him to adapt a little style, it is by now apparent that Lennon held the reins in on McCartney's cutsie-pie, florid attempts at pure rock muzak . . . None of the Beatles is a truly self-sufficient artist . . . in this light, Paul has simply proven to be the most vulnerable . . . *McCartney* and *Ram* both prove that Paul benefitted immensely from collabora-

tion and that he seems to be dying on the vine as a result of his own self-imposed musical isolation.[42]

Thus the scenario is straightforward. The Beatles formally broke up; Lennon and McCartney stopped writing together; Lennon by himself created music of almost "monomaniacal intensity"; Paul quickly degenerated to "cutsie-pie . . . pure rock muzak." Paul was especially helpless without John, and was "dying on the vine" without him.[43]

However, the historical facts of McCartney and Lennon's songwriting do not support this scenario. Lennon had said earlier, in the pages of the *Rolling Stone*, that the breakup had not come in 1970, but years earlier, in 1968, when the White Album was being recorded. McCartney and Lennon had been writing many songs separately even in the early Beatles era. Certainly, some songs were written with thoroughgoing or "finishing" collaboration during that period. But Lennon and McCartney wrote more and more separately as they left those early albums and began producing their middle-Beatle era masterpieces.

If Landau's close-collaboration dependence theory had been valid, the incompleteness of McCartney's art should have been obvious in the McCartney songs from *Revolver* onward, especially in the White Album, and in the McCartney songs on following albums. The worst songs should have been found on *Abbey Road* and this album should have been one of the Beatles' worst.

The opposite, of course, is true, as we've mentioned earlier.[44] The White Album and *Abbey Road* have been highly regarded by the rock critical consensus.

---

[42] Landau, Review of *Ram*.

[43] The influential biographer Philip Norman is similar: After the breakup, Paul's songs "were always catchy, always pleasant, always empty of real content and lacking that extra effort and edge that used to come from John peering over his shoulder." *Shout*, 2003 ed., 486.

[44] See above, for a rough consensus of rock critics. In the two *Rolling Stone* polls I summarize, the White Album is ranked at 10 and 5; *Abbey Road* is 14 and 6.

Other details argue against Landau's scenario. First, many of the songs on Paul's first two solo albums (e.g., "Hot as Sun," "Teddy Boy," "Junk," "Back Seat of My Car") had been written much earlier, when he was a Beatle; when he was working in the physical presence of John. Some of them were even written in India.

Second, John attacked Paul in long interviews for the influential American rock magazine, *Rolling Stone*. The longest interview was conducted by the main editor of the magazine, Jann Wenner, and was published as a book. The weight of *Rolling Stone*'s influence was given to John and his side of the Lennon-McCartney conflict.

Third, rock critics have had a tendency to emphasize lyrics in their reviews. In Paul and John's early albums, Lennon's lyrics were forceful and compelling; Paul, however, was primarily a musician, and his lyrics were often secondary, sometimes deeply felt and creative, but sometimes following the Buddy Holly school of rock lyrics.

Fourth, Paul's instrumentation obviously changed after the technical Beatle breakup. The concise power of a four man rock group was replaced by more intricate textures of keyboard and acoustic guitar, often with background female vocals. The "surface" of the music certainly had changed.

Looking at the individual authorship of the Beatle songs will lead us to understand the solo Beatles better, to thoroughly re-evaluate the artistic achievement of the Beatles after the breakup. The technical dissolution of the Beatles in early 1970, after *Abbey Road*, is an extremely artificial line of demarcation, if we look at songwriting. The idea then, that there was a severe drop-off from the last Beatle albums to the first McCartney solo albums (as expressed by Jon Landau, among others) is a version of the popular "magical synergy" theory. But Paul and John had been writing increasingly separately for years as the Beatles produced their middle and late period masterpieces.

Hopefully, as we progress ever further from the partisanship of the Lennon-McCartney early breakup era, we will start to look at the accomplishments of John and Paul, as individual songwriters, with fresh eyes.

And this will certainly lead us to reassess the Beatles' solo albums and solo careers. There is a positive continuity between John (as individual writer) and Paul (as individual writer) before and after the breakup, rather than a sudden, complete drop-off in spring 1970.

McCartney and Lennon certainly influenced each other deeply. Lennon said, in 1969, "We [Paul and John] inspired each other so much in the early days. We wrote how we write now because of each other. Paul was there for five or ten years, and I wouldn't write like I write now if it weren't for Paul, and he wouldn't write like he does if it weren't for me."[45] Linda referred to Paul and John as mirroring each other. Paul said, "The thing about me and John is that we were different, but we weren't that different. I think Linda put her finger on it when she said me and John were like mirror images of each other. Even down to how we started writing together, facing each other, eyeball to eyeball, exactly like looking in the mirror."[46]

Despite this enormous mutual influence, John and Paul were individuals, and they developed in different ways. Their songs became increasingly idiosyncratic as the Beatles progressed from album to album. If we take Paul and John seriously, we will look at their individual contributions to the Beatle canon, rather than continue to accept a version of the flawed "magical synergy" theory, and a view of the breakup which is dependent on a conventional version of this theory. John, Paul, George and Ringo are all much more than their few years with the Beatles.

---

[45] Fallon, "Will the Real John Lennon."
[46] Wilde, "McCartney: My Life in the Shadow of the Beatles," 245.

BIBLIOGRAPHY

Adams, Sean. "Paul McCartney discusses songwriting and RAM with Mansun's Paul Draper." Drowned in Sound website, May 28, 2012. At http://drownedinsound.com/in_depth/4145012-paul-mccartney-discusses-songwriting-and-ram-with-mansuns-paul-draper (accessed Sept. 28, 2012).

Agueras, Juan and Javier Tarazona. "A Meeting with George Martin." At http://www.beatlesnews.com/georgemartin.htm (accessed March 14, 2008).

Aldridge, Alan, ed. *The Beatles Illustrated Lyrics.* NY: Delacorte Press, 1969. 156 pp.

———, ed. *The Beatles Illustrated Lyrics 2.* NY: Delacorte Press, 1971. 123 pp. plus index.

———, ed. *The Beatles Illustrated Lyrics.* Boston: Houghton Mifflin Books, 1991. Combines the 1969 and 1971 eds. 267 pp.

———. "Beatles Not All That Turned On." A Paul McCartney interview. Published in the *Washington Post,* 1969, reprinted in Eisen, *The Age of Rock,* 138-46.

Alterman, Loraine. "The Beatles: Four Smiling, Tired Guys Talk About Their Music." *Detroit Free Press,* August 19, 1966. Via *Rock's Backpages.*

Aspinall, Neil. "George's California Trip." *The Beatles Monthly Book* no. 51 (October 1967): 25-26, 31.

———. "Neil's Column." *The Beatles Monthly Book* no. 33 (April 1966): 6. On "What Goes On."

———. "Neil's Column." *The Beatles Monthly Book* no. 38 (Sept. 1966): 25. On "Tomorrow Never Knows" and "Yellow Submarine."

Asher, Peter. Introduction to performance of "Nobody I Know," 2015. Youtube video, at https://www.youtube.com/watch?v=aJo-11BBDps (accessed Dec. 17. 2016).

Babiuk, Andy. *Beatles Gear: All the Fab Four's Instruments from Stage to Studio.* 3rd Revised edition. San Francisco: Backbeat Books, 2009.

Bacon, Tony. "Paul McCartney - Meet The Beatle." *Bass Player* (July/August 1995). At http://www.macca-central.com/macca-archives/bassplayer.htm (accessed April 14, 2008).

Badman, Keith. *The Beatles: Off the Record: Outrageous Opinions & Unrehearsed Interviews.* London: Omnibus Press, 2000.

———. *The Beatles: The Dream is Over: Off the Record 2.* London: Omnibus Press, 2002.

Baird, Julia with Geoffrey Giuliano. *John Lennon, My Brother.* NY: Henry Holt, 1988.

Baker, Geoff. "Paul McCartney." *The Street* 3 #10 (Nov. 1990): 10, 11, 22.

Barnes, Anthony. "Sinatra Rejected My Song, Says Sir Paul." May 17, 2003. At http://www.macca-central.com/news/1245/ (accessed Oct. 16, 2016).

Barrow, Tony. "The Lennon and McCartney Songbook." *The Beatles Book Monthly* 113 (Sept. 1985): 17-21.

———. "Why John and Paul Started Writing Songs." *The Beatles Book Monthly* 114 (Oct. 1985): 16-21.

———. "The Songs John Wrote." *The Beatles Book Monthly* 115 (Nov. 1985): 14-19.

"Beatlemania Strikes Again." Includes quotes from McCartney. *Melody Maker* (June 18, 1966): 1, 15.

"Beatles Get Back, Track by Track: Fab Four 'kick out the jams' on upcoming LP." *Rolling Stone* 42 (September 20, 1969): 8.

Beatles-unlimited.com website, at http://www.beatles-unlimited.com/mamboarchive/SiteArchive/prlibncut.htm (accessed August 26, 2012).

The Beatles. "Beatles Interview: Bahamas, Promoting 'Help' Movie - May 1965." At Beatles Ultimate Experience website, http://www.beatlesinterviews.org/db1965.03help.beatles.html (accessed Oct. 16, 2016).

————. "Press Conference in New York City (1966 August 22)." At http://www.beatlesinterviews.org/db1966.0822.beatles.html (accessed Oct. 16, 2016).

————. Indianapolis Press Conference, September 3, 1964. Available at the Ultimate Beatles website, at http://www.beatlesinterviews.org/db1964.0903.beatles.html (accessed Oct. 16, 2016).

————. Interview, Dunedin, June 26, 1964, with Bob Rogers, New City Hotel. At http://www.dmbeatles.com/forums/index.php?topic=4084.10;wap2 (accessed Oct. 16, 2016).

————. Interview, February 22, 1964. Pathe News and BBC television. At http://www.beatlesinterviews.org/db1964.0222.beatles.html (accessed Oct. 16, 2016).

————. Interview, Top Gear program, July 14, 1964. Available on http://www.youtube.com/watch?v=SnhT2BaxE9k (accessed May 20, 2013).

————. Interview. Klas Burling, August 23, 1963, Bournemouth. At http://www.beatlesinterviews.org/db1963.0823.beatles.html (accessed Oct. 16, 2016, 2008).

————. Press Conference, Adelaide, Australia, June 12, 1964. At http://www.beatlesinterviews.org/db1964.0612.beatles.html (accessed Oct. 16, 2016).

————. Radio Interview, October 28, 1962 at Hulme Hall in Port Sunlight, on the Wirral in England. Monty Lister, with additional questions from Malcolm Threadgill and Peter Smethurst. Available at http://www.beatlesinterviews.org/db1962.1028.beatles.html (accessed Oct. 16, 2016).

————. *The Beatles Anthology*. San Francisco: Chronicle Books, 2000.

The Beatles Bible, a website. http://www.beatlesbible.com/ (accessed June 23, 2013).

The Beatles for the Record. NY: Totem Books, 1982.

The Beatles Ultimate Experience website, at http://www.beatlesinterviews.org/ (accessed Oct. 16, 2016).

Beathoven, a website. At http://www.geocities.com/hammodotcom/beathoven/because1.htm (accessed via Wayback Machine on May 6, 2013).

Best, Pete and Patrick Doncaster. *Beatle! The Pete Best Story*. NY: Dell, 1985.

Bibliography

Benitez, Vincent Perez. *The Words and Music of Paul McCartney*. Santa Barbara, CA: ABC-CLIO, LLC, 2010.

Black, Johnny. "John Lennon: From the Quarrymen to the MBE." *MOJO* (October 2000). Via *Rock's Backpages*.

Blackburn, Robin and Tariq Ali. "Lennon and Ono interview," Jan. 21, 1971. *Red Mole* (underground, left-wing newspaper). At http://www.counterpunch.org/lennon12082005.html (accessed March 11, 2008).

Bonici, Ray. "Paul McCartney Wings It Alone." Interview with Paul. *Music Express*, #56 (GG70470) (April/May 1982). At http://beatles.ncf.ca/mpl.html (accessed April 23, 2008).

Boyd, Pattie. *Wonderful Tonight: George Harrison, Eric Clapton, and Me*. NY: Harmony Books, 2007.

Bramwell, Tony, with Rosemary Kingsland. *Magical Mystery Tours: My Life With The Beatles*. NY: Thomas Dunne Books/St. Martins Press, 2005.

Braun, Michael. *Love Me Do: The Beatles' Progress*. London: Penguin, 1964.

Brightwell, Andrew. "Hunter hits the mark with talk on his memoirs." *Ham&High* (March 25, 2005). At http://www.hamhigh.co.uk/content/camden/hamhigh/news/story.aspx?brand=NorthLondon24&category=Newshamhigh&tBrand=northlondon24&tCategory=newshamhigh&itemid=WeED24%20Mar%202005%2016%3A17%3A02%3A410 (accessed April 9, 2008).

Brown, Geoff. "McCartney: Life after Death." *Melody Maker* 49 (Nov. 30, 1974): 8-9, 63.

Brown, Mick. "A Conversation with George Harrison." *Rolling Stone* #289 (April 19, 1979). Via *Rock's Backpages*.

Carvill, John. Review of Peter Doggett, *You Never Give Me Your Money: The Battle for the Soul of The Beatles*. *Oomska: an Online Arts & Pop Culture Magazine*, March 22, 2010. At http://www.oomska.co.uk/2010/03/ (accessed Apr. 13, 2014).

Cashmere, Paul. "George Harrison Gets 'Undercover.'" Interview with Harrison, 1996. Transcript at http://abbeyrd.net/harrison.htm (accessed April 23, 2008).

Coleman, Ray. "Beatles Say—Dylan Shows the Way." *Melody Maker* 40 (Jan. 9, 1965): 3.

———. "George Harrison—Exclusive!" *Melody Maker* 39 (Mar. 21, 1964): 10-11.

———. "Here We Go Again." *Melody Maker* 40 (Feb. 27, 1965): 12-13+. Also in Sander-combe, *The Beatles*, 115-16.

———. *Lennon*. NY: McGraw-Hill, 1985.

———. "Life with the Lennons." *Melody Maker* 40 (April 10, 1965): 11+. Also in Sander-combe, *The Beatles*, 122.

———. *McCartney: Yesterday … and Today*. Los Angeles: Dove Books, 1996. First published London: Boxtree Limited, 1995.

———. "Wish Elvis All the Best in *Aladdin*." *Melody Maker* 40 (Jan. 16, 1965): 8.

Coleman, Ray and Chris Roberts. "What Makes a Beatle Beat?" *Melody Maker* 38 (Aug. 3, 1963): 6-7.

Bibliography

Compton, Todd M. "Lennon-McCartney Song Database." At http://toddmcompton.com/beatlesongschronprint.htm (accessed March 5, 2017).

Conners, Peter. *White Hand Society: The Psychedelic Partnership of Timothy Leary and Allen Ginsberg.* San Francisco: City Lights Books, 2010.

Connolly, Ray. *The Ray Connolly Beatles Archive* (Plumray Books 2011). This includes a 1970 interview with John Lennon (pp. 101-11) that Connolly recorded while working with Aldridge on *The Beatles Illustrated Lyrics.* It sometimes duplicates Aldridge, and sometimes has material not in Aldridge.

Cott, Jonathan. "John Lennon: The Last Interview." *Rolling Stone* (Dec. 23, 2010), as found at http://www.rollingstone.com/music/news/john-lennon-the-last-interview-20101223 (accessed 10-31-2015).

————. "The Rolling Stone Interview with John Lennon." Interview dated September 28, 1968. *Rolling Stone* No. 22 (November 23, 1968): 1-4.

Cott, Jonathan and David Dalton. *The Beatles Get Back.* Unpaginated. London: Apple, 1969.

Cott, Jonathan and Christine Doudna, eds. *The Ballad of John and Yoko.* Garden City, NJ: Dolphin Books, Doubleday & Company, 1982.

Covach, John. "From 'Craft' to 'Art': Formal Structure in the Music of the Beatles." In *Reading the Beatles: Cultural Studies, Literary Criticism, and the Fab Four,* ed. Kenneth Womack and Todd F. Davis, 37–54. Albany: State University of New York Press, 2006.

Cowan, Philip. *Behind the Beatles Songs.* London: Polyantric Press, 1978.

Davies, Hunter. "All Paul." *Sunday Times.* An interview with Paul which took place on Sept. 18, 1966. Reprinted in Davies, *The Beatles,* 2nd edition, xxii-xxiii.

————. *The Beatles, the Authorized Biography.* 2nd rev. ed. NY: McGraw-Hill, 1985. Originally published in 1968.

————, ed. *The John Lennon Letters.* NY: Little, Brown and Company, 2012.

Dawson, Jerry. "Lennon's Eye View." *Melody Maker* (Nov. 13, 1965): 3+.

Dean, Johny. "Editorial." *The Beatles Book Monthly* 49 (August 1967): 2.

deCurtis, Anthony. *In Other Words: Artists Talk about Life and Work.* Milwaukee, WI: H. Leonard, 2005. June 1987 interviews with Paul and George, 55-64 and 65-71. First published in *Rolling Stone* (Nov. 5, 1987).

————. "Beatlemania strikes again." An interview with McCartney. *MacCalls* 115 (Apr. 1988): 36.

DiLello, Richard. *The Longest Cocktail Party: An Insider's Diary of the Beatles, Their Million Dollar Apple Empire and Its Wild Rise and Fall.* Chicago, Ill.: Playboy, 1972. Reprinted [U.S.]: Mojo Books, 2001.

The Dingles Fairground Heritage Center website. At http://fairground-heritage.org.uk/learning/ (accessed June 13, 2013).

Doggett, Peter. *Abbey Road/Let It Be: The Beatles.* Classic Rock Albums series. NY: Schirmer Books, 1998.

———. *You Never Give Me Your Money: the Beatles after the Breakup.* NY: HarperCollins Publishers, 2009.

———. *The Art and Music of John Lennon.* NY: Omnibus Press, 2005.

Doherty, Pete. "Pete Doherty meets Paul McCartney." *Guardian* (Oct. 14, 2007). Available at http://music.guardian.co.uk/pop/story/0,,2188017,00.html (accessed April 14, 2008).

Douridas, Chris. Interview with Paul McCartney, May 25, 2002. Episode of NewGround at KCRW. At http://www.kcrw.com/music/shows/chris-douridas/paul-mccartney (accessed Sept. 30, 2016).

Dowlding, William J. *Beatlesongs.* NY: Simon & Schuster, 1989.

Du Noyer, Paul. *Conversations with McCartney.* NY: The Overlook Press, 2016.

Earle, Steve. "The Ten Most Important Beatles Songs." In Sawyers, *Read the Beatles,* 308-10.

"Early Beatle Songs" website. At http://earlybeatlessongs.weebly.com/just-fun.html (accessed June 28, 2012).

Eisen, Jonathan, ed. *The Age of Rock: Sounds of the American Cultural Revolution.* NY: Vintage Books/Random House, 1969.

Elson, Howard. *McCartney: Songwriter.* London: W. H. Allen, 1986.

Emerick, Geoff and Howard Massey. *Here, There and Everywhere: My Life Recording the Music of the Beatles.* NY: Gotham, 2006.

Engelhardt, Kristofer. *Beatles Undercover.* Burlington, Ontario, Canada: Collectors' Guide Publishing, Inc., 1998.

Evans, Mal. "'The Beatles Get Back': August LP Surprise." *The Beatles Book Monthly* 72 (July 1969): 22-29.

———. "Diary Extracts." Timeonline, March 20, 2005. At http://www.timesonline.co.uk/tol/life_and_style/article424669.ece (accessed March 12, 2008).

———. "John and Yoko's Toronto Concert." *The Beatles Book Monthly* 76 (November 1969): 6-14.

———. "Mal's Diary." *The Beatles Book Monthly* 62 (October 1968): 11-12.

———. "The Eighteenth Single." *The Beatles Book Monthly* 62 (September 1968): 6-11.

———. "Thirty New Beatles Grooves on Double Disc Album." *The Beatles Book Monthly* 64 (November 1968): 7-14.

———. "Your Album Queries." *The Beatles Book Monthly* 67 (February 1969): 7-13.

Evans, Mal and Neil Aspinall. "Magical Mystery Tour." *The Beatles Book Monthly* 53 (December 1967): 6-13.

———. "Mal and Neil Tell You How 'All You Need is Love' was Recorded." *The Beatles Book Monthly* 49 (August 1967): 9.

———. "New Single Sessions." *The Beatles Book Monthly* 57 (April 1968): 11-14.

Everett, Kenny. "Beatles' Dinner Party." *The Beatles Book Monthly* 48 (July 1967): 25.

———. Interview with Paul McCartney. Recorded June 26-30, 1967. BBC Radio 1.

———. Interview with the Beatles, June 5, 1968. At The Beatles Ultimate Experience website, http://www.beatlesinterviews.org/db1968.0605.beatles.html (accessed Oct. 15, 2016).

Everett, Walter. *The Beatles as Musicians: Revolver through the Anthology.* NY: Oxford University Press, 1999. [Cited as "Everett I"]

———. *The Beatles as Musicians: the Quarry Men through Rubber Soul.* NY: Oxford University Press, 2001. [Cited as "Everett II"]

Fallon, B. P. "Will the Real John Lennon Please Stand Up? Part Two." *Melody Maker* (Apr. 19, 1969): 16-17.

Farrow, Mia. *What Falls Away: A Memoir.* NY: Doubleday, 1997.

Fawcett, Anthony. *John Lennon: One Day at a Time*, revised ed. NY: Grove Press, 1981.

Fitzgerald, Jon. "Lennon-McCartney and the "Middle Eight." *Popular Music and Society* 20.4 (1996): 41-52.

Flanagan, Bill. "Boy, You're Gonna Carry That Weight." *Musician* #139 (May 1, 1990): 40-42, 44, 46, 48, 50, 52, 54, 56.

Fontenot, Robert. "Francie Schwartz: The About.com Interview." 1999. At http://oldies.about.com/cs/theculture/a/schwartz.htm (accessed Apr. 23, 2013).

Forsyth, Ian. "The Alistair Taylor Interview." 2002. http://beatlesnumber9.com/taylor.html (accessed Aug. 10, 2012).

Forte, Dan. "George Harrison." In *Secrets from the Masters: Conversations With Forty Great Guitar Players, from the pages of Guitar Player Magazine*, edited by Don Menn, 101-8. San Francisco: Backbeat Books, 1992. Originally published as "The Jungle Music & Posh Skiffle of George Harrison." *Guitar Player* 21 no. 11 (Nov. 1987): 83-97.

Friedman, Bernard Harper. *Tripping: a Memoir of Timothy Leary & Co.* Provincetown, MA: Provincetown Arts Press, 2006.

From Rio . . . to Liverpool. TV documentary. MPL Communications LTD., 1990. Available on You Tube.

"From 'You To Us' Inspired 'From Me To You'." *New Musical Express*, May 10, 1963, page 10. As cited in http://www.geocities.ws/pisces2878/OA/May1063.html (accessed Oct. 17, 2016).

Gambaccini, Paul. "A Conversation with Paul McCartney." *Rolling Stone* 295 (July 12, 1979): 39-46.

———. "The Rolling Stone Interview: Paul McCartney." *Rolling Stone* (Jan 31, 1974): 32-34, 38-46. The interview took place in December 1973. At http://www.rollingstone.com/news/profile/story/9359339/the_rs_interview_paul_mccartney (accessed Feb. 1, 2008).

———. *Paul McCartney, In His Own Words.* NY: Flash Books, 1976. These interviews were done mostly in November and December 1973; after page 86, they were done in the summer of 1975.

Garbarini, Vic. "Paul McCartney: Lifting the Veil Off the Beatles." *Musician* #26 (Aug. 1980): 44-51, 98. Reprinted in Tony Scherman, *The Rock Musician: 15 Years of Interviews: The Best of Musician Magazine* (NY: Macmillan, 1994), 17-42. Released as a record, *The Paul McCartney Interview*, Columbia 36987 (1981).

Garbarini, Vic and Jock Baird. "Has Success Spoiled Paul McCartney?" *Musician* #76 (Feb. 1, 1985): 58-64.

Garcia, Gilbert. "The Ballad of Paul and Yoko." *Salon* online, Feb. 20, 2008. At http://dir.salon.com/story/ent/music/feature/2003/01/27/paul_yoko/index.html?pn=2 (accessed April 23, 2008).

Gass, Glenn. "Interview with Hunter Davies." June 2002. At http://www.music.indiana.edu/som/courses/rock/davies.html (accessed April 3, 2008).

"George Martin on the Beatle Days." *Rolling Stone* 71 (Nov. 26, 1970): 14.

Ghosh, Palash. "The Beatles In 1960 Liverpool: Royston Ellis Remembers." Jan. 8, 2013, http://www.ibtimes.com/beatles-1960-liverpool-royston-ellis-remembers-996876 (accessed May 6, 2013).

Gilmore, Mikal. "Why the Beatles Broke Up: The Story Behind Our Cover." *Rolling Stone*, Aug. 18, 2009. At http://www.rollingstone.com/music/news/why-the-beatles-broke-up-the-story-behind-our-cover-20090818 (accessed Apr. 14, 2014).

Giuliano, Geoffrey. *The Beatles: A Celebration.* Toronto: Methuen, 1986.

Giuliano, Geoffrey and Brenda Giuliano. *The Lost Beatles Interviews.* NY: Penguin Books USA Inc, 1994.

Glazer, Mitchell. "Growing Up at 33 1/3: The George Harrison Interview." *Crawdaddy* (Feb. 1977): 32-41.

Gobnotch. "Recording Sessions Update." At http://whizzo.ca/beatles/rs/gobnotch.html (accessed March 11, 2008).

Goldman, Albert. *The Lives of John Lennon.* Paperback edition. NY: Bantam Books, 1988.

Goodman, Joan. "Playboy Interview: Paul and Linda McCartney." *Playboy* 31.12 (Dec. 1984): 75-110.

Goodman, Pete. "Norman Smith Continues Talking About Balancing the Beatles." *The Beatles Book Monthly* 23 (June 1965): 13-15.

Google Groups, rec.music.beatles, paramucho, 8/3/99. Citing a Lennon interview, "September 28, 1974, New York Radio in GST362." At https://groups.google.com/forum/#!topic/rec.music.beatles/jrMlMHaRy0I%5B151-175%5D (accessed Dec. 3, 2016).

Greene, Joshua M. *Here Comes the Sun: The Spiritual and Musical Journey of George Harrison.* Hoboken, NJ: John Wiley & Sons, 2006.

Greenfield, Robert. *Timothy Leary: A Biography.* Orlando: Harcourt, Inc., 2006.

Grow, Kory. "McCartney Shares His Touring Secrets." *Rolling Stone* (July 13-27, 2017): 26.

Haglund, David. "The Forgotten Songwriter Who Inspired the Beatles." *Slate*, Feb. 11, 2013. At http://www.slate.com/blogs/browbeat/2013/02/11/arthur_alexander_and_the_beatles_forgotten_songwriter_also_inspired_the.html (accessed Apr. 7, 2013).

Harrison, George."By George." *Mersey Beat* (Feb. 13, 1964). At http://www.triumphpc.com/mersey-beat/archives/bygeorge.shtml (accessed March 27, 2014).

———. *I Me Mine*. NY: Simon and Schuster, 1980.

———. Interview with Johnny Moran, March 11, 1970. Partial transcript at http://lifeofthebeatles.blogspot.com/2006/11/interview-george-harrison-london-march.html (accessed Oct. 22, 2013).

———. Interview with David Wigg, Apple Offices, London, October 8, 1969. Transcription at http://www.beatlesinterviews.org/db1969.1008.beatles.html (accessed Oct. 22, 2013).

———. Discusses writing "Something." At the BBC Song on Song website, http://www.bbc.co.uk/radio2/soldonsong/songlibrary/something.shtml (accessed March 31, 2014).

Harry, Bill. "Billy J. Kramer." At http://www.sixtiescity.com/Mbeat/mbfilms95.htm (accessed July 12, 2012).

———. "Cilla Black." At http://www.sixtiescity.com/Mbeat/mbfilms83.htm (accessed July 12, 2012).

———. "Fourmost." At http://www.sixtiescity.com/Mbeat/mbfilms96.htm (accessed July 12, 2012).

———. "George Harrison, Songwriter." At http://www.beatlefan.com/harrisonsongwriter.html (accessed March 11, 2008).

———. "Jane & Paul: A Love Story." At http://www.triumphpc.com/mersey-beat/beatles/janeasher-paulmccartney.shtml (accessed Apr. 13, 2013).

———. Email on George Harrison. Posted January 31, 2008 at http://www.dmbeatles.com/forums/v-print/m-1189852901/ (accessed March 11, 2008).

———. *The Paul McCartney Encyclopedia*. London: Virgin, 2002.

Hennessey, Mike. "Lennon: the Greatest Natural Songwriter of Our Time. *Record Mirror*'s Great Ones, Number Three, John Lennon." *Record Mirror* (Oct. 2, 1971): 11-13.

———. "Who Wrote What: For the First Time John Lennon Breaks Down the Lennon-McCartney Songs Into Who-Wrote-What Form." *Record Mirror* (Oct. 2, 1971): 14.

Hieronimus, Bob. Interview with George Martin re *Yellow Submarine*, November 12, 1995. At http://www.21stcenturyradio.com/NP8-22-99-1.html (accessed March 14, 2008).

Hilburn, Robert. "From 'Yesterday' to Today." *Los Angeles Times*, Calendar section, Nov. 19, 1989, 75.

Hilton, Simon. *Chaos and Creation at Abbey Road*. TV movie of a concert by Paul McCartney given on July 28, 2005. Released on February 27, 2006.

Bibliography

Hodenfield, Chris. "George Martin Recalls the Boys in the Band." *Rolling Stone* 217 (July 15, 1976). Available at http://www.rollingstone.com/music/features/george-martin-recalls-the-boys-in-the-band-19760715 (accessed Oct. 16, 2016).

Howlett, Kevin. Liner notes for *On Air—Live at the BBC Volume 2* (Apple 2013).

Hull, Dave and Derek Taylor. "The Beatles: Let's Talk With Paul." *KRLA Beat*, 21 April 1965. As found in *Rock's Backpages*.

Hunt, Chris. "The Story Of Hey Jude." *Mojo* Beatles Special (February 2002). At http://www.chrishunt.biz/features01.html (accessed March 7, 2008).

Hutchins, Chris. "The Lennon Interview." *New Musical Express*, No. 1000 (March 11, 1966): 3. At http://www.beatlesinterviews.org/db1966.0311.beatles.html (accessed Feb. 11, 2014).

Hutton, Jack. "Protest palls: Says Paul." *Melody Maker* (Oct. 2, 1965): 1.

"In The Beatles' Song Writing Factory." *Melody Maker* (July 16, 1966): 10. Available in Sandercombe, *The Beatles: Press Reports*, 171.

Interview: Apple Offices, London, October 8, 1969. As transcribed in The Beatles Ultimate Experience website, http://www.beatlesinterviews.org/db1969.1008.beatles.html (accessed July 12, 2012).

"Interview with Peter Asher, half of legendary duo Peter & Gordon." At the Rock&Roll Hall of Fame website, http://rockhall.com/blog/post/interview-with-peter-asher-of-peter-and-gordon/ (accessed March 8, 2014).

Interviews 1967, a bootleg. Lazy Tortoise.

Irvin, Jim. "Get It Better: The Story of *Let It Be . . . Naked.*" *MOJO* (2003). As found in *Rock's Backpages*.

———. "George Martin." *MOJO* (January 2007). As found in *Rock's Backpages*.

James, Frederick. "Beatles Talk." An interview with the Beatles. *The Beatles Book Monthly* 39 (October 1966): 11.

———. "Beatles Talk." An interview with the Beatles. *The Beatles Book Monthly* 41 (December 1966): 6.

———. "Beatles Talk." An interview with the Beatles. *The Beatles Book Monthly* 42 (January 1967): 7.

———. "Beatles Talk." An interview with the Beatles. *The Beatles Book Monthly* 44 (March 1967): 24.

James, Frederick. "Lennon & McCartney (Songwriters) Ltd." *Beatles Book Monthly* 2 (September 1963): pages unnumbered (at about p. 20).

———. "Revolution Report: How the Beatles Recorded Their New Single." *The Beatles Book Monthly* 60 (July 1968): 6-8.

"John Lennon and Paul McCartney Interview." *Flip Magazine* (May 15, 1966). At http://www.dmbeatles.com/interviews.php?interview=47 (accessed Oct. 16, 2016).

"John Lennon: Biography." No date. At http://www.rollingstone.com/music/artists/john-lennon/biography (accessed Apr. 13, 2014).

Jones, Peter. "Northern Songs Ltd. for Beatle Songs Unlimited." An interview with Dick James. *The Beatles Book Monthly* 21 (April 1965): 9-13.

Kelley, Harold. Interview with the Beatles. Armed Forces Network, Paris January 24, 1964. As transcribed on Beatles Ultimate Experince website, at http://www.beatlesinterviews.org/db1964.0124.beatles.html (accessed Oct. 17, 2016).

King, Bill. "'Shout!': An Interview with Author Philip Norman, part 2." *Beatlefan* #17 (August 1981): 10-12.

King, Larry. "Paul McCartney Discusses 'Blackbird Singing.'" Interview with Paul McCartney. CNN, Larry King Live, June 12, 2001. Transcript at http://transcripts.cnn.com/TRANSCRIPTS/0106/12/lkl.00.html (accessed Oct. 17, 2016).

Kozinn, Alan. "Meditation on the Man Who Saved the Beatles." *New York Times*, Feb. 7, 2008. At http://www.nytimes.com/2008/02/07/arts/music/07yogi.html?_r=0, with appended pdf by Alex Mardas (accessed Apr. 30, 2013).

Landau, Jon. Review of *Ram*, by Paul McCartney. *Rolling Stone* 86 (July 8, 1971): 42.

Leigh, Spencer. "Cavern King," Interview with Bob Wooler. *Record Collector*, no. 227 (July 1998) at http://www.tropeamagazine.it/thebeatles/cavern/rcollectori.htm (accessed June 26, 2012).

Leitch, Donovan. *The Autobiography of Donovan: Hurdy Gurdy Man*. NY: St. Martins Press, 2005.

———. "Poet John." In *Memories of John Lennon*, edited by Yoko Ono. NY: HarperCollins, 2005.

———. *Uncut* interview, September 5, 2005. At http://www.uncut.co.uk/music/donovan/interviews/8599 (accessed April 21, 2008).

Leng, Simon. *The Music of George Harrison: While My Guitar Gently Weeps*. Milwaukee, WI: Hal Leonard Corp., 2006.

Lennon, Cynthia. *John.* [London:] Hodder & Stoughton, 2005.

Lennon, John. Interview with Miles, September 1969, the "Oz Interview." http://unfinishedno9.blogspot.com/2007/11/oz-interview-1969.html (accessed October 22, 2013). See also Miles, "My Blue Period."

———. Interview with Tony MacArthur, late September, 1969. http://www.youtube.com/watch?v=x9E1TV5cLwo (accessed Oct. 22, 2013).

Lennon, John. Rolling Stone Interview, Dec. 1970, 5-part BBC podcast. I cite from this recording whenever possible. Transcriptions in Wenner, *Lennon Remembered* and Yoko Ono's Imagine Peace website, http://imaginepeace.com/archives/4385 (accessed Jan. 19, 2017). However, long passages in the interview cannot be found in the recording, in which case I cite *Lennon Remembered*.

Get Back to Let It Be . . . Dissected, blog, at http://letitbedissected.blogspot.com.co/ (accessed Nov. 29, 2017).

Lewisohn, Mark. *The Beatles: All These Years. Volume 1, Tune In.* NY: Crown Archetype, 2013.

————. *The Beatles: All These Years. Volume 1, Tune In*. Extended edition. London: Little, Brown and Company, 2013.

————. *The Beatles Recording Sessions: The Official Abbey Road Studio Session Notes, 1962-1970*. NY: Harmony Books, 1990. Originally published in England in 1988 as *The Complete Beatles Recording Sessions*.

————. Liner notes from The Beatles, *Anthology 1* CD (Apple/Capitol 1995).

————. "The Paul McCartney Interview." In Lewisohn, *The Beatles Recording Sessions*, 6-15.

Liner notes from *Doris Troy* (Apple 1970). At http://www.applerecords.com/#!/albums/Doris_Troy (accessed March 21, 2014).

Liner notes from Billy Preston, *Encouraging Words* (Apple 1970). At http://www.applerecords.com/#!/albums/Album_EncouragingWords (accessed March 21, 2014).

Lost Lennon Tapes. A weekly radio show with 218 episodes, from January 24, 1988 to March 23, 1992. Includes many interviews with Lennon and others. Written by Laurie Kremie, narrated by Elliot Mintz. A presentation of the Westwood One Radio Network, produced in cooperation with the John Lennon estate.

Lydon, Michael. "Lennon and McCartney: Songwriters—A Portrait from 1966." Unpublished, March 1966. As found in *Rock's Backpages*.

MacDonald, Ian. *Revolution in the Head: The Beatles' Records and the Sixties*. London: Fourth Estate, 1994.

Madinger, Chip. Liner Notes to *The Family Way* soundtrack album (Decca 1967). At http://varesevintage.wordpress.com/2011/06/15/paul-mccartney-the-family-way-soundtrack/ (accessed June 13, 2013).

Matovina, Dan. *Without You: The Tragic Story of Badfinger*. Frances Glover Books, 2000.

Martin, George. Audio at Sold on Song Top 100, "66 Strawberry Fields Forever." http://www.bbc.co.uk/radio2/soldonsong/songlibrary/strawberryfieldsforever.shtml (accessed Apr. 17, 2013).

————. "George Martin Interview." No date. At http://members.tripod.com/~taz4158/martin.html (accessed April 23, 2008).

————. *In My Life* album (MCA 1998), cover notes. At http://albumlinernotes.com/In_My_Life.html (accessed Oct. 5, 2015)

Martin, George and Jeremy Hornsby. *All You Need Is Ears*. NY: St. Martin's Press, 1979.

Martin, George and William Pearson. *With a Little Help from My Friends: The Making of Sgt. Pepper*. Boston: Little, Brown, 1994.

Mascaró, Juan. *Lamps of Fire: the Spirit of Religions*. London: Methuen, 1958.

Matthew, Brian. "Interview with Paul McCartney & John Lennon." March 20, 1967 - 7:00 P.M. at Studio Two, EMI Studios, London, United Kingdom. Broadcast March 27, 1967, 2:00-3:00 P.M., on BBC Light Programme, The Ivor Novello Awards for 1966.

McCabe, Peter and Robert D. Schonfeld. *Apple to the Core: The Unmaking of the Beatles*. NY: Pocket Books, 1972.

————. *John Lennon: For the Record*. A 1971 interview. NY: Bantam Books, 1984.

———. Interview with John Lennon, Sept. 5, 1971, in the Sept. 1984 *Penthouse*. As published in http://www.beatlesinterviews.org/db1971.0905.beatles.html (accessed July 22, 2012).

McCartney, Linda. *Linda McCartney's Sixties: Portrait of an Era*. Boston: Bullfinch Press, 1992.

McCartney, Paul. "Autobiography." Date unknown. From Paul's page on myspace.

———. "Interview with Derek Taylor." March 3, 1965, Bahamas. Transcribed at http://members.aol.com/dinsdalep/650303b.txt (accessed March 7, 2008). [note, superseded by Hull and Taylor, "The Beatles: Let's Talk With Paul."

———. "Interview with Klas Burling," July 29, 1964. For background, Winn, *Way Beyond Compare*, 223.

———. "Interview, Observer Music Monthly." September 18, 2005. Transcript at https://www.theguardian.com/observer/omm/story/0,,1571996,00.html (accessed Oct. 17, 2016).

———. Interview with Radio Luxembourg, November 20, 1968. At The Beatles Ultimate Experience website, http://www.beatlesinterviews.org/db1968.1120.beatles.html, (accessed Oct. 16, 2016).

———. Interview. *USA Today* (Dec. 19 1985): 2.

———. Letter to John on John's induction to the Rock 'N Roll Hall of Fame, January 19th, 1994. At http://beatlesnumber9.com/letter.html (accessed April 15, 2008).

———. "On-line chat with Paul McCartney." At the Bishopsgate Memorial Hall, London, Saturday 17 May 1997. In Harry, *The Paul McCartney Encyclopedia*, at the entry "Internet, The."

———. OobuJoobu. In which Paul served as DJ for a radio show. 1995.

———. "Press Conference, 1 May 1993, Georgia Dome, Atlanta." Included in Harry, *McCartney Encyclopedia*, at the entry "Georgia Dome, Atlanta, Georgia."

———. Self-interview. Insert for *McCartney* (1970).

"The McCartney Recording Sessions." http://webpages.charter.net/ram71/1970.htm (accessed May 24, 2013).

McGrath, James. "Cutting Up a Glass Onion: Reading the Beatles' History and Legacy." In *50 Years With The Beatles: The Impact of The Beatles on Contemporary Culture*, edited by Jerzy Jarniewicz & Alina Kwiatkowska, 303-26. Łódź: Łódź University Press, 2010.

McLean, Ralph. "Stories Behind the Song: 'Strawberry Fields Forever.'" At http://www.bbc.co.uk/northernireland/music/story_behind/strawberryfields.shtml (accessed April 22, 2008).

Merritt, Mike. "Truth behind ballad that split Beatles." "As stripped-down version of last Beatles album is re-released, Paul McCartney tells of writing The Long And Winding Road in Kintyre." *Sundayherald*, Nov. 16, 2003. A Scotch independent newspaper. At http://web.archive.org/web/20060427062227/http://www.sundayherald.com/38051 (accessed Feb. 13, 2008).

Miles, Barry, compiler. *Beatles in their Own Words*. 1978. NY: Omnibus Press, 1978.

———. *Paul McCartney: Many Years From Now*. NY: Henry Holt and Company, 1997.

————. "My Blue Period: John Lennon." *MOJO*, (November 1995). Interview with John Lennon conducted on Sept. 23-24, 1969. Via *Rock's Backpages*.

————. "The Way Out Is In." Interview with George Harrison, *International Times* (May 19, 1967). Accessed via *Rock's Backpages*.

Miles, Barry, with Jason Beard and Stephen Coates. *The Beatles: A Diary: an Intimate Day by Day History*. London: Omnibus Press, 1998.

Morse, Tim. *Classic Rock Stories: The Stories Behind the Greatest Songs of All Time*. NY: St. Martin's Griffin, 1998.

Newborn, Brant. "Ringo in the Afternoon." *Rolling Stone* 342 (Apr. 30, 1981): 28-31, 61

Newman, Ray. *Abracadabra! — The Complete Story of the Beatles' Revolver*. Web-published, at http://www.revolverbook.co.uk/abracadabrav1.0.pdf (accessed February 5, 2008).

Norman, Philip. *John Lennon: the Life*. NY: Ecco, 2008.

————. *Shout!: The Beatles in their Generation*. NY: Simon & Schuster, 1981. A revised updated edition is NY: Simon & Schuster, 2005.

O'Hare, Kevin. "McCartney on McCartney." Interview for *The McCartney Years* DVD. At http://blog.pennlive.com/thrive/2007/12/paul_mccartney.html (accessed April 23, 2008).

Okun, Milton. *The Compleat Beatles*. 2 vols. Greenwich Ct.: Cherry Lane Music Co., 1981.

"Paul Joins Band." *Melody Maker* (July 6, 1968): 2.

"Paul McCartney and John Lennon at the Tonight Show, with Joe Garagiola," May 14, 1968. Transcript at http://www.dmbeatles.com/interviews.php?interview=64 (accessed April 14, 2008). Also in *Record Mirror*, May 25, 1968, as found in Sandercombe, *The Beatles*, 238.

"Paul McCartney: Let It Be." *Record Mirror* (April 18, 1970). In *Rock's Backpages*.

"Paul McCartney Reveals Photo Inspiration for Lady Madonna." Nov. 1, 2017, at _/ (accessed Dec. 3, 2017).

The Paul McCartney World Tour. 1989. Tour booklet. See an interview, "Paul McCartney in Conversation," pp. 36-97.

Pawlowski, Gareth L. *How They Became the Beatles*. NY: E. P. Dutton, 1989.

Pearson, Stan. "Paul's Shout Up at Shipley." *Melody Maker* (July 13, 1968): 10.

Pedler, Dominic. *The Songwriting Secrets of the Beatles*. NY: Music Sales Limited. Omnibus Press. 2003.

Peebles, Andy. *The Lennon Tapes*. London: BBC Publications, 1981. Now reprinted as *The Last Lennon Tapes*. This interview was conducted two days before Lennon's death in December 1980.

Peel. Ian. *The Unknown Paul McCartney: McCartney and the Avant-Garde*. London: Titan Books, 2013.

Pinch, Trevor and Frank Trocco. *Analog Days: The Invention and Impact of the Moog Synthesizer*. Cambridge, MA: Harvard University Press, 2002.

The Plastic Ono Band Unfinished Discography, http://homepage.ntlworld.com/carousel/pob/pob04.html (accessed May 7, 2013).

Bibliography

Pollack, Allan. *Notes on … Series*. A thorough musicological analysis of all the Beatle songs. 1989-2001. At http://www.icce.rug.nl/~soundscapes/DATABASES/AWP/awp-notes_on.shtml (accessed Apr. 19, 2017).

Pritchard, David, and Alan Lysaght. *The Beatles: An Oral History*. NY: Hyperion, 1998.

Quantick, David. *Revolution: The Making of The Beatles' White Album*. London: Unanimous Ltd., 2002.

Radice, Gary. "A Welter Of Helter Skelters." At http://www.joylandbooks.com/themagiceye/galleries/helterskelters.htm (accessed May 1, 2013).

Radio Luxemburg interview with John Lennon, to promote Abbey Road, September 1969, broadcast on Sept. 27th, available on the bootleg LP *Abbey Road Talks*. As transcribed in http://beatlesong.info/mg/sun_king_deciphered.html (accessed Oct. 17, 2016).

Read, Mike. "McCartney on McCartney." Interview with Paul McCartney. BBC series, 8 episodes, March 25, 1989 to May 13, 1989.

Renard, Gail and Thomas Shnurmacher. "Eight Days in Montreal with John and Yoko." *The Beatles Book Monthly* 74 (September 1969): 23-24.

Riley, Tim. *Tell Me Why: A Beatles Commentary*. NY: Knopf/ Vintage, 1988.

Robbins, Fred. "Interview with John Lennon." October 29, 1966. Beatles Ultimate Experience website. At http://www.beatlesinterviews.org/db1966.1029.beatles.html (accessed Oct. 16, 2016).

Roberts, Chris. "How to Write a Hit:" Interview with John Lennon and Paul McCartney. [Or "Lennon and McCartney Tell You . . . How to Write a Hit."] *Melody Maker* 39 (Feb. 1, 1964): 11.

Rybaczewski, Dave. "'Kansas City/Hey-Hey-Hey-Hey!' History." *Beatles Music History* website. At http://www.beatlesebooks.com/kansas-city (accessed Dec. 4, 2016).

Rock's Backpages. Database. At http://www.rocksbackpages.com/.

Rorem, Ned. "The Music of the Beatles." In Eisen, *The Age of Rock*, 149-59. First published in the *New York Review of Books*, January 18, 1968.

Rowland, Mark. "The Quiet Wilbury." *Musician*, #37 (March 1, 1990): 30-36, 97.

Salewicz, Chris. *McCartney: the Definitive Biography*. NY: St Martins Press, 1986.

———. "Paul McCartney: An Innocent Man?" *Q* (October 1986). As found in *Rock's Backpages*.

———. "Tug of War: Paul McCartney Wants to Lay his Demons to Rest." *Musician* #96 (October 1986): 56-69.

Sandercombe, W. Fraser. *The Beatles: Press Reports, 1961-1970*. Burlington, Ontario, Canada: Collector's Guide Publishing, 2007.

Saltzman, Paul. *The Beatles in Rishikesh*. NY: Viking Studio/Penguin Putnam, 2000.

———. Excerpt on "Ob-La-Di Ob-La-Da." At http://www.thebeatlesinindia.com/thebook/ob-la-di.html (accessed Apr. 22, 2013)

Sann, Paul. "The Beatles: The Intimate Portrait." *New York Post*, September 14, 1964. Available at http://www.paulsann.org/beatles.htm (accessed Feb. 8, 2008).

Sauter, Donald. "One John Lennon, with sound bites." http://www.donaldsauter.com/john-lennon.htm (accessed Oct. 17, 2016).

Sawyers, June Skinner, ed. *Read the Beatles: Classic and New Writings on the Beatles, Their Legacy, and Why They Still Matter.* London, Penguin Books, 2006. Excerpt of McCartney *Uncut* interview, July 2004, at pp. 243-53.

Scaggs, Austin. "Ringo Starr." *Rolling Stone* #1044 (January 24, 2008): 22.

Scorsese, Martin. *Living in the Material World.* DVD. HBO, 2011.

Schaffner, Nicholas. *The Beatles Forever.* Harrisburg, PA: Cameron House, 1977.

Schreuders, Piet, Mark Lewisohn and Adam Smith. *The Beatles' London: A Guide to 467 Beatles Sites In and Around London.* Northampton, MA: Interlink Books, 2009.

Self, Joseph C. "The 'My Sweet Lord'/'He's So Fine' Plagiarism Suit." First published in *The 910* magazine in 1993. At http://abbeyrd.best.vwh.net/mysweet.htm (accessed Aug. 29, 2012).

Sennett, Sean. "At Last, They Let It Be." *The Sydney Morning Herald (The Sun-Herald)*, December 1, 2003. At http://www.smh.com.au/articles/2003/11/30/1070127259589.html (accessed April 1, 2008).

Shea, Stuart and Robert Rodriguez. *Fab Four FAQ: Everything Left to Know about the Beatles--and More!* NY: Hal Leonard Books, 2007.

Sheff, David. "John Lennon and Yoko Ono: Candid Conversation." *Playboy* 28:1 (Jan. 1981): 75-114, 144.

———. "All We Are Saying: Three Weeks With John Lennon." Interview with David Sheff, excerpts from his interview with John Lennon. NPR, October 8, 2010. http://www.npr.org/templates/story/story.php?storyId=130429818 (accessed March 9, 2017).

———. *The Playboy Interviews with John Lennon & Yoko Ono.* NY: Berkley Books, 1981. Edited by G. Barry Golson. The interviews took place in September 1980. Reissued as *All We Are Saying: The Last Major Interview with John Lennon and Yoko Ono* (2000).

Shepherd, Billy. "Beatles on Holiday." *The Beatles Book Monthly* 12 (July 1964): 7-13.

———. "Filming with the Boys in *A Hard Day's Night.*" *The Beatles Book Monthly* 11 (June 1964): 13-15, 21-23.

Shepherd, Billy and Johnny Dean. "Behind the Spotlight." *The Beatles Book Monthly* 24 (July 1965): 23-24.

———. "Behind the Spotlight." *The Beatles Book Monthly* 31 (Feb. 1966): 21-22.

———. "Behind the Spotlight." *The Beatles Book Monthly* 32 (March 1966): 21-23.

Sholin, Dave and Laurie Kaye. "John Lennon's last interview, December 8, 1980." Audio and transcription at http://www.beatlesarchive.net/john-lennons-last-interview-december-8-1980.html (accessed March 2, 2014). Also transcribed at http://boythewayglennmillerplayed.blogspot.com/2009/12/last-interview-part-i.html (accessed March 25, 2014).

Shotton, Pete & Nicholas Schaffner. *The Beatles, Lennon and Me.* NY: Stein and Day, 1984. Orig. *John Lennon: In My Life.* NY: Stein and Day, 1983.

Bibliography

Sliwicki, Susan. "The Beatles' second single put the band on the map." December 12, 2011, at *Goldmine*, http://www.goldminemag.com/article/excerpt-the-beatles-second-single-put-the-band-on-the-map (accessed Sept. 5, 2012).

Smith, Alan. "At a Recording Session With the Beatles." *Mersey Beat* (Jan. 3, 1963): 4. At http://www.triumphpc.com/mersey-beat/archives/recording-session.shtml (accessed March 31, 2014). Also in Sandercombe, *The Beatles*, 14.

———. "Beatles Almost Threw 'Please Please Me' Away." *New Musical Express*, No. 843 (March 8, 1963): 10. As found in *Rock's Backpages*.

———. "Beatles Music Straightforward On Next Album." An interview with John Lennon. *New Musical Express*, No. 1164 (May 3, 1969): 3. Reprinted in *Hit Parader* (December 1969) (U.S.). At http://www.beatlesinterviews.org/db1969.0503.beatles.html (accessed Feb. 11, 2014).

———. "Close-up on a Beatle: George Harrison." *New Musical Express*, No. 866 (August 16, 1963): 2. Available at http://thateventuality.tumblr.com/post/58389142430/close-up-on-a-beatle-george-harrison-nme-16 (accessed Feb. 11, 2014).

———. "Close-Up on Paul McCartney, a Beatle." *New Musical Express*, No. 865 (August 9, 1963): 10. Via *Rock's Backpages*.

———. "Lennon: Doing The Rounds For Publicity." *New Musical Express* (July 31, 1971). Via *Rock's Backpages*.

———. "My Broken Tooth." *New Musical Express*, No. 1015 (June 24, 1966): 3. Via *Rock's Backpages*.

———. "Ringo Played Cards As Others Sang 'Paperback'!" *New Musical Express*, No. 1014 (June 17, 1966): 3. Via *Rock's Backpages*.

———. "Throat Sweets Keep Us Going Say Beatles!" *New Musical Express*, No. 849 (April 19, 1963) , p. 9. Via *Rock's Backpages*.

———. "You've Pleased—Pleased Us! Say the Beatles." *New Musical Express*, No. 838 (Feb. 1, 1963): 9. Via *Rock's Backpages*.

Smith, Howard. "Interview with John Lennon and Yoko Ono." Dec. 12, 1970, for Radio Station WPLJ. At http://homepage.ntlworld.com/carousel/pob21.html (accessed April 18, 2008).

Smith, Joe. Edited by Mitchell Fink. *Off the Record: An Oral History of Popular Music*. NY: Warner, 1988. Interview with McCartney, 199-202, with George Martin, 202-4, with George Harrison, 260-62.

Snow, Matt. "Paul McCartney." *MOJO* #24 (November 1995). Consulted in *Rock's BackPages*.

———. "We're a damn good little band." *MOJO* (October 1996). Consulted in *Rock's BackPages*.

Soderbergh, Steven and Richard Lester. *Getting Away With It: Or, the Further Adventures of the Luckiest Bastard You Ever Saw*. London: Faber and Faber Limited, 1999.

Somach, Denny, Kathleen Somach, and Kevin Gunn. *Ticket to Ride: A Celebration of the Beatles Based on the Hit Radio Show*. NY: William Morrow, 1989.

Bibliography

Song on Song website, BBC, at http://www.bbc.co.uk/radio2/soldonsong/ (accessed Oct. 17, 2016). This has clips from interviews on a few Beatle songs.

Stahl, Jeff D. "The Lennon/McCartney Collaboration." 1998. At http://jeffdstahl.com/worksfiles/lennonmccarney.pdf (accessed Aug. 11, 2012).

Stormo, Roger. "Lennon's first published song." October 22, 2010, at WogBlog - all things Beatle, http://wogew.blogspot.com/2010/10/lennons-first-published-song.html (accessed Dec. 2, 2016).

Sulpy, Doug and Ray Schweighardt. *Get Back: The Unauthorized Chronicle of the Beatles' Let It Be Disaster.* NY: St. Martin's Griffin, 1999.

Tannenbaum, Rob. "Paul McCartney Reveals the Stories Behind the Beatles' No. 1 Hits." *Billboard*, Nov. 12, 2015, at http://www.billboard.com/articles/events/greatest-of-all-time/6760851/billboard-cover-paul-mccartney-on-beatles-number-one-hits (accessed March 22, 2017).

Tate, Phil. Interview for Pop Chat, BBC, July 30, 1963. The Beatles Ultimate Experience website, at http://www.beatlesinterviews.org/db1963.0730.beatles.html (accessed Oct. 17, 2016).

Taylor, Alistair, with Martin Roberts. *Yesterday: The Beatles Remembered.* London: Sidgwick & Jackson Ltd, 1988.

Taylor, Derek. "Congratulations on a hit, everybody!" *Disc and Music Echo* (July 26, 1969). At http://homepage.ntlworld.com/carousel/pob/pob01.html (accessed March 31, 2014). Also in Sandercombe, *The Beatles*, 272.

"Thingumybob." In *Scraping the Barrel: An Apple Singles Collection Catalogue*, at http://apple.relocution.com/wiki/index.php?title=Main_Page (accessed April 14, 2008).

Thomson, Graeme. "Paul McCartney," interview. *The Word* (October 2005). Accessed via *Rock's Backpages* database.

Tillekens, Ger. "Word and Chords: The semantic shifts of the Beatles' chords." At www.icce.rug.nl/~soundscapes/VOLUME03/Words_and_chords.shtml (accessed July 25, 2016).

Tobler, John and Stuart Grundy. "George Martin." Chapter from *The Record Producers*. London: BBC Books, 1982. Via *Rock's Backpages*.

Torrance, Kelly Jane. "Don't Let It Be." *The American Spectator*, Dec. 29, 2003. At http://spectator.org/archives/2003/12/29/dont-let-it-be/print (accessed Aug. 27, 2012).

Turner, Steve. *A Hard Day's Write: The Stories Behind Every Beatle Song.* 3rd edition. NY: Harper, 2005.

Unterberger, Richie. *The Unreleased Beatles.* San Francisco: Backbeat Books, 2006.

Vozick-Levinson, Simon. "Q&A: Paul McCartney Looks Back on His Latest Magical Mystery Tour." *Rolling Stone* (July 25, 2013). At http://www.rollingstone.com/music/news/q-a-paul-mccartney-looks-back-on-his-latest-magical-mystery-tour-20130725 (accessed Nov. 3, 2013).

Walsh, Alan. "George—More to Life Than Being A Beatle." *Melody Maker* (June 25, 1966). In Sandercombe, *The Beatles*, 167.

———. "Will the real Richard Starkey please stand up?" *Melody Maker* (March 16, 1968): 12-13. In Sandercombe, *The Beatles*, 231.

"'We Can't Please Everyone' says Paul." *The Beatles Book Monthly* 40 (November 1966): 9-10.

Wenner, Jann. *Lennon Remembers: New Edition.* NY: Rolling Stone Press, 2000. Originally published in 1971. The post-breakup Lennon interviews in the *Rolling Stone*, which took place in December 1970.

———. "One Guy Standing There, Shouting 'I'm Leaving'." *Rolling Stone* 58 (May 14, 1970): 1-6.

———. "The Rolling Stone Interview: John Lennon." *Rolling Stone* 74 (Jan. 21, 1971): 32-42; 75 (Feb. 4 1971): 36-43.

White, Timothy. "George Harrison Reconsidered." *Musician* no. 109 (Nov. 1987): 50-60, 62, 65-67. Also in White, *Rock Lives*, 151-74.

———. "Paul McCartney: Farewell to the First Solo Era." *Musician* #112 (Feb. 1, 1988): 44-60, 62, 64, 66, 68. Sometimes I quote from the fuller version of this interview in White, *Rock Lives*, 122-150.

———. "Paul McCartney On His Not-So-Silly Love Songs." *Billboard*, vol. 113, issue 11 (March 17, 2001): 1. Also at http://www.billboard.com/articles/news/80344/paul-mccartney-on-his-not-so-silly-love-songs (accessed May 24, 2013).

———. *Rock Lives: Profiles and Interviews.* NY: Henry Holt, 1990. This includes the interviews first published as "Paul McCartney: Farewell to the First Solo Era," 122-150 and "George Harrison Reconsidered," 151-74.

———. "The Billboard Interview With George Harrison." *Billboard* (June 19, 1999). Available at http://www.fortunecity.com/victorian/canvas/103/george.html (accessed Oct. 17, 2016).

Wiener, Allen J. "Interview with Ringo Starr." *Goldmine Magazine*, Issue 310 (June 12, 1992). At http://www.beatlelinks.net/forums/showthread.php?t=17239 (accessed March 11, 2008).

Wigg, David. Interview with Paul McCartney, September 19, 1969, at Apple offices in London. Published on BBC Radio-One program 'Scene and Heard.' At Beatles Ultimate Experience website, http://www.beatlesinterviews.org/db1969.0919.beatles.html (accessed Oct. 17, 2016).

Wikipedians, eds. *The Beatles.* PediaPress. No date. Available at Google Books.

Wilde, Jon. "McCartney: My Life in the Shadow of the Beatles." In *Read the Beatles: Classics and New Writings on the Beatles, Their Legacy*, edited by June Skinner Sawyers, 243-53. NY: Penguin 2006. Originally in *Uncut*, July 2004.

Williams, Richard. "John & Yoko (part 1)." *Melody Maker* (December 6, 1969). Via *Rock's Backpages*.

———. "John & Yoko (part 2)." *Melody Maker* (December 13, 1969). Via *Rock's Backpages*.

———. "Produced by George Martin." *Melody Maker* 46 (August 21, 1971): 18+, (August 28, 1971): 24+, (September 4, 1971): 25+. Available at http://aboutthebeatles.com/biography_georgemartin_mminterview.php (accessed Oct. 18, 2016).

Winn, John C. *Way Beyond Compare: The Beatles' Recorded Legacy, 1957-1965.* NY: Three Rivers Press, 2003.

———. *That Magic Feeling: The Beatles' Recorded Legacy, 1966-1970.* NY: Three Rivers Press, 2009.

Womack, Kenneth. *Long and Winding Roads: The Evolving Artistry of the Beatles.* NY: Continuum International Publishing Group, 2007.

Wyndham, Francis. "Paul McCartney As Songwriter." *New York Herald Tribune Magazine* (Dec. 26, 1965): 26-27.

Yorke, Ritchie. Interview with George Harrison, September, 1969. Transcription available at http://beatles.ncf.ca/gharris.html (accessed February 28, 2008). Parts of this, edited, appeared in "George Harrison on 'Abbey Road': 'Newer' LP will precede 'Get Back.'" *Rolling Stone* 44 (October 18, 1969): 8.

INDEX

www.ingramcontent.com/pod-product-compliance
Lightning Source LLC
Chambersburg PA
CBHW071855090426
42811CB00004B/611